Actions and Passions

Actions and Passions

Passions

NOTES ON THE
MULTIPLE REVOLUTION
OF OUR TIME
BY

MAX LERNER

KENNIKAT PRESS/PORT WASHINGTON, N. Y.

ACTIONS AND PASSIONS

Copyright 1949 by Max Lerner
Reissued in 1969 by Kennikat Press by arrangement with
Simon and Schuster, Inc.
Library of Congress Catalog Card No: 76-86037
SBN 8046-0569-6

Manufactured by Taylor Publishing Company   Dallas, Texas

ESSAY AND GENERAL LITERATURE INDEX REPRINT SERIES

FOR

JOHN P. LEWIS

who edited a fighting paper

TABLE OF CONTENTS

PART II

Movers and Shakers:
Notes on Economics and Politics

PART III

Empire, Chaos, or Law:
Notes on America among the Powers

As life is action and passion, it is required of a man that he should share the passion and action of his time at peril of being judged not to have lived.

—Justice Oliver Wendell Holmes, Jr.,
Memorial Day speech, 1884.

I rely on a story which I once heard, how Leontius, the son of Aglaion, was coming up from the Peiraeus, close to the outer side of the north wall, when he saw some dead bodies lying near the executioner, and he felt a desire to look at them, and at the same time felt disgust at the thought, and tried to turn aside. For some time he fought with himself and put his hand over his eyes, but in the end the desire got the better of him, and opening his eyes wide with his fingers he ran forward to the bodies, saying, "There you are, curse you, have your fill of the lovely spectacle."

—Plato, Republic, Bk. IV,
A. D. Lindsay translation.

FOREWORD

Meeting daily deadlines is one of the necessities of being a working news-paperman. Seeing some of your deadline-products gathered within the covers of a book is a shameless luxury which few newspapermen allow themselves. This is the second time I have indulged myself in this luxury. Like my earlier collection of pieces, Public Journal (1945), these were also originally written for the New York newspaper PM. They combine ele-ments of the signed editorial, the commentary column, and the short per-sonal essay, in what I hope is something of a fresh amalgam.

I have, of course, made a selection. From among the pieces I wrote over an exciting period of almost four years—November, 1944, to August, 1948 —I have picked some two hundred which seemed worth rescuing from the dark oblivion that engulfs newspaper print. The earliest pieces included here are a group on the American river valley developments toward the end of 1944. The last pieces are those I wrote in August, 1948, after PM had changed management and entered on a new phase of its history as the New York Star, and after the 1948 political conventions had been held. I felt that these events marked a logical stopping-point for the present vol-ume, and I interrupted a longer work on the analysis of American civiliza-tion in order to edit and prepare these pieces for the press.

It may be argued—and has been by some of the reviewers of the earlier volume—that pieces written for the daily breakfast table should not be preserved for the years on the library table and the bookshelf. I consider this a curiously narrow and mechanical view, and I want to break a lance here for the art of the essayist and commentator in the periodical press as not necessarily an ephemeral art. The test is not how frequently the pieces were written, but how they stand up a year, three years, five years, or even a decade later. My own training before I became a journalist was an aca-demic one, from my graduate-school days, 1923–25, and my work as an encyclopedia editor, 1925–30, to my college teaching and academic writing for the decade from 1932 to 1943. To me any journalistic "event" is the converging-point for streams of tendency that reach far back into the past and can be projected into the future, and reach out into far areas of impli-cation for politics and economics, psychology and ethics.

To vary the figure, an "event" is like a detail in a mural, and is meaning-less unless you try to see it within its larger frame of cultural values and as part of the long campaign of history. When you do make that effort, the reserves of implication you can squeeze out of an event—a battle, a speech, a public controversy, a Congressional act, a new movie or book, a Supreme Court decision, the death of a statesman, a Cabinet change, a ballet performance, an episode on a college campus, a primary campaign, a holiday— are bounded only by the limits of your thinking. The event itself is transitory, in the sense that other events crowd in upon it, and the newspaper in which it was first blazoned grows yellow and brittle with age. But the implications of the event are suspended in time, and are as little enduring or as greatly enduring as the quality of the reflections brought to bear on them. On that the reader must be his own judge.

The years to which these pieces are footnotes were years as fateful as any in our era. They saw the closing of a war, the death of Roosevelt, the collapse of Nazi power, the opening of the atomic age, the emergence of the two giant powers on the world scene, the growth of tensions between them, the envelopment of the world in fear, the years of the Big Money in America, the closing in of the walls on political and economic heterodoxy, the flaring up of a half-dozen civil wars over the surface of the world, the birth and swift decline of the United Nations, the breaking and the making of nations. To live in such a time and to write about it is an experience that kindles the imagination while it benumbs the sense of being able to do very much about it. These proved to be years therefore of ferment in political life without a corresponding ferment in thought, years of widespread cynicism and moral nihilism, years of the decline of political writing.

To do a running commentary on events in such a time meant to live a precarious intellectual life. It involved the attempt to hew out a theory of social forces and social action firm enough to keep from dissolving into impressionism and adventurism, yet flexible enough to admit the lessons of a rapidly shifting social experience. It meant the willingness to challenge the tyrannies of opinion on both the Right and the Left at a time of sharpened crisis when each side demanded rigorous adherence to a credo and a cult. It meant a willingness to challenge the slogans by which political armies try to mass their followers for battle—even the slogans on the side one had come to consider one's own. It meant an effort to cleave to intellectual integrity at a time when every compulsion was toward running with your crowd at the cost of integrity.

I do not pretend to be certain that I was right on all, or even most, of the issues contained in these pieces. I hope that the lapse of years will not prove me too badly wrong. But right or wrong, these are the things I thought.

I have grouped them under three broad categories: the first dealing with intellectual, cultural, and moral values; the second dealing with economic and political issues on the American national level; the third dealing with the world of the Great Powers and the struggle between what I have called the choices of empire, chaos, and law. I have not arranged the pieces chronologically but in a rough topical sequence inside each category, but the reader will find at the end of each piece the date when it first appeared. In many cases I have taken two or three pieces, and sometimes as many as four or five, and grouped them under a single title because—while written and published on different days—they formed themselves naturally into a cluster around a single basic issue or theme. In such cases I have set off the component pieces in the larger cluster by arabic numerals, and sometimes by a subheading which may have been its original title. In many cases—and especially where I have run a number of pieces together—I have cut whole sentences and even paragraphs, either to avoid repetition or because the passages dealt with matters too ephemeral to keep. Here and there I have changed a phrase or a sentence because it was too carelessly composed, and in many instances I have pruned and tightened my writing. But I have been careful not to seem too much wiser after the event than I was at the time. And especially since this book may be read in the future as a sort of documentary—however unimportant in itself—on an important time, I have here and there indicated in footnotes the points at which my views have changed since I wrote the pieces, and at which the event proved me wrong.

For what is important in an era like ours is not the pretense of prescience or the saving of face. It is not even the art of persuasion, although I should be pleased if some readers considered the basic philosophy behind these scattered pieces a persuasive one and worth testing for themselves. What is crucial for me—and one can never go beyond one's own sense of the crucial—is that, at a time when history seems to be shaped by vast and even malignant forces beyond our control, one should feel that men can act with a sense of pattern amidst the chaos, with a sense of togetherness amidst the moral nihilism, and that, whatever comes, one has—in Justice Holmes's phrase—"shared the passion and action" of one's time.

PART I

Look to the Source: Notes on Culture and Ethics

The Human Heart and the Human Will [1]

THE WORLD of actuality has for the first time outstripped the imaginative world of the artist. Nothing—not even the nightmares of H. G. Wells's early scientific romances—has equaled what soldiers and reporters have seen in the starvation camps like Belsen and Buchenwald and the annihilation camps like Maidanek. Wells was obsessed with the destructiveness of science. He foresaw the chance that we would contrive weapons of war so deadly that, in the sequel, civilization would be destroyed, and only a few pitiable men would be left to grub amidst its ruins. But what the Germans did to Jews and political prisoners and prisoners of war had very little to do with Wells's fantasies of rocket warfare or chemical warfare.

It is not science that has destroyed the world, despite all the gloomy forebodings of the earlier prophets. It is man who has destroyed man. He has destroyed him face to face, with forethought and without pity. And he has not needed the newest weapons of science. He has used the oldest weapons of hunger and bludgeon and fire.

This should be a spur to the artist and the social thinker. If the reality can outstrip both the individual and social imagination, then there is something wrong with the imagination. It must stretch out to new horizons and create new worlds.

The basic assumption of twentieth-century social theory has been that mankind is caught in a tragic paradox: that man's brain creates the things his will cannot control. This has been proved true by the event. But what we must now add to it is that man's will creates the things that paralyze his brain and brutalize his heart. And we must add that man's heart has proved to be a soil in which it is possible for evil to flower.

We are the fortunate survivors who are able to witness the crumbling of the fascist house of death. But we must not allow ourselves to forget that the men who built this house of death were also men. Their impulses were our impulses, their instinctive endowment ours, their biological inheritance ours, their historical memories ours. De te fabula must still be our cry to ourselves as we reflect on the meaning of the fascist story.

This has nothing to do with the guilt of the German nation; its guilt is beyond argument. But the German nation is part of the Western world,

[1] In this case, as in the piece that forms the Epilogue of this book, I have used an editorial of mine contributed to the American Scholar. This is from the summer, 1945, issue.

and the German people belong to the human race. That is the harsh fact we must face if we are to be honest with ourselves.

We have been too long concerned with only the human brain, and with the science and the social construction it has created. The axis of our interest will now have to shift to man himself and his essential nature. And it must shift to the way in which man can organize his collective will so as to create a genuine society of men and a genuine community of nations. Scholarship can have no other function in the generation to come. Poetry and the arts, when they have lifted themselves from the nightmare that will oppress them for some time to come, will turn the nightmare symbols into symbols of the human heart that has triumphed over its always potential evil.

1945

America in the Sunlight [1]

THE FIRST THING I encountered when I got off the boat at New York and stepped out into the street was a cop bawling out a taxi driver. The first words anyone said to me were about Mayor La Guardia and the curfew. The evidence was unmistakable. I was back in my own country.

It was several weeks ago, on one of the early spring afternoons, and there was a sultry germinal feeling in the air. I liked being back. I didn't even feel the sense of strangeness I was supposed to feel after Europe. The only shock I got was in seeing the streets filled with well-dressed, well-fed, prosperous-looking people. This was like nowhere else in the world today. No ruins. No shabby, strained look. No dead. Only sunlight streaming on millions of people—America in the sunlight.

I thought: this is the same sunlight that is streaming on the rest of the earth—on battlefield and ruined city and sea-lane scattered with wreckage. But only in America do you have the feeling that the sun is not ironic.

I bought a lot of newspapers and magazines. The American Labor party and the Liberal party still were fighting. So were John L. Lewis and the

[1] I wrote this on my return from fifteen weeks in Europe as a war correspondent for *PM*.

coal operators. I read again of the nefariousness and malevolence of Russia. Governor Dewey had fallen in love with the CIO. The Dillings and Gerald Smith had fallen in love with no one. Bill White had written a book saying the Russian women looked shabby. Advertisements showed American women looking anything but shabby in their newest sartorial creations. What kind of legs for wounded veterans? The last prize fight, and the newest book of poetry. Theater first nights, and what the reviewers said. The new crop of Hollywood's slick mystery products. The "power-drunk Big Three." The smell of a Hearst paper. Who is biting whose back and who is scratching ditto?

Did I resent all this? I did not. I wallowed in the luxury of it. I, who had been away less than four months, got a taste of what a homecoming might mean—with a pleasure twenty fold my own—to a soldier who had been away in the South Pacific theater for years. The jangle of voices I knew to be a cacophony, but it was so good to hear them again that the sounds almost blended into a harmony. This, I told myself, is what you return to. This is what you will be coming back to no matter how widely or for how long you wander over the seven corners of the earth. Wherever you go you will only, like the traveler in Oliver Goldsmith's poem, drag a lengthening chain behind.

This is where the soldiers came from. This is America, passionate for freedom and riddled with unfreedoms, generous and insular together, far-roaming yet deep-rooted, rich beyond the dreams of men yet fearful lest its men will not have jobs. All that massed power of tanks and guns and men and supplies that I saw in Germany—this is what backs it up. All that mixture I saw in the American soldiers of confusion and simplicity, geniality and roughness—this is where it comes from.

And this is where the soldiers want to return. I looked about me and was struck again by the sheer paradox of us. America has wealth, and spends it lavishly on almost fantastic creature comforts while millions of beings as human as ourselves go starving and in tatters all over the world. America is the symbol of immense and unified power, yet remains in essence a collection of small towns. America is trying painfully to build a culture, and in doing so it is reaching out to other lands to find what other men have thought and wrought. Yet this same America shudders at anything alien, and when it wants to shut its mind against any man's ideas it calls him a foreigner.

It was good to be back in my study, surrounded by my books. I took one of them off the shelf. It was *Marius the Epicurean*, Walter Pater's too cloying and prettified but unforgettable re-creation of what Rome once meant to a young man growing up in the Roman world. There too was a glittering culture to which everyone was drawn, which built on the riches of the world and dominated it with its fame and power. I recalled a conversation I had in Paris with a young Englishman, one of the deftest and subtlest minds I had met. "You Americans are Rome," he said to me. "We English are Greece." I thought what had happened to Rome: how it had flung its armies over the world, built cities everywhere, fashioned administrative constructions, developed codes, but had never created great tragedy or philosophy or undying values; and how it had finally grown fearful of the barbarians, and disintegrated before their vigor. I was not sure I liked the Englishman's historical parallel.

Then I thought of the wounded with whom I had come back on the ship, and I was consoled. I shall never forget the cry that arose from them as they stood on their crutches at the portholes, ready to greet New York and its haven. "See the old lady with the torch," they said, and the sentence was echoed by hundreds of throats. Nobody but an American would think of calling his national symbol of liberty "the old lady with the torch."

What was the deep painful yearning of these boys to get home? Their forefathers yearned for the undiscovered, the thrust into the unknown. For us, America has become the home carved out of the wilderness of the world. The more of the world the American soldier sees, the more of a jungle it seems to him. And the more he wants to get back to the place and the ideas he can hold on to when everything else in the world seems to be reeling.

APRIL 10, 1945

The Postponed Generation

HUNDREDS OF THOUSANDS of American soldiers are streaming in from the European theater.[1] This is the big furlough time for them. Our young men are home from the wars—but only for a brief, all-too-brief spell. America is not their destination. Japan is their stopping-point. America is only a way-station.

Many of them have been fighting a long fight. Out of the line they come

[1] This was written in the period between VE-day and VJ-day.

piling and out of the planes, out of the tanks and half-tracks and jeeps and trucks, out of the mud and the artillery dug-outs, some of them out of the hospitals or the German prison-camps. They are glad, for a brief moment, to turn away from all that. From the dying and the killing, and from the callousness against both that you grow as a protective skin, keeping always a saving tithe of the sense of horror at the way life is being mutilated.

They will not easily forget. Even the joking and the parties and the casual bantering talk will not blot out the memories they bring back with them: of months of training in England and the warning blast of sirens; the first glimpse of the African shore, with the surf beating against wrecked boats; the feel of the ground under you that is to be your first battlefield; the agony of Kasserine Pass, the bitter taste of retreat; the crossings always in the dark, the landings, and the first fighting always in the dawn; the crooked, dust-choked mountainous Italian roads; the withering fire at Anzio and later at Omaha Beach; the battle of the tanks on the French plains; the stalemates and the breakthroughs; the river-crossings, the parachute-landings, the tension and waiting in the pitchblack German night; the long lines of German prisoners, the full savor of victory, the rotting sights and smells of the concentration camps, that sicken even the victors to the point of despair.

Sometime, between clean sheets in secure beds, the nightmare horror will revisit them. They will jump up with flailing arms to ward it off, and will find they are among loved ones. They will go back to sleep, knowing they have a respite, but that the nightmare will wait for them. That is part of the big furlough time.

I saw some of these men in Germany, after they had been in the front lines for months. It seemed to them that they were doomed to fight to the end, that no reprieve would ever come until death itself offered it. Now they know they were not forgotten. The greeting kiss welds them again to the life of which they once formed part. That, too, is part of the big furlough time.

So many of them are still kids, but am I wrong in thinking that there are more of them than before with faces on which the months have left an imprint? Sometime we will see more clearly what the war has done to them. Perhaps they will have become men who, like Tennyson's Ulysses, "cannot rest from travel." In the meanwhile, it is good to see them back. It is good to watch the couples walking along the street, hand clasped in hand, clinging to each other with an utterly unselfconscious candor, knowing they must crowd so much living into so small a stretch.

But this is also the heartbreak of the big furlough time. They have waited so long, and it isn't only for baseball games and the theater, for fishing trips, for late nights, and the luxury of late rising. It is for these, yes, but also for more.

They have waited so long that they have piled up their demands on life, and somehow life doesn't always pay off to those who are most insistent. To be sure, I have seen youngsters together whose eyes tell whomever it may concern that the reality does not fall short of the dream. But I have also watched others whom the tension of waiting has made more exacting than is good for them. They count off every moment as it passes, subtract it from the meager total sum they have at their disposal, eat their hearts out when it lacks the surpassing quality they feel they must squeeze out of this brief gleaming interval between two darknesses.

It is all too easy for us to say that they ought to expect less, contain themselves. They are young, and have lost so much time already.

Later, when they have moved on to other battle-areas and are back at the grim war business, all the youngsters will think back to this as the halcyon period. It will be a foretaste of what they can do with life when they have more time, less feverishness. They deserve a nation that has the will to make sure they will achieve it.

For the big furlough time is not only a brief rest between two spells of war. It is a savoring of how good life can be sometime when we don't have to purchase a few moments of it by killing men in an anarchic world.

Congress is back in session, and one of the tasks it will have to face is to prepare a real homecoming for the "conquering heroes." The kind of homecoming I mean is not the fanfare and parades that the home town always whips up for Eddie Bracken in the movies. Far better than that is Bernard Baruch's report to General Omar Bradley, the new head of the Veterans Administration. Baruch says the "human side of demobilization is being neglected tragically." He suggests a hard-headed program for fitting veterans into hometown life again. And he warns that if we fail, the veteran may nurse his grievances apart from the rest of the nation, "his feelings an explosive fuel ready to be ignited by some future demagogues."

After World War I the generation that fought it came to be called the "lost generation." How will the historians refer to the present generation of homecomers from the war?

I should myself be inclined to call them the postponed generation.

Whenever I have talked with them—during the lulls on the front, and on the boat coming home, and in the hospitals—and whenever they have written to me, the strongest feeling that emerged was a yearning to resume their peacetime experience, a consuming hunger to sit once more at the table of life. They want to be wanted, to be used and useful, to court and marry and bring up healthy children, to run a farm or machine or open a business.

Four years taken out of any life is a big chunk. Out of a young life it is a monstrous one. They are impatient to be men again, and not killers and survivors. They want to experience the ordinary actions of peacetime and not the abnormal passions of the battlefield.

They have waited a long time. If we help them to create a decent framework in which they can live, not as soldiers or even as veterans but as citizens, then they will be only the postponed generation. Otherwise they will again be the lost generation.

JULY 11, SEPT. 6, 1945

The Face of Evil

"APRIL IS the cruelest month," wrote T. S. Eliot, and the aching beauty of the American countryside gives me a glimpse of what he meant. But every day our correspondents in Germany send us reports of another sort of cruelty, not nature's loveliness but man's ugliness.

Now all the things that Americans had been hearing about German sadism are coming home to them. They had heard it from the French and Belgians, from the Poles and Jews and Russians. It had all seemed a bit distant, as other people's atrocity stories always are. We had even discovered about Japanese cruelty at first hand. But Germany itself remained for us the country about which others complained.

The reports we are getting now form a sort of course in German history and psychology. Only we are having to read it backward. We have seen newspaper photographs of Americans whom our armies have released from German prisons, looking like macabre X-ray versions of themselves, with their skeletal structure showing through and practically nothing else on their frames. This should prepare us to believe the stories that are piling in about Russian and Polish slave-workers and Russian prisoners of war, and how the Germans treated them, reducing them to the level of animals battling with each other for meager and dirty scraps of food. And now the correspondents with the American armies, as they go deeper into Germany, are meeting people who give them eyewitness accounts of how the Germans herded tens of thousands of Jews within barbed-wire enclosures, and burned and machine-gunned them.

We shall be getting other stories soon, as our correspondents dig back further into the history of the fascist era. We shall learn how the Germans treated Germans—trade-unionists, Communists, Social Democrats, liberals, just ordinary decent people who dared speak out. We shall have stories of the concentration camps. We may catch up with Nazi history, and we may even end up by tracing it back to its source when we get the records (if any are left) of the alliance between German big business and German political gangsterism out of which the whole movement sprang.

More important, however, than the stories that will be written are the stories that will never be written. You cannot write stories about the nameless dead, whose bodies have long ago been reduced to ashes and become part of the uncomplaining earth.

We are seeing finally the face of evil. The big thing that has happened to the Western world is that it has finally explored man's inhumanity to man, and found how far it reaches. It is a benumbing experience. If the era of fascist power had done nothing else, it would still be notable for bringing the problem of evil back into the center of our thinking.

I say "back" because the Greek tragedians and philosophers and the Jewish prophets and the Christian fathers knew what evil was and wrestled with the problems it raised about man and his nature. It was the centuries of enlightenment and progress, with their basic premise of a mankind that was growing better and better every year, that dissipated this insight. It has taken little over a decade of Nazi activity to restore a fresh sense of the impact of evil. The long process of constitutionalizing politics and humanizing war, which had taken a succession of centuries, came to an abrupt break with the Nazis.

This is the thing itself. This is evil, formerly a word the theologians used in their drowsy sermonizing, or that decadent French poets played with in the wake of Baudelaire in order to shock the bourgeois. This is evil itself, positive, brutal, aggressive, organized. It is not simply power, but evil power. It is not simply evil, but powerful evil.

We must face its meaning. Don't fall back on your catchwords, O cultured progressive, brought up in the tradition of liberalism. Don't say it is due to the social environment or to faulty education, or to unemployment, or to the lack of religion. Those are masks that you put on the face of truth so that you can hide its ugliness. Don't say this is the way Germans act but no others, this is the way the Nazis act but no others. The Germans, even the Nazi Germans, also started as human beings.

The fact is that evil and good are both basic thrusts in human nature. We had almost forgotten about evil and how powerful it is in all of us. The whole of social organization is a way of curbing it, channeling it. The civic in us is what keeps the tiger in us slumbering. All the decencies toward each other that we build up painfully in daily life—these are the connective tissue of any community. When it breaks (as it did in Germany) man has nothing to confront but his own unchecked brutish nature.

I think back again to the German landscape I saw, as bleak and devastated a landscape as the world has ever offered. I thought at the time: See how the machines of war have broken down a whole society and reduced it to wreckage. But I see on reflection that I was wrong. German society had long ago been reduced to wreckage—long before the war machines came over Germany and dropped their bombs. Even when Nazi Germany was still whole, it was only a primitive landscape, with animals prowling around dressed like human beings.

The final sin of the fascists is that they unleashed the evil that is part of man. To face the fact of that evil is the beginning of political wisdom.

APRIL 11, 1945

Politics and the Connective Tissue

THERE IS, of course, more involved in the question of politics and ethics than the evil things that fascists do. There is the fact of power politics in our own antifascist world, of the Russian one-party system and British imperialism, of the vicious American habit of alternately playing God with the world and ignoring it. There are economic exploitation and political corruption. There are double-talk and double-cross.

What shall decent, sensitive men think and do about this? That is the big ethical question which faces our generation. Do we not, in using a lesser evil to fight a bigger one, destroy the old meaning of our victory?

The easiest course—and one which many intellectuals are now pursuing

—is to condemn everyone and everything, fascists and communists and democrats alike, and live in solitary splendor with your own esteem, writing articles and reviews which are love letters to yourself. The next easiest course is to accept supinely whatever is thrust upon you, on the sleazy principle that you must compromise with "realism."

I want to set down my own guiding ideas tentatively on this problem of politics and ethics.

Do not confuse power with evil. The fact that Roosevelt, Churchill, and Stalin are powerful men, the heads of powerful states, does not mean that what they do is therefore evil. What they do must be judged in itself—in its nature, its intentions, its alternatives, its fruits. Power may be evil, and then it must be fought. But it may also be a way of avoiding evil (would that we had used it thus in the 1930s—unfortunately we did not, and we allowed fascist evil to grow) or it may be a way of crushing evil.

When you choose the lesser of two evils, always remember that it is still an evil. You may have to make the choice, but do not fool yourself into thinking that it is therefore a good. But also do not confuse yourself into thinking that whatever displeases you must therefore be evil.

Do not reject partial or gradual solutions because they are partial or gradual. The test is not whether they are complete and immediate, but whether they are moving in the right direction, and moving quickly enough to avert disaster.

Do not let your principles grow too rigid to be useful in a real world. Principles—and I have in mind such principles as states' rights or national sovereignty or the free market or pacifism—have a way of drying up while the sap of life goes flowing in another direction. All theory is gray, said Goethe, and only the tree of life stays green. This is foolish if it leads you always to reject the rational, but it contains a deep truth when you consider how many people are more interested in a lifeless, logical symmetry than they are in experience. Thurman Arnold once wrote a book called *The Folklore of Capitalism*, in which he mercilessly flayed American "liberals" who would rather not achieve their ends at all than achieve them in a way they had not contemplated. His criticism is still true. That is what I mean when I say that I set more store by values than by principles, more store by the quality of life than by its blueprint.

Do not reject an imperfect ally when you are working for a common aim in a time of great danger. That was the mistake which both the Communists and the Socialists, the liberals and the conservatives made during Hitler's rise to power in Germany. It was a mistake the French Resistance did not make when Hitler occupied France.

Do not confuse your vested interests with ethics. Do not identify the enemies of your privilege with the enemies of humanity. Thus there are many writers who are convinced that all economic control and planning are evil, or that all capitalism is evil. Thus, what should be settled as an item of policy on the score of wisdom and unwisdom becomes an item of ethics on the score of good and evil.

But with all warnings against hysteria, don't lull yourself into thinking that good and evil are thereby explained out of existence. They do exist. When you find something that is, in truth, evil—as fascism is, as lynching is, as terrorism is—then you will know it, because there are the darkness and distance of the pit between you and it.

The final test of social evil is whether it breaks the connective tissue that joins man to man and thus forms a society. I choose my friends and give my allegiances among those who have my own values. But I manage to live and get along with those who don't have these values—with reactionaries and fools and snobs. When I see someone hurt, I take his side against those who are hurting him. When he is unjustly spoken of, I speak out in his defense. But what gives me the freedom to speak and act against injustice is the fact that I have tolerated differences in my fellows and agreed to accept partial solutions—the fact that I have joined with them to get a consent on common values. Together we thus manage to keep the connective tissue of society strong and alive.

Why not apply this on the international level as well? One of the curious things about us is that we demand of our political life greater certainty and greater perfection than we demand of our personal life. We are far less tolerant in our political life than we are in our personal life. We are much more intemperate on the international and national levels than we are in our own ordinary relations.

Our problem is to develop a connective tissue between nations which will be as real as the connective tissue between individuals in a society. Once we have done that, we can throw our weight around with far less danger than now. For we shall have a framework within which the evil in man can be controlled, and the good and the creative developed.

APRIL 12, 1945

On a Smashed Cyclotron

IN JAPAN the American occupation forces, by order of General MacArthur, have destroyed four Japanese cyclotrons, or atom-smashing machines. In Tennessee, the Association of Oak Ridge Scientists, which includes ninety-five per cent of the men who helped produce the atom bomb in the big Oak Ridge plant, has called the act of destroying cyclotrons "wanton and stupid to the point of constituting a crime against mankind."

These are worth some pondering: the act of the man of war and that of the men of science. Their importance goes beyond four smashed machines and a hot statement of protest. Each of them is a deeply symbolic act. Pitted against each other, they dramatize the current struggle between two contrasting views of the world.

The Oak Ridge statement points out that the four cyclotrons have been under American observation; that the Japanese have only an infinitesimal fraction of the material it takes to make an atomic bomb; that the cyclotrons could be used only for nuclear research, in the interest of a common fund of science; that in any event we could have taken them over and operated them ourselves. Given these facts, the act of wrecking them is the act of a blind and unknowing destructiveness which does not discriminate between what is hostile in Japan and what is human, between what is potentially dangerous to the peace of the world and what belongs to the heritage of all men.

The military man may say that it is not his business to make these distinctions. But in a world in which the things that can destroy us and the things that can give us life flow from the same source, it is the business of all men to separate the two streams and to cherish the life-giving one. The Oak Ridge scientists are right in saying that to wreck the cyclotrons is as bad as it would be to burn the Japanese libraries or smash the printing presses. The same blind and unknowing fury could some day, in our own country, be directed against books and laboratories, against schools and unions.

Turning from the man of war to the men of science, it is good to know that there are men who care enough about reason and the human spirit to speak up for a smashed cyclotron in a vanquished country. And it is especially important because these men are also the men who brought the bomb into being. Their statement may be—as the skeptical psychologist might perhaps put it—a gesture of compensation for their own brooding sense of guilt. But whatever the motive, the act and its meaning are all to the good.

For the Oak Ridge statement is a valuing statement. It says, in effect, that a human being with values does not smash things wantonly; that he does not smash things unless he has to, by a tragic necessity; that all destruction—unless it is to save ourselves from a worse destruction—is so much taken away from the common fund of knowledge and reason; that this fund, as science, knows no national boundaries; that it belongs not to Americans or Japanese, but to humanity.

It is good to have these things said finally after years during which men have had to give themselves over to destruction. It is good to have them said at a time when so many men have only contempt for the intellect, and flout reason, and when man's inhumanity to man no longer makes many mourn.

What has happened to awaken the men of science, to make them among the most militant leadership-groups in our democracy? It was their own atom bomb that gave them the final jolt. But it could not have had that effect on them had they not, during the years before that bomb exploded, already been jolted by the explosive force of the hatred and evil in men.

Here is a group which, until now, seemed to be like the engineers and the lawyers: men endowed by big industry, to work for big industry, and to think in big-industry terms or, to put it more precisely, endowed to stick to their last and let big industry do their social and world thinking for them. One of the things that the reactionaries had counted on was the social passivity of the men of science. That passivity has now been broken.

The men of science are now doing some clear social thinking about the world control of the atom bomb, and about the use of industrial atomic energy to get abundance for all the people. Naturally this causes pain and dismay in the hearts of the vested interests and their honest mercenaries. "These are experts in science," they say scoffingly. "What do they know about social affairs?" To which the answer is: Who has a greater stake in controlling the atom bomb than those whose child it is? Who has a better right to be heard about the things in our system of economic power that determine the uses of science than the scientists themselves?

I hope that the scientists, having made this start, will go further as thinking, valuing men. I hope they will give some thought to the relation of the Government to scientific research and its subsidizing. I hope they will think about what happens to science when discrimination is practiced against minority groups in medical and engineering schools, and about the relation of a healthy school system to the spirit of free inquiry. I hope they will turn their minds to the whole enveloping universe of imperialism and nationalist rivalries and racist hatreds in which, as in a dark and gusty night, the candle of reason flickers.

When they have done that they will have built a bridge between their specialty and the world's framework, between what they know about as technicians and what they care about as human beings. That is all that any of us can do in the end. But it is what can make each of us a whole person.

NOV. 27, 1945

The Imagination of H. G. Wells

IN THE FACE of his approaching death, H. G. Wells prepared a literary testament, *Mind at the End of Its Tether*. In it he despairs of the human animal, and predicts that "he has to give place to some other animal, better adapted to the fate that closes in." Watching the political and moral blindness that has closed in on the spokesmen of the Western world, I am not inclined to quarrel too violently with him.

What is the quality of Wells's gift? What is it that made this London cockney, this draper's clerk, this hack science-assistant, into a mind that was at once the whiplash and the mirror of the world's urgencies?

I have been reading the new edition of Wells's 1933 book, *The Shape of Things to Come*. That far back Wells not only foresaw the approximate year when the second World War would break out, but predicted a third one just about now. He had many things wrong, too, and there is the off-scale feeling you get in reading old prophecies that fell flat. But by and large it is a sturdy and swaggering "history of the future" up to the twenty-second century, better worth reading than dozens of the predigested tracts that pass for social thinking in these days.

Wells does these things better than most. In 1900, in a book called *Anticipations*, he took a long look across the threshold of the new century, and saw the military plane and the armored tank. In 1913 he "wrote on a sudden impulse in the Alps, where the air is overconfident," a book called *The World Set Free*, about the "sun snares," who find the secret of atomic energy, and how a world government is the outcome. An inspired amateur at social theory all his life, Wells always had hold of one crucial truth: that there is an organic relation between man's tools and man's fate, that a world technology means either a world government or world suicide.

But Wells's enduring value does not lie in his diatribes and his apocalyptic visions, in his Cassandra role or his brilliant Nostradamus guesses. It lies rather in his novels of science, and in the kindling imagination and the storyteller's art which make each of them a creative miracle. I came to these scientific romances very late, reading them one after another through the whole of a Williamstown winter in 1941. I have kept coming back to them since on nights when nothing will do for me imaginatively except the magic of a world not our own.

There is *The Time-Machine* in which an invention zooms you into the future, and you find that man has subdivided over the years into a species that governs and a curious subterranean species that is specialized only to labor. There is *The Island of Doctor Moreau*, with its ghastly imagining of the "beast folk"—in which parts of animals have been grafted together into the human form. There is *The Invisible Man*, known to all moviegoers by now. There is *The War of the Worlds*, about the invasion of the Martians which (in the Orson Welles radio version) sent the New Jersey folk into a panic. And, best of all, there is *The First Men in the Moon*, the best of Wells's books in its blending of science, imagination, and adventure, the book in which you travel to the moon in a sort of plane made of a metal called cavorite, which is impervious to gravity—and you find the moon inhabited.

What gives these books their quality is that they have each of them at the kernel a scientific idea (and always one within the possible limits of science), but it is an idea with which Wells plays around to his full bent, whereas in his social books it is always some political idea that he belabors. In one set of books he is fancy-free; in the other he is flagellant. It is the difference between the storyteller and the prophet. I prefer the former.

And so, I suspect, will readers for some generations to come. I am glad that *The First Men in the Moon* has been put into a Viking Portable book called *Novels of Science*, along with three others in the same genre by other writers. I think that the editor is sound in saying that Wells—even more than Jules Verne—created the basic patterns in this area that others have followed.

I do not say that Wells's scientific romances lack social meaning. My point is only that the meanings come naturally out of the story and are not forced. By setting his story in another time, on another planet, Wells achieves the detachment that makes great social satire. Capitalism, religious superstition, the savagery and inanity of war, the illogic of economic power over others—Wells's sharpest shafts are aimed at these institutions of ours, and always reach their mark. I recall, for example, the wonderful bit in *The First Men in the Moon* about how the Selenites, when they have no work for their workers to do, simply drug them and put them out of commission until the next job comes along.

Yet Wells's real shafts are aimed not at man's institutions but at man himself, as an incident in biological evolution. His seemingly harmless romances show man that he need not consider himself the Lord of creation and the center of the only possible social system; that other universes are possible, and that in these other universes man may turn out to be only the animal that time and change have left behind.

That is why Wells is at his best in envisaging the breakdown of the social fabric. We seem so confident about our technical apparatus and our complex social organization, as if the water supply and the state would go on forever. Wells has dared imagine them breaking down, under war and famine and pestilence. He has dared depict the world—even America—with only a handful of straggling survivors left, trying feebly to start over again the connection of man with man.

NOV. 16, 1945

The Machine Explodes

THEY DON'T KNOW quite what caused that explosion in Los Angeles that killed scores of people and leveled several city blocks. They don't quite know what caused the crack Pennsy train to leave the tracks at Altoona, killing and injuring many people. They don't quite know just what happened in the series of current airplane crashes.

I have a fantasy about it, and I have a theory. First, the fantasy. It is that the machines are in revolt against us. They have had about all that they can stand. E. M. Forster once wrote a short story called "The Machine Stops" (which you can find in his volume of collected stories, *The Eternal Moment*). He stretches his imagination to embrace a completely mechanized world, and the moment in it when the machine runs down. I premise not a stopping of the machine, but an explosion of the machine—in a burst of rage and futility.

At what? I think the machines are enraged at being so completely taken for granted. The relation between Americans and the machines has been one of the great love affairs of history; each took to the other with that completeness of passion which makes lovers feel that aeons of time have wheeled in their cyclical course only in order to bring them together. But love cannot tolerate complacency. No lover likes to be taken for granted. And it is true that we Americans have been assuming a world in which we are safe with the machine, in which we don't have to take any real trouble to master its way, or to set up the controls which will marry the industrial machine to the people's needs or the war machine to the people's survival.

I don't think the machines have made their final decision to revolt. They are waiting first to see whether there is any hope for the world of men. What has been happening recently has been the sporadic revolt of individual machines, too impatient to await the final order. When that order comes, the machines will stand at Armageddon and battle against their former lords and masters.

Is this all fantasy? I am not certain it is. Back in the old days, forty or fifty years ago (which David L. Cohn has described so nostalgically in his social history of the American automobile, *Combustion on Wheels*), the people accustomed to a horse-and-buggy culture thought the auto a contrivance of the Devil and a violation of human nature. The Almighty, they argued, had never intended his creatures to tear along the countryside at fourteen miles an hour. We laugh now good-naturedly at this folly, and we half suspect that a future generation will laugh equally at our own fears as to whether we have been intended to cleave the heavens at six hundred miles an hour or build complicated dynamos on which whole cities depend for their power, or lay out networks of rails along which high-powered trains zoom.

Perhaps they will laugh. Yet the fact is that the faster and more powerful and yet more delicate the machine becomes, the narrower grows the margin for error, and the greater become the machine's destructive possibilities. That is the big fact we don't quite face about the machine in our time. We have learned, in a life of limited possibilities, to set limits for most things. We set no limits to the machine. We assume it will go on forever; that it will never end, never explode, never revolt; that we can go on indefinitely piling up new structures of machine-risk on the same narrow base of human intelligence, human instinct, and human will.

The fact is that we cannot, and the sooner we face it, the healthier will our future be. We often laugh at the eighteenth and nineteenth centuries because they so uncritically accepted the doctrine of unending progress.

Yet I doubt that we have cause to laugh. For to those centuries the machine was a new and exciting thing; they saw it moving forward, and they thought that the inevitable march of the machine was a phase of the inevitable march of human progress. They were wrong. But are we not just as wrong in taking the march of the machine so completely for granted that we grimly calculate how many human lives have to be lost before the airplane or the atom bomb has become human-error-proof?

Our greatest mistake is to think they will ever become error-proof. Our instincts are not geared to a foolproof machine-age. I don't say they can't be. The annihilation of world after world, and the survival and inbreeding only of the mechanical superman, may in time produce the kind of race Huxley once satirized in *Brave New World*, or that Gerald Heard is now writing about in his fantastic romances.

That certainly is one choice. The other—and the only other one—is to shift the emphasis from inventing the machines to running and controlling them, from mechanical invention to social invention. Either a set of new instincts or a set of new controls. As for myself, I can only be grateful that we have not yet become wholly machine-men. The way to the human ant-state does not lie along the road of social controls, but along the road of a blind reliance on machines alone.

FEB. 26, 1947

The Ethics of the Dust

1. The May-Garsson Case [1]

THE IMPACT of political scandals and revelations is generally that of shock without surprise. The current disclosures of the Mead Committee in the May-Garsson business are no exception. All through the war years one got a strong whiff of the stench of easy war-contract money. Everyone spoke of the "contract brokers," of the men who had "inside connections"— which could only mean Congressmen and high Army officers—of favoritism and protection, of shoddy standards and materials, of padded payrolls

[1] The Senate War Frauds Committee, under the chairmanship of Senator James M. Mead of New York, turned up evidence implicating Representative Andrew May of Kentucky, and a war-contract firm run by the Garsson brothers. They were later indicted and convicted.

and "fixed" cost items, of mushrooming fortunes and easy financial and political morals. Everyone said: "Wait till some of these things break." Senator Mead's Committee is now breaking them. Yet how curious Americans are about such matters. We·are always ready to think the worst, and we are always shocked to find we are right.

If the evidence given by the Committee witnesses stands up, and if the May-Garsson case was a symptom and not a solitary episode, we had better do some heart-searching about our Army officers, our Congressmen, our businessmen.

More dismaying, perhaps, than anything else is the evidence that high Army officers were willing to play around with the businessmen on whose bids for war-contracts they had to pass; were willing to be entertained by them, to have their hotel bills paid by them, to accept favors from them and grant them favors. The historian of the Era of the Big War Money may explain this by the suction force of the wasteful to-hell-with-what-it-costs war attitude. But to explain is not to condone. Those to whom we entrust the lives of our young people owe us a more exacting code of public conduct.

The case of the Congressmen is more complicated in practice, if not in principle. A Congressman is usually an ordinary man who is where he is because he is a genial, not-too-critical fellow, willing to make promises and lend a helpful hand. If he has a core of strength and rightness in him, he will have no difficulty in drawing the line between being helpful and "exerting undue pressure"—especially if the latter leads to lining his own pockets. If he is weak and loses his head, the moralities of ward politics can easily carry over into his Congressional work, and then he is only a cheap and pliable politician who carries on his trade in Congress. It is part of the tragedy of American politics that the codes of the political sub-moral world do spill over into high office.

There remains the question of business morality. There has been a good deal of talk about the "paper empire" of the Garssons. This is one phase of the case that may lead us away from the central issues, and up a blind alley. There can be little question that the Garssons started their war-contract operations on a shoestring. But that is scarcely unique in the history of American business enterprise, and it accords with the American myth of quick and staggering success. The Garssons did not have to start with the massive strength of the big corporations; but while one may blame the Army officials for not asking better guarantees of performance, one can scarcely blame the Garssons because they were small fellows. The fact that they started with almost nothing is not the real count against them. It is rather the charge that they bought military and political favors.

A broad view of the role of the war contractors in the war economy would show the largest proportion of them, no doubt, doing the best possible job according to their lights. Yet the records of the War Frauds Bureau of the Justice Department show that in many instances their standards were even more lax than those of the Army officers and the Congressmen. Joseph Loftus of the New York *Times* has had the happy idea of going through the War Frauds Bureau activities in order to get a framework for the May-Garsson case. He has found that at every stage in the history of the war contracts, from the original bids to the contract re-negotiations, the Government has had to contend with widespread attempts at fraud, padding, deception of accounts. It was only when a test-case was made and a contractor and his accountant sent to jail that many of the contractors took fright, and the Army was flooded with requests to change the renegotiation estimates.

It is this record which is, in one sense, even more frightening than the May-Garsson evidence. For every individual instance of corruption flows from a whole reservoir of loose and anarchic standards.

2. Sons and Brothers

I WANT to turn to the story of a fellow called Joe Keller and his sons and all men's sons. Joe Keller is a creation of Arthur Miller's fine play, *All My Sons.* I find, from the theater gossip columns, that the two leading contenders for the coming prize awards by the Critics Circle and the Pulitzer Committee are Eugene O'Neill's *The Iceman Cometh* and Miller's *All My Sons.*

I should not myself find it hard to choose between them. The O'Neill play is good theater, but its theme that you must not strip a man of his pipe-dreams seems a curiously futile one in an age when the major nations on the world stage seem to be moving trancelike toward a common disaster which—when it comes—will be no pipe-dream. The Miller play has dramatic stature because it grapples with the central moral problem of our world: the betrayal of men's brotherhood, the question of whether the fabric of brotherhood can be rebuilt. Count this as a piece of electioneering for *All My Sons.*

The whole history of American practicality—a combination of the business spirit and "common sense"—is distilled in Joe Keller. He is not what we should call an evil man. He is looking out for the main chance: how to make money for his family, how to give his sons a start in life, how to build up a business and keep from being broken by life. In the process he manufactures defective airplane parts during the war, and sells them to the Government, and sends them off, knowing that they may cause the deaths of young Americans like his own sons, but hoping that they will not.

They do. And when one of his sons discovers it, he kills himself. And when another discovers it, he turns against his father with the agonized passion of one for whom the moral issue transcends the family tie.

The play has been highly praised, and with justice. It has generally been approached as a study in the moral responsibility that each person must bear for his acts, even in a world where responsibility is carried lightly, and where you can twist out of it by telling yourself that you are doing only what everyone else is doing.

But I should like to approach it somewhat differently. There have been many works of art, in the history of our Western culture, dealing with the virtues of courage and loyalty, patriotism and fortitude. We discovered during the war how plentifully men are endowed with these qualities— perhaps because they have been so long celebrated that they have become bone of our bone, perhaps because men have been conditioned to associate them with their sense of manliness.

Here is a play that takes these virtues for granted, and celebrates a virtue of a very different sort. It is hard to find a name for it: "brotherhood" sounds too mawkish, the "sense of society" sounds too abstract. But whatever the name, the quality is real: the sense of whatever it is that links man to man. Chris Keller, the son, discovers it during the war when one of the men in his company gives him his only pair of dry socks before he goes off to battle. Joe Keller, the father, knows it only in a narrow sense: the blood-kinship and blood-loyalty of members of a family. "Nothin's bigger than that," he insists. "I'm his father and he's my son, and if there's something bigger than that, I'll put a bullet in my head." At the end, too late, he discovers that they were all his sons, all the twenty-one who died because of the faulty cylinder-heads he furnished for the P-40s.

This dawning sense of the linkage between all men, this sense that all men are sons and brothers, is the new thing that Miller's play has brought to the jaded playhouses of Broadway. How curious that so old a theme— as old as the Judaeo-Christian myth—should seem new and even daring. But in our celebration of the tribal virtues of courage, we have forgotten about the inner sense of kinship that crosses all tribal boundaries and makes them seem puny. The play has its faults, of course. We learn to see

Joe Keller from the inside, and to understand his feeling for the "practical." We never see his son Chris from the inside; we do not see the developing process by which he comes to grasp the great and simple truth that he does; so that when it comes upon us, we are unprepared to believe it.

But that is a necessary fault of the play. For Chris Keller is not alone in having no preparation for the sense of society. That is true of all of us and of our children. And because it is, the tribal passions that are now loose in the world may have their way.

3. The Case of General Meyers

Major General Bennett E. Meyers is in trouble, and plenty of it. The Senate War Investigating Committee has dug up enough dirt about his double life as Air Forces procurement official and as contractor-speculator-profiteer to smother even the hardiest reputation.

General Meyers himself is of little importance, and will soon be forgotten.[1] What will not easily be forgotten is the symbolic meaning of the charges against the general—and the admissions by him. What do they show about life and striving in these United States under the spur of the Big Money and the passion for profit?

Throughout the Committee hearings the fierce glare of public exposure has been focused—and rightly—on an individual. But all the time the press has been silent about the unlovely light which the investigation has shed upon the major incentives which move men in our vaunted system, and the ethics which flow from it.

Consider some of the things that have emerged from the hearings. Here was a two-star general, who had served in the Army all his life, and had become commanding general of the Army Air Forces Materiel Command. His was the big voice on procurement and contracts. Yet it has been disclosed—and the disclosures have not been seriously challenged—that he talked about loans and postwar jobs with the heads of corporations over whose contracts he had a perhaps decisive control; that he held corporate stock whose extent he did not reveal to the Army; that he set up his own company to manufacture electrical gadgets, operated it under dummy con-

---

[1] For the record, he was tried and convicted of "inducing a former business associate to lie under oath to the Senate Investigating Committee" and given a sentence of twenty months to five years.

trol, and had contracts and sub-contracts allocated to it; that he set up the company with thirty thousand dollars and got millions in Government contracts; that when his own company engineers figured that fuse-boxes for airplanes should be sold to the Air Forces for eleven dollars each he had them jack up the price to four times that amount.

It will not do to dismiss this as an abnormal case. No one can tell how characteristic it was or wasn't, but it is hardly likely that conduct of this sort was a solitary weed in an otherwise perfect garden. General Meyers himself seems to believe it was normal and natural, and (according to UP's Frederick Othman) he said things at his press conference after one hearing—an almost incredible melange of big names and the Big Money and sex—which no newspaper would dare risk libel in printing.

Is it so hard to recapture how such things might happen—how a man, looking around him and seeing the Big Money flowing and big fortunes made almost overnight and a moral code an obstruction to be sidestepped and integrity a bugbear for fools, might decide he would be a fool not to cut himself into an easy thing and a good thing? This is the moral air which big men and little men breathe in a grab-and-hold system; this is the moral soil out of which the weeds of profiteering and corruption grow.

The whole episode sets one's mind astir. How does a man get that high up in a crack military organization without revealing his basic fiber to his associates and superiors? Why do they, at the end of the war, pin a Distinguished Service Medal and a Legion of Merit decoration on him? Why, when they received a tip-off on his activities, did they file instead of investigating it? What about the businessmen with whom he had dealings—official and social? Were they naïve enough never to suspect anything, or was there so much swag around for everyone to cut into that suspicions could be brushed aside—and the job of asking questions left safely to a Senate Committee several years later?

I suppose there was worse corruption during the war. I have dug up out of the newspaper files an item from July 12, 1943, about a Senate Committee report on the aircraft industry. The head of the Committee was a man called Harry S. Truman, and it was a great Committee. The report had to do with unsafe materials used in making airplane engines, falsified tests, forged inspection reports—and, as a result, flying coffins in which young Americans died. Curiously in my newspaper clips the name of the then Brigadier General Bennett Meyers appears as one of the Army big shots who backed up the high corporate officials involved. The current disclosures, at least, deal only with extra money made at the people's expense—not with the lives of their sons.

One thing is to be said for the real Army career officer of the old school: he holds all such goings-on in horror. But the last two wars have shown pretty well that the integrity of the old school stands very little chance when it comes up against the ethics of the Big Money. In a profits civilization even the most austere activities take on the complexion of the passion for profits—and Army officials have not remained untainted.

As I see the shapes that loom in the future, the real threat will not be a military caste, in the sense in which the German Junkers had one. America is not the right soil for that kind of caste. A much bigger threat will come when the authority with which the Army is invested combines with the swinishness of the profiteer and the drive of Big Business. That will bring us dangerously close to what the great English prophet, John Ruskin, once called "the ethics of the dust." [2]

[2] This piece of mine on the General Meyers case evoked an angry editorial in *The Saturday Evening Post*, Dec. 20, 1947. The gist of it and the nature of my reasoning in reply are given in the following excerpts from my piece, "The Ethics of the Satevepost" (Dec. 18, 1947):

I wrote about the case of General Bennett E. Meyers, and said rather harmlessly that the case was not only about him but also about "life and striving in these United States under the spur of the Big Money and the passion for profit." I added that, culpable as Meyers was as a person, the case also shed an "unlovely light upon the major incentives which move men in our vaunted system, and the ethics which flow from it." This latter, with its red-flag-to-the-bull word "system," is what irks the *Satevepost*. They say there are rotten apples in every barrel (granted), that there is corruption in Russia (decidedly), and in England (of course), and besides, do "the Lerners et al." want us to give up our freedom and "submit ourselves to some other system?"

The answer is No.

I do not want America to give up its freedom. What I should like to see, however, is something better than the ethics of the dust that flows from the cupidity for the Big Money. What surprises me is the candor with which the *Satevepost* equates freedom with acquisitiveness. What its editors seem to say—otherwise there is no point to their editorial—is that any attack on the forces in our society that make for the economic hoggishness of profiteers and monopolists is at the same time an attack on political freedom. In short, that the only freedom there can be is the freedom of the trough as it flows over with the Big Money. Is that the ethics of the *Satevepost*?

I will match my regard for democracy and freedom with that of the *Satevepost* editors. But I have not so stupefied my thinking as to conclude that democracy and freedom can exist only as a by-product of the economics of the jungle. I do not believe that democracy and freedom come to us only by courtesy of the aluminum monopoly, or the present black market in steel, or the current orgy of inflation profiteering, or the rumblings about commodity speculation by both Administration and Congressional "insiders."

If I were giving a Christmas gift book to the editors of the *Satevepost*, it would be the great English classic, *The Sickness of an Acquisitive Society*, by R. H. Tawney. From it they might learn to distinguish between the freedom and democracy which are crucial in the life of a moral man, and the obsession with money-as-the-prime-good, which is the least attractive element in a material culture. The failure to make this distinction not only leads to blunders like that of the *Satevepost* editorial, but it might also lead to the rejection of all reform measures in our economy on the ground that they destroy our freedom.

4. *Look to the Source*

WE ARE DEALING in all this with a coarsening of the human conscience that is not only America-wide but mankind-wide.

Even a random sampling of recent events will disclose how deeply this corrosion has eaten into American political ethics. Take Senator Bilbo's victory in the Mississippi primaries, on the basis of the most open incitement to anti-Negro hatred since the era of the night riders. Take the economic Bilboism that strangled the Fair Employment Practices Committee and allowed it to die with scarcely a quaver of regret. Take the moral obtuseness of the Senators and Congressmen who were willing to gamble with runaway price inflation and the destruction of the people's living standards because they cared more about pleasing the business lobbies. When Representative May said in his naïve way that he had done nothing that other Congressmen were not doing all the time, he was—in a deeper sense than he knew—giving the whole ethical show away.

The story goes beyond Congress. The political orators deliver glittering periods about the war veterans and how much the nation owes them. One thing the nation owes them is housing. Yet the major organizers of the housing blockade are the banks and insurance companies and trust companies who control the flow of mortgage money. A special grand jury in New York was adjourned for a month after Wall Street pressure was applied to forestall a criminal indictment. We have the inglorious spectacle of the New York State Superintendent of Banks pleading against a criminal indictment on the ground that it may undermine public confidence in the banks!

This sums up the current state of public morality: let truth go begging for statement, let the skies of the veterans' welfare fall—but let no harsh words be allowed to tarnish the interests of the American banking fraternity.

I do not say these things are new and unexampled. They follow all too closely the pattern of American public and political ethics after World War I, in the incredible twenties of Teapot Dome, in the era of Warren Gamaliel Harding and the Big Money. Go further back into American history to the period that followed the Civil War, and you get to the tawdry ethics of the Grant Administrations, the Crédit Mobilier scandal, the fake land-booms nourished on bribery—the whole era that Mark Twain in one of his bitterest novels called the Gilded Age.

Is the main indictment then against capitalism? Is the root of political corruption to be found in the cash-nexus? That is too easy an answer—as the whole recent experience of Russia shows. The Russians have done away with capitalism and the private business system. Yet they too, as the current news-items document, have their public graft scandals and their private greed for money and power. Even the severest penalties imposed by the Party and the State have not been able to prevent Russian officials from yielding to bribery and lining their own pockets at the public expense. The Communist philosophy of legislating political ethics from above has proved as leaky as our own noble experiment in the twenties of legislating temperance habits. The values men live by come from deeper sources than the commands of a Congress or a Politburo.

What is happening today is that the faiths are failing—whether they be the faiths of capitalism or socialism or democracy. In their traditional form they are proving an insufficient cement to hold men together in a structure of social decency.

To many people the answer will seem to lie in a return to religion. The trouble is that the religious faiths have failed too. They depend too much on the inner personal conversion of the individual considered by himself. If humanity moves away from the corrupt and the bestial it will be not by individual conversion but by the re-establishment of the sense of society— the sense of what ties men to other men. A local community, for example, in which men have come together to work out the housing problem or the task of crushing the fascist virus in the schools, is worth all the sermons in the book. This functioning sense of society, at the level of daily living, is the source to which alone we can look.

JULY 29, 1946; MARCH 19, NOV. 19, 1947; JULY 9, 1946

Sports and the Big Money

THE WHOLE EPISODE of the attempt to "fix" a championship football game, and its dramatic discovery, is evidence of the contradictory beats of impulse in American life today. On the one hand we have turned our sports into Big Business professionalism, with the gambling sluices wide open and the Big Money pouring into them. On the other hand we still cling fiercely to our old ideal, carried over from a simpler society and a slower tempo, that the games must stay straight and clean. When our ideal collides with our practice, we feel bruised and shocked. Which does us honor. But it ought also make us think a bit, and take stock of what is happening to one of the best and most vigorous aspects of American life—mass sports.

Most Americans still live bemused in the dream-image of the sports contest as a fight for glory between two traditional college rivals. Actually the professional spirit has invaded even the colleges, where it is no secret that in many cases of college football the coaches have to find some way of recruiting their best players by buying them without actually paying cash. And now the shadow of corruption looms over professional sport.

We get the picture of a gambler like Alvin Paris—perhaps fronting for a syndicate of bigger gamblers—who entertained key members of a big professional football team at night-clubs; of players like Merle Hapes and Frank Filchock, who listened to his proposal to pay them for throwing the game, and—while rejecting it—failed to report it to League officials; of a Football League commissioner who had not succeeded in making such reports an instinctive part of player habit and League discipline; of mysterious messages almost unintelligible to those who do not know the sports bookies' code, coming over wires tapped by police; of police conferences in the mayor's office important enough to absorb Mayor O'Dwyer for the better part of a day and night.

Behind all this is the fact that we are a nation of sports spectators, so that baseball, football, fighting, basketball, have all become Big Business; and we are also a nation of sports gamblers, so that we have a second Big Business piled on the first. The sports writers estimate that there was a minimum of twenty million dollars bet all over the country on the Giants-Bears game, on which the bribe try was made. Almost every newspaper carries the betting-odds and the margin points for every important game. The odds are fixed by a big syndicate in Minneapolis, and followed by thousands of bookies all over the country.

The business of the bookies is illegal, but so deep have the roots of sports betting gone in American life that the attempt to enforce the laws would meet the same fate as the attempt to enforce Prohibition once met. ·It must be said for the bookies that their profits come from having the games played straight and not from having them played crooked. The impulse toward crookedness comes from the professional gamblers who, unlike the amateur bettors, see a chance to sew up a game tight.

In the light of these facts, there ought to have been less surprise at an episode like the Paris case. Yet it easily made front-page headlines everywhere. Why? I think it is because Americans, who know perfectly well how seamy their business and politics are, still regard sports as their great area of integrity. Millions of Americans are sports spectators, and they want to watch a contest, not a conspiracy. Millions are bettors, and they don't like to think of themselves as suckers—which no doubt they very often are.

We are not wholly innocents. We have a curious grading of our sports on the score of integrity. No one expects wrestling to be honest. Very few expect boxing to be wholly honest. Basketball, which is one of the new Big Business betting games, did run into trouble several years ago on the Brooklyn College affair, and has since been on shaky ground. But we still cling to it as we do to baseball and football as untouchable. The flagrant and classic affair of the Chicago White Sox in 1919 was a form of shock therapy for baseball. Everyone hopes that the present Giants-Bears episode will be equally healing for pro football. But behind the hope there is the acid knowledge that in a society where the siren song of the Big Money is so sweet and insistent, there will always be some who will not stop up their ears.

DEC. 18, 1946

Leo Durocher and Burt Shotton

FOR MOST AMERICANS the gladiators who count are those of the baseball diamond, not those in the Berlin corridor;[1] and the generals who count are not the grim and bestarred ones but the men who guide the destinies of the ball clubs. Say Lucius Clay and Curtis Lemay to the fellow next to you in the bleachers and you'll get a blank look. But say Leo Durocher, Burt Shotton, or Branch Rickey, and the ecstasies will soar or the expletives crackle, depending on whether you have chanced upon a Guelph or a Ghibelline of the baseball feuds.

I prefer it that way. I would rather have pop bottles busted than heads, and home run records atom-bombed than cities. These baseball generals are more fun than the grimmer ones, and (I venture) healthier for the republic. On front stoops and in backyards, on the beaches and at the bars, the hot discussion has been not about the B-29s on their way to Europe, but about the great baseball shuffle. Which is the best safety valve I know for the midsummer madness of the Berlin war.

[1] This was written at the time the Russians cut off transport from the Western portions of Berlin.

Not that the baseball titans are innocents. They could probably give the Kremlin and the Pentagon some pointers on power politics. Baseball is run on the principle of a big feudal empire, each major league club having a lot of satellite clubs like satrapies in the provinces. Players are owned, bought, sold, bartered, and released as if they were serfs in the Middle Ages or slaves on the auction blocks of the old South. The man at the top is a boss without a Politburo. If you don't follow his orders you are out of baseball, and a broken man. Take the Ed Stanky affair, which was the Tito episode of the Rickey empire. Like Tito, Stanky showed some rebelliousness of spirit, but Rickey cracked down, banished him from his beloved Brooklyn, only to find him nettlesome still.

Or take the strange case of Mel Ott, the erstwhile manager of the Giants. He asked for his own death sentence, as if he were one of those self-lacerating defendants at the Russian purge trials. When Stoneham asked him what the club needed most to get out of its doldrums, Ott said "A new manager"—which is surely Dostoevskian in the depths of its self-punishment.

Finally there is the Great Shuffle proper, with Durocher being fired from the Dodgers, Ott replaced by him at the Giants' helm, and Durocher replaced by Burt Shotton. As a way out of several impasses, the Great Shuffle was as slick a diplomatic maneuver as anything the striped-pants boys have worked out. With the excitement it has stirred up it should pay off in the turnstiles of both clubs, and go down in history as baseball's Marshall Plan for the care and feeding of hungry magnates.

As for the debate on Durocher vs. Shotton, the real issue seems to be whether you want a quiet fellow like Omar Bradley to mastermind your baseball strategy, or a blood-and-guts brawling fellow like Georgie Patton. Durocher has the blitz tactics of a Patton, the same weakness for dramatics, and the same knack for keeping things at a high tension. His is a St. Vitus generalship. His strategy is that of shakeup and violence, with catchers playing the infield, infielders catching flies in the outfield, pitchers following each other in dizzying succession, and pinchhitters appearing dramatically to turn a tide that doesn't turn. The method is exciting, but no player lasts anywhere long enough to prove himself, find himself, be himself. The first requirement of a baseball player, like the rest of us, is peace of mind—not a piece of his manager's.

If Durocher makes the players jumpy and neurotic, Shotton is like the psychoanalyst on whose shoulders they pour out their troubles. He is the great white father, the authority principle itself. He too is cunning at manipulating, shaking up, improvising, but he does it in a quiet way. His record in the major leagues was mediocre. Then he went into a retirement, and came back from it after a long spell like a Lazarus come back from the dead. I don't suppose that baseball managers have time to read Toynbee. If they did, they would find in one of his volumes a long section on what he calls withdrawal-and-return, a sort of period of exile and brooding after which a leader comes back a better and deeper man. Durocher had it for a year, Shotton had it for more than a decade. Each may have used it to discover something about himself.

But baseball should have room enough for the methods of both a Durocher and a Shotton. That is why the Great Shuffle, which leaves them both at the head of competing teams, was a good thing. Both will be scrutinized jealously in the most critical democracy of all—the democracy of the fans. Without the great cementing force of the fans, baseball would be only a collection of petty despotisms held together by the lure of the Big Money. With it, it has become one of the great popular arts of America. It is an art in which all the performers are judged finally by the suffrage of the fan, who is passionate in his hatreds and his loves, but passionate also in his sense of justice.

That is what makes baseball the only empire which can carry on power politics without destroying the world. And that is why I would rather have our eighteen- and nineteen-year-olds in the stands and on the sandlots where they belong, rather than at the draft boards and on the plane carriers, where they so tragically but so surely are going to be.

JULY 20, 1948

I'm Dreaming of a Bright Sweepstake

THEY HAVE STARTED the drawings on the Irish sweepstakes for the English Derby races. We shall now be treated to the customary stories of New York City washerwomen whose Cinderella dreams have come true, and mechanics on whom have been showered the riches of Croesus. The newsreels will show their traditional picture of a prizewinner, surrounded by wife and children, still breathless with an incredulous joy, explaining how he will spend the money that has fallen to him. And the audience will laugh, partly in unbelief, mostly in envy.

But something has happened to the Irish sweepstakes. They are no longer the solitary big events they used to be. Our American culture has caught up with them. There are the radio give-away shows, where you don't even have to make an initial investment for a lottery-ticket, but require only a radio, a telephone listing, and patience. There is the numbers game—or the "policy" racket—where you can play for the sweepstake prizes with a newly welling hope every day. There are the daily race-track betting ventures, so widespread that millions of men and women all over the nation wait with suspense every day to learn how a horse they have never seen makes out on a track they have never attended.

Then there is, of course, the market. The heavy volume of recent stock-market sales seems to indicate that the professionals are no longer alone in the market, and that the amateurs have begun to move in again. The smell of the 1920s is in the air. Those in the know tell me that this is getting to be a "People's Market" again, as it was in the halcyon days of Coolidge and Hoover, and that the irrepressible impulse to get rich quick is stirring once more.

One wonders why it took so long to come back. Most people were thoroughly shaken by the 1929 market collapse, when paper dreams as well as profits were wiped out. But it is almost twenty years now, and the memories of 1929 have gone frayed around the edges. The new generation of amateur market players is about ready for action.

Up to now the market quotations have not kept pace with the obvious boom in industrial production and profits. There are signs that—even with margin restrictions and all—the speculative interest is kindling again. Maybe it is because people expect the heavy war-contract orders to go on for some time, maybe it is because they expect the election of a Republican who will be nice to business and its profits. Or maybe it's only one of those mysterious collective hunches that come out of the air, sweep through merchant, lawyer, doctor, stenographer, clerk, and finally push stock prices out of all relation to industrial reality.

If you ask me, the whole thing is a sort of glorified numbers game. But don't expect me to be censorious about it, and to utter stern warnings about the dire things that will happen to the economy and the suckers. I do think they will happen, but I don't see why we should raise our hands in horror at the market sweepstakes when the sweepstake element is so much a part of the whole fabric of our society. Let us at least have a frankness about the get-rich-quick behavior in our culture equal to the frankness that a man called Kinsey is teaching us to have about sexual behavior.

At the root of the sweepstake-impulse is the fact that everything in our mode of living makes us hungry for the big prizes. Even in the richest country in the world, life for most people is in reality nothing like the sensuous, glamourized version of it that they find in the movies and the picture-magazines, and out of which their dreams are woven. In this land of opportunity we have never lost hold of the myth that *anything is possible.*

We wait for the Florida and Bermuda vacation to happen, for the dream house to happen all complete with electric refrigerators and television sets, for the golf-club membership and the country-club dances to happen, for the sizable bank account against the uncertain future to happen. They don't happen to happen. We wait and dream and stay in our rut. Only one thing can pull us out—the phone-call for the radio jackpot, the lucky sweepstake number, the fifty-to-one long shot in the horse race, the stock market killing.

There is no sense in becoming preachy about it. The fact is that life has become a sweepstake. Millions of people who have lost the sense of being able to make anything of the collective effort of shaping their economic society, now expect fortune to descend like pie from the sky. Except that it is no longer pie they are expecting. It is the chromium-plated, newest-gadget dream of the Big Money.

MAY 28, 1948

The American Look

I CAME upon a missive the other day from one of the big department stores of our town. Along with a sadly unpaid bill from which I averted my gaze, there was an enclosure that caught it: a reprint of a large advertising spread for college girls' clothes. In a bold diagonal sweep there were three young heads haloed in an incandescent magic; and in a transverse line cutting across them were four young bodies dressed with a jaunty but fetching casualness. The motto in the center said: THE AMERICAN LOOK; and underneath it the words: "It's in her face, in the way she dresses—youth, freedom, gaiety, naturalness—typically American traits."

You may dismiss this as simply the ebullience of the advertising copywriter's art, or as a distressing instance of a brash nationalism that has burst its way into the garment trades. But if you stop there you will be making a mistake. For this is a case where the copywriter, in the pursuit of profit, has stumbled on a social and psychological truth. There *is* an American Look.

For America has become one of the civilizations that leaves its mark on history, and every civilization has a style of its own that shows itself in its outward form and in its inner spirit, in its architecture and its literature, in its work life and play life. Why should it show itself less in the silhouette of the American woman than in the skyline of the American city? Both are equally products of American nature and American art.

We have all seen the American Look, whether or not we have recognized it as such. Into the making of face and figure have poured the life-strains of many nations and races and peoples, crossing and recrossing in this "nation of nations." Into the making of the clothes and styles has poured so much of our resources and our resourcefulness. Into the matching and synthesis of the whole has gone so much of the energies of the woman herself. Her time and intensity are sunk in it, her anxieties and fantasies are woven around it. With so much attention lavished on it, it would be surprising if the American Look were not a thing of glamour and wonder.

Some of our latter-day moralists (Philip Wylie notable among them) have written some bitter things about the way the glamour-ads play on the sex-fears and the sex-fantasies of women. Yet the fact remains that, whether by art or nature, we have succeeded in creating in our minds a type-image of how the American woman should look. Like as not she doesn't look that way at all, but that's the way we think of her as looking, especially when we are deprived of her for a time.

Our soldiers, wandering perforce among all the distant places of the world, sought the American Look the world over. They found no dearth of women, and they found good qualities in them—a worldly wisdom, a strength in meeting adversity, a willingness to bear their own loads, a dedicated cherishing of the male—to a greater degree perhaps than the American women possess these qualities. But they did not find the American Look. And for want of it, despite all the little accumulated memories that will stab their hearts for years to come, the world for them was an empty place full of foreigners.

Some of these men are back now, and the rest will follow. The streets are beginning to be alive with them again. They have come back hungrily to many things, but what they devour most is the American Look.

For realism's sake, I must add a postscript. I think back to the times when I have had occasion to loiter about in the shops where the American women flocked to seek the American Look. It was then that I understood how cruel are Beauty and Smartness as gods, especially to those who can approach them only from a distance. The not-so-young, the scarcely-gay, the far-from-natural: these were the women who sought most frantically to buy the appearance of qualities whose loss they long ago should have acknowledged.

As I watched them in their assorted sizes, ages, silhouettes, and as I saw the feverish eagerness with which they pursued the American feminine ideal, I blanched a bit. I felt the pathos of life in a glittering consumer's civilization, the thousands of little tragedies that counterbalance the few dazzling successes. But I also doff my hat in admiration for the unquenchable spirit of American women who will admit of no obstacles and shrink from no heroic sacrifices in the tireless pursuit of such goals as they have.

Actually it is one of the great paradoxes of the world that the American Look should be what it is. Take again the adjectives I have quoted from the advertising copy. Youth—in a country which is a young country, but which is clinging to an old system of economic and social power long after it has become archaic everywhere else in the world. Freedom—in a country which is politically freer than any other, but where men and women alike are tied to tyrannous conventions and are the captives of iron fears. Gaiety—at a heartbreaking time when millions all over the world face a winter of blank destitution, and the world has grown gray with the breath of the atom bomb. Naturalness—in a machine culture which is the most standardized in history.

From which I conclude that all is not wholly well even in the land of the American Look, and that part of our gaiety is a brave effort to still the unquiet spirit and heal the soul's schism in a troubled time.

NOV. 9, 1945

The Fortress of the Collyer Brothers

SOME SORT of climax, if not end, has come to the saga of Homer and Langley Collyer and to their Harlem hermitage which has become so dear to newspapermen and to crowds of spectators. Homer is dead, and Langley is missing, and crews of unfeeling police have dug their way into the sacred tunnels of what has been the Collyer fortress against the world since 1909.[1]

The ranks of gaping citizens who keep a kind of death-watch over the house obviously find in it an inexhaustible store of nourishment for their

[1] The reference is to two brothers who had become legendary for their withdrawal from the world. The piece was written before Langley was found—as he was several days later—dead under piles of the debris.

jestings and their sense of the bizarre. But I wonder whom the joke is on, the watchers or the watched?

Let us take a closer look. The watching crowd sets down the Collyer brothers as crazy, cracked. I suppose it is right. The story of their infancy experiences, their dreams and desires as young men, the psychic hurts and lesions which jolted them into the grooves they were to keep for forty years: all that would make a psychoanalyst's bonanza. I can't do even an amateur's job on them, and I don't propose to try.

But one can see clearly enough what it is that has captured the public imagination. First of all, we laugh at grown men who piled up so much useless and irrelevant junk and lived among it. Chandeliers, rotted bicycles and rubber tires, dressmakers' dummies, baby-carriages, mounds of old newspapers and magazines, cartons of paper scraps, old lampshades, old-fashioned hats, a Ford chassis, boxes of human excrement. All abnormality is simply an extension into the fantastic of the things we call normal. Which of us, in all honesty, is free from the itch to collect things which by the furthest stretch of the imagination we shall never have use for, and pile them up in closets and attics? The Collyer brothers (driven by what obscure and now buried impulsions?) took this hoarding-instinct of ours and carried it to its logical and morbid end.

But this is only the surface. The Collyers were more than hermits living a retired and cobwebby existence. The point is that they were ingenious and belligerent hermits.

Their lives were organized militantly around the campaign to keep out the world. They fought an unceasing guerrilla war against the world and its pace and its values. It was a losing war, which is what gave it the touch of pathos. But who can doubt that in their own way (Homer had graduate degrees from Columbia, and Langley was a chemist, a pianist, and an engineer) they put as much sheer psychic intensity into their defense plans as the general staffs of the Great Powers are now spending in mapping out the strategies of the war to come?

Their father, it is reported, was a well-known doctor. Their grandfather was one of America's foremost shipbuilders. They inherited money, realty, the habits of a cultivated family. But for some reason they could not cope with the world, and they withdrew ever further from it in a womb-retreat. My guess is that it was a protracted withdrawal: shutting off first one whole story of the house while they lived on the others, then confining themselves to a single floor, then to a single room, then perhaps to only a corner of the room. This is, of course, what all psychiatrists recognize as the familiar retreat from the reality principle, but a retreat acted out in this case with a frightening literalness.

They made earthworks out of their possessions, like the street revolutionists of 1848, before modern artillery made such earthworks archaic. They built barricades, they hollowed out tunnels through the piles of newspapers, they contrived crafty entrapments for the enemy that never came. They had, of course, a few well-publicized encounters, with tax officials and with the encroachments of a bank that wanted the site of their house. But for the most part they were like characters in one of Kafka's tales, haunted by pursuers whose reality lies in the fact that they have created them.

For most of us, what is so curious about the Collyers is that they should have counted on such pathetic earthworks. But isn't that true of us, too? We stow away our bric-a-brac not in our houses, but in the lumber-rooms of our minds—useless items we call facts, jumbled and unexamined prejudices, archaic mementos of what our ancestors once used and believed in our ancestral world, unprobed hatreds and fears, garments of ideas thrown, not around a living reality, but around stuffed dressmakers' dummies, racial and national and religious myths that are the excrement of past eras.

Let us look at ourselves. We are a nation of readers, but we have closed our minds against the reality principle of a world in change. We pride ourselves on collecting "facts," but we do nothing to relate them to a central social purpose. We keep out "foreign" immigration, "foreign" ideas. We are prisoners in our own national house, locked behind our own barricades, bristling against a phantom enemy outside, fearful of exposing ourselves to fresh ideas or impulses which may reach and release our moral imaginations.

Instead of laughing at these Collyer brothers, we might make them our patron saints. I propose that we build a statue to them, and in it worship ourselves.

MARCH 27, 1947

The Epic of Model T

AT THE TURN of the century, in Detroit, an American mechanic who had spent most of his nearly forty years tinkering with machines made a decision in whose shadow we have all lived since. He broke with the men in his company who saw the newly emerging automobile as a luxury product to be made at high prices and high profits for the few. He decided on the mass-production of a car for the many, at low cost and with a slim margin of profit per unit on a large volume of production. Out of that decision came the epic of the Model T Ford, what has been called "the Tin Lizzie Revolution," which transformed American production methods and set a new cultural pattern for an America on wheels.

Henry Ford has never been one of my heroes. He was—on all the things that matter in our world of values—too ignorant, too gullible, too much of a social primitive. But now that his death gives us a chance to assess his total impact, it would be stupid to allow the memory of Ford's racist and reactionary views to distort our perspective on his achievements as a technician and an industrialist.

Ford's talent as a mechanic was in line with the great American tradition of the tool-makers and inventors—a tradition which includes Whitney and McCormick, the Wright brothers and Edison. In that field they were greater than he. But where he went beyond them was in his genius for going straight to the jugular on the question of how capitalist enterprise was to be organized.

His core-idea was mass-production. From that everything else in his economic methods flowed. To get mass-production you had to have a single and simple model with replaceable parts: hence Model T, imperishable and omnipresent; so standardized that you could get it in any color provided it was black, and could fix it in its frequent breakdowns with parts bought at the corner store or the crossroads garage. Also to get mass-production, you had to have a high-speed production belt-line, where a man did a single operation and had to keep up with the tempo set by the gods of the machine. And to get men to do this, you had to pay them high wages (remember Ford's $5.00 a day when the prevailing rate was $2.34), even though this meant a slimmer rate of profit on a large volume.

Mass-production, standardization, high-speed belt-line, high wages, large volume: these were the elements of the economic concept summed up in Model T. For a time, in the years just before and just after World War I, they seemed just as indestructible and irresistible as Model T. There was the general feeling in the twenties that the problems of the prosperous economy and the good society had been solved by this "New Capitalism." The men who felt this were as naïve in their way as Ford in his. The Great Depression wrote the epitaph of their hopes. For it proved that what one man might decide in a moment of insight was not the way of business enterprise as a whole. Businessmen *ought* to see that with high wages and low prices, they can do a bigger volume and get their products sold for a greater total profit. But as recent events have shown, their impulse when left to themselves and when given power over prices is to boost prices and profits per unit, even if it dries up the golden well.

Thus, even in economic terms, Ford's philosophy was the light that failed in the history of capitalism. When Model T came to an end in 1927, and Ford came out with a smoother, slicker, and better-looking car, he lost his dominance and distinction in the automobile age. The others had caught up with him, and he no longer had the genius to strike out on new lines and forge ahead of them.

Yet we cannot help looking back at the Age of the Tin Lizzie in an elegiac mood. There was something about her that caught the affection of the American people. She was crotchety and exasperating. There were others more beautiful than she. But there was an indomitable quality about her that made her not just another car but something of a folk-heroine in the American mind.

The rest of Ford's story is too shabby and stupid to have even the quality of tragedy. In our culture we make heroes of the men who sit on top of a heap of money, and we pay attention not only to what they say in their field of competence, but to their wisdom on every other question in the world. Henry Ford was one of the victims of this strain in us.

He came to see himself as a prophet on everything. His "Peace Ship" to Europe was a fantastic failure, yet what he brought back with him was even worse—the forged Protocols of the Elders of Zion, and the conviction that the root of all evils was "the international Jew," who was at once a communist and an international banker. His *Dearborn Independent* was largely the work of W. J. Cameron, and by 1926 Ford had to retract everything it had said about Jews; yet its work had been done, and the sewer of filth pouring out of it had poisoned enough minds from Argentina to China to make Ford a hero of the fascists. On another front, under the tutelage of Harry Bennett, he became a violent enemy of trade-unions.

This was Ford, brilliant in technology, a genius in organization, his mind a jungle of fear and ignorance and prejudice in social affairs. Can we perhaps find in him a mirror of the American problem today?

APRIL 9, 1947

Will We Be Saved by Print?

I AM TOLD by my publisher friends that a book isn't a book these roaring days unless it sells at least a million copies. There are three main sluices through which the new millions of books are pouring into our minds. One is the old best-seller, which has now reached new sales magnitudes. The second is the mail-order book-club, with several of them over or near the million mark in membership rosters, and others coming up. The third is the cheap reprint, especially the paper-backed glossy-covered book at a quarter, that now sells some fifty million copies a year and may soon be sending a hundred or even two hundred million copies a year into the American mind.

This raises some reflections. Will we be saved by print? We have a habit of measuring a people's inner cultural health by its percentage of literacy—especially book-literacy. Judged by that standard we should now be well on the way to salvation. If we lived once among mounds of print, the mounds have become mountains. We have become a nation of readers.

This could mean that we shall become a more mature nation—better informed, more reflective, more responsible, more creative. It could—but will it? Let me say straight off that I am unimpressed by the new publishing figures, viewed merely as figures. The American worship of bigness is one of our more adolescent characteristics. I am left cold by the reflection that a moronic mystery which once sold ten thousand copies now sells a million. I am equally unmoved when I hear that some mediocre mixture of sex and adventure, washed down by history, which might once have reached twenty-five thousand readers is now distributed by the mailman through a book club to a million doorsteps and R.F.D. boxes.

I have watched the consumption of these books. The readers treat them on the principle of democracy in the book-world: that all books are born free and equal. No sooner is one glamorous female adventurer or stale whodunit or senseless western consumed than another is taken up. I have seen chain smokers and I have seen chain coffee-drinkers. But must I now count it a sign of progress that we are treated to the spectacle of chain readers of second- or third-class drivel, just because that drivel is inside book-covers rather than in magazines or newspapers or on the airwaves?

41

To this some of my publisher friends will—and do—reply that commercially they have to publish a lot of drivel in order to be able to publish some good stuff; and that the crucial thing is to establish the book-reading habit. The argument is that once you have the habit you will make the transfer from Perry Mason to Edward Bellamy, or from Max Brand to Tolstoy. Perhaps.

But the dismaying fact is that it may work the other way, for there is a sort of Gresham's Law of the mind as well as of economics: bad books often will succeed in driving out good. I can say for myself that I have in the past few years consumed so many second-rate mysteries that my taste for other books is being debauched by them. In another field, one of the reasons usually given for the decline of our theater is the similar debauching of our creative sense—both of authors and critics and audiences—by the slick and sleazy Hollywood stuff.

No doubt we should be thankful that some of the cheap editions that sell in millions, regardless of their quality, are tapping a reading public they did not have before. No doubt also they are a good index of American reading tastes. But if American publishing is to perform a creative rather than a passive role in fashioning a humanism for the millions, it must help form new reading tastes rather than merely mirror the existing tastes. It must help create an intellectual discipline and integrity. The enemy of culture is not simply illiteracy. It is intellectual and moral slackness.

Some of the new publishers see this—Penguin Books, for example, whose list of new titles includes Walter Lippmann's *Public Opinion*, George Gamow's *Birth and Death of the Sun*, and (best of all) Ruth Benedict's brilliant *Patterns of Culture*. These books will not sell as easily as Ellery Queen does or James Hilton or Erich Remarque or the latest lady novelist whose boom is based largely on her bust. But at least a segment of the American future depends on getting books like these out of the sacred circle of the illuminati who have hugged them privately for years, and into the broad and popular market-place of ideas.

As we go further I should like to see the book people muster up courage enough to publish quarter editions of old and new books in the battle of political ideas. The American newspapers are flunking the job of providing a competition of ideas. The magazines do better, but the people need something more basic than the surface stuff of the magazines and the digests. The publishing of cheap books, and of pamphlets like the now classic *Races of Mankind*, may well prove to be the last citadel of the struggle for the human spirit.

But this will happen only if the publishers show daring in taking commercial and political risks, and only if the new millions of readers show a growing maturity by demanding books that are not an insult to their intelligence. In England the Labor party victory had the ground prepared for it by Fabian Society pamphlets and the Left Book Club books and by the reading and discussion groups built up around them all over Great Britain. In America we cannot expect to short-circuit the process by gaining new millions of readers for the romance of the girl who became embroiled with the court chamberlain of Charles the Wag, or for the Case of the Sleepwalker's Great-Aunt.

APRIL 29, 1946

On Dreiser

To READ of Theodore Dreiser's death was like saying good-bye to a whole age; or better, to some impersonal force which, like the vast aggregates of our cities, we had come both to scorn and to love as part of the American landscape. Dreiser seemed somehow imperishable. He had been with us for three-quarters of a century; had been writing novels among and about us for half a century. It had become oh, so easy to be oh, so smart about how bad he was as a writer, how inept as a technician in the literary machinery, how primitive and blundering and mastodon-like as an intelligence. All these adjectival judgments have become worn with the years, and I have encountered them again and again until I am thoroughly weary of them.

For the fact is that Dreiser, granted all his crudities, was the greatest American writer we have had in this twentieth century. He came out of our people, out of our soil, out of the granite rock of the American experience and the American plight. It took him half a century to hew his sculpturings out of that rock, but now they are there they will stand every change in the climate of ideas, every buffeting of the political tempests. The reason he wrought enduringly was not that he was a fancy craftsman— he was not: but because he was an honest one, because his chisel was governed by a passion of his brain and heart.

If you have never read Dreiser's first novel, *Sister Carrie*, then read it before anything else of his. I read it again after I had heard of Dreiser's death —ten or twelve years after my first reading—and it was even more moving than before. Dreiser wrote it just at the turn of the century, when he was twenty-eight. It had a curious publishing history: brought into print by the enthusiasm of Frank Norris, himself a young genius of American realism, condemned by the shocked assessment of the publisher's wife, and withdrawn from circulation for a decade. But that does not matter here, except as it showed the emergence of a new American writer who knew his country and the human heart, and was implacably determined to tell the truth.

Where had Dreiser quarried this knowledge, this determination? He was an Indiana boy, who had the small-town Midwestern childhood that so many American writers had: outwardly bleak, yet rich with inner brooding; religiously narrow, with the rigors of German Catholicism, not of Bible-belt Puritanism.

Yet in a boy's mind the two merged, and the adolescent sense of rebellion and of self-discovery became permanently fixed as Dreiser's basic attitude. It was an adolescence filled with hungers—for gentility, for advancement, for ideas, for beauty, for sexual fulfillment. Dreiser has set down these hungers in his books more unsparingly than any American writer, for his books are all self-portraits.

He was largely self-taught (he had only a year at college), and one traces in his books the marks of the self-taught man who cherishes ideas others have come to take for granted, and who quotes passages out of chemistry and biology books, and out of Spencer and Darwin. The ideas of these men wrought the profoundest influence on him; the break from life viewed as a religious and moral code to life viewed as an evolutionary process was for him the crucial break. Yet he was not a bookish man. His real schools were the great schools to which so many American writers have gone: the life of the giant city—Chicago, New York—viewed through the wide-eyed wonder of a small-town boy; and the training-ground of American journalism—the newspaper days in Chicago, St. Louis, Pittsburgh, New York.

This was the knowledge that was poured into the pages of *Sister Carrie*, and into the books that followed. Yet these outlines of Dreiser's "education" do little to explain (who can "explain" such matters?) how it was exactly he who happened to have the rugged honesty and the massive patience to set down what he saw in American life, and to fight it out with the censors and the prudes and the aesthetes. Two of his books—*Sister Carrie* in 1900 and *The Genius* in 1915—became *causes célèbres* in the long-drawn-out war for honesty in American writing; but every one of his novels was something of a battleground in this war.

He has been called the Zola of the American novel, and there is a sense in which it is true, not that he derived from Zola (Dreiser is strangely underived from anyone), but that the same forces that produced a Zola in France came, a quarter-century later, to produce a Dreiser in America. The literary movement that both represented has been called sometimes "realism," sometimes "naturalism." Zola theorized a good deal about it; Dreiser did not. He simply wrote—about himself, about how men and women live in America, about what is in the human heart, and about why we live at all. He was a realist in that he set down the actual life that he saw, without equivocation, without prettying-up. He was a naturalist in that he saw the human being as still part of a world of nature, obeying its laws, caught in its plights. His view can best be put in a sentence of his out of *Sister Carrie*: "Our civilization is still in a middle stage, scarcely beast, in that it is no longer wholly guided by instinct, scarcely human, in that it is not yet wholly guided by reason."

There had been others who had sought to write thus about American life: men like Henry Fuller and Stephen Crane and—above all—Frank Norris, whose *McTeague* and whose epic novels of wheat might have been forerunners of a more mature genius. But their promise never reached a fruition. Dreiser's did. The big fact about him, as Justice Holmes once said of John Marshall, is that in the campaign of history he was *there*, and he stayed there.

It is almost impossible to think ourselves back to an American fictional art without Dreiser—impossible to imagine what our literature would be like today without Carrie and Hurstwood, without Jennie Gerhardt, without Cowperwood, without Eugene Witla, without Clyde Griffiths. Take Hurstwood, who breaks his career and life in two for Carrie, and whose deterioration and doom proceed with the inevitability of a Greek tragedy: he is one of the great character-creations of our time. Cowperwood, the hero of Dreiser's two novels [1] of the financial community, *The Financier* and *The Titan*, was drawn from the life of Charles T. Yerkes, the traction magnate of Philadelphia and Chicago; yet in the act of transposing a man from the newspaper files to his novels, Dreiser created a man as well as a symbol of business power. Witla, the "genius," is perhaps of Dreiser's great characters the least successful. Clyde Griffiths, in *The American Tragedy*, was taken out of the court records of a murder trial in Herkimer, N. Y. Yet Dreiser invested the skeleton of his story with the living flesh-and-blood of what it is like to be a middle-class boy in America, and to hunger for success and power, and to be caught between sexual hunger and the allurements of wealth.

James Farrell has called Dreiser the great type of the plebeian artist in

[1] This was written before the third (posthumously published) novel of the Cowperwood trilogy appeared—*The Stoic* (1947).

America, and in a sense he is right. Dreiser came of the people, and for all his wanderings in the morass of New York's intellectual life, he never lost his sense of the people. He never became sophisticated. His knowledge came out of the life around him, and his sense of detachment in studying and describing that life went along with a sense of pity about not only the American tragedy but the human tragedy.

Where he was weakest was in his social and political thinking. Here his instincts were honest enough—the instincts that led him to fight on the side of the people, and led him militantly even as far as Communism. But he had no innate sense of the contours of political ideas as he had of the contours of character. He tried to go at the problem of the American political and social dilemma in much the way he wrote his novels—by sheer assault, without fear and without probing into what other men had tried to do in figuring out the age-old difficulties. And it didn't work. Aside from some of his blundering anti-Semitism, I respect the integrity of his political thinking, but I find little illumination in it.

But there is illumination and to spare in the novels and the autobiographies. Now that Dreiser is gone, he leaves a void in American life that will take a big novelist to fill—one who, with all the pity he has for his characters, is pitiless in setting down what he sees.

DEC. 31, 1945

Camus and the Outsider

I FIRST HEARD of Albert Camus when I spent a month in Paris in January of 1945. Every morning I would go out and buy an armful of the many wretchedly printed single-sheet Paris papers, and always I would find that what stayed longest in my memory was a daily piece, half-editorial, half-essay, running all the way down the left-hand column of *Combat* and finishing on the other side. I sought out the author, badgered him with questions, involved him in a long conversation. Several days later there arrived in my room at the correspondents' quarters a neat package from Camus, containing the three books he had published—a volume of plays, one of essays, a novel.

Camus' novel, *The Stranger*, has been translated and published (Knopf,

$2.00). The interest in it is, I suspect, largely due to the current literary cult, barbarously called "existentialism," which has spread like a fog from Paris to New York, and with which Camus' name is linked along with that of Jean-Paul Sartre. When I enter a room these days and hear the gorgon-word "existentialism," I recoil and flee for my very life. But I like Camus (not least because he hates cults and has dissociated himself from this one), and I find strangely moving his spare, underwritten, closely wrought story.

It is the story of a little clerk in Algiers whose crime is that he is too numb and dehumanized to pay lip-service to the conventions of civilized life. In that sense, wherever he may be, he is the Stranger, the outsider. (I should have preferred *The Outsider* as the translation for Camus' title *L'Étranger*.) Because he cannot support his mother, he sends her to a home for the aged. When she dies, he cannot show a grief he does not feel. He enjoys swimming with his girl and sleeping with her, but when she badgers him about "love," he cannot wrap himself in that garment; when she speaks of marriage he agrees—not because it means anything to him, but because it will please her.

When a next-door lodger speaks to him of being "pals," he nods an absent-minded assent, not because friendship means anything to him, but because the fellow is so urgent. But somehow he gets embroiled with the man and his affairs, gets caught up in a senseless quarrel that has nothing to do with him, and, with the hot Algerian sun addling his senses, he shoots and kills an Arab. At the trial his lack of emotion about his mother's death is distorted into proof of his depravity, his easy relations with his girl are made into something monstrous, and he is sentenced to death by decapitation.

What Camus is saying is, I think, that the man who cannot fake the social ties of family, love, marriage, friendship, civic obligations, gets caught in an absurd unbreakable web. Camus' Outsider, let me make it clear, is not a conscious rebel in the Promethean sense or the Byronic. He is not out to assert anything or reform anything. He is a curiously passive creature. He wants only to be let alone. He resists nothing. He does not live: to use a phrase of W. H. Auden, he is lived.

But where Auden's plea is for finding an active spiritual life in God, Camus' Outsider rejects that, too, along with the other trappings and illusions. In the months he spends alone in his cell, he comes as close to finding himself as anyone can in Camus' philosophy. The only burst of rage he shows is against the priest who seeks to tell him that he is leaving nothing valuable behind, and that what counts is how he will face God.

bears in their own minds than by prisons and chains. He keeps them continually haunted by the ghosts of the dead and by the sense of remorse. They are crippled men, living in the dark cave of the lies that have been told them by their master and his high priests. They practice, as Zeus puts it, "the good old piety of yore, rooted in terror." They live in the kingdom of fear, and wear the clanking chains of original sin.

This is piercing political insight. As the author of *Portrait of the Anti-Semite*, Sartre understands that the most atrocious evils today are committed and permitted by men whose minds have become dungeons of fear.

But while the fascists and the communists have cast an organized spell over their people, we in America also live in an age of fear. The campaign which is softening up the American mind for the coming struggle with Russia is one of the slickest and smoothest efforts in history to cast the combined spell of government, press, radio, the churches, the schools, business, and the armed forces over a tortured and credulous people.

Does this mean that Sartre has written a tract for liberalism? It does not. This is a shaking play for liberals to see, for Sartre blows their pet illusions as sky-high as he does the nightmare world of the reactionaries and propagandists.

The liberals believe that reason and reasonableness will conquer all. Sartre does not. Orestes' tutor is ridiculed as a rationalist liberal—the man who has brought Orestes up to see that all ideas and all cultures are relative, who implores him to be tolerant, who wants him to get away from Argos and its festering environment. The tutor is the typical liberal who believes that all crime comes from social environment, that men's hearts are a clean tablet on which society does its writing, and that men are somehow exempt from the tragic inner conflicts which rage in every heart.

Throughout the play Sartre is canny in his refusal to accept the liberal and Marxist clichés. He does not let Orestes (like his sister, Electra) succumb to the sense of pity for the people and to self-pity, the sense of guilt and repentance. He does not depict the Argive people in flattering or heroic terms; they have allowed themselves to become slaves in spirit, and no good can come from their paltriness of spirit. You cannot, Sartre is saying, find your solutions simply by invoking "the people." You cannot resort only to mass techniques. You cannot pool your collective enslavements and thereby become free.

What then remains for Orestes and for Sartre? Only the individual knowing in his own heart that nothing can shake his freedom. Aegisthus, the king of men, asks Zeus, the king of the gods, to "fell Orestes with a thunderbolt." For, reasons Aegisthus, "a free man in a city acts like a plague-spot. He will infect my kingdom and bring my work to nothing."

But Zeus cannot. "Once freedom lights its beacon in a man's heart," he says, "the gods are powerless against him. It's a matter between man and man." Zeus can regulate the stars in their courses, and the revolutions of day and night—but not a man who has once grasped that he is free.

This may seem arid doctrine to the men of our time who must act together to prevent their world from being handed back to the animals. It seems to reduce everything to the individual atom, to a great man acting from intuition. And that is Sartre's weakness—this high-sounding individualism that seems so futile in a world of corporate monopolies and state monopolies, of famine and war.

But don't dismiss his basic truth. It is exactly in a world of tyranny that we must come back again to the free man, exactly in a world of fear that we must get back to the solid core of conviction that links men to each other as it did in the resistance movements and will do again. Sartre's Orestes is not a world to himself. As the play ends he exhorts the people of Argos to stop crouching in their cave of fear, to stand up straight. He has committed his crime, he knows its consequences, he is willing to face them. As he leaves Argos, he takes the flies with him, so that the people, too, can win freedom for themselves.

What Sartre is saying, I think, is that the unbreakable sense of freedom within each man can in the end be linked with the unbreakable sense of the common plight and common freedom of all men.

MAY 14, 1947

Koestler on Terrorism

A GROUP of young men, along with a girl, carrying satchels into a railroad station in Palestine. A phone call to British authorities—certain to be heeded now—to evacuate the building. Then the blast and the dead. Then the arrest, the round-up of suspects, the futility of seeking the culprits when a whole people is arrayed against you in stony hatred. A few days later—at a bridge, a trestle, a British headquarters of some sort—the incident is again enacted. Thus the iterated ritual of terrorism in the passion of a people for a free home to which they can bring their brothers.

Is terrorism ever justified? That is the root problem with which Arthur Koestler deals in his novel about Palestine, *Thieves in the Night.*

On its face, Koestler's book is political history dressed up as fiction, the history of a Hebrew commune in Galilee called Ezra's Tower, from the night in 1937 when a truck convoy of armed settlers first plow it up under the watchful eyes of sentries, to the night two years later when a group from Ezra's Tower moves on to build another commune.

I agree with the reviewers who say that Koestler's Palestine story is not a particularly good novel. Joseph, the chief figure in the story, is wooden and without magic—a convenient abacus on which the author makes his moral calculations. Except in one book—*Darkness at Noon*, dealing with the Russian purge trials, and its massive figure of Rubashov— Koestler has generally failed in the novelist's godlike task of creating people. The fact is that he is less a novelist than a seismograph—to register the convulsive upheavals of the liberal mind and conscience. He turns ideas round and round artfully, to see how they glisten and what consequences they have for the human spirit.

There can be little doubt about where his sympathies lie in the battle of strategies inside Zionism. They lie not with Weizmann, the official statesman of world Zionism, but with Jabotinsky, the "direct action" revisionist, to whom the book is dedicated; not with the spokesmen of the Jewish Agency (whom he parodies cruelly in the figure of Glickstein), but with Baumann, the man in the leather jacket who knows how to command, who deals in mobile radio transmitters and machine guns, who believes that "we have to use violence and deception to save others from violence and deception," who swears youngsters into his underground army by secret rites, and who knows how to use the irrational and the heroic in the human animal.

Being rooted in the liberal tradition, Koestler's terrorists are tortured at the thought of death as means. But they face the Medusa-head without turning to stone. On the road that leads to the King David Hotel there are no logical stopping-places. And in the face of Arab terrorism, British betrayal, oil power-politics, callousness about the "floating coffins" waiting outside the ports, they embrace the only language (as Baumann puts it) that is understood universally from Shanghai to Madrid, the Esperanto of the machine gun.

What is most surprising about Koestler's trend is that it seems to reverse what he has said in every book from *Darkness at Noon* through *The Yogi and the Commissar*. In those books he attacked the Communists because they acted on the principle that the ends justify any means. Yet here, as a Zionist revisionist, he is invoking sympathetic understanding for a gang which defends terrorism as a means toward the sacred end of national liberation.

There is a possible way out of Koestler's dilemma. It is to make a distinction between terror by the state against dissenting groups (as in Russia, and even more in fascist totalitarianisms), and terror by a small desperate people struggling against imperialist oppression, as formerly with the Irish, and now with the Palestinian Jews.

Another approach is to say, as Koestler does, that we live in a political ice age; and that until the ice clears away, only the glacial elements of the human spirit have any chance of surviving. The Talmudic student with his lovelocks, who can repeat the manual of arms by singsong rote, is no more a paradox than the absent-minded scientist who creates in his laboratory the ultimate weapons of atomic energy or germ warfare. All war is legalized terrorism, and in an age when the preparation for war forms the logic of statesmanship and science, it is too much to expect the completed nation-states to have the monopoly of terrorism. The nation-state struggling for being is bound to be infected by it.

All this can be argued, but in the end the decision will not be made by those who stand by as observers, but by the Palestine Jews. It is they who will have to die or kill, they who will have to make the stony Palestinian earth yield enough to sustain their brothers from Europe if they can get their brothers in.

NOV. 13, 1946

The Budenz Conversion Story

WHILE I WAS reading this book,[1] I found myself turning back to a book, published in 1902, dealing with the vagaries of the conscience and of conversion, with religious turns and returns—the great Gifford Lectures of William James, *The Varieties of Religious Experience*. For me, the James of 1902 shed a good deal of light on the Budenz of 1947.

As James puts it, there is in all religious men an abiding sense of "the More" and a persistent drive to a "union" with it. Budenz happens to have come out of a devout Catholic home in Indiana, and his sense of "the More" takes, therefore and quite naturally, the symbolic figure of the Immaculate Virgin, to whom he dedicates his book. Had he been born in

[1] *This Is My Story*, by Louis Francis Budenz (Whittlesey House, $3.00).

India or China, in a Chassidic village in Russia or in the Arabian desert, his hungering religious spirit would have taken quite different forms.

But I think he would still have been a zealot, the sort of person who overstates whatever he believes in at the time with a passion that excludes the possibility of any other belief, the sort of person who—when he turns his back on one belief to embrace another—must magnify the new good which was once evil and vilify the new evil which was once good. Else he has no peace.

Budenz started as a devout Catholic, became a devout labor organizer on the fringes of the revolutionary movement, went on to embrace Communism and to thunder away at the wickedness of a capitalist world and has now come back to Catholicism. In his pre-Communist-fringe days, when his friends prophesied he would join the Communist party, he would mockingly characterize his course as "from Rome to Moscow and return." What was meant as a crack has survived to describe his life-cycle.

You may read his book for various reasons. You can read it—as most of its readers will hope to—as a sort of Dies-Rankin-Wood-Thomas report on the nefarious plotting of the Communists to destroy America and hand over the broken shards and fragments to Moscow. If you do, you will be disappointed. For, while Budenz is very clear in his mind that American Communists are part of a world-wide conspiracy to do Russia's bidding, there are very few sensational exposures in his book.

You may read the book for its intra-party gossip. That was part of its interest for me, but it was terribly meager pickings. Two hundred of the 370 pages of the book are devoted to the ten years (1935–45) when Budenz was a Communist functionary in the next-to-the-top ranks. It is clear that he was never really in the highest ranks of the Communist hierarchy. He was useful to the party and was used by it, most of the time passionately eager to be used. But you get the sense throughout that, even when he was a member of the Central Committee, he was not a policy-maker, not a mover and shaker, only an able man who was told what to write.

We learn, for example, that the Communist leaders have to watch carefully the speeches made by Russian leaders and the articles in Russian publications for hints of the shadings of the current party-line.

Budenz evidently believes there are also more direct links between the Communists here and "the East" (one of the phrases he quotes as being used for Moscow), but his evidence is nebulous. He cites a few phrases let slip by Communist leaders in their unguarded moments, but most of them indicate what all of us know—that American Communists are always eager to find out what the Russian line is, so that they may follow it.

His most serious new evidence lies in the encounters he relates with a succession of mysterious emissaries from Russian headquarters, whom he knew only under the false names of "Edwards," "Richards," "Roberts" and other "men of the mist," who seemed to come out of nowhere and vanish into nowhere and whom Budenz furnished with information on American affairs. One of these men, he is convinced, organized the assassination of Leon Trotzky. It is to this group of Soviet undercover agents, Budenz maintains, that "Berger"—or Gerhard Eisler—belongs.

It is not a pretty picture that Budenz draws of the group of men with whom he worked and lived for ten years—and, I cannot help feeling, of himself as well. Much of it is, I am convinced, overdrawn. I doubt that the "men of the mist" were always powerful secret agents sent over here to run the party; they were, more likely, special secret emissaries sent here on particular missions for the Russian group, who didn't mind acting big once they were here among the Marxian provincials and throwing their weight about.

I doubt that the American Communist leaders have made up their minds that they are part of a conspiracy to destroy America in the interests of Russia. More likely they are muddled little men, who are so wrapped up in the *mystique* of the Marxian tradition that they have convinced themselves that what is good for Russia must of necessity be good for America, too.

I doubt even that the men on "the ninth floor" at Communist headquarters are quite as powerful as they think or as they would have liked Budenz to think. (Budenz seems afflicted with an awe for the authority and ritual of any hierarchy, whether Communist or Catholic, and his obsessive dwelling on the "big decisions" and the turns of line and the reports and conclaves of the Communist leaders seems an inverted form of respect for their power.)

I have always felt, and still feel, that the American Communist leaders are a pitiable group of second-rate men with no roots in American life, with no sense of the American mind, with no self-respect as free men, with no largeness and generosity of view, turning and twisting in the gyre of their fettered dogmas, hating each other and hated by each other, nourished only by the vision of themselves as militants and revolutionaries and by their contempt for "liberals," fascinated by the Russian image and tied, in the end, to whatever their Russian heroes think good for both countries and the world.

But Budenz himself is much less free of their basic attitudes than he supposes. He has written a conversion story, and he therefore plays up, as far as possible, his differences with his former colleagues. Yet it is hard to feel that he has escaped the "intellectual strait-jacket" which he describes the Communists as wearing. His whole life seems to have been a quest for the authority-principle, whether in the Catholic discipline or the Communist.

The book strikes me as that of an essentially naïve man, for whom every half-truth and quarter-truth is inflated to a super-truth, a naïve man who enrolled in an army (for that is what the Communist party is) and now laments that everyone in it takes orders. I find it hard to feel deeply about the obvious agonies of his disillusionment; for the original illusion with which he clad himself seems to me one that a man with any intellectual complexity could have avoided.

And I find distasteful the manner in which the news of his joining the Communist party was staged, with a deliberate delay to have it break at just the right time, and equally distasteful the way he lingered on for months as editor of the *Daily Worker* ("fingering a rosary," he tells us, while going through the motions out of which the heart had ebbed), so that the news of his conversion by Monsignor Sheen could break on the world with the maximum effect.

Despite his references to Cardinal Newman, I find no parallels at all in their conversions. John Henry Newman was a sensitive and great spirit who acted out of the deepest passions of his heart, not to achieve institutional effects. I regard his *Apologia pro Vita Sua* as the product of a first-rate mind and a magical style. This book reveals neither.

MARCH 16, 1947

Conspiracy and the Neurotic Dream

Do you know about the case of the mysterious "blond spy"? And about the "ranking New Dealers" whose "confidante" she was? If you don't you are probably just as well off, for what isn't sheer hokum is a small core of fact inflated by the poisonous gases of sensational headlines into a big spy scare.

The blond spy's name has now been revealed as Elizabeth T. Bentley, aged forty, a native of New Milford, Connecticut. The Thomas Committee, which has been trying to get her as the star of its show, released her name.

Back in the days of the great depression, a small-town New England girl graduated from a woman's college in New York. She was filled with the vague idealism of those days of hope and confidence in a new social order. She moved around in the shadowy world of bohemian aimlessness, loose revolutionary talk, and reckless half-baked action which is to be found on the fringes of every new movement. She became a member of the Communist party. She met up with one of the boss-men of the party, and found herself a part of a web of secret transactions of which he was the center.

She became, as the story continues, a member of the very small Communist group which in every country is used to make more or less secret contacts with Communists from other countries. During the war, although Russia was our ally, it was not fully in our confidence. This girl, who was known only as "Mary" even by those who worked with her, insists now that she was used to help transmit to the Russians whatever information they wanted.

Presumably some of it was picked up from various agencies and minor officials of the Administration—which is where the charges about "New Dealers" come in.

The girl's Party comrade died. She found herself cut off from the projects with which she had formerly been connected. She started thinking about the past and future. She got frightened, and perhaps also she got conscience. She went to see the FBI agents in her home state. They are said to have laughed unbelievingly at her story. Finally they started to investigate and took it seriously. The trouble was that she had no proof that could stand up in a court case on espionage. So they sent her back to the Communist party to see whom she could implicate. They photographed every move of hers, and every person she talked with, but either her "contacts" had never existed, or else they had become too wary to be snared in this fashion.

This is what the grand jury had to work with, in the sessions that lasted a year and a half. They had a witness, but her lurid story had no supporting evidence. The grand jury grilled a number of the people she named, but with no results. Since they could not prove her story in court, she was judicially more or less of a flop. Hence the indictment of the twelve Communist leaders was restricted only to the "conspiracy" to rebuild the Communist party, and had no mention of espionage.

But the investigating committees of Congress do not suffer from the need to prove their stories in court. They can operate in committee rooms where the laws of evidence and the rule of law do not apply. And they can operate in the tribunal of the press, a large part of which is anxious enough to smear "New Dealers" with the stigma of pro-Russian espionage.

I don't know how many of the girl's charges are true. Maybe all, maybe none, more likely there is a core of truth and the rest neurotic fantasy. But the whole episode shows how much the tensions of our time can do to corrupt the basic material of our culture.

By one of those crazy turns of history that make the study of society so entrancing, the New Deal is having its Riom Trial ten years after the event. It isn't really a trial, but a series of political accusations and revelations. Yet the intent is clear: to besmirch the whole New Deal chapter of American history by writing across every page of it, in big letters, the now nasty nine-letter word "Communist."

The Republicans have taken President Truman at his own word—that Communism is a treasonable conspiracy—and have opened closets whose skeletons lugubriously intone that the New Deal was riddled with Communist cells and run by a Communist underground. Thus the answer to the Republicans cannot come from Truman. It must come from those Americans who, while differing sharply with the Communists and refusing to work with them, believe also that it is no crime to be a Communist, and that the whole Bentley-Chambers-Budenz affair is a dramatic show by political neurotics for political neurotics.

The revelations by Whittaker Chambers don't make a pretty picture, either of his own role or that of the men he accuses. Yet one must note that he does not accuse them of espionage—a subject which belongs in a courtroom and not in a committee room.[1] Chambers talks of Communist infiltration into the Government, which is a proper—if not a fruitful—subject of investigation. It is not a crime—not even under the Smith Act, which talks of overthrowing the Government, not of helping to run it. There have been many charges of infiltration in the past—infiltration by businessmen under the NRA, by Catholics in the State Department and the foreign service, by Jews, by the Missouri gang, by the generals. I would myself say that the most dangerous New Deal infiltration was by men who at heart were Republicans.

Even if you assume—what is not thus far proved—that Chambers'

[1] Whittaker Chambers, after having been a Communist for some years, renounced the party. Asserting that he had tried without success to convince high federal officials of the facts of Communist infiltration into the Government, he made open accusations before the Thomas Committee against a number of people, including a former State Department official, Alger Hiss. He denied that he had any proof of espionage, although he admitted having himself been a spy-courier for the Communists. In later developments, in the course of a libel suit by Hiss, Chambers introduced microfilm of documents taken from top-secret State Department files of 1937–38, and which he had kept hidden for a decade. Chambers resigned as an editor of *Time*. The whole Chambers-Hiss episode is still (December, 1948) in flux.

charges are true, what do they really show about the New Deal? They show that in the most far-flung administrative organization in the world, employing hundreds of thousands of men and women, there were some Communists. Budenz says there were many. Perhaps. Chambers says they had a grand design to get themselves into high places in the Government. No doubt they wanted to, and perhaps in some instances they did.

But the argument cuts both ways. For the New Deal was an impressively successful enterprise. If I were a Communist, I would be very flattered by these revelations. They might convince Americans that the people who got them out of the depression, put through the most constructive social program in American history, rebuilt the fabric of American life, and won the war against Germany and Japan were the Communists.

The ironic fact is, of course, that the New Deal was the biggest single effort the world has seen since 1917 to undercut Communism and make it unnecessary. If some Communists helped in that effort, and thought they were being heap-big conspirators, then the more fools they.

We seem to have taken the Communist renegades to our breasts, and are making near-heroes of them. They were not heroic to me when they were Communists and are not heroic now. I hope young Americans won't conclude that the formula for success is to become a Communist, have a high and heady fling at conspiracy, and then tell all and receive not only absolution but canonization.

I fear that American political life is coming to be the perfect image of the neurotic fanatic dream. The materials of it are sin, guilt, hysterical confession, and the compulsive conviction that everyone must join with the repentant sinner on the road to salvation. Through the whole dream there runs that sense both of conspiracy and of diabolism which religious fanatics share with pipsqueak revolutionaries.

No doubt the world of Whittaker Chambers and Louis Budenz is a world still filled with these symbols, for in stripping oneself of a near-lifetime of Communist fanaticism, one does not strip oneself of the habit-pattern of seeing the world as a network of conspirators and saviors, devils and angels. One simply reverses the pattern.

But for the American people as a whole the neurotic dream is no solution, whether it be Communist or anti-Communist. You can't run a society as a peep-show plus a sawdust trail, and still expect it to make sense as a society.

AUG. 1, 5, 1948

The Lost Age of Confidence

I WENT to the City Center to see and hear Marc Blitzstein's "play in music," *The Cradle Will Rock*. What interests me most is the sharp difference between the social climate and moral atmosphere that surrounded the play in 1937 and that surround it now in its revival. More than a decade separates the two dates. They seem to belong to different eras.

The best way to describe the era in which the play was written and first produced is to call it the Age of Confidence. Consider what was happening. The New Deal was in full swing, FDR had been elected for a second term, and the program of reform legislation which his first Congress had eagerly passed was evidently on the statute-books to stay. Political, economic, and legal institutions were being reshaped. Even the Supreme Court was feeling the tremors of the confident upsurge of mass opinion. The big organizing drive to create an industrial unionism in America was getting under way. No one knew how far it might go. There was, of course, the cloud of Hitlerism in Europe, but the angel of American democracy was still looking homeward, and troubled itself very little about world affairs. The Popular Front unity of liberals and Left Marxists was still intact, and Russia still seemed to merit the high hopes that most liberals had for it. The world was awry, but liberals were confident that the way to set it straight was along the highway of militant unionism.

What Blitzstein gave us in 1937 was a semi-opera on a contemporary theme and in an American idiom—a *Waiting for Lefty* in music. All was wrong with capitalism ("there's something so damn low about the rich"), its power was based on nothing more than cupidity ("I can see the market rising like a beautiful bird"), murderous terrorism (the workers are framed, bombed, pushed into machinery that crushes them), and the manipulation of the law, the press, and the church. The capitalist is pictured as a power-mad bully, his wife as an ignoramus and a tease, his daughter as a frustrated neurotic, his son as a lecher.

The middle-class people come in for even more savage analysis. Whether they are the lawyer, the doctor, the preacher, the teacher, the college president, the painter, the musician, the druggist, they are cowards, sycophants, lap dogs, prostitutes, pimps. They are the "Union of Associated Stooges," "stuck like a sandwich between the top crowd pressing down and the bottom crowd coming up" ("What do you wanna be, hamburgers?").

As for the workers, they are uniformly victims, but victims in whom alone the great hope rests. Their plight is all pathos ("Joe Worker gets gypped; for no good reason, just gypped"). Moll, the prostitute who is "an amateur in the company of all these professionals" of the middle class, is simply a worker deprived of the chance to make a living. She dreams pathetically of finding "a nickel under my foot." Larry Foreman alone is neither victim, executioner, nor stooge. He is not afraid, does not oppress, does not betray. He organizes—and is confident. Once he even seems to deny the existence of capitalism as a real force ("There ain't no Mr. Mister"). But the rest of the time he is confident that its days are over:

> *That's thunder, that's lightning,*
> *And it's going to surround you . . .*
> *And when the wind blows, oh, when the wind blows,*
> *The cradle will rock . . .*
> *When the storm breaks*
> *The cradle will fall.*

There is a moving simplicity about all this—a simplicity that characterized the lost Age of Confidence. We lack it now.

We have seen, in the intervening decade, that terrorism is not the exclusive province of the capitalists—that workers' governments can use it against their enemies, and find rationalizations for it. We are learning, from Europe's history in the past decade, that the roots of evil will be found not only in institutions, but that—like the roots of decency—they reach deep into the human heart. We have lost our innocent contempt for everything middle-class, our innocent belief that unionism will solve all.

In one sense we are worse off. The loss of innocence has meant the loss of unity. The labor movement is deeply split, and its splits run several ways. Russia has lost whatever magic it once had for the thinking Left. The liberal can accept uncritically the leadership neither of the Russian police-state nor of America's unplanned and chaotic capitalism. He is still deeply pro-labor, but he has no illusions that the human material in a worker is any better or any different from the human material in the rest of us.

But in another sense this is all to the good. The Age of Confidence was always looking for solutions from the outside. It was always some vast external force like the revolutionary labor movement, or the leadership of Russia, that was going to do the trick. We know now that there are no solutions from the outside, that we shall have to construct our American democracy out of the materials we have—including the management groups and the middle-class groups as well as labor. We know that the change in institutions will come slowly and painfully.

I don't mean this to sound optimistic. Our world is still reeling from the impact of the last war, and already we feel ourselves on the brink of another. The United Nations, which so many millions of men gave their lives to create, is being used by each of the giant Powers as a club with which to beat the others.

Men are dreaming up newer and more barbaric weapons with which to kill their brothers. In America itself reaction is still on the march, and many of those who should be fighting back against the threats to our freedom are bent on appeasement and willing to surrender.

But even at this moment in mankind's long night, an episode out of Xenophon's *Anabasis* comes to my mind with force. Xenophon tells of the little band of Greek soldiers marching through Asia Minor, trying to get to their homes in Greece. During the night their generals have been treacherously murdered. They huddle together, looking at each other in dismay. They know now what it means to be leaderless in an alien land, thousands of miles from home. But most of them have been trained in the great tradition of Greek democracy. They find unsuspected leadership potentials in the men, they choose new leaders and lay out their hard course ahead, they regroup their forces, and finally through wild terrain and unknown dangers they make their way home.

Our leaders, too, have been cut off in the night. With them have gone some of the clear and simple ideas that moved and guided us. But, like Xenophon's men, we have fewer illusions now. We know the paths are treacherous. We can regroup our forces and with a new and less naïve confidence find our way home.

NOV. 27, 1947

On Dimly Remembered Reading

READING A NOTE that E. L. Voynich, after a silence of decades, had published a new novel called *Put Off Thy Shoes* sent my mind back to one of the novels she wrote in her heyday. It was called *The Gadfly*, and it is part of my all-but-lost treasury of dimly remembered reading.

Every reader has such a treasury, particularly after he has crossed the

magical threshold of forty, and the books read in childhood take on the
nostalgic glow of childhood sweethearts. As also with sweethearts, one is
well advised to be content with the fragments of a memory, and not to put
it in jeopardy by any revisiting of the reality.

I was eight when I first read *The Gadfly*, and all I can remember of it
now is that it was about a revolutionary conspirator, and a priest whose
son he was. I remember in the final throbbing pages how the priest, in the
midst of a mass he is celebrating, confesses his sin, and laments that he has
allowed his only begotten son to die. No doubt there was much more in
the book than that final scene, shot through with human melodrama and
Church Latin. But I do not recall it.

You will say that this was pretty strong stuff for a boy of eight. But I
was like Crusoe marooned on an island having to eat whatever fruits grew
there. My father, with some scraped-together savings, had made a hapless
purchase of a farm in the Catskills from a patriarch with a white beard.
The patriarch's old-maid daughters left behind them a small shelf of the
popular novels of the decade, which I found on ransacking the attic. In
addition to *The Gadfly* there was a book called *Ishmael*. And there was a
novel by Marie Corelli—I think it was called *Buried Alive*—whose opening sentence, "I who write these words am dead," still resounds in my
mind. Each night after I had read this book I would lie in bed shaking
with fear, but each day I would return to its flamelike fascination.

My reading memories then jump to the age of ten, when we moved to
New Haven. There were, of course, the Henty adventure stories, for me
almost wholly forgotten now. There were also the Horatio Alger books,
which left their hooks in my mind. I wanted passionately at that age to
believe that virtue somehow triumphs in the end, that mortgages do get
paid off, that wicked uncles and scheming lawyers are defeated, that Phil
the Fiddler and Paul the Peddler rise on a steadily ascending scale from
fifty cents a week to a modest fortune, that boys who are left to sink or
swim manage to swim, and that through pluck rather than luck they not
only survive but they marry the boss's daughter.

That was about the time my sister bought three sets of novels from a
book salesman, and we paid for them on easy instalments. There never
was a happier purchase. There were ten or a dozen volumes in each. There
is not a novel in Scott's Waverley series that does not yield a memory,
especially the haunting *Bride of Lammermoor*. Cooper's stories, *The
Leatherstocking Tales*, were similarly devoured. I don't recall much more,
however, than the unjustly suspected spy, and Natty Bumppo's forest wisdom, and Chingachgook, and the bad Indians who lurked in the forests to
slay the noble-born white maidens, and the good Indians who saved them.

I have since read Mark Twain's murderous attack on "Fenimore Cooper's Literary Offenses" and D. H. Lawrence's analysis of his inner dream-life. I have read them, but I have not dared go back to *The Deerslayer* and *The Pathfinder* for verification, lest my own remembered dream vanish.

But best of all was the Dumas—not the *Musketeers* or its sequel (I did not read them until later)—but the Marguerite de Valois series. I panted through a maze of court intrigues and amours, was caught in the toils of Catherine of Medici, followed the exploits of Henry of Navarre. Most of the details have vanished from my mind, save two. One was of the Huguenots being pursued in the massacre of Bartholomew's Eve, the long night of the knives. The other was of two friends who were put on the rack by the Inquisition. One had his bones crushed; the other was saved because he had once spoken a kind word to the man who now had the power of death over him.

I have heard it argued that children at eight or ten should be reading useful civic things, like the romance of trolley cars and how the egg gets from the chicken to the dining-room table. I doubt it. At that age I am for fiction rather than fact. It is a good age, in which everything is possible. That being true, why spoil it by sticking to the earth-grubbing things? Bulfinch's *Age of Fable* is better, or "Snow White and Rose Red" and "Rapunzel" in Grimm's *Tales*, or the bird-girl Rima in W. H. Hudson's *Green Mansions*.

But best of all are the great romances of the courts and the forest, swashbuckling, bloodcurdling, lyrical, melodramatic. Childhood is a time to rejoice or weep over the imagined things that seem real. When you grow up it will be time enough to break your heart over real things that are fantastic enough to have been left to the imagination.

AUG. 6, 1945

Murder at Fourteen

EVEN IN OUR nightmare world, in which the worst horrors have come to seem normal, the brutal killing of an eleven-year-old boy by a fourteen-year-old boy is gruesome enough to evoke some shudders.[1]

---

[1] Eleven-year-old Jackie Preston was lured to an abandoned ice house by fourteen-year-old Fred Smigelski, and killed. In May, 1948, the New Jersey State Supreme Court ruled that the fourteen-year-old boy must stand trial for his life.

The first impulse on the part of the victim's family and on the part of society is for revenge. But from the standpoint of the community, what a paltry solution it is to take revenge on a fourteen-year-old, with his warped and befuddled mind. The assistant prosecutor of Hudson County says he will ask for the death penalty. Does he really think that it will serve any purpose, except to add a second death to a first, a second social enormity to a ghastly personal tragedy?

Our first duty in the case of Fred Smigelski is to do some thinking about how he came to kill his victim. The assistant prosecutor seems to think it is simple. Fred, he says, has reached the "age of reason." Fred planned the crime, and carried it out in cold premeditation. He re-enacted it coldly for police officials. Hence he must be tried for his life. And that, I suppose, finishes the story.

But the story isn't as simple as that. Fred Smigelski's crime was a monstrous crime, and one recoils from it as one recoils from the image he has revealed of his twisted little personality. But what was it that shaped Fred Smigelski's mind? Don't dismiss his own answer, which is as good a clue as one could ask for. He felt humiliated, he says, because his mother made him do a girl's chores at home. He wanted to prove to himself—and no doubt to others—that he was "not a sissy" but a male, a he-man. The ultimate proof of maleness, in his distorted thinking, was to kill someone who was helpless—someone who "could be handled."

It must be clear that this is one of the most damning indictments that has been uttered of our civilization. In the jungle that our society has become we lay inordinate stress, from the earliest years, on "not being a sissy." We teach our children to be tough, ridicule them when they show signs of sensitiveness or humane feeling. And even when the family does not teach this—as in Fred's case it evidently did not—the boy gets it from all around him. The whole civilization in which we live is shot through with the violence of man against man. Our movies have it, to the point where we no longer consider a movie a good one unless it has several deaths in it, each of them so completely stripped of feeling that it has become a counter in a game. Our crime and gangster programs on the radio have it. Our magazine pulps have it, and our comic strips with their super-human—and therefore dehumanized—achievements. Our business mentality has it, setting itself stonily against anything that does not pay off in the toughest terms. Our whole culture has it, with its emphasis on man wreaking his power on man.

Well, Fred Smigelski is the pay-off. We can't reject him—because in a real social sense we have created him. There will, of course, never be a culture without abnormal people and abnormal children. But the form that their abnormality takes is shaped by the kind of society they live in. Fred Smigelski is the moral death's-head that looks out at us as we look at the mirror.

I don't say it is easy to deal with his kind of boy. I do say that transferring him from the juvenile courts to the regular adult courts, with their open trials and their fierce publicity, is the wrongest way possible. Obviously the boy relishes the publicity. After re-enacting his crime, he asked to see what the papers said about him. He has dramatized himself in the role of kidnaper and killer. If he goes through an open trial—even assuming he is not electrocuted—that image of himself will be burned into his mind all the more sharply. The only way to treat him and others like him is on the assumption that a boy's mind is still a confused jumble of dreams and poses, fears and identifications. A boy like Fred is as sick as a boy can be. He needs more than juvenile courts. He needs study by mature people, and prolonged treatment by psychiatrists who will not turn him loose until he is cured.

But we need something too. We need to look at our own civilization, and the tensions it sets up in children as well as adults. We need to consider seriously whether we can continue to pay the social cost of the interior violence of our culture, of which the violence of our movie and radio programs is a symptom.

SEPT. 17, 1947

Violence without Meaning

SOME OF MY FRIENDS seem surprised and a bit shocked because pickets and deputies have been slugging each other in the jurisdictional inter-union fight in Hollywood. Doesn't it strike you as a paradox that we should find anything strange about violence in Hollywood? Every day, on hundreds of thousands of screens, Hollywood unfolds to us scenes of mayhem and death whose victims, if they were real, would fill more hospitals than Los Angeles contains. But when Hollywood becomes part of our real world of labor conflict we rub our eyes as if we were emerging out of the darkness of the theater into the garish heat and sweat of the street.

Nothing could more strongly underscore a fact about the Hollywood film and its American audience that we sometimes forget: that we don't draw a connecting line from the Hollywood image to the world of our experience. The two worlds are kept distinct. We commute between them. The morning after we have seen Humphrey Bogart battered about in an alley by the yeggs of the night-club proprietor, we go about our routine business with never a thought that in the doorway we have just passed, perhaps, a "shamus" looking like the rugged Bogart might be going through the same epical battering.

This does not in any sense mean that the current increase in sadistic thriller-films is harmless. In fact, the harm may be all the greater because of the very split in us that I have described. We keep our imaginative movie-life in one compartment of our minds, and our everyday experience in another: as a result the impressions left by the movies can get by our inner censor, which might otherwise stand guard critically to sift what is believable from what is unbelievable. Having got by our censor, the impressions of senseless violence, of cruelty without meaning and ceaseless action without upshot, pile up in us, layer upon layer. At some point they break out, on subjects that are seemingly wholly unrelated to their source: in a hysterical outburst on Russia, perhaps, or in an impassioned verbal lynching of Negroes or of "labor agitators."

It would be a mistake to put the burden of this on Hollywood alone. The fact is that our whole national life is shot through with "action" and violence. Hollywood has come around to mirroring it, and relatively late at that. But having caught up, it has caught up with a vengeance.

Recent moviegoers have been treated to pictures like *The Stranger*, *Notorious*, *The Killers*, *Crack-Up*, *Martha Ivers*, and *The Big Sleep*. We do these things terribly well; even the most critical of the movie critics have had to admit the high technical quality of most of these pictures.

Why do we do them well? My hunch is that it is because they reflect the things that characterize our whole culture. Action, swiftness, violence, power: these are native, homegrown American qualities, derived from the vast continent that has been ours to open up, and the big prizes that have made our economy into a jungle where the law is eat or be eaten. Hollywood makes up its stories, but it can't make up the qualities that give its pictures strength and skill and appeal. Those qualities come from the civilization itself. Humphrey Bogart, for example, dominates the screen today as he does because in his genius for tough, self-possessed and meaningless action he mirrors the American male.

I say "meaningless" action. That is where the danger lies—in the signs that the films are giving us violence without an ethic. In *The Stranger*, for example, we see Loretta Young finally shrinking in revulsion from Orson Welles because she finds he is a Nazi mass-killer—yet there was no shrinking when she thought he was only a simple murderer. In *Notorious* we are treated to the spectacle of Ingrid Bergman marrying the Nazi as a deliberate trick, in an unscrupulous end-justifies-the-means episode. Worst of all, in *The Big Sleep* there is a succession of killings that are wholly amoral, and that leave the principal characters and the audience unmoved because they are so pointless.

There can be clean and meaningful violence, when a great cause is at stake, when a man has reckoned the consequences and made his moral choice. But action without meaning and violence without point are the materials out of which mass sadism can grow.

OCT. 10, 1946

Gods of the Marquee

READER, have you never walked along Broadway and gazed with fascination at the sybarite splendors portrayed on the signs in the movie lobbies?

As far back as I can remember, these signs—whether on Broadway or Main Street—have proved irresistible. When I passed them on my way to high school they used to furnish a kindled memory which I could store away in my mind, and by which I could warm my spirit while the teacher droned on about algebra and the hoyden next to me adjusted the brace on her teeth. Even now, with the monitory gray hairs reminding me that I must make stern use of the hurrying years, I can never walk down Forty-second Street or Eighty-sixth Street without loitering a minute to inspect the lusty gods—and the luscious goddesses—whose names grace the movie-palace marquees.

Or are you, reader, one of the latter-day Malvolios who take a stern view of such tawdry fripperies?

That admirable movie critic, Manny Farber, strikes out passionately in the *New Republic* against what he calls the "signs of the double cross." In a walk down Broadway he notes that the theater sign for *Counter Attack* shows the heroine "in black negligee, leaf-patterned brassiere and panties, chained to a dungeon wall," while in the actual picture "she never is seen in less than the full outfit of a Partisan." The ad for *Colonel Blimp* shows a blonde about whom the aged Tory is presumably dreaming, and a duel, with the motto "a fighting fool about women"; whereas in the picture itself "there is no lust, no blonde, no fighting fool."

I agree with Farber that this is shoddy stuff. It is bad enough, in terms of a mature movie art, for Hollywood to turn out infantile sex tripe; it is worse when the pictures that show adult emotions are bedizened with the gaudiness of a street-walker. It is bad enough for Hollywood to make a cult of sadistic violence; it is worse when even the saner pictures are sold with a nightmare band of terror about them: with poster-details lavished (as Farber says) on "guns, the fright or cruelty in a character's eyes, the hands of a strangler."

But I wish Farber had gone further, and had seen that our movie signs—like most of our movies—are an expression of our values and our hungers. Ours is a culture in which the double cross pays, and whatever pays is valued. To be sure, a lot of hardened movie-goers have had their fingers burned many times by the deception of the signs, and have grown wary of their flame. But the sign-makers go right on.

Why? Well, one reason is that we have developed a going understanding that the advertisers don't have to be truthful and we don't have to believe them. It is all a sort of play in which it is one man's role to lie and the other's role to be skeptical. Ours is a culture in which salesmanship continues to have a throbbing life of its own even when cut off from substance and truth.

Nor is this true only of movies. I have seen a woman go through the pages of *Vogue* or *Harper's Bazaar*, entranced by the dazzling shimmering beauty of the dress creations advertised there, even though she knows perfectly well that (if she has the money to buy them) she will never look the way the model or the drawing does. As for me, I have become a hardened skeptic about all the fancy promises in life, whether it is the shoes that will make me look taller, or the collar that will make me look handsome, or the "Hayek way" which will keep me off the road to serfdom, or the movie posters showing Esther Williams and Van Johnson in the bursting sexuality of a swimming-suit clinch.

Thus are cynics made. And yet we go on listening to the more vapid commercials and reading the more idiotic books and attending the cruder and more infantile movies. Which is what the technicians of the slogan and the picture counted on in the first place.

The fact is, let me repeat, that movies and movie signs mirror our values and minister to our hungers. A theater-owner has his eye on the customer. His posters reflect not what is on the screen, but what is (or what he thinks is) in the mind of the movie-goer. He goes on the assumption that the things valued most in our culture are sex and nakedness, and the light falling on the curves of a dress, and gun-play and violence and death. He is right.

You will say, these form a curious combination of qualities: Nineveh and Sparta, luxury and violence. They do. The reason is that we are a frontier nation that has moved—more swiftly than any in history—from hardihood to wealth, from the timberlands to the big money. Our living-standards are higher than in any other country in the world, but there is also a greater gap between lowest and highest than anywhere else. Ours is the land of success, but for every successful man there are hundreds unsuccessful. We have deep psychic hungers, all of us—hungers for money or power or dazzling beauty or acclaim. The movies, with their glamour and their violence, minister to our hungers. For two hours in the darkness of the theater we seem to realize our heart's desire, and when we emerge we feel somewhat slaked.

Perhaps it is better thus. It is better to have glamour on the screen than only a manic hunger for it; better to have violence in the films than in fact; better to have death in fancy than death on the streets. Call this, if you will, the safety-valve theory of the movies. For most people it is a true one. It does not make art, but it fulfills hungers.

The pity of it is that so much of it should be based on lies like those on the posters. But the lies would not be on the posters if they were not, to start with, in our hearts.

JUNE 6, 1945

Chaplin: Death as Business

THEY ARE TRYING to draw a ring of hostility around Charlie. As William Bolitho once said of him in a memorable essay: "Charlie makes Chinese laborers laugh, and Kaffirs in the compound of the Rand." Such a man is obviously dangerous, for he is too close to the hearts of the world's folk, too capable of reaching them. Hence the effort that has been made to alienate people from him.

I think I understand the fears of Chaplin's enemies better now that I have seen his current picture, *Monsieur Verdoux*. It is a withering dissection of business-for-profit, murder-as-business, and a civilization founded on both.

The bluebeard hero who marries women for their bank accounts has been done in a story stylized as never before. A former bank-clerk, he lost his job in the mass layoffs of the depression, and turned into a prowling ruthless killer in an economic jungle not of his making. Chaplin has given us as elaborate and satiric a *Theory of Business Enterprise* as Thorstein Veblen ever dared write. I was not overly taken with the talky parts of the picture, which make everything much too explicit, and smell of the amateur philosopher. The strong meat is what is implicit in the story itself and the way Chaplin acts it, or rather dances it, for Chaplin has never ceased being the great mime, and in this picture all his acting and action are a grim dance of death.

Take, for example, the way he counts the mounds of thousand-franc notes which are his booty from the murder of his "wives." Here he is a dead-serious bank-technician, with lightning fingers and passionate precision. When he flicks the pages of a directory to find the address of an intended victim, there is the same speed (time is money), efficiency (no room for dawdling and sloppiness in business), detachment (no room for sentiment either).

Every gesture of his is grotesquely "businesslike." One remembers at random the dispatch with which, after each murder, he phones his broker to give instructions about his investment portfolio. There is not a surplus word. One remembers him as the dapper sea captain who has married a loud-laughing perfervid lottery winner, played by Martha Raye. On his periodic homecomings to her he hangs up his hat in the hall with the contained tension of a man arriving for a big-business conference involving corporate mergers rather than corporeal embraces. And when Martha is foolish enough to fling her money away on phony schemes for turning the ocean's waves into electric power and salt water into gasoline, Chaplin's righteous sense of outrage is in the best tradition of sound business principles.

Charlie's wooing-scenes often seem overdone and farcical. Yet remember that they are no more farcical in their fanatic fury than the stock market scenes which are newsreel shots. Charlie takes his sex not as erotic experience, but as a business pursuit. This is not the financier who is a lover in his hour of diversion or out of his need for expressing his power. He is the lover as financier. He uses a different technique and puts on a different personality with each woman, just as a salesman varies his approach to each customer. But underneath there is a terrifying strain of sameness. There is in Chaplin's wooing the same detached and single-minded pursuit of the object that you will find in the lives of big businessmen like Drew, Rockefeller, or "Jupiter" Morgan. And the object is not love, but booty; not welfare or production, but money.

The ways of business enterprise are not easy. "Business is business." You must sweat at it, as Chaplin does at his love-making, racing from one city to another. You must call in the help of science, as he does when he extracts from his druggist boon companion the formula for a death that will look like a heart attack. You must put up with disappointments and frustrations, as in the hilarious and painful failures in the murder attempts on Martha Raye. You go about distracted, harried, fury-driven.

Why? In Charlie's picture, you do it for the security of your family, in the hope that some day you can retire from ruthlessness. But you find that there can be no security even for the most protected in this jungle-world. Even your genius in never allowing a *corpus delicti* to be found does not avail you. And when the end comes you turn from hollowness to nothingness with a sense of inexpressible relief. Not even religion has much relevance (Chaplin has done a priest-repentance scene to end all priest-repentance scenes), for Chaplin's bitterness is directed at the man-made institutions, and help must come not from above, but from within.

Lest anyone say that Chaplin has told only one man's story, that of an inhuman murderer, he makes his Verdoux a sentimental family man entertaining neighbors at dinner, very much as Rauschning describes Hitler and his associates sipping tea and eating cookies in bourgeois fashion while they chat about their plans for mass-extermination. And Chaplin's newsreel shots of roaring crowds and grimacing dictators are outwardly no less funny than his own scenes. His point that all business is in essence ruthless, and that private madness is small-shot stuff compared with public madness, would be hard to deny. In an atom-bomb age, his parting "I shall see you all very soon" has monstrous overtones. And as he walks to the guillotine, all his feverish energy is gone, and he is once more the old baggy broken little man who must carry the crushing burden of human guilt and human sadness.

This is Chaplin's art. It is dangerous as all great art is dangerous. The classic Chaplin mask—the famous figure of "Charlie" that has made history—was in its origin a fusion of three strains: the stock figures of the Italian tradition of the *commedia dell' arte*, the training in English music halls, and the wardrobe of a Hollywood studio lot in the Keystone days. But what fused these strains was the human fervor of Chaplin himself. When he depicted his little man, he was a rebel, the "poor man's artist." He has said that it was not he that put an end to the forlorn little man, but FDR. Yet even during the New Deal, Chaplin—changing his mask—continued a rebel: against the dehumanizing mass of the big city, against the machine in modern time, against dictators. He is still a rebel as he faces the impending mass-murder of his time.

That is his crime. That is why, unable to hit at his art, the stupid attacks are made on his private life. As for myself, I am content to take him as an artist, and to face the criticisms of our institutions that his art implies. I judge him in terms of how successful he is in creating a universal language that ties us all together in our common plight.

Where he makes his money and how he spends it, what he did or did not do about the war, what he thinks of Russia or Communism: these are his affairs, not ours. This hounding of him is unclean. To my view, Chaplin's weakness lies not in his rebellion, but in his despair. His final outlook is not Communism, but a moral anarchism.

Yet, given the obscene spectacle of his attackers, who can say that Chaplin's despair is wholly without foundation?

APRIL 17, 1947

On the Ballet

THIS IS a report from an enchanted palace. For two nights I have been a prisoner of the ballet—a delighted prisoner loath to break away from the enchantment. I write as a layman in these matters, a complete innocent—which is what almost every other American is as well. But one need be no professional to fall under a spell that has lasted centuries and crossed national boundaries at will, and that needs to attach the layman to itself, else it will die.

I went to the ballet skeptically. I dislike cults, and I have always despised the combined fanaticism and exclusiveness in the so-called "balletomaniacs." I dislike the transplanted, and I saw no reason why an art form that had once possessed roots in the Russian cultural soil should necessarily find any in the American. I dislike the uniform and the mechanical, and the imprisoned rigor of the classical ballet seemed one kind of uniformity I could stay clear of. Finally, like so many middle-class parents who flirt with the idea of giving their children accomplishments, I still remembered the times I had called to take one of my daughters home from her ballet classes, and the imprint of the tortured and unwilling torsos I saw there had stayed with my mind.

If I write differently now it is because there is an inherent beauty in a great dance form which survives cultists and transplantation and even the folly of parents. That beauty the ballet has. I didn't really care about the tragic story of Giselle and Albrecht: it was only the traditional shell, the frame. The thing itself was the dancing, completely stylized yet infinitely fluid, the swaying rhythms of the young bodies, the bold leaps like tongues of flame, the tiny formal steps which are somehow transmuted into a long sweep, the stilted grace and the disciplined pirouettes, the sense at once of flying and of being rooted—"as if" (in William Bolitho's phrase) "the actors were only attached to earth on a moving pivot."

I am conscious that my words come with difficulty here. In the dance, as in political thought, it must take years to build a vocabulary before the words come readily. I am also conscious that the dancing I saw did not come readily. Every step that seemed so effortless was the product of a dedicated discipline to which the youngsters had given themselves. I am not speaking only of the mechanical timing and co-ordination: no doubt you can get greater drill-perfection at Radio City from the Rockettes. But there was a tension not only of body, but of will and mind, which you cannot evoke from people unless they have behind them a continuous and heroic tradition.

There were, of course, during two evenings long stretches of slackness. The O. Henry story of the *Gift of the Magi* seemed irrelevant, *On Stage* and *Tally Ho* were weak and never caught fire with at least one lay observer, and even *Firebird*—for all the magic of the music and Markova's dancing and Marc Chagall's decorations—made me squirm with the uneasy sense of watching a cluttered-up pantomime instead of a free-moving dance. But all this is merely to say that the classical ballet transferred to the American stage is still groping, and has not yet acquired good new material to work with.

Which brings me to the question of why the ballet form should still be so cut off from the lives of millions of Americans, why it is considered so alien and forbidding. Some day it may be thought natural to go see the ballet as it is now to listen to serious music. Perhaps the further development of television, which can bring the whole perfect pattern of a ballet into every American home, may witness a new flowering of the art.

Certainly there is nothing inherently alien to the American spirit in the ballet. It was born in the romantic Russian tradition, and it is a form capable of holding the lustiest energies of any people. Beneath the deceptive smoothness and grace I felt at times a potential of violence in it. And so we need not be surprised that it can contain the robust sailor-strength of *Fancy Free*, or the psychological tension of *Undertow*.

Tolstoy used to feel about ballet, as he did about opera, that it was a social waste because it did not express the life of the people or aid their causes. If you turn to his long essay, *What Is Art?*, you will find him saying that "the ballet, in which half-naked women make voluptuous movements, twisting themselves into various sensual writhings, is simply a lewd performance." He thought of the people who worked to make this performance a success, and concluded that "art is not so important that such sacrifices should be made for its sake."

This is, of course, the view of an impassioned and embittered Christian Socialist, but it is wrong from any angle. Every great art form starts from a living civilization, and has its roots in a living need. Later it tends to become a mere shell, although a beautiful one. The Russian ballet started with the great Russian folk-traditions. Torn from those it becomes only hollow, and needs revitalizing, needs to kiss the earth again from which it sprung. (Chagall, who knows the Russian folk-myths, almost did that alone with his sets for *Firebird*.) The question now is whether it can kiss the American earth.

It will not do this by becoming the exclusive plaything of a cultivated audience which views the ballet with the possessiveness of owners. Nor will it do so by developing a group of ballet jitterbugs, who crowded in at the pit to applaud Eglevsky's execution of a double something-or-other very much as I have seen the bobby-soxers in another medium overwhelming Sinatra.

The new sources of strength lie elsewhere. That was why *Fancy Free* seemed so important to me. It catches so completely the folklore of the American sailor at a bar—his truculent camaraderie, his predatory piracy among the heavily freighted girls, his swagger, his brawling and, above all, his trousers. For those trousers, whose very form-constricting tightness makes them impossible as garments, are by the same fact heaven-sent for the ballet. The natural habits and habitat of the American sailor were caught by this ballet form and imprisoned in a timeless mold. Thus is a folk-institution made permanent; thus is a form given life.

OCT. 26, 1945

The Muzzling of the Movies

1.

THE CURRENT HEARINGS on "Communism" in the movie industry by the House Committee on Un-American Activities [1] could be pretty funny if

[1] This Committee was in direct line of succession from the Dies Committee, and was headed by Representative J. Parnell Thomas, Republican, of New Jersey.

they were not so genuine a threat to American freedom. The spectacle of a number of Congressmen, investigators, and Hollywood celebrities turning themselves into sleuths in an effort to track down the footprints of Karl Marx in movieland—all done under klieg lights and with grinding cameras—is one of those macabre incidents of mild insanity that makes cultural life in America a gay and somewhat cockeyed affair. Some day it may turn up in some future photograph-album like the current *I Remember Distinctly*, on a par with college boys eating goldfish, and prohibition agents smashing up furniture. But until the time when we can safely look back and laugh, it is the grimmer and more sinister aspects of the hearing that must concern us.

The impression that emerges from the results of the first two days of the hearing is that of almost complete irresponsibility. The Committee hearings are obviously being used to air personal feuds that belong inside the industry, trade-union jurisdictional disputes that occur in every industry, personal rivalries and hatreds, as well as clashes of political ideas.

Add to this the almost incredible looseness with which terms are used in the Committee hearings. Adolphe Menjou, for example, avers that "Hollywood is crawling with un-American, anti-capitalistic, anti-free-enterprise influences." I remember that Menjou, during the war, became apoplectic at President Roosevelt's suggestion that wartime incomes be limited to $25,000. It was, he said both privately and publicly, anti-capitalistic, anti-free-enterprise. From which one can only conclude that it was un-American and that anything is un-American which does not fit Menjou's scheme of economics. Menjou has his right to his somewhat moth-eaten opinions. But his insistence that anyone who deviates from them is un-American—perhaps a Communist even—would be humorous if it did not fit so completely into the whole intellectual atmosphere of the Committee hearings. The one "free enterprise" that neither Menjou nor Chairman Thomas seems much concerned about is the freedom of movie-making from control, intervention, snooping, and terrorism.

This leads into the real intent of the inquiry. The target is not Communism in itself, which has no substantial roots in the American mind. The real objective is the muzzling of the movies. The men whose names are being mulled over again in this hearing, as in earlier investigations, may or may not be victimized and thrust out of movie-making.[2] But the larger purpose being aimed at is the silencing of Hollywood on any topic that has to do with an examination of the American conscience. The purpose is to strike terror into the hearts of the big movie-producers and directors, so that these men—few of whom have ever been distinguished for their bold-

[2] Ten of them were, as it later turned out.

ness—will no longer dare to make another picture like *Crossfire* or *Gentle-man's Agreement* about the disease of anti-Semitism, or another picture like *Fury* about a lynching-mob.

If it be asked whether Congress does not, after all, have the right and duty to inquire into the use of propaganda in the movies, the answer must be clear. It is the function of Congress to legislate, and to make inquiries that will help it to legislate. But this function must be carried on inside the safeguards of the Bill of Rights. There is nothing in the Congressional investigating power that gives a committee of Congress the right to interfere with free expression in American life. If Congress were to pass a law stating that men with liberal or even Communist views on economics could not be employed in the movie industry, it would be fantastic to think that the courts would ever let such a law stand. It ought to be clear enough that Congress cannot legally, by investigation and its consequent terrorism, muzzle people whom it could not muzzle by legislation.

As soon as you get into movie-making, radio-broadcasting, book-publishing, newspaper and magazine writing, you are in the realm of speech and opinions and their public expression. This is the most delicate area for governmental intervention of any kind. It is also the most delicate area for the conducting of prosecutions by Congressional committees. Nothing that the Committee has done so far is as potentially destructive of freedom of expression as is this foray into Hollywood.

Because the Committee has taken so much power into its hands, and because of the current anti-Russian hysteria under the cloak of which it operates, those who dare oppose it will need courage. There will be a tendency among some liberals to complain that the Committee is confusing Communists with the ordinary garden-variety of liberal, and that it must discriminate more closely. Yet that does not touch the real issue. Obviously there are some Communists in the movie industry, as there are some in the theater, in the radio industry, or on newspapers, or among the writers of books. It will not save American freedom to say that the Constitution protects non-Communists but does not protect Communists. If the principle of freedom has any meaning, it means that the Constitution applies to all: that just as Congressmen are not above the Constitution, so Communists are not below it. The problem of freedom in America is that of maintaining a competition of ideas, and you do not achieve that by silencing one brand of idea. The problem of freedom in America is that of maintaining the safeguards that prevent one group of men from falling into the category of second-class citizens, while the rest remain first-class citizens.

In meeting this threat to freedom of expression, conservatives as well as liberals must stand together. I felt dismay when I read that a man as powerful in the movie world as Louis B. Mayer had called for outlawing the Communist party, and for legislation which would deny to Communists private employment as well as public. There is very little danger that Mayer will be mistaken as a Communist, and that goes for all the other movie producers. It is hard to see what prompted them to so drastic a proposal, unless it is the belief that the hounds of Congress might be diverted by throwing them this bit of prey.

It is a curious illusion—this illusion that the way to win freedom is to cut it up piece by piece. That was not the advice that Wendell Willkie gave to the movie industry when an earlier investigation threatened. He met the peril of muzzling the movie-makers, and he met it squarely, standing on the only possible ground—the ground of freedom for all.

2.

EVEN THOUGH the Thomas Committee had to suspend its Hollywood investigation, it came out the victor. If its chief purpose was to strike terror into the hearts of the major producing and distributing companies of Hollywood and their lawyers and financial advisers and front men, it has succeeded. For the big movie moguls, closeted for several days at the Waldorf, finally emerged with their decision. They are firing the ten Hollywood employees who were cited for contempt by the House. They promise never again to hire a Communist. And they plead with Congress to pass a law which will "assist the motion-picture industry to rid itself of subversive, disloyal elements."

Representative Thomas and his cohorts must be in ecstasy. William Randolph Hearst must be giddy with one of his biggest personal victories. There is plenty of joy in the kingdom of reaction because the film industry —the mighty film industry, the vaunted King of Swat—has struck out without even swinging very hard.

Why? It looked for a time as if the Thomas Committee had been met and mastered and had ingloriously yielded the field. The best of the newspapers, including the conservative ones, had seen that the threat to the freedom of the movies was a threat to all media of mass opinion and communication. The irresponsible methods of the Committee had evoked disgust. But it is one of the attributes of the masters of reaction that, like Hitler, they know the uses of fear and of a persistent and unremitting war of nerves. The Thomas Committee threatened to return to the attack.

The Hearst papers ran a daily feature-and-editorial exposing the "Holly-wood Reds" and, in the name of freedom, calling for Federal censorship of the movies. They knew how to seek out and play on the most sensitive nerve-ganglia of the Hollywood moguls, who have always lived in night-mare terror of censorship. All of which was too much for Hollywood.

In surrendering, Messrs. Louis B. Mayer, Jack Warner, Edward Man-nix, Barney Balaban, Spyros Skouros, and their Brain Trust of Eric John-ston, James F. Byrnes, and Paul V. McNutt, used some pretty fancy and high-flown language. "We are not going to be swayed by hysteria or in-timidation from any source," their statement reads. And it goes on bravely and gallantly: "There is the danger of hurting innocent people. There is the danger of creating an atmosphere of fear. Creative work at its best can-not be carried on in an atmosphere of fear. We will guard against this danger, this risk, this fear."

But they have fired The Ten. And they have promised, in effect, never again to employ anyone who does not conform to the prevailing winds of political doctrine. And they have asked Congress to pass a law defining for them exactly whom the movie industry, as a private industry in a free-enterprise economy, may or may not employ.

I can understand timidity, especially business timidity. Few men are brave, and the money nerve is a sensitive nerve, and if a man or an industry wants to retreat, that's that. But what I cannot quite stomach is a craven retreat in fact which is dressed up in the fancy highfalutin' language of social militancy.

The movie industry is a privately owned and operated industry, like the press. It is also one of the major opinion-forming agencies in the country, and as such both its freedom and its creativeness are of first importance to the democratic forces of the nation. The movies have always lived in fear of government censorship and of private pressure groups. They have adopted a policy of self-regulation—housecleaning and moral policing from within—which is best described in Ruth A. Inglis' *Freedom of the Movies* (University of Chicago Press), one of the volumes prepared by the Hutchins Commission on Freedom of the Press. The industry censors its own movies under the Production Code Administration (PCA), which is run by Joseph I. Breen. In addition there are state and city censor-ship boards whose authority the industry has never dared challenge in the courts. The biggest fright the industry got was in the early 1920s, when a campaign of criticism resulted in the establishment of the Hays Office; and in 1934, when a campaign by the Legion of Decency scared Holly-wood and resulted in the present form of the PCA. The current Thomas-Hearst scare is the third big one in the history of the industry.

It is clear then what the masters of Hollywood are afraid of—the censorship threat, the threat of boycott of movie theaters, and—most of all—continued Congressional investigations with their attendant unfavorable publicity. To ward these off the masters of Hollywood have given in to them.

But in their fear they have jeopardized more than the movie industry. They have placed freedom itself in jeopardy.

No one can doubt the right of Congress to investigate—within its constitutional limits. The whole question at issue is: What are those constitutional limits? The Ten who have been cited for contempt chose to test those limits in the legal American way. They did it on the ground that whatever the investigating power of Congress may be, it does not include the right to inquire into the political opinions of private citizens. I think that many constitutional lawyers would probably agree with them; I think that a good case for their view could be made out in the precedents of constitutional law; and I think that a majority of the Supreme Court justices may well, in the end, hold that the Committee exceeded its powers or failed to operate under adequate safeguards.

A reasonable man can scarcely dismiss the action of The Ten as either seditious or disloyal. I have heard a good deal recently about the fact that they made a lot of noise in defending what they conceived to be their constitutional rights. But since when has the noisy defense of a man's rights been considered un-American?

If these men are Communists I think they have hold of a wrong philosophy. But they have the right to be wrong. The Communist party is not outlawed. It has not even been declared seditious by the Supreme Court.

The movie industry prides itself upon its self-regulation. But is it really self-regulation to surrender at the point of a gun? Eric Johnston and the other spokesmen of Hollywood talk a good deal about not having an atmosphere of fear in Hollywood. The firing of The Ten, the commitment to toe the line politically in the future—these are not exactly the way to evoke an atmosphere in which great pictures can be produced by men who need only think of their art and their product. Eric Johnston and the other Hollywood spokesmen have gone beyond self-regulation of industry when they ask Congress to lay down clear and exact definitions of whom they may or may not employ in the free-enterprise industry of the movies. A police-state is none the less a police-state when the victim begs for the whip.

OCT. 22, NOV. 26, 1947

The Unbroken Web

HOLLYWOOD IS MORE than a sprawling collection of studios, movie-lots, mansions, swimming pools, directors, stars, and hangers-on. It is more even than an industry, and more than an entertainment and an art. It is a powerful social force—the most powerful force in education for good or ill that America possesses. Here is a medium that overleaps the barriers of semi-literacy or illiteracy and the restrictions of words, gives immediacy to actions and emotional content to ideas. It is potentially the great mass-art of our century and civilization, the unacknowledged legislator of what we feel and think.

The pity of it is that Hollywood has so frequently squandered or fallen short of its potential as a social force, lacked the courage to say something maturely to mature people. It has not been as craven as the radio industry, which is, with a few honorable exceptions, an insult to the American intelligence. But it has proceeded on much the same theory—that you must take no chances, step on no toes, steer clear of ideas, aim only at "entertainment" for people of adolescent minds and emotions, skirt the surface of life, never dig into the subsoil or reach for the heights.

That is why *Gentleman's Agreement* is an important event. It reduces to drivel the chestnutty old argument between "entertainment" and "message." It represents a marriage of Hollywood's best technical skill—and how good Hollywood can be at its technical best—with a theme that has meaning for democracy and human life in America. It shows that Hollywood could grow up if the people in Hollywood had the courage to grow up. It grasps the nettle of one of the most "dangerous" issues in Hollywood today—that of anti-Semitism in these United States—and out of it fashions a work of art that will have a more powerful effect on the social thinking of Americans than all the preachments, committees, conferences, and stuffed-shirt good-will-ism, whether you roll them together or lay them end to end.

What makes this picture tick as it does? It shows how lovingly a team of skilled Hollywood craftsmen can work together when they are given a big theme to work on and the green light to go ahead. In this case they had something creative to work on—the central dramatic conception of Laura Hobson's novel: that you can't understand anything about the collective disease called anti-Semitism until you have made a complete identification of yourself with the victims of that disease. This is in line with the key tradition of American pragmatic philosophy—that a knowledge of values can come only directly out of experience.

This brings me to the question: What are the values in *Gentleman's Agreement*? And are they valid as ideas, or is this just an emotional binge in a "good" cause?

Unlike *Crossfire*, *Gentleman's Agreement* has no overt violence in it. Some will, for that reason, think it too "talky," and this is true of one or two of the speeches toward the end. Yet as a whole the picture has drama of the most intense kind—the drama of ideas and emotions in action. The violence is not that of the killing of the body, but of the mutilation of the spirit. It is the violence of the thousands of daily slurs, insults, repulses, exclusions, condescensions, discriminations, to which Jews are subjected.

As I understand the movie, what it is saying is not that the physical violence doesn't count—obviously it does—but that there is no basic difference *in kind* (there is, of course, in degree) between the physical and the moral violence. It is the principle of the *unbroken web* between the various forms of anti-Semitism. It is an unbroken web that ties together the remembered comment of the ambulance-man on the battlefield about the dying Jewish soldier ("Give me a hand with this Sheeny"), with the epithet "Dirty Jew" flung at Phil Green's son at school when his schoolmates hear his father is Jewish, with the restaurant scene where the drunken soldier expresses his dislike for officers "especially when they're Yids," with the Flume House scene where the manager of the "restricted" hotel turns Green away, with the sneering assumption by one of the magazine's executives that of course Green had been in "Public Relations" in the Army, with the "Jewish anti-Semitism" of Green's own secretary. I have listed these incidents on a descending scale of intensity, as we generally measure it; yet the point of the movie is that they are all tied together.

Sometimes the movie—like the book—seems to be saying that the anti-Semitism of the people on the sidelines, who abet the Gerald Smiths by their silence and inaction even while they scorn him, is more dangerous than the anti-Semitism of violence. But I should, for myself, rephrase it somewhat as follows: Obviously, the dangerous anti-Semitism is the organized kind—that of the lunatic fringe, that of political demagogues and movements. But in America this can thrive only when it is nourished in the soil of the anti-Semitism of the "respectable" people, who wouldn't be caught dead at a rabble-rousing meeting, but who have formed a conspiracy of silence about the whole issue. And in a real sense the soil of cowardice and blindness is more dangerous than the flower of evil that sends its roots down into it.

On one important score I am delighted that *Gentleman's Agreement* pulls no punches—the question of the moral ground on which anti-Semitism must be fought. John Garfield puts it well when, as a Jewish soldier, he says to his Christian comrade: "It's your fight, brother. I'm on the sidelines." The problem of anti-Semitism is a problem for all Americans, but primarily it is a problem of the Christian conscience, and of the democratic civilization within which it functions.

In *Crossfire*, as in so many "tolerance" speeches I have heard and on which I am fed up, the big argument given for Protestants and Catholics to join in the fight against anti-Semitism is that once injustice starts it may spread to them as well, and they may become its victims. This is the argument of self-interest, and it has some validity. But I am happy that *Gentleman's Agreement* does not resort to it. For at bottom it is a morally inadequate argument. The reason that you must join hands with the Jews—because "some day this may happen to you"—is a spurious reason. The real point is that we must stand up and fight against injustice no matter to whom injustice happens in our civilization—whether to the Jew, the Negro, the worker, the child, the alien. We are all involved in this, not in order to save our own precious skins, but because we are human beings with human dignity, and because moral values do exist.

NOV. 12, 1947

Night-Riders of the Spirit

A MAN who used to be called "His Majesty, Imperial Wizard, Emperor of the Invisible Empire, Knights of the Ku Klux Klan," has died obscurely in an Atlanta hospital. His name was William Joseph Simmons. His death calls to mind one of the maggoty chapters of American history, now ended. Or is it?

The man who would be emperor was a broken old man when he died. His empire had been taken away from him by a fellow-rival for the chieftaincy of the racist hoodlums. He himself had been sick for some years before his death. Even his death was not reported to the press for several days—whether from obscurity or design does not appear. But his story is worth retelling, even in a year that has taken in its stride the death of much more resounding Klansmen called Hitler and Mussolini and the collapse of their not-so-invisible empires.

Simmons started the "modern" Klan in 1915, at a time when there was considerable talk about the foreign-born and one hundred per cent "Americanism." He seems to have been compounded of equal parts of mystic, spellbinder, adventurer, and knave. He was a tall, thin-lipped, emotional Southerner in his middle forties, had been a Methodist circuit-riding fundamentalist preacher, had picked up a few dollars as traveling salesman and promoter of fraternal organizations, had even taught Southern history in a little Southern college.

The thing that people talked about when he was a boy in the South was the old Ku Klux Klan, organized by a group of former Confederate officers a few years before Simmons was born, and glorified in the *Birth of a Nation* film. Simmons got the idea of reviving its secrecy, its pageantry, its mumbo jumbo, its night-riding terror. He took out papers of incorporation for the Knights of the Ku Klux Klan, and he and a few friends put on bedsheets, masked their faces, went to the top of Stone Mountain outside Atlanta on a Thanksgiving night, burned a fiery cross, and swore a terrible oath to obey the commands of the Imperial Wizard and maintain complete secrecy about the new organization.

For five years the Klan crept along at a sluggard pace, and in 1920 it had only four or five thousand members. Simmons hoped to create something like the German mediaeval V*ehmgericht* or secret drumhead courts that were reputedly founded by the Emperor Charlemagne and flourished from the twelfth to the fifteenth century. One student and former member of the Klan states that the title "Wizard" came from the "wissende" or initiated of the Vehme. But though Simmons dreamed himself another Charlemagne and orated with the passion of the great Southern tradition of spellbinders, he did not know how to promote membership.

The turning point came in June, 1920, when Simmons signed a contract with Edward Y. Clarke and Mrs. Elizabeth Tyler, who were both streamlined promoters and saw the limitless possibilities for making money out of an organization that combined secrecy, fanfare, white supremacy, religious hatreds, and sadism. They mapped out the job of getting new members at ten dollars a head. There was an Imperial Kleagle (Clarke), who was in charge of recruiting. The country was divided into eight "domains," or sections, with a Grand Goblin at the head of each. The domains, in turn, were divided into "realms," or states, with a King Kleagle in charge. Within each state the legmen, who had the job of talking at meetings and of house-to-house soliciting, were called Kleagles.

Within fifteen months the organization had grown to hundreds of thousands. Men were kidnaped by it, terrorized, flogged, tarred and feathered, branded with acid, mutilated, killed. The slogans and speeches that preceded these acts were always highly patriotic and moral. Simmons always insisted that the Klan was only a "patriotic and fraternal organization," dedicated to the purposes of Americanism and the purity of American womanhood. In fact, however, the reason for its success was not only the structure of salesmanship that Clarke and Mrs. Tyler built up, but the appeals to anti-Catholic, anti-Negro, anti-Semitic, anti-labor, and nativist hatreds among the poor whites in the South and the lower middle class throughout the country.

The storm broke over the Klan when the New York *World* decided to look into the Invisible Empire. The series of twenty-one front-page articles began running September 6, 1921, and dozens of other papers carried the *World* stories, including Southern papers.

The investigators of the Klan found a sickening hypocrisy in it. Despite the phony idealisms of the Klan spokesmen, the Kleagle promoters and local leaders stirred up violent hatreds as a way of swelling their movement. The *World* found also that Clarke, the Imperial Kleagle (or boss organizer), and Mrs. Tyler, the chief of the women's section who made much of the purity of Southern womanhood which had to be protected by white supremacy, had not been very pure themselves. According to police court records, they had been arrested two years earlier for immoral conduct after a raid on a "notorious underworld resort," which the lady ran in Atlanta.

The investigators found financial corruption. Of the ten dollars collected from each new Klansman, four dollars went to the Kleagles, one dollar to the King Kleagle, fifty cents to the Grand Goblin, and the rest to Simmons and others at the central offices in Atlanta. They found that the Klan controlled an invisible political empire, with mayors, governors, and judges jumping at its command. They found, back of all the power, the terrorism of the few and the insecurity and cowardice of the many.

The newspaper exposure was followed by a Congressional investigation. Simmons handled himself shrewdly on the stand. He was all compact of innocence. "My disposition from boyhood," he said, "has been tinged with a distinctive streak of timidity." And when questioned about the Klan's secrecy, he answered, "Our mask and robe, I say before God, are as innocent as the breath of an angel."

It was this same Simmons who two years later made a speech in Atlanta in which he shouted: "When the hordes of aliens walk to the ballot box and their votes outnumber yours, then that alien horde has got you by the throat. . . . Americans will awake from their slumbers and rush out to battle, and there will be such a stir as the world has never seen the like. The soil of America will run with the blood of its people."

Nothing came of the Congressional investigation. Nor did the *World* exposé break the Klan; instead it gave it priceless publicity. By 1924 John M. Mecklin, the shrewdest student of the Klan, estimated a membership of close to five million. This was not restricted to the South, but had spread through the Middle West and reached the Far West.

But the American conscience, stirred by the exposure, did not wholly slumber. The boom prosperity of the next five years, moreover, weakened the Klan's roots in middle-class insecurity. By the time of the depression the Klan had been further weakened by internal disruption. A dentist called Hiram Wesley Evans moved in on a good thing and took Simmons's job as Imperial Wizard. From that time, Simmons moved in a twilight world of failure. He formed a series of rival organizations, among them the Knights of the Kamelia, the Knights of the Flaming Sword, and the White Band. But for all the flummery of names, the old magic was gone. Finally he sold his interest, got ninety thousand dollars in cash, pulled out entirely, and spent his remaining days feeding on the bitterness of his heart.

The Klan itself was drawn increasingly into the struggles of an industrial culture. It was used for breaking strikes, frightening labor organizers out of factory communities. It turned up in the automobile union struggle in Detroit. It distributed widely the early anti-Jewish writings of Henry Ford's *Dearborn Independent*, until a chastened Ford published a letter asking that further distribution be stopped. It made an alliance in New Jersey with the German-American Bund, and its leaders appeared on the same platform with Bundists. When the Detroit race riots broke out and Negroes were clubbed and shot in the streets, it was generally accepted that the Klan was involved, but no proof developed. Throughout the country, whenever violence broke out, people thought of the Klan— whether justly or not. It was this fact that spelled its collapse.

The Klan no longer exists as a strong organization. But the hatreds and insecurities on which it fed are still present in the American scene. But the day is far from over for the night-riders of the spirit. New organizations have sprung up which inherit the Klan's outlook and its methods. They are waiting for the day when new insecurity, created by new unemployment, will give the night-riders of the future the chance to ride again.[1]

MAY 24, 1945

[1] After this was written, there were scattered attempts to revive the Klan. In a number of states (notably in California, under the leadership of Robert W. Kenny as State Attorney General) moves were made to revoke the Klan charters. For the recent history, see Carey McWilliams, *A Mask for Privilege: Antisemitism in America* (1948).

The Loomis Story: The Lumpen-Leisure-Class

WHAT MAKES a fascist adventurer tick? Croswell Bowen has put this question and has come up with rewarding material in the life story of Homer Loomis, Jr.[1] Loomis dreamed up the Columbians as a fascist organization, and hoped to build an anti-Negro and anti-Jewish popular movement that would mushroom out from Atlanta, dominate Washington, and march on New York. He never got farther than a squalid Atlanta meeting-hall, a dismal barracks-dormitory, some planted tear-gas bombs, a cache of dynamite, a few cheap and nasty efforts at terrorizing Negroes, an inglorious fizzling-out of his movement in a Georgia court.

The story is of a man at once evil and stupid. Loomis and his Columbians are in themselves paltry stuff. But as symptoms they are worth some reflection.

The most striking phase of Loomis' story is what is generally called its "Park Avenue" background. Up to now the would-be *Fuehrers* have generally come from the rural regions, the small towns, the urban lower middle class. Loomis comes from a group which—to borrow from the term *Lumpenproletariat*—I can only call the Lumpen-leisure-class. It is a world of emptiness, excesses, frustrations; a twilight world of functionless people who are the real wasteland of American life.

We have often thought of fascist leaders as the incarnation of hatred. But in Loomis' case it is clear that the hatred of Negroes and Jews is secondary—a convenient instrument, not a fanatic passion. Here, coming out of a group accustomed to success and rule, was a man whose life was a succession of failures. And so he cooks up a hotchpotch assortment of crazy ingredients drawn from the surrounding atmosphere—racial "purity," white supremacy, anti-Jewish myths, sexual asceticism, class-war, army discipline, the cult of violence. Stupid though he is, he has enough sense to turn to rootless and functionless young veterans for his support. He knows—what other fascist adventurers know—that his only chance for power lies in turning their habits of war violence into habits of criminal violence.

I find an alarming theme in the material Bowen has dug up from a Princeton paper, showing that many young men of the leisure-class have

[1] This story appeared in *PM*, Jan. 12, 1947.

the conviction that they belong to an elite group; that, without doing anything useful in their nation, they are the natural rulers of the masses, by divine right of property, race, breeding, leisure. From there it is only a step toward the effort to manipulate the masses in order to serve the power-lusts and the revenge-impulses of the self-styled elite who are only empty-minded boys in an empty world. What America contributes to the natural history of fascism is this progression from night-club nuisances to street political hooligans.

There is little question that the human material for fascism is present in American life, both in the form of power-hungry adventurers and the mass-hatreds and middle-class frustrations which they know how to exploit. This is the real enemy we must face—this and not the scares about "Reds" and "Left Wingers" which the press and the politicians and the reactionaries of church and business spread and which the fascists use.

We are sometimes misled into shrugging the native fascist movements off because they are led by men like Loomis and Gerald Smith, like the Klan's Doctor Green, like the ex-priest Terminiello; and because thus far they are mainly a matter of hate-rantings and some dynamite. But behind this paltry stuff there is always the shadow of the annihilation camps and the human furnaces to which German fascism led. Once a nation submits to the fascist idea, it cannot stop short of mass bestiality. And let us remember that whatever Americans have undertaken—capitalism, war, unemployment, gang violence, mass production—they have done on a far larger scale than any other nation. That would go for fascism too.

I have said that the Columbians are important only as a symptom. The social conditions for a real fascist movement can exist only when adventurers like Loomis gain the support of the big corporations and the Army. That was the basic pattern of fascism in Germany—the Unholy Alliance of army, big business, and storm-troopers. The thing to guard against is the emergence of the same pattern and the same alliance here.

Obviously the Columbians did get some corporate money. As Governor Arnall has put it: "I know that such organizations as the Columbians, and such peddlers of hate as the hundreds of slimy little racial and class sheets that are distributed and broadcast throughout our common country, cost a great deal more money to support than the riffraff that front for such groups can raise from deluded and neurotic followers." But the corporate money has not yet started flowing in big amounts. And there is as yet no tie-up with Army leaders, as there was between Hitler and the *Reichswehr* generals. That is our margin of safety. It can be maintained only as long as we maintain jobs and peace.

JAN. 12, 1947

Immigration and Racism

TRIPPING UP a blind man, stealing money from a beggar, kicking a man when he is down: these are some of the traditional American expressions for acts that come from mean spirits and sawdust hearts. They are also good descriptions of the trick that the United States Senate has played on the displaced persons (DPs) of Europe, in passing the Wiley-Revercomb Bill. For the provisions of the bill form a package whose outer wrapping seems to be all generosity, but when you open it what explodes in your face is Hitler's principle of racist discrimination.

The history of the effort to pass a decent bill for admitting DPs beyond the current immigration quotas goes back to the end of World War II. At the end of December, 1945, President Truman, by executive order, asked for the expediting of visas for DPs within the quotas of the central European countries. The result was almost negligible. Then a movement was started to admit 400,000 of them beyond the quota, over a four-year period. Nothing came of that. Now the Republican Senate leadership has come up with a bill to admit 200,000 in a two-year period. But there are cruel jokers attached to it.

The best analysis of those jokers will be found in a statement made by Earl G. Harrison, former Commissioner of Immigration and now Dean of the University of Pennsylvania Law School. He is chairman of the Citizens Committee on Displaced Persons, which has spearheaded the fight to open America's gates to some of the survivors of the Nazi terror. Here are the jokers:

Fifty per cent of the DPs must come from countries which have been "annexed by a foreign power." This means, of course, Latvia, Lithuania, Estonia, and Eastern Poland, all annexed by Russia in 1939. These are the Baltic countries. They furnish only a small percentage of the total number of DPs and thus are made the darlings of the Wiley-Revercomb Bill. There are few, if any, Jewish DPs among them, and scarcely any Catholic DPs. It is almost incredible that these countries should get this sort of preference, which is a direct slap at two great religious groups in America. It is even more incredible in the light of the widely known and documented fact that among these Baltic DPs are many who collaborated with Hitler's invasion armies and had a hand in the Nazi racist massacres.

The bill says half the DPs admitted must be farmers. Actually only a small percentage of the DPs in Europe are farmers. The percentage is even smaller for the Jewish DPs. The result and (I suspect) also the intent of this clause seem clearly racist.

To clinch the racist character of the bill's provisions, there is one giving the former German Nazis a special break. It provides that "all persons of German ethnic origin," no matter what country they may have been born in, shall be considered Germans and admitted under the German quota.

This means that we have now taken over Hitler's concept of the *Volksdeutsche*—those who are German because they have German (ethnic) *blood* in them, regardless of their *place* of birth. It is *Mein Kampf* written into the American statute books. Many of these people formed part of Hitler's movement in the countries of their birth, and later found their way to Germany and Austria. We are now proposing to give them preference over those whom their philosophy victimized.

The cruelest joker of all is the one directly aimed to exclude all but a small number of Jewish DPs. No one will be eligible for the DP visas who came into the DP camps after December 22, 1945. Why that date? Because the big stream of Jewish refugees started moving into occupied zones of central Europe *after* December, 1945. Before that date there were only ten thousand Jewish DPs in the camps.

There are other jokers, but I have given enough of the crucial ones to show the Wiley-Revercomb Bill is one of the slickest and most cynical measures in the racist tradition that has ever been passed by a legislative body. Dean Harrison says: "No bill at all would be better than this so-called DP bill." I agree.

We had a chance to break with the racist trend in immigration policy that set in under the 1924 Act which established carefully chosen national quotas. For the first time in almost a quarter century there was a popular movement under way to go back to the non-discriminatory pre-1924 policy. There was a pressing human need. There was a dramatic symbol of the results of racial oppression—the symbol of the DP camps. There was a renewed insight which the war against fascism gave us—an insight into the inner nature and the consequences of the principle of racism. All of these together might have led to a generous new DP immigration measure that would have reaffirmed the American belief in the equity of all human beings under God, and the historic mission of America as a refuge for the oppressed.

Instead of that the Wiley-Revercomb Bill is a slap in the face to those in the DP camps who hoped for America as a refuge, and to those in America who are jealous of American democratic honor.

I don't see how the Republican Senate leadership can escape the responsibility for this outcome. Senator Taft did make a plea on the floor of the Senate, asking his colleagues not to approach the DP problem "in a trivial way." Yet it was he, along with the other Senate Republican leaders, who assigned Senator Revercomb to make a study of the DP immigration problem which he submitted as a report to the Republican Steering Committee in December, 1946. The whole tone of that report was racist. The only admissible tests for any DPs we may admit into our country is whether they will make good citizens and be useful and democratic Americans. To add the kind of tests which will exclude most of the victims of Nazism is a sorry kind of victory over people who have had to encounter and survive a more ruthless racism than even the Wiley-Revercomb Bill embodies.

JUNE 8, 1948

The United States as Exclusive Hotel

ONE OF THE indirect results of our country's being the United Nations capital may be to win us back to a great American tradition that we have been steadily pushing aside. I mean the tradition of friendliness and welcome to people of foreign birth. Once we owned that tradition and lived it. Now we own it as you might be said to own a discarded garment that is still in your closet, but that you no longer wear.

What do you think of when you think of the American nation? Do you think of it as being all the people? Or do you think of it as an exclusive hotel, catering only to those who had the luck to be born here?

I put these questions to you because I have had an exchange of letters with an eminent American literary critic on the subject of who belongs in America. I do not now mention his name, because it has been a private exchange. But the subject is of very wide import.

He started by arguing that some of my utterances (he referred to a long essay I once wrote as an introduction to the Modern Library edition of Machiavelli) have been "inflammable." I think he is wrong, and am ready to argue it out—but that isn't the crucial point.

He went on to argue (and this is crucial) that since I was born in Russia, and did not come to America with my family until I was four years old, I have no right to be "censorious." I asked him whether he really meant that we who have known other countries as well as America (he, too, is foreign-born) do not have the same right to examine American institutions as do the native-born. That would, I argued, put us both in a lower category of American citizenship. I stand, and shall always stand, on the great tradition of an inclusive and not an exclusive American-ism—one which asks of a man not where he was born or any other extraneous question, but only whether he is dedicated to fighting for humanist values according to his best lights.

His answer raises a crucial issue. This is, he says, a "nation," not an "international lodginghouse." "Every hotelkeeper," he goes on, "knows the difference between a person who behaves as a permanent guest and a person who behaves as a transient. The permanent guest, even so, is not as involved as the home-keeper."

This is interesting. Let me start by saying that I recognize fully the right of every national government to decide the conditions on which it will accept aliens into citizenship. That is part of our Constitution, and there is a large body of Supreme Court interpretation of it.

The real question is whether we shall draw a distinction *between American citizens* on the basis of *their birth*. This is not a question of racism or blood-thinking. My friend, the critic, is deeply anti-Nazi and anti-racist. He would include native-born Negroes and native-born Jews in his category of the "home-keepers." But he seems to believe that those citizens who are foreign-born and therefore "guests" (either permanent or transient) have less right to freedom of discussion than those who are the "home-keepers." They must, presumably, stay away from critical discussion of basic political and social issues, any comments on the house-rules of the "hotel."

I dissent, thoroughly and completely. If these remarks came from a ranting Congressional primitive I should not pay any attention to them. They come, however, from a humane and distinguished critic who believes himself a thoroughgoing democrat with a small *d*. They show therefore how far the idea has gone that there is a birth-line cutting America in two. Disraeli once said that England was two nations, not one; and he was talking of the class-structure. Shall we now say that America is two nations, not one, on the basis of birth?

In my thinking America is neither an exclusive hotel nor an international lodginghouse. We cannot divide Americans into home-keepers, permanent guests, and transients on the accident of birth. America is a passionate idea or it is nothing. America is a human brotherhood or it is a chaos.

When you look back at the American tradition you find that the life-blood of it is the concept that men must be free to think, to talk, to criticize, to dissent. It is those who would balk criticism, smother dissent, who place themselves outside the American brotherhood. It is they who endanger the survival and flowering of the American idea. A foreign-born American who believes in the competition of ideas is of far more value to our common country than a native-born American who would drown out that competition.

We shall not have an enduring peace until the world has moved much further toward becoming a society in which men are linked with men *because of what they are.* And our first step must be to make our own nation into a true society.

MARCH 27, 1946

The Shame of the Deportations [1]

I WISH that Attorney General Clark and President Truman would read a book. The book I have in mind is Zechariah Chafee's classic study, *Free Speech in the United States* (Harvard University Press, 1941). They would find in that book, among other episodes of attacks on American freedom, an extended account of the deportation follies of 1920. At that time there was an Attorney General named A. Mitchell Palmer, now happily forgotten, except for the idiocy of his raids upon alien radicals. It was Palmer's quaint idea that the way to get rid of the Communist party (which had at that time just split off from the Socialists) was to round up and arrest all alien radicals and send them back where they came from. Palmer's deportation blitz came in January, 1920. Thousands were arrested in Communist and trade-union meetings or dragged out of their beds at night; they were handcuffed, kept in dirty and crowded jails, "tried" administratively without the right of counsel. The whole business came to an inglorious end because the Labor Department, which at that time had final jurisdiction, refused to carry through the dirty affair, and only a small fraction of those arrested were actually deported. But the memory of the "Palmer raids" remains as the low point in the history of

[1] This was written in the early spring of 1948, about deportation arrests that had been going on through the winter.

the Justice Department, and the dramatic proof of how far hysteria can carry arbitrary men and arbitrary methods before the basic common sense of a democracy asserts itself.

Tom Clark is no Mitchell Palmer. In the matter of technique he has learned a thing or two that Palmer didn't know. He doesn't arrest thousands for deportation in a single month, he doesn't round up all the obscure little people who attend radical meetings, he doesn't dispense with warrants, he doesn't boast (as Palmer did) of the network of Government spies in radical organizations. He doesn't even assert that he is saving the nation from Communism.

He plays it all deadpan. He arrests only the key figures who are alien radicals and who are strategically important in the Left Wing trade-unions. He carries the arrests out one at a time, spacing them carefully at irregular intervals so that while the potential victims know a blow is impending they never know just when it will fall or where. He picks up his people suddenly—one on the way to work, another in the midst of trade-union bargaining. His game is often big game, and always lands on the front pages. He doesn't talk about a crusade against Communism, but presumably is only carrying out his lawful duty as the chief justice officer of the nation in executing a law of Congress. One cannot but feel that the Department of Justice has left behind the primitive methods of the Mitchell Palmer days. Everything now is so much slicker and so much more sophisticated. In a decade that has carried the techniques of death in war to their utmost refinement, one expects—and gets—the same kind of refinement in the techniques of political persecution.

But it is political persecution nonetheless. These men and women have been living in the United States for many years, and those who are Communists have been known as such for many years. There have been dossiers on them in the FBI files. Why has the Government suddenly decided that they are undesirable aliens? Why has the Government suddenly decided to deport them under the Alien Registration Act of 1940? The answer is clear. This is, as President Truman and Attorney General Clark see it, a way of showing the Russians and the world Communist forces that we too can be tough. This is their way of cracking down on the Communist party, which Truman and Clark hold largely responsible for engineering the Wallace split. This is, finally, their way of trying to harry the Communists out of whatever strongholds they still retain in the American trade-unions. In short, these are not ordinary deportation cases but a political maneuver.

One of the meanest phases of these political deportation cases is the denial of bail, which keeps the victims shut up at Ellis Island, away from their families and their work, until they are either deported or released. Legally the Justice Department can grant or deny bail at will, for deportation cases do not count as criminal actions and therefore the Constitutional guarantees of bail do not apply to them. The vengeful nature of these particular cases is shown by the Attorney General's rigid resistance to allowing any bail, as if these men were dangerous criminals who must be kept locked up while their fate is being settled. The hunger strike that they have been staging at Ellis Island is a protest against this injustice, and —in so far as it dramatizes the injustice—a valid protest.[2]

How about the larger Constitutional issue? There is no question that every government has the right to deport aliens, but a government of free people must use that right sparingly, and only in the spirit of freedom. That is not what we have done. The Deportation Act of 1918 was severe enough, that of 1920 was made more severe, that of 1940 was hysterical. Yet even under that Act, it is still uncertain whether the Justice Department has a Constitutional right to deport men for Communist party membership.

The Act does not mention the Communist party, but only membership in an organization which advocates the overthrow of the Government by violence. The question of whether this applies to Communist membership has not been decided by the Supreme Court, although the lower Federal courts have tended to say yes. Obviously the problem is not one of deciding what the Russian Communists or the Czech Communists advocate, but what applies in the American case at the present time. Until the Supreme Court decides, Tom Clark's whole deportation adventure is a shot in the dark. If he genuinely wanted to test the law, he could have made one arrest and made a Supreme Court test case out of it. The fact that he is making arrest after arrest, and denying bail although it is obvious that the deportations cannot be carried out until the Supreme Court has finally passed on the issue, leaves only one conclusion: that the Administration's intent is political suppression and political vengeance.

That is exactly where the futility and danger of the whole procedure come in. Americans, perhaps exactly because they are a nation of immigrants, have a more bristling attitude toward aliens than you are likely to find in any other democracy. Many Americans express their frustrations and hatreds in alien-bating. After reading the debates on the 1940 Alien Registration Act, Professor Chafee wrote: "Congressmen have taken a savage joy in demanding bigger and better deportations. I never realized how Nazis feel toward Jews until I read what Congressmen say about

[2] The legal case on bail was later argued before the Federal Court, and bail was granted.

radical aliens." There is a general feeling that you don't have to worry about denying freedoms to aliens, because—after all—they are not citizens, and do not have the rights of citizens. The Justice Department is exploiting this feeling, made all the more tense and explosive now by the brink-of-war psychology on both sides of the Russian-American world struggle.

But it is a dangerous attitude to exploit. The difference between the democratic concept of the nation and the totalitarian is that one is broadly inclusive, the other narrowly exclusive. We must count as part of the American community not only those who share our political ideas but also those who challenge them, provided they do so without violence. We must count not only native-born and citizens, but also the foreign-born and those who—for whatever reason—have not become citizens. In the case of Communists, it is unjust to blame them for not having become citizens when the fact is that they are refused naturalization when they do apply. Moreover, the arbitrary procedures that the Justice Department is using might—as they did in Palmer's day—land citizens in the same net with aliens, subject to the same indignities until citizenship was proved. Let us remember that aliens, as well as citizens, are human beings, and that injustice directed at them will corrupt the whole of our culture.

Many who will go along with me up to this point may nevertheless say: "But the Communists, wherever they are in control, have no such scruples about injustice. We must fight them with their own weapons, lest they get a chance to use them against us." This seems to me a deadly doctrine. Communism has no roots in the American mind, and there is no present danger that it will strike such roots in our time. The best way to play into the hands of the Communists is to weaken our own democracy by abandoning our democratic convictions. The surest way to give a martyrdom to their ideas is to subject them to political persecution. "Justice," wrote William Bolitho, "must never use injustice in its fight on injustice—for fear of making it just."

I want to quote an anecdote from Charles P. Howland, an American lawyer who wrote about the 1920 deportation follies. "A Dukhobor tried to go naked in the streets of London. A policeman set out gravely to capture him, but found himself distanced because of his heavy clothing. Therefore he divested himself, as he ran, of garment after garment, until he was naked; and so lightened, he caught his prey. But then it was impossible to tell which was the Dukhobor and which was the policeman."

MARCH 7, 1948

Scars on the American Conscience

IT IS NOT a simple and easy thing for a people to be free. I have just finished reading a remarkable Government report which documents that fact. It is called *To Secure These Rights*, and was released by the President's Committee on Civil Rights. It does not dig deep into the psychological roots of the bigotry, apathy and personal frustration which are still dangerous enemies of American life: that is a job for the psychologists and the social thinkers. But it does give a remarkably candid report on the scars on the American conscience, on what it is that still stands in the way of our achieving freedom from fear.

There is none of the double-talk you generally find in Government documents. It gives facts and figures, concrete instances of injustice, detailed recommendations for practical action. It is as much a landmark in the understanding of the conditions of American freedom as the Temporary National Economic Committee report, in the heyday of the New Deal, was a landmark in the understanding of the American economy. One could not ask for a more adequate answer to the hysteria on the Hollywood inquiry, nor for a better frame of perspective within which to estimate the threat contained in the irresponsible methods of Representative Thomas and his comrades.

For what the report does is to show how precious is the American heritage of civil liberties and how fierce a pride we may take in it as a heritage. Yet, as Jean Jaurès once said, we must take from the past its fires, not its ashes. Never in our history have we been in as great a danger of scattering our heritage to the wind. The report does no flag-waving and gives us no ground for smugness despite the obvious fact that we have more freedom than you will find in any totalitarian system.

Consider the current record. Lynching of Negroes has declined, yet it is still practiced and is still the worst scar on the national conscience. The murder of four Negroes at Monroe, Georgia, is still fresh in our memories. Negro prisoners are still killed by armed guards in forced labor camps, as in the Glynn County instance, and the protection of Negro rights in Southern courts is a mockery. It is only a few years since American citizens were brutally torn away from their homes and jobs and roots because they were Japanese in descent. It is still true that Negroes are kept from voting in Southern states by the device of "white primaries," [1] and that low-income whites, as well as Negroes, are cheated of their suffrage in seven remaining poll-tax states. We still practice segregation and discrimination against Negroes in the armed forces. There is still job discrimination in our industries because of a man's color and religion. Those in the minority groups are the last to get hired in prosperity and the first to be fired in depression. Their children have a harder time getting into colleges and professional schools and if they are colored they have the rawest deals in elementary schooling. They are Jim Crowed in housing almost as badly in the North as in the South and are segregated even in public housing. Their doctors and their sick don't get a chance in the hospitals.

The record goes on wretchedly. Jim Crow stalks the trains, the buses, the theaters, the restaurants, the hotels. In the case of Northern resorts it affects Jews as well as Negroes. In the national capital itself, Washington, D. C., a Negro must change to a Jim Crow train going south, can find no place in a restaurant, movie, or hotel in the downtown district, must live in crowded slums, send his children to Jim Crow schools, and be content with the substandard medical service.

This is America. Oliver Cromwell once asked his portrait painter not to leave out his wart. The President's Committee on Civil Rights has had the courage to do a portrait which shows the ugly wart on the face of America. Or perhaps the figure should be stronger. We are dealing with nothing less than a cancerous growth on the body of American freedom.

And because it is that, it cannot be cured merely by words or pious wishes. A cancerous growth must be cut out while there is still time. The Committee's recommendations are no namby-pamby affair. Put an end to segregation of all kinds—whether based on race, color, creed, or national origin. Pass the Federal Fair Employment Practices Committee act. Set up state commissions to deal with cases of discrimination in education— and to prosecute them. Outlaw restrictive covenants in housing.[2] Pass a Federal law banning Jim Crow in interstate transportation. Pass state laws banning Jim Crow in restaurants and stores and places of recreation. Pass a Federal anti-lynching law. Clear up the discrimination in the nation's capital. Pass a Federal primary law and an anti-poll-tax law. Set up clear standards on loyalty tests for Government employees. Use the method of disclosures rather than the method of hysteria and censorship in fighting totalitarian ideas on the Right and Left. Put teeth into the

---

[1] These were declared unconstitutional by the Supreme Court, but in practice some of the Southern states have found ways of evading the decision.

[2] In 1948 the Supreme Court held that agreements embodying restrictive covenants are not enforceable in the courts.

whole program by strengthening the Federal civil rights statutes, and by setting up a full-fledged division on civil rights in the Justice Department, and a standing joint House and Senate committee.

This is good medicine because it is strong medicine. Nothing less will do. It will not be done overnight, but it can and must be achieved in our decade. What we need is to make our Bill of Rights come alive. If we do not, all our talk about the lack of civil rights in foreign countries will be a mockery, and the promise of American life will prove a delusion.

The report has political dynamite in it. If President Truman and his Administration accept it, they can use it as the Democratic answer to the Republican philosophy of fear and repression now being placed on the record by the Thomas Committee. But the Democrats carry on their shoulders the oppressive burden of Southern reactionaries, to whom this report—with its clear thinking, plain speaking, concrete action—will be the Devil himself.[3]

OCT. 30, 1947

The Negroes and the Draft

ONE OF THE most impressive and courageous statements ever made before a Congressional committee by any man, white or black, was made on March 31, and it has not received nearly as much attention as it deserves. For it opens a new chapter, not only in the history of the American Negroes, and of American military measures, but also in the history of the deadly serious struggle for American democracy.

The two Negro leaders who made the statement are A. Philip Randolph and Grant Reynolds. Randolph has been in many battles for Negro freedom and trade-union rights. He is the head of the Union of Sleeping-car Porters. Reynolds is a member of the New York State Commission of Corrections. But both men mean what they say when they speak out against Jim Crow in the Army. Recently they saw President Truman, and Randolph told him that "Negroes are in no mood to shoulder an-

[3] As it turned out, the support President Truman gave the Report helped produce a rebellion of Southern Governors and Senators against him and led to the formation of the so-called Dixiecrat Party in the 1948 campaign. But Truman's increased strength among the liberals and the minority groups gave him the victory.

other gun for democracy abroad while they are denied democracy here at home." Truman blew up and said he didn't like to listen to that kind of talk. The delegation asked him whether he did or didn't want to know how the Negroes felt. They were reporting a hard fact to him, and he could take it or leave it.

But when Randolph and Reynolds came up before the Armed Services Committee of the United States Senate, they did more than report. They took a stand. Randolph pledged himself to advocate and support among Negro youth an "organized refusal to register or be drafted" unless the draft and the universal military training acts embodied specific provisions against Jim Crow. He talked of a possible "mass civil disobedience movement along the lines of the magnificent struggles of the people of India against British imperialism." He added: "I personally pledge myself to openly counsel, aid, and abet youth, both white and Negro, to quarantine any Jim Crow conscription system." He said that the Negroes had fought in the war against the Nazis because they saw it as a war against Hitler's racism. "This factor," he said, "is not present in the power struggle between Stalin and the U. S."

This is not idle talk, and Randolph and Reynolds showed that they had coldly measured its consequences, for themselves and for the large mass of Negroes whose view they undoubtedly express. When Senator Wayne Morse of Oregon showed his sense of shock at the testimony, and pointed out that this might be prosecuted under the legal doctrine of treason, Randolph answered that he knew there would be terrorism against the Negroes, but "we would be willing to absorb the violence, absorb the terrorism, face the music, and take whatever comes. . . . I think that's a price we have to pay to get our democratic rights."

Whether you are sympathetic with Randolph, or are shocked as Senator Morse was shocked, you must recognize two facts about it. First, that it is a historic statement, one that took the kind of courage of going into battle in the face of enemy fire. Second, that it presents a far more important question in the security of American democracy than all the debates about the draft, universal military training, atom bombs, and a larger air force that are now occupying the military minds. Morally Randolph and Reynolds are right, and they have gone far deeper into the relation of democracy and national security than any of the military men or the Congressmen have gone. What they are saying is that you cannot brush aside the struggle for democracy on a plea of a national security emergency. For it is not the armed forces which can protect our democracy. It is the moral strength of democracy which alone can give any meaning to the efforts at military security.

On this score even a general who is unlike his fellow generals—Dwight Eisenhower—showed a narrowness and blindness when he defended the current system of Army segregation. Eisenhower is a former Chief of Staff, he is now a university president, and he is a man whose mind is obviously on the move and whose social philosophy is in the making. I suggest to him very strongly that he go to school to these two Negro leaders, and learn a few things from them about democracy which his military experience has not taught him.

We can all learn from them. And they in turn have learned something from Gandhi. We shall be adding up the total of the full effect of Gandhi's teaching for many years to come. On this score Gandhi taught two things: that nothing is more important than the moral conviction of an individual; and that in the face of the organized passive resistance to evil—a resistance flowing from that moral conviction—no amount of violence or terrorism will ultimately prevail.

This is, in my memory, the first time that responsible Negro leaders, who are not playing the Communist game or being stooges for a strategy not their own, have talked out so clearly and unmistakably on so fateful an issue. I know that there are many other Negro leaders who feel that this goes much too far, and who regard the Randolph-Reynolds statement as a mistake. Yet I think there can be no question that Randolph and Reynolds come closer to the true feeling of the masses of American Negroes, in the North as in the South, than their more cautious and circumspect colleagues.

Something has happened to the American Negro in the era of the New Deal and of World War II, and it is something that will have to be reckoned with by those who are measuring forces in World War III. They have found a moral and political principle that can only be expressed in the words Thomas Wolfe once used: a principle

> *Whereon the pillars of this earth are founded,*
> *Toward which the conscience of the world is tending—*
> *A wind is rising, and the rivers flow.*

That principle is, of course, the principle of a democracy which is not qualified by race or color or any other stupid irrelevance. It is idle to point to the undoubted fact that the position of the American Negro is slowly improving, that the injustice to him is being diluted, that the lynchings are fewer, that the discriminations are slowly being whittled away. You cannot answer a plea for equality by a half-inequality; you cannot answer a demand for justice by meting out injustice somewhat more carefully. Equality is a passion that feeds on itself. The taste of democracy becomes a bitter taste when the fullness of democracy is denied. That bitterness has been increased by the hypocrisy we have shown in fighting racism abroad while we tolerate it at home. It has been increased by the experience our Negro GIs had when they were sent abroad, and found there were countries in which they were treated as human equals, and where the black badge of color did not blot out the red badge of courage. Democracy makes many claims, and talks very loudly about itself. It must also face the music, and pay the reckoning.

When Senator Morse asked Randolph whether he would advocate mass civil disobedience if the Russians should attack us, Randolph's answer was a good one. He said there was still plenty of time for Congress to attack Jim Crow in the armed services before the Russians attack us. The whole idea of a Russian attack is under present conditions fantastic, and the tension of our relations with Russia has been used much too often to obscure issues of democracy as well as of peace.

I can add another answer to the one Randolph gave. The threat of civil disobedience undoubtedly weakens the military front we present to Russia; but what weakens us far more is the fact of racist discrimination. What the generals and Congressmen don't know—and even a liberal like Senator Morse does not seem to know it—is that in its deepest sense World War III will be fought out all over the world as an ideological war. It is a naked struggle for power, but the weapons with which it will be fought will be ideological weapons.

And in such a struggle one of the real enemies within is Jim Crow. It is Jim Crow who will be committing treason, who has already committed treason.[1]

APRIL 11, 1948

"Certain Unalienable Rights"

HE WAS A young man of thirty-three, a tall, red-haired, freckled Virginia gentleman, who knew the classics, played the violin, and had fastidious tastes. He had left his estate at Monticello, and his ailing wife and young daughter, to travel to Philadelphia where the Continental Congress was

[1] Some months later, after the Truman Administration had moved to correct some of the more flagrant Jim Crow practices in the armed services, Randolph and Reynolds announced that their immediate purpose had been achieved, and called off their passive resistance movement.

in session. He was not a ready talker or debater, but he had a strong, graceful, and pungent pen. When the time came to decide on the issue of independence, the other four men on the drafting committee left the job of drawing up the declaration to the studious young Virginian, whose name was Thomas Jefferson.

He worked at his draft (see Dumas Malone's first-rate biography, *Jefferson, the Virginian*) from the middle to the end of June, in quarters at Seventh and Market Streets rented from a bricklayer called Graff. In the parlor on the second floor, using a folding writing-box to work on, consulting no books but drawing on his stored-up reading and the general ideas available to a cultured man of his day, he set down the case for American independence.

On July 2, 3, and 4 the members of the Congress dissected and debated, with a critical scrutiny that made the young author writhe, every sentence and phrase he had written, beginning with "When in the course of human events" and ending with "We mutually pledge to each other our Lives, our Fortunes and our sacred Honor." On July 4, twelve states (New York did not vote) accepted it.

I know that one could make out a case to show that the men who signed the Declaration were largely conservatives, men of substance; that the decision was forced on them by a stupid king and his arrogant ministers. Yet it remains true that the Declaration of Independence was an act of revolutionary boldness.

These men risked death, disaster, and disgrace. It was, I suppose, a form of midsummer madness for them to think they could get away with it. But they were bold men, living in a great time. What Jefferson wrote in the Declaration was more than a manifesto of independence; it was a radical democratic credo that American life has been trying to catch up with ever since.

The root idea in the Declaration is the idea that no government can separate a man from his rights as a man—the "certain unalienable Rights," including "Life, Liberty and the pursuit of Happiness." Not only then must government rest on "the consent of the governed": in a free society, men are the governors as well as the governed; and the famous right of revolution, with which Jefferson embarrasses the fat cats of this day, is the right of men to fashion their own destiny and reshape their own institutions. What an irony it is that at a time when these fat cats are hunting dangerous and subversive thoughts, they must celebrate a document containing the most dangerous thought of all.

If you look for Jeffersons of today, you are unlikely to find them in America. You may have a better chance of finding one in India, in Burma, in Indonesia, in Israel—wherever men can still find unity in throwing off the shackles of other men's oppression. In the farthest corners of the world, the phrases of Jefferson have lighted fires in the hearts of yellow men and brown and white, of Hindus and Jews and Christians. Their will marches to the beat of his ideas.

Yet they are doing little more than rounding out the cycle he began. They are the last embers of the fires he lit—the fires of nationalist democratic independence.

That is no longer the central problem of human affairs in our age, as it was in the eighteenth century. They were the happy men, for they had a concrete external enemy to fight—a tyrannical king the calendar of whose oppressions could be set down with eloquence. They had a new and vibrant philosophy to draw on—that of enlightenment, to which the Declaration gave magnificent form and synthesis. As for us, the tyrannies are not external, but are in ourselves—in the smugness and anarchy of our society. And no new philosophy of enlightenment has risen to stir us.

Jefferson wrote a Declaration of Independence. Ours must be, in this century, a Declaration of Interdependence. The problem is no longer centrally one of the alienation of rights from man, but the alienation of man from man. Even when men are tolerably free, as they are in America, they act like free beasts in a jungle. Even when nations are sovereign and independent, they are at each other's throats.

Our current philosophies, whether of rugged capitalism or rugged communism, are not much more than competing versions of how power can be organized and men exploited. They do not tackle the root question of how men can live together in a world society, and lead productive lives, and not be rent asunder from each other.

Some day another Jefferson will draft another Declaration. I want to be around when he does.

JULY 4, 1948

The Loyalty Hunters

THERE ARE SEVERAL extremely dangerous elements in President Truman's executive order for a loyalty purge of Federal officials.

First: the wide net it casts. To the question of who is disloyal and who is subversive, the answer used to be one who believes in the overthrow of the

American Government, or who belongs to an organization that does. That is the wording of Section 9A of the Hatch Act and also of the riders to Congressional appropriation bills denying the use of any of the funds to disloyal employees. Up to now those have formed the legal basis for loyalty tests. Yet now we have an executive order from the President extending disloyalty and subversiveness to mean "sympathetic association" with any group the Attorney General may designate as subversive.

I think a good argument could be made out that a man's disloyalty ought to be proved as a personal fact; that to brand him with disloyalty because he belongs to a suspect but still legal organization is to strip him of the chance to compete for Federal employment on an equal basis with others, and therefore to strip him of a basic right as an American. But even if you waive this reasoning, there are still several removes between membership in the Communist party and "sympathetic association" with some group which in turn might once have been used by the Communists or fought for some specific reform alongside them. But no matter how many removes there may be, and no matter how loose or vague the linkage, the executive order blithely makes the leap. I know of few non-party-line, non-fellow-traveler liberals worth their salt who would not at some time in the course of the last fifteen years have made themselves vulnerable to this wide net.

Second: the executive order sets down as law the worst rather than the best of the practices of the past years. In Washington you will hear the argument that there is nothing in the executive order which has not been a matter of recent routine practice, and that all it does is to standardize what is currently being done. That may possibly be its intent. But if the security officers of the ten Cabinet departments have been purging people because of "sympathetic association," they have had no basis for it either in the Hatch Act or in the appropriation riders. They have been doing it on the cuff, and now the same on-the-cuff rules are being extended to all the independent agencies and officially embraced by the President. Instead of defending the new executive order on the ground that it embodies current practices, it would be better to criticize those practices on the ground that they had no authority.

Third: the fate and fortunes of several million Federal workers are being turned over to the whim and mercy of a single man—the Attorney General. Part V, Section F of the order gives the Attorney General the power to decide what shall be the groups and organizations for "sympathetic association" with which an employee may be branded as disloyal and have his career destroyed and his life blasted.

I am, of course, aware that a man will first be investigated by his department's security officer, or by the Civil Service Commission operatives, or by the FBI; that if he insists on appealing, he may appeal to his department head, and then beyond him to a Loyalty Review Board. But their decisions will have to be within the framework of interpreting the executive order; and that order gives not to them but to the Attorney General the power to decide what are the organizations with which any contact is so leprous as to infect a man. The whole elaborate system of administrative appeal and review becomes only a series of frantic efforts by poor cornered animals to find crevices in a steel trap that only one man can fashion and only one man can change.

I don't know Attorney General Clark, but even if he were wiser than all the Eastern sages, juster than Solomon, and more passionate in his devotion to freedom than the heroes of Greek and Roman fable, he would still not fill this assignment. For in a democratic system no man—not even the President, and certainly not one of his deputies—should be given that much power over human lives and hopes.[1]

Fourth: the executive order imposes what amounts to criminal penalties without providing for any sort of judicial process. Again I am aware of the series of appeal possibilities I have mentioned above. But none of them are judicial. I don't mean that they are carried on outside the courts. I mean that they are carried on within the administrative system without the most elementary protections to the accused.

Let us be very clear about it: to dismiss a man from Federal employment with the brand of disloyalty and subversiveness is not merely, as the defenders of the President's program state, an administrative act. It is a lethal penalty which as surely smashes a man's life as a prison sentence would. The ordinary man doesn't draw subtle distinctions between administrative and judicial penalties. To him a dismissed Government worker is a traitor.

Yet the fact is that we are branding men as traitors without open and impartial hearings, without the right of cross-examining hostile witnesses or even of knowing who they are.

Fifth: we are in danger of taking a big step toward the creation of a police-state. Everyone knows that one of the characteristics of the police-state is that you place all government servants under the continuous surveillance of a political police. That, in effect, is what we are now entering on. I don't know just how much share the FBI will have in the surveillance, and how much the Civil Service Commission operatives, and how much the departmental investigators. But between them the ordinary Govern-

---

[1] Attorney General Clark later made public several lists of "subversive" organizations.

ment employee will find his workday harassed, his hours of rest shadowed, his inmost thoughts guessed about, his whole life made intolerable.

You can't have an efficient body of Government employees under these conditions. To a great extent the survival of democracy in our time has come to depend on the ability of an administrative organization in running the social services of a crisis economy. We can be fairly certain now that this ability will stay out of Government service, or will be used only for reactionary ends.

MARCH 25, 1947

The Professor as Political Eunuch

H. L. MENCKEN once insisted that there are three sexes: male, female, and professors. If some of the people who throw their weight around in the control of American colleges have their way, this will turn out to be true— at least politically. Judging from some of the recent episodes in the campaign of repression being waged against Wallace supporters on college faculties, the kind of professor some of the college moguls want is a political eunuch.

The most flagrant case is that of Doctor George Parker, professor of Bible and philosophy at Evansville College, in Indiana. He was chairman of a Wallace meeting at Evansville which was attacked by hoodlums. For the crime of presiding at a political meeting to which the local bigwigs were opposed, President Lincoln Hale of the college fired Parker from his job. It was as simple as that and as crass as that. The two historic figures whose names he bears—Hale and Lincoln—had died to establish a freedom to which their namesake and the men whose bidding he follows are oblivious. The Klan spirit in Indiana does not always have to hide behind a white sheet. Sometimes it dons the robes of academic office.

Episode Number Two took place at Chicago. The Wallace party leaders in Illinois had decided to put up their own candidate for the United States Senate, to oppose reactionary Republican "Curly" Brooks and liberal Democrat Paul Douglas. It was a move which I consider a serious mistake and a disservice to liberalism—but that's part of another story. The man they picked out and put into the race was another Professor—Curtis

McDougall, of Northwestern University. A few weeks later McDougall re-tired from the race, still attacking both Brooks and Douglas, but with a not too cryptic announcement that he had to retire for personal reasons.

What were the personal reasons? It turned out that McDougall had a choice between dropping out of the senatorial race and dropping out of the University, and he chose the former. At that point one asks whether Northwestern University makes it a rule not to allow any of its faculty to run for political office. The answer is given in a recent column by Milburn P. Akers, in the Chicago *Sun-Times*. It seems that the dean of Mc-Dougall's faculty—Dean Olson—stated (I am quoting Akers) that "Mc-Dougall's candidacy would have been different had it been on the Demo-cratic instead of on the Progressive ticket." Which reveals the whole episode as another shabby case of the use of economic pressures on profes-sors by a university administration which finds truth only in the heaven of orthodoxy.[1]

Episode Number Three is of a different sort. This time the college au-thorities stand behind the professor in question, and it is the college alumni who are out to get him fired. The case is that of Professor Frederick L. Schuman, of Williams College. Since Williams was the college where I did my most recent spell of teaching I can testify to Schuman's brilliance as a teacher and his fearlessness as a political fighter. He wrote a review of James F. Byrnes's book, *Speaking Frankly*, which he called "The Devil and Jimmy Byrnes" and which was published in *Soviet Russia Today*. George Sokolsky, writing in the New York *Sun*, attacked him in a series of columns; and since many of the Williams alumni use the *Sun* as their gospel, a flood of alumni letters came streaming into the office of the col-lege president, James P. Baxter, III. Not only had Schuman committed *lèse majesté* on Byrnes, but he committed the even more unpardonable crime—in the eyes of the alumni—of being very articulately for Wallace.

The pay-off came on an issue so blatant that it might have come directly out of the pages of Upton Sinclair's *The Goose-Step* or Thorstein Veb-len's great classic, *The Higher Learning in America*. Some of the alumni pointed out to President Baxter that Williams had not only Schuman, but also a building fund drive for two and a half million dollars, of which only a little over a million had been subscribed. They made it clear that the college would have to choose between Schuman and the building fund. To which President Baxter, who has been writing mollifying letters to the alumni, has nevertheless made it clear that he will stand by

---

[1] Several months after this was written Professor McDougall re-entered the senatorial race, stating that he was risking his teaching job, but that the stakes of war and peace were higher than any personal risk.

Schuman and academic freedom; and the student paper, the Williams *Record*, has backed him up.

These three episodes—of a professor fired, a professor who has been compelled to withdraw from a campaign, and a professor under intensive alumni attack, all because of their activity in the Wallace campaign—could probably be matched by dozens of other cases that do not reach the newspapers.

They show up much of the hypocrisy of what is supposed to be the system of free higher education in the United States. One of the arguments always given against state control of colleges and universities is that it will mean political control. And largely that is true. But it comes as a weak argument from colleges and trustees and alumni bodies that are already exercising political control over their faculties. Here and there a college administrator whose backbone is not carved out of a banana may be able to make a stand for academic freedom. But in most cases the pressures are there—the pressures which Veblen described when he subtitled his book "A Memorandum on the Conduct of Universities by Businessmen." And in most cases the pressures triumph so completely that they don't even have to be exerted openly.

This is an issue that reaches far beyond the question of the Wallace campaign and its wrongness or rightness. I have my differences of opinion from the professors I have named, and I have had my quarrels with them. But the trouble with our colleges is not that there are professors for Wallace, but that the whole atmosphere is so tense and tight that very few of them dare to speak out their convictions. They know that if they do, they will in one way or another be victimized.

American colleges are supposed to represent a competition of ideas. How can you teach students when one strain of political thinking is snuffed out on the campus whenever it appears? American teachers are expected to teach social reality. How can you expect them to teach it when you frighten them away from participation in the life of the nation? American students are supposed to learn something about freedom. How can you expect them to have any respect for freedom when they see it despised and rejected on their own campuses?

Or is it possible that the men who run the colleges, and the men behind them, are scared to death of the very ideas in which they are supposed to be dealing?

MAY 2, 1948

Letter to College Students

Dear College Students:

How do you like being told what speakers you can listen to and what speakers you must shun like lepers?

The incidents of the banning of speeches on college campuses by men branded with the suspicion of "subversiveness" are piling up. Columbia University barred a speech by Howard Fast. The College of the City of New York took similar action to prevent CCNY students from having a chance to listen to Arnold Johnson, Communist party legislative director. The University of Wisconsin has ruled against a speech by Carl Marzani. A pattern is being set.

What is the pattern? What are the reasons given for putting blinkers on each side of your face, and Keep-Off-the-Grass signs on certain intellectual pastures where you may not roam?

In the Fast case Columbia pleads a "University precedent that no person under indictment" may use University facilities. This is a personal rather than an organizational test. Fast has been convicted of contempt of Congress in a case involving the Committee on Un-American Activities.[1] But there are many honest and conscientious Americans—non-Communist and even anti-Communist—who believe that the Thomas Committee has exceeded its constitutional powers.

In the CCNY case, where the speaker barred was an avowed Communist, the reason given is that "the Communist party is now identified as subversive to the best interests of the country." "Our action," the college representative continues, "follows the statement issued last Thursday by Attorney General Tom C. Clark." This is, of course, the giveaway. The Thomas Committee cites ten Hollywood writers for contempt, and straightway their Hollywood bosses fire them. The Attorney General lists seventy-eight organizations as "subversive"—and zingo, CCNY claps down a ban on a speaker belonging to one of them. The colleges are evidently falling in line just as avidly as the movie studios. University administrators are just as anxious to please the ruling powers as are the big private employers of talent.

[1] Howard Fast, a well-known novelist, was also active in left-wing organizations, including the Anti-Fascist Refugee Committee, whose directors were cited for contempt by the House Committee on Un-American Activities.

110

A college is supposed to be the custodian of truth, and its administrators ought to be trained to handle facts with precision. Yet Dean John J. Theobald, who made the announcement for President Wright of CCNY, missed several crucial facts. I cannot find that he told you that Attorney General Clark's list, while provided for in President Truman's executive order, does not have the force of law. Nor did he tell you that it was intended solely as advisory guidance in cases of Federal employment only; and that even within that area Attorney General Clark carefully denied that he intended the doctrine of "guilt by association." It is not the Attorney General, but the college Dean and the college President, who have applied the list to college speakers, who have given it a legal standing it does not have, and who have underwritten the doctrine of "guilt by association."

The University of Wisconsin case goes even further. Marzani had been allowed to speak at Columbia last summer, and at CCNY recently. He is now barred from Wisconsin by the University's Administrative Committee "because of the moral implications involved in sponsoring a man of Marzani's record." [2] Here there is not even the pretense of using the Attorney General's list. There is no citation of legal grounds, but only a reference to moral ones; no citation of facts, but only a reference to "implications." The field for further action in the same direction is wide open. The sky is the limit. The United Press story from Madison notes that one of the sponsors of Marzani's talk was the AYD (American Youth for Democracy), which in turn was one of the groups on the Attorney General's list. Here is guilt by association at still a further remove—not the speaker but the sponsors of the speakers are to be found on a list.

A strong trend has set in against freedom on the college campus. If I were a college student today I would speak out clearly, in classroom and in student organization, against the forces that are turning the once free campus into an intellectual drill-ground. The issue here is much bigger than that of a gag on particular speakers. The issue is that of the right of the college student to learn the truth by comparing and sifting competing versions of it. It is not only the right to speak that is being denied but— even more important for an educational system—the right to listen: to listen and learn, to reject or accept, to sit as judge and jury (as every student must who is worth anything) of his world and his society.

The apologists for these bans will try to get you into arguments about the merits or demerits of Fast, Johnson, Marzani, and the organizations

[2] Carl Marzani was a State Department employee during World War II. He was later indicted and convicted of perjury in failing to disclose what the Government contended was a record of past Communist activity.

with which they are connected. Don't let them get you off the crucial issues. I disagree sharply with the views of these men—but that isn't the point. So do most of you—but that isn't the point either. Nor is the fact that the AYD is obviously a Communist front organization any reason why you should be prevented from hearing its speakers if you wish to—with full knowledge of its origins and nature. The question is whether we will let the loose, cowardly, and hysterical use of the term "subversive" or "disloyal" destroy the chief function of the college in a free and creative society. For the chief function of the college is to give you competing views of what the great traditions are to which you will be the heirs, what the forces are that are active in our world, what the potentials are for making it a better world. To shut out any of these competing versions, however extreme and however controversial, is to destroy the function of the college.

It will be argued that the college does not have the obligation to teach views it regards as wrong. True: but no one is arguing that the colleges ought to hire as professors the men we have been discussing. The college administrations generally do their best to keep the teachers fairly "safe," to expound the truth within the conventionally accepted limits. But if the students, through their own organizations, want to supplement the college intellectual fare by inviting speakers from outside, they exercise a sacred and necessary right. Even political governments recognize the necessity for an opposition as well as an administration view: and the British even pay their opposition. Surely the colleges cannot be less liberal in the defense of competing truths than some of the politicians are.

Don't let yourselves be stampeded or cowed. I want you to believe in the potentials of America as a democratic society. You will have to achieve this belief by yourselves—in spite of the example your elders are setting.

DEC. 11, 1947

Goebbels: The Delusion of Thought Control

THE SUPREME EXAMPLE of a system of thought control based on the Great Fear of Communism is the system of Joseph Goebbels. I want to examine it in the light of the *Goebbels Diaries* (edited and translated by Louis P. Lochner), a book which needs to be brought home to the current problem of civil rights in America.

It is now clear that of the whole group that built up the Nazi movement and ran the Nazi state, Goebbels was second in importance only to Hitler. The Nazis operated on a simple principle: The way to destroy a people is first to prepare their minds for destruction, then break their will to resist. This applied not only to peoples outside of Germany, but to start with it had to be done to the German people themselves. The storm-troopers, the Gestapo, the Army, and the whole apparatus of force were, of course, the final instrument. But the initial instrument was the propaganda apparatus, and the continuing force that was to hold Hitler's power together was thought control. Here the directing genius was Goebbels. One of the ablest of the Nazis, he thought of himself—and Hitler evidently thought of him—as one of the keys to the whole system of Nazi power.

The big fact that emerges from these diaries of Goebbels' is how utterly delusive is the belief in thought control. The diaries cover parts of the years 1942–43, which were the years of testing for the Nazis—the years when the war turned from victory to defeat. From page to page the note of confidence becomes one of doubt, and the note of doubt one of desperation. We can see from our vantage point of history what Goebbels himself was unwilling and unable to see: that Germany's failure was not only the failure of armies and generals and leadership; that it was, at bottom, the failure of a social system that proved utterly hollow when put to the test because it rested on a basic contempt for people.

"In London," writes Goebbels on March 6, 1942, "they are at present busy threatening further air attacks on the Reich. I won't let reports of that kind get into the German press, because there are still dumbbells among us who fall for such threats." This contempt for his own people went so far that Goebbels did not even allow the relatively high Government and party officials to read the summaries of war developments or the monitored accounts from the foreign radio and press. Only a handful could be trusted, if they; and if Goebbels had had his way, no one would have been trusted with the facts except the *Fuehrer* and himself—and perhaps not even the *Fuehrer*. The people and even their rulers were, for this master of the thought-control machine, only the targets for his propaganda, the objects of his idea-manipulation. At bottom he hated them, as one always hates pliable material. "The human being," he wrote in a moment of great self-revelation, "makes me sick to my stomach."

What was the riddle of a man like Goebbels? What sustained him through the trials and crises these diaries describe, and through such barbarisms as the massacre of Europe's Jews—a massacre of which he was one of the most fanatic proponents.

A faith of some kind there was—even a stoicism of some kind, for here was a man who remained cool when other Nazis grew panicky, and who in the end carried out his vow to kill himself.

But faith in what and in whom? It was not a faith in the people. Nor in Germany as a mystical abstraction. Not even in race, for Goebbels despised Rosenberg, the apostle of racism. It was not a faith in the party, most of whose leaders seemed to Goebbels to be merely playing at power. It was certainly not a faith in the generals, whom Goebbels hated and despised as part of the old blundering Junker aristocracy. It was not even a faith in Hitler's social program, much as Goebbels talks about it in these war diaries, and pants for the peace days after victory when the Nazis would be able to forget the color of Russian snow and the sound of British and American bombs, and get down to the tasks of reshaping the conquered world. Actually Goebbels had started as some sort of radical, had been appalled at one stage in his career by the reactionary character of Hitler's program, and had survived as a devoted Nazi only after a sharp conflict of conscience.

Here we come to what really fascinated Goebbels: Hitler himself. It was not that he had faith in Hitler. It was rather that Hitler was the mirror of Goebbels' own lust for power and manipulation. Remember that Goebbels was a frustrated intellectual, who had once learned the humanist attitudes about freedom and democracy. Being frustrated he had grown to hate them. He was fascinated by Hitler's ability to turn them topsy-turvy. When he attached himself to Hitler, he attached himself as the man who could manipulate people's ideas to the man who could break people's wills. It was the perfect marriage of the two destructive principles that make up any kind of totalitarianism.

Goebbels hated people. And the hatred of people—especially of your own people—is deeply a form of self-hatred. Since he could not face the self-hatred, he channeled it into a lust to kill and destroy, a lust to wreak his vengeance on history by bending history to his purposes. He fed his power-lust in the only way he knew, and for which he had a genius: by getting inside the minds and passions of people, by telling them what they could or could not read, say, even think; by seeking to provide *all* the furniture and furnishings and motive-power of their minds and wills. It was the devil playing God, and when he found that he could not shape the universe of people's minds after his own will—when he saw the German people crumbling, the end came for him. He could not admit defeat, for to admit defeat was to negate his whole reason for existence. So he killed himself and his family, and all that was left behind was the shambles of Germany, and some dirty sheets of diary-paper lying in a German gutter to be picked up by a ragseller.

Goebbels never lived to understand the sources of his failure. He believed, like all believers in thought control, that you can play God with people, and shape them to the purposes of human power. But when the furniture he had put into their minds didn't conform to the facts of the world, the people were lost, for they had no will left to furnish their own ideas and form their own opinions. This is the central fallacy of the loyalty-hunters and the would-be thought-controllers of America as well.

Lincoln put it best when he said: "As I would not be a slave, so I would not be a master." The worst slaves, and the worst masters, are those in the kingdom of uniformity of thought.

MAY 20, 1948

The Seven Deadly Press Sins

THE HISTORY of press criticism has entered on a new phase. The days of Upton Sinclair's *Brass Check* and George Seldes' *Lords of the Press*, with their muckraking fervor, are over. The new kind of criticism is best found in the corner of the *New Yorker* where A. J. Liebling conducts his "Wayward Press" department; in the earnest and careful tomes of the Hutchins Commission on the Freedom of the Press; in Don Hollenbeck's weekly radio herd-riding on the errors and sins of newspapermen; in the publications of the group of Nieman Fellows who do postgraduate work in journalism at Harvard under the excellent shepherding of Louis Lyons. The new tone is less strident, more sophisticated, more concrete and scholarly, more humorous at times than the old. What it has lost in sheer power and passion it gains in indirection and persuasiveness.

There was never a time when irresponsible press power could do as much as it can do now, in a brink-of-reaction America which forms part of a brink-of-war world. There was never a time, therefore, when it was more important to tell the unadorned truth about the press.

The Big Press is less sinned against than sinning. It has many merits—a broadly flung net of newsgathering efficiency, a split-second haste in getting the latest reports to you, a mastery of the typographical arts, an almost incredibly workmanlike plant. But once these merits have been set down, what remains is less flattering.

There are what I should like to call the seven deadly press sins—the dangers both to press freedom and to the great role that the press can play in the American civilization:

The first is the *concentrated power* of the Big Press. It is part of the general trend toward centralized economic power, but however dangerous this trend may be in aluminum, steel, electrical appliances, banking, it is a hundred times as dangerous in the press because these other commodities are only commodities while the press forms ideas and beliefs. The Hutchins Commission Report, however mild it was in its conclusions, did have the forthrightness to set down the facts about what it called "the communications revolution" and about the new "communications empires." More than half the newspaper circulation of the country is controlled by chains—national, regional, and local; less than half is independent. Only fourteen owners control twenty-five per cent of the daily circulation. The Hearst, Scripps-Howard, McCormick-Patterson, Gannett baronies represent the new feudalism; in their wake are the empires of the press associations and the syndicates; linked with them are the accompanying baronies of the banking and corporate groups.

A related deadly sin is the *passing of competition and the coming of monopoly*. William Allen White noted this in his time, and Morris Ernst has documented it richly in his book, *The First Freedom* (Macmillan, 1946). The fact is that most of the Americans who live in small cities have only one newspaper to turn to. The others have been crowded out, either by the chains or by their stronger competitors, and the advertisers find it convenient to get their coverage by only one set of ads. But whatever the causes, the results are clear: if by "freedom of the press" you mean access to competing newspapers and to competing ideas, then most Americans do not enjoy freedom of the press.

A danger that grows partly out of this is *governmental control* of the press—a sin not of the press but against it. The best treatment of this, by far, that I have ever come across is the recently published book by Zechariah Chafee, Jr., the two-volume *Government and Mass Communications*, one of the Hutchins Commission series (University of Chicago Press, 1947). Chafee, who wrote the classic *Free Speech in the United States*, is one of those rare persons—a scholar with courage and a lawyer with passion. He asserts—and he is right—that the danger from the Government is only ten per cent of the problem of a free press in America. But, as he writes: "Totalitarianism, like Spanish influenza, is not confined to the countries of its origin, and America is not wholly immune. Powerful intellectual influences have a way of jumping supposed boundary lines." And he asks: "How long will our present freedom last?" My own feeling is that it is unlikely to survive either the next depression or the next war. The extremes of both the Right and the Left, in Europe, have shown that a state press is one of their characteristic instruments. The current Hearst cry for censorship of Hollywood shows how blind the press itself can be in invoking this danger upon itself.

The fourth press sin is *timidity*, especially in the face of group and corporate pressures. It is always hard to trace these. But every newspaperman knows that, when there is the question of outraging some powerful pressure-group by telling the truth, one can (to adapt Theodore Roosevelt's phrase) "carve out of a banana men with more backbone" than the publishers and editors of the Big Press. Their investment—like the investment in the radio and the movies—is too big to risk by this sort of rashness.

This brings me to the fifth sin—the fact that *the Big Press has a Big Business mentality*. It is one of the cardinal errors of the American liberals that they attribute the reactionary character of the press mainly to the influence of advertising. I note an article in the current issue of the *Guild Reporter* which attributes the low state of journalism to this source. I think this misses the mark. A really liberal editor or publisher is a poor creature indeed if his conviction cannot stand up against advertisers. A reactionary publisher does not have to stand up against them. For he is completely with the Big Corporations. Their mentality is his. He does not need to be corrupted. When he is a groveling lickspittle servant of the vested interests, it is because their intellectual and moral universe is also his.

The sixth deadly sin is the clannishness among the newspaper publishers that has prevented them from criticizing each other. This *immunity from mutual criticism* has also led to a stagnation of self-criticism. Here is the point at which we are now making the greatest progress. One man to whom we owe it is A. J. Liebling, who has now collected his *New Yorker* pieces and the story of his newspaper education in *The Wayward Pressman* (Doubleday, 1947). Liebling knows how to strike at the jugular in every case, as I must myself admit, somewhat wryly, because some of his barbs at me have struck home. His fault, if any, is that he tries to be a bit coy in a fight in which the enemy uses cold steel and glittering gold. But he is a good man to have on the side of honest professionalism in the press. And what he says in the end, I take it, is that there cannot be a great press unless the men who run it and write in it have a sense of craftsmanship they are proud of.

This is also the theme of *Your Newspaper*, written by nine Nieman Fellows, and edited by Leon Svirsky (Macmillan, 1947). These younger newspapermen and newspaperwomen have a sense of craft integrity, as is shown by their survey of the shortcomings of the press.

This survey points up the seventh of the deadly sins that concern the American press—its *social blindness*. In most of the news stories which the Nieman group and Liebling analyze as having been overplayed or underplayed or distorted or wholly muffed, the fault can best be traced back to a myopia of social vision,-a lack of perspective about the nature of news and about what the really important issues are in a democracy. What is required here is more than newspaper craft; it is an intellectual and moral education—especially for the publishers whose concentrated power controls the situation.

The best hope I can see is in the fact that the youngsters, like the Nieman group, are discontented, that they are watchful and critical, that they are dreaming up visionary newspapers after the shape of their heart's desire. When the young men still have visions, all is not yet lost.

DEC. 4, 1947

Yardstick Freedom: Self-Audit and Self-Control

1.

I WRITE THIS to my fellow newspapermen in America—publishers, editors, and rank and file, New Dealers and Old Dealers, Republicans, Democrats, and Socialists alike.

The Russians have made an attack on those who control and those who write for a section of the American press.[1] They accuse that section of the press of publishing murderous libels on Russia, full of hatred and incitement to war. They call these attacks criminal, and propose some sort of international control to check it.

It is easy for the American newspaper community to hurl these charges back at the Russians, with derisive remarks about the rubber-stamp press as it functions in a Communist state. It is even easier to wrap ourselves up in our mantle of virtue as the freest press in the world, in the sense that we are the least subject to Government controls. And having wrapped ourselves in this mantle, it is easy for us to go on smugly exactly as we were.

[1] The reference is to a sensational speech delivered at Lake Success by Andrei Vishinsky.

This would be the routine course, and would take the minimum of brains, imagination, and sense of responsibility. But I think the American press will be making a tragic mistake if it lets it go at that.

The fact is that while the Russians scarcely have the moral right to be throwing stones at the irresponsibility of the press of other nations, the substance of what they charge is unfortunately true. The usual fanatic fringe of the press has, on the question of Russia, become more than a fringe. It is true that men who ordinarily have a sense of civic honor, and who would never dream of inciting their readers to kill an individual adult or a child, are day after day inciting their fellow Americans to what can only become an atomic-bomb war that will kill tens of millions of individual adults and children. In doing this they lose their perspective and their sanity, they distort facts, they betray all the best traditions and the honor of their newspaper craft.

The central fact about the American press is its freedom from Government control, whatever the business and party controls it is still subject to. We cannot and will not abandon that freedom. The Russians ask for checks and controls on the press by some international authority because that is the way their minds work—in terms of governmental controls. We cannot possibly submit to that.

But does it therefore follow that our only alternative as newspapermen is to stand pat? If we do, the Russian charges will remain to plague us in the eyes of the world and in our own consciences.

There is another choice, that does not involve political controls on the one hand or complete irresponsibility and press anarchy on the other. It is to clean our own house, and help the newspapermen of other countries to clean theirs. It is the method of self-criticism, self-control, self-policing by the newspaper community.

More than twenty years ago the newspaper editors of America did draw up and adopt such a code of ethics, but it has lain moldering in somebody's file ever since. I see no point in adding one futile and unobserved code to another.

My proposal is different. It is for an active system of self-policing by the American newspaper community, and the extension of the system on a world scale. After all, even the Hollywood movie industry, which has sometimes been regarded as the lowest form of organic life in the opinion industries, has worked out an ethical code and a way of policing it. Newspapermen could do worse.

But I am not proposing the Hollywood method; I don't like its emphasis on box-office morality, or its fear of church and state censorships, or its power handed over to a single dictator.

The model I have in mind is the United States Supreme Court. It has enormous power. That power, to be sure, rests formally on its constitutional position and on its being backed up in the end by Government force. Actually, however, it rests on the respect the people—lawyers and non-lawyers alike—have come to hold for its opinions.

No one who has studied the history of the Supreme Court can deny that it has achieved its great present position by its great tradition; and that the greatness of its tradition is due to the fact that decade after decade a group of masters in the law have scrutinized in case after case what their fellow craftsmen in the law have been doing, have given reasoned statements of their views, have built up a body of precedent, have been subjected to a running fire of surveillance and criticism from the other lawyers and the community at large.

I don't see why the lawyers should have it over the newspapermen, or the courts over the press. A shyster lawyer or a corrupt and irresponsible judge is immediately caught up—not so much by the power of the Government as by the tradition of the legal community. But a fanatic newspaper, a megalomaniac publisher, an irresponsible editor: these fellows get away with it. The rest of the press maintains a conspiracy of silence about them, on the ground that there ought to be no internal quarrels in the profession. And if the hatreds that fill the hearts of the fanatics, the irresponsibles, the megalomaniacs, happen to be shared by the power-groups in the nation, they can infect the whole people.

My proposal, in short, is for the newspaper editors and publishers to get together and set up a sort of board of review from among the best and most respected people of their own number—men whom both the liberals and the conservatives would join in honoring because their integrity is beyond question. Let them adopt a code of newspaper ethics on such questions as inciting to group hatreds, inciting to racist discrimination, inciting to international war. Let the board of review hear the cases where accusations are made that the bounds of integrity and craftsmanship have been violated on these matters. Let them give the reasons why they agree or disagree. Let a body of critical precedent be built.

These men should have no power, should not be connected with the Government. Their sole power must be the force of opinion inside the press profession itself and in the nation as a whole. When we show the way in setting up such a group, we can extend its scale and make it international, and call the Russians and others to task for violations both of press ethics and of press freedom itself.

There are many difficulties about this proposal, and many weaknesses. But its core assumption I would defend: that newspapermen—at least the best among them—have an instinct of workmanship as well as a passion for the survival of their world.

2.

THE AMERICAN CIVIL LIBERTIES UNION and its director, Roger Baldwin, have contributed to our social thinking one of those monstrously rare things—a fresh idea on the techniques of freedom. The Union is digging into the possibility of setting up "a commission of disinterested citizens to sit in Washington and hold hearings on the Thomas Committee's procedures."

To get the full force of this suggestion one must remember how sterile the whole controversy about freedom and unfreedom has been for years. Why do Americans give so little attention to creative social thinking, and so much to vacuous gossip and snarling hatreds?

In very few areas has political thinking been bogged down as badly as on the question of freedom. Its champions—and I honor them—have not gone beyond the terms in which Justice Holmes stated the high stakes of individual freedom of thought some thirty years ago, and in which it has now been restated in pages as diverse as those of the *New Yorker* and the Report of the President's Committee on Civil Rights. Its detractors—and I dislike them—still use the maggoty procedures of the Thomas Committee as they once used the Lusk Committee, and still speak with the idiot gibberish of the Hearst press, now as then.

The arguments based on reason deal with the right of the individual to his opinions, the danger of splitting American citizenship into a first-class brand and a second-class brand, the intellectual and moral lifeblood which a stream of dissenting thought gives to any society of men. But no argument based on reason will have much sway in the minds of the primitives. Their thinking is stuck for good, because it is not thinking at all but herd-emotion. But most Americans don't fall either into the class of the primitives or into the class of the dedicated champions of freedom. Most Americans are men and women of good will, caught in doubts. They suspect the Thomas Committee's procedures, but they are afraid that denouncing the Thomas Committee will play into the hands of the Communists. They fear the Communists even more than they fear the Congressional primitives. So they end by saying: "I don't know and I don't care," and they withdraw into what David Reisman of Chicago University has well called "the protective sheath of apathy."

What I like about the Civil Liberties Union's suggestion is that it breaks through some of the prison walls that surround the ordinary American's mind on questions like the Thomas Committee. It is hard to question the power of Congress to investigate dangers to the nation. But one can and must question the procedures a Congressional committee uses, especially when they may be a greater danger to the nation than the objects of investigation are. Eventually the Supreme Court will pass on some of those procedures. But that will take a long time, and meanwhile we must have some other yardstick. Why not use the yardstick of open hearings by respected Americans who are neither Congressional wolves nor Supreme Court guardians, but who do care about the nation and its liberties?

It is an attractive idea. Instead of letting the Thomas Committee hog the whole Washington show in something like the movie industry hearings (are the theaters next or the book industry?), there will be another and more respected group of men sitting in Washington at the same time, holding hearings on the Thomas Committee hearings, judging what is fair and what is dangerous, letting the American people know.

A similar yardstick can be used to measure the distortions practiced by the Big Press in America. I once suggested that the newspaper profession set up its own autonomous critical board—a sort of supreme court of independent outsiders, who would judge the performance of newspapers by the profession's own stated ethics. A similar suggestion has just been made by Chancellor Robert M. Hutchins of the University of Chicago. I feel in good company because to my mind no university head today is showing anything like the social and moral courage Hutchins is showing. Hutchins calls for "an independent agency freely evaluating and criticizing the press's performance."

Here again is an idea which breaks through the prison walls surrounding the American mind. On the one hand is the massive concentration of press power in the hands of a few big publishers and their corporations. On the other hand there is the danger of government censorship if, as the Russians suggest, you try to use the government to curb the press.

One of the hoary defenses of the Big Press for its own excesses is that the newspaper readers are themselves the best judges of the merits of the press. "Why, Doc," says a *Daily News* editorial in answering Hutchins, "this agency . . . is already in session. . . . It consists of perhaps sixty million Americans who read the newspapers from coast to coast." Which is like saying that the best judge of cyanide is its victim, that the best jury for opium and heroin are the millions of dope-addicts from coast to coast, that the best answer to the marijuana problem is to leave it to the kids who smoke it. The *Daily News* has a simple solution for an old problem: once you have made a man a drug-addict, his continued pleasure at being fed repeated doses of racism, jingoism, national hatreds, freedom-baiting, is itself proof that it is good for him.

I want to add a third idea in the yardstick approach to freedom. It has been applied in several communities—once in July, 1947, at Stamford, Connecticut, and later at Montclair, New Jersey. The civic groups at Montclair, headed by the American Veterans Committee, got together, held an open town meeting, and conducted what amounted to a grass-roots audit of the civil rights of the community. They asked about how much freedom and how much discrimination were being practiced in the schools, churches, factories and offices, stores, hospitals; how much racist segregation was being practiced; how much equality of opportunity there was.

I should like to see the Montclair idea taken up by every American city and town. I should like to see it become the focal center of infection for spreading freedom. For it shares with the other two ideas I have discussed the merit of building freedom without the help of the Government and without surrendering it to the jungle-world of indifference and to the mercies of the big corporate groups. Every one of these ideas involves a self-audit of American civilization, made by the people themselves. It involves self-control by the collective action of decent people, without surrender to either the Big Corporation or the Big Government.

OCT. 2, DEC. 31, 1947

Racism at the School Grassroots

1. The Silent Quotas

I HAVE BEEN reading an article that contains the biggest open secret in the U. S. A. It is Benjamin Fine's first-rate piece of journalism in the New York Times, on the Dodson report [1] that has been presented to the Hughes Committee on Unity in New York City.

What is this secret? It is the fact that most of our privately endowed colleges and professional schools—our so-called "institutions of higher learn-

[1] "Inequality of Opportunity in Higher Education," by Professor Dan W. Dodson. This was made public July 1, 1946.

ing," about which we pretend to be so proud—have really only a qualified respect for learning and equality and democracy. That they judge their applicants for admission on the principles of Hitler's racist doctrine. That much of their high-flown talk about democracy and learning is cant. That in determining whether they will admit your son or your daughter, they don't go by scholarship and ability and character. That they have a quota system for Catholics, and for Jews, and for Negroes. That they care more about that quota system than they do about teaching or learning, and more about racist and religious discrimination than they do about the principles of this Republic.

This has been known "in the trade" for many years. But our educators, for all their pretended boldness, have never had the boldness to let the American people as a whole know it. Their nice-nellyisms prevailed over their candor, and their clannish vested interests prevailed over their sense of integrity. So they kept quiet.

Of course, every now and then someone has blundered. For example, there was the notorious case of Ernest Martin Hopkins, President of Dartmouth College, who was rash enough to write a letter defending the principle that there must be a Jewish quota at Dartmouth, otherwise the Jews will hog the professions and (sic!) anti-Semitism will result. In short, Hopkins was telling the Jews that it was in their own interests that he was discriminating against them. There was a great outcry, but it missed the point. For the outcry was against Dartmouth and Hopkins. It should have been against the same system in all the colleges and professional schools. Hopkins was only the man who had been foolish enough to blurt out the true facts.

There has been a lot of to-do recently in the educational world about "philosophies" of education. There has been a big, theoretical fight between the "traditionalists" under Hutchins of Chicago, and the "progressives" under John Dewey. There was a fanfare of trumpets over a long report proposing a new philosophy and a new curriculum for Harvard. And the amazing thing to me was that everyone played these controversies deadpan. It was all carried on like a Chinese ceremonial drama, with routine gestures and stereotyped words. Never did anyone sweep the cobwebs away and ask all the fine gentlemen what use these philosophies of education are so long as you hide behind a screen the basic fact that our higher education is racist.

In Poland, even before Hitlerism came to Europe, they had a *numerus clausus* (Latin for *closed number* —i. e., quota system) for Jewish students in the universities. In the United States, according to the Dodson report, it is the common practice in all privately endowed institutions of higher learning to apply a rigid quota system to Jews, Catholics, and Negroes. This is particularly true for any youngsters who happen to fall in these groups if they live in New York City. Then they are doubly discriminated against. That applies even, as a matter of common knowledge, in New York City's own privately endowed university—unidentified in the *Times*, but known to be Columbia University. It applies in the professional schools throughout the nation, but is especially bad in medical schools and engineering schools. It has applied for generations, but has grown steadily worse during the last decade—the decade in which the shadow of Nazism hung over the world. It is a fact now that Jewish, Catholic, or Negro boys who have come back as veterans from a war against racist ideas, and who want to get into medical school or other professional schools, have two strikes against them from the very start.

I can speak from personal knowledge here, as well as from hearsay. I have studied and taught in a number of privately endowed colleges and professional schools, and have lectured in others across the face of the country. I have known very few to which the statements of the Dodson report did not apply to a greater or lesser degree. Some of the presidents and deans and trustees and faculty were brazen about it, some secretive, some shamefaced and full of self-hatred over it. But none has challenged it publicly, none has had the courage to speak out against it and brand it for what it is: Public Enemy Number One of American higher education.

What can we do about it? The first step seems to me utterly clear. Racism is utterly against all the principles of our Government and tradition and belief. Individual Americans can, if they wish, nourish their private prejudices. But when they make it a matter of actual institutional practice, they have no right to public funds and public support.

My first proposal is therefore simply this: Withdraw from every privately endowed institution of higher learning the tax-exemption which the communities grant it as a matter of public subsidy. Racism is against our Constitution and our creed. It is public insanity to continue subsidizing it with our funds. Let every community appoint a fact-finding body whose purpose it will be to read the charter of the tax-exempt institution, and find whether that charter empowers and directs it to discriminate against youngsters by reason of their birth, color, religion. And let them act accordingly.

My second proposal is that we cease to place our main reliance on privately endowed institutions, since the canker of racism has eaten so deeply into them; and that we extend the area of state-supported higher education.

My third proposal is that the Federal Government move into the field of higher education. It can do this by Federal subsidies to state institutions which live up to certain standards, but are situated in impoverished states. And it can do it also by setting up Federal universities with Federal funds. There is a great danger of political control, in both state and Federal institutions. But it can be met by establishing the precedent of granting complete autonomy to recognized educators, who will run the schools with freedom as long as they live up to the standards of democratic decency.

It is time that we awakened to the danger confronting us: that by practicing racism upon our youngsters who want to get a chance at higher education, we are poisoning the American future at its grassroots.

2. We Teach What We Are

LET ME CONSIDER an immediate legal difficulty on the first point of my program above. An able and progressive lawyer has written me, pointing out that there is already a New York State provision (section 4(6) of the State Tax Laws) which prohibits nonsectarian tax-exempt institutions from "denying the use of its facilities to any person otherwise qualified, by reason of his race, color or religion." But what happens? Does the aggrieved person sue? Or does the State Tax Commission revoke the tax-exemption on its own?

Thus far there has been no test case. Obviously the effective way is not an individual suit, but action by the Commission. Bills have been introduced at Albany to provide for this. But at this point we hit a Constitutional snag. My lawyer friend writes me that the New York State Constitution (Art. XVI, sec. 1) guarantees that there can be no repeal of tax-exemption in institutions exclusively used for "religious, educational or charitable purposes as defined by law."

Note the phrase "as defined by law." This throws the burden back at the State Legislature. The framers of the Constitution obviously could not have meant to say that tax-exemption, once granted, was guaranteed forever no matter what the colleges and schools did. It is for the Legislature to state clearly what is the definition of an "educational institution" for purposes of tax-exemption. In framing the tax law I quoted above, the Legislature clearly meant to make nondiscrimination part of the definition. But in the light of the Constitutional clause it needs to be made so crystal clear that even the blindness of racist and religious bigotry can read it on the run.

Let me put the question negatively. *Question:* When is an "educational institution" not being used for education? *Answer:* When it is being used for discrimination. Morally and intellectually that is already clear as a bell. We have the right to ask our legislators to make it just as explicit in legal terms.

To fight along this line does not mean excluding a parallel fight along the other lines I have proposed. The bill for a new university for New York State is one. The youngsters from our state who have been off to the wars, and who have come back hungry for education, are part of the postponed generation. Their chance to get at a normal peacetime life has already been shelved for five years. The time to renew their education is now.

But here we must make an extra effort to think clearly. There are people who will be content with setting up a state university and who will think it solves the problem. It does not. To build state universities, in New York or any other state, is to create islands of refuge from Nazi racism in our privately endowed colleges. But the islands of refuge are only that: they do not solve the problem of the corruption and the pestilence outside. A state university is a solution only when it is part of the larger attack on racism in education. Standing alone it is itself in great danger of succumbing to the general infection. I have had, for example, letters citing instances of the *numerus clausus* practiced even in medical schools that are part of state universities.

That is the nub of the whole question. We are not dealing simply with isolated practices of discrimination, that can be grappled with in an isolated way. We are dealing with a cast of mind that is shaped by a deep bias in our social system, and which in turn corrupts the whole ethos of our life. It is infected and infecting, corroded and corrosive.

I have heard it argued that the men who are at the head of our great privately endowed universities are men who believe in democracy and hate the principles of racism. I do not doubt it. But they have a chance now to subject their words to the acid test of action.

They, and many others like them, are caught in a vicious system. Their universities have long been practicing discrimination. The silent quotas are there. As for rationalizing them, no university president is at a loss for that. From my teaching days I recall one of the dodges: that Harvard (or substitute any other Eastern university) is a national institution; that it must therefore encourage the entrance of boys from fine Midwestern communities and limit the entrance of boys from New York, et cetera, et cetera. But why is Des Moines any more America than New York is? It is time to lay bare these dodges and devices for what they are: a conscious or unconscious screen for racist ideas.

America is not geography, either physical or social. America is equality of opportunity for the youngsters who make the American future. To keep out the groups that don't make the religious or racial or social grade is to smother the American dream and make a Nazi nightmare out of it. It is not only to break the hearts of those who are kept out, but to poison the entire atmosphere for those who are admitted.

It comes down to the question of action. In the end, as any successful teacher will tell you, you can only teach the things that you are. If we practice racism then it is racism that we teach—between every line of every book, in every intonation of every lecture. We have our choice: to act so that we teach racism; or to act so that we teach a heroic grappling with the tragic discrepancy between our professions and our behavior in a democracy.

If we mean what we profess, the youngsters will know it. If we don't, they will know it too. The classroom for this lesson has moved. It has become the whole nation. The classroom is ours.

3. *The Dissipation of Talent*

YOU MIGHT FIND it somewhat hard to explain to a visiting foreigner why the news accounts of the President's Commission on Higher Education have created such a stir in the press. Thus far [1] the publicity has centered on three proposals that seem so simple as to be self-evident. One is the proposal that the Southern states repeal their segregation laws against Negro college education. The second is the proposal that the discrimination of colleges and professional schools against Negroes, Jews, and other minorities be ended in practice as well as in theory. The third is the proposal for Federal funds to provide college scholarships on a large scale for young Americans who want and deserve to go to college but can't afford it.

These are straight, fair, and sensible suggestions. All they add up to is the proposition that democracy should rise higher than racism and higher than poverty. The State Department is making a big fuss all over the world, insisting that the democratic principle be adopted universally. If our visiting foreigner takes the diplomats at their word, he may well ask: Why then all the fuss about these simple and obvious democratic proposals of the President's Commission?

---

[1] This was written when only the first two volumes of the six-volume report, *Higher Education for American Democracy*, had been released.

The clue, of course, is that there is a vast gap between the theory and the practice of democracy, and it applies as much in education as anywhere else. The ingredients of the gap are indifference, class interest, fear of the people, and—downright hypocrisy. That is why we all stare with disbelief when anyone seriously proposes to bridge the gap. When an official governmental group—a President's Commission—makes the proposal, it becomes an act of courage.

Not all the members of the Commission are equally militant in defense of democracy in education. Four of the twenty-eight—educators in St. Louis, Arkansas, Georgia, and a Virginia historian—have written in Volume II a dissenting opinion to the section on "Racial Discrimination." It is a "Yes—But" dissent. It does not challenge any of the facts or figures in the report, and presumably it accepts them. It does not challenge the fact that Negroes are basically as educable as whites; nor the fact that the segregation policy has victimized the Southern Negro, so that far more is spent on educating whites than on educating Negroes (in the extreme case of Kentucky, the ratio is 42 to 1); nor the fact that Negroes have almost no chance in graduate and professional schools. What the four dissenters do is to call these hard facts "pronouncements" of the Commission, and to refer ironically to "the high purpose and theoretical idealism of the Commission's recommendations." But they insist that whatever is done in the South should be done "within the established pattern of social relationships, which require separate educational institutions for whites and Negroes."

This difference between the dissenters and the rest of the Commission goes to the root of the whole problem of an educational New Deal in America. It not only involves segregation, but all other phases of educational democracy; not only Southern social practices, but Northern social practices as well. For it reaches to the crucial question of the relation of education to the rest of American life. What the Southern dissenters are saying is, in effect: "It's all right to talk about educational reforms, but don't let any real action disturb the peculiar institution of Southern Jim Crow." What they are saying is that you can try for educational reforms while leaving the rest of the social body as is. They are arguing that education can and must be separated from life.

I think they are wrong. You can't talk about educational reform in the South while leaving Jim Crow in Southern colleges and in the rest of Southern life. If you try to, your educational reform becomes a hypocrisy and a monstrosity.

This becomes clear for the North as well when you approach the question of the "quota system" for Jews and Negroes. The report has the honesty and courage to recognize that the quota system exists, and is widespread in its use. It calls boldly for its abolition, and proposes that no Federal funds be given to institutions that continue this form of discrimination. Yet I wonder how many Northern college administrators, in addition to the excellent ones on the Commission, will have the courage to go along with this. I wonder even how many of them would be honest enough to express their dissent as openly as the four Southerners did, and on grounds as cynical. I don't have any illusions about how easy it will be to put the report into action, in North as well as South. Yet the fight must be made, and the report is a brilliant beginning. For you cannot, in a democracy, set the educational sights higher than they have been without at the same time setting the sights higher in actual social living.

That part of the report which has the best chance of being adopted is the one that deals with Federal funds for college scholarships. It is always easier to take money than to take action, and the privately endowed colleges are notoriously hard up in these days of rising costs. The Commission's proposal for an average scholarship of four hundred dollars a year for three hundred thousand needy college non-veteran students, and for fifteen hundred dollars a year fellowships in graduate study for an initial ten thousand graduate students next year, is in the best tradition of Thomas Jefferson. That Virginian, you will remember, once developed a scholarship plan for his own state, writing:

"By that part of our plan which prescribes the selection of youths of genius from among the classes of the poor, we hope to avail the state of these talents which nature has sown as liberally among the poor as among the rich, but which perish without use if not sought for and cultivated."

There is the nub of a democratic philosophy of Federal scholarship aid. Its purpose is not to send every boy and girl to college. Its purpose is rather to make sure that no American boy or girl who wants to go to college, and who has the ability to make use of an education, shall be denied the chance because of belonging to the wrong income-group. It is not only a way of preventing broken hearts and frustrated ambitions. It is also a way of preventing that dissipation of talent and energy which is the cruelest feature of a class society.

4. *The Chance at an Education*

THE CHANCE at a college education is an important part of the American image. That is why it is more heartbreaking for a boy or girl to be turned away from the college and university gates in America, through no fault of his own, than it would be in any other country. I am happy that in our own State of New York the educators and the Governor have finally been moved to take some action on the long-festering question of educational opportunity and educational discrimination. The Young Commission has been working on some first-rate recommendations, and if they go through and lead to some action, those who want to go to college in New York should have a happier time of it than they have thus far had.[1] The heart of the Commission's plan is a network of "community colleges" in various parts of the state. Both the phrase and the idea are taken from the report of the President's Commission on Higher Education. It is good to see a Truman-appointed national commission and a Dewey-appointed state commission agreeing on so creative a plan. Here is another instance where professional technicians can get a meeting of minds when the politicians cannot.

The "community college" is, quite simply, a college that does not restrict itself to the turning out of scholars, but tries to serve the educational needs of the whole community. Most boys and girls don't need four years of college, and don't want to spend so long a time, but do want some preparatory training for jobs and for life. The community college provides them with two years of training—"terminal" education, as it is now coming to be called. This does not and must not mean a duplication of the freshman and sophomore years of the usual liberal arts college. The curriculum must be replanned, so that the two years are spent partly in basic studies that will liberalize the social thinking of the students and make their lives deeper and richer; and partly also in the type of semi-professional education that so many young people want these days—which will train them for jobs as technical and laboratory assistants in expanding fields like medicine, dentistry, science, aviation.

But the community college must deal with more than these two preparatory years. It has the chance of becoming the kind of real educational center which so many American communities need, and which so many of the present liberal arts colleges do not provide. It is not only young Americans who need education. American adults need it as well. The community college can serve as the sort of adult educational center which the New School for Social Research has become in New York City, under the leadership of Alvin Johnson and now of Bryn J. Hovde, operat-

[1] The report of the Temporary Commission on the Need for a State University, headed by Owen D. Young, was made public on Feb. 16, 1948. It recommended a N. Y. State Fair Educational Practices Law. The basic proposals were embodied in the Steingut-Feinberg Bill, and passed on March 11, 1948.

ing on the assumption that men and women do not abandon either intellectual curiosity or intellectual hope when they leave their teens.

Beyond the community college is the four-year college, and beyond that the graduate and professional schools of the university. The Young Commission plan calls for some sort of provision for full liberal arts education under state auspices, and also for the creation of a professional-school network, including dental schools and at least two medical schools.

But this is only one phase of the problem the Commission has grappled with. The second is that of discrimination against Negroes, Jews, and other minority groups in both private and public colleges in the state. This is even more important than the creation of new colleges and universities, because the question of the basis of admission into existing college facilities reaches deeper into the malady of American privilege and injustice than does the question of building new facilities. Let me put it thus: the shortage of facilities is the excuse generally given for the rejection of students when the actual reason for that rejection is religion, color, race.

If the Young Commission had dealt only with a state university, it would have muffed the larger part of its task. The great danger was that if nothing was done about existing discrimination, the new state universities and colleges would have received only the rejects and the so-called "undesirables" from the present ones, and would have become minority-group educational ghettos. By dealing with the deeper problem the Commission has done much to avert this.

The Fair Educational Practices Law which the Commission is backing is, in its proposed form, a good one. It provides for a special division in the Education Department of the State, under an Associate Commissioner of Education; it aims to forbid the current discriminatory educational application forms; it aims to strike a blow at the existing quota system, by state investigation of charges of discrimination against any nonsectarian school, public or private; the cease-and-desist orders would be enforceable by court injunction, and failure to comply would mean the penalties for contempt of court. It is not yet clear whether the Commissioner would himself have the power to start investigations, or whether he must wait for complaints from students. The former would mean a far more effective setup. But I am glad to see that the Commission has been discussing a law with teeth in it.

I wish that the Association of American Colleges, which is now finishing up its annual meeting at Cincinnati, would be bitten by either the President's Commission or the Young Commision—or both—so that it might be infected with at least a fraction of the courage and the insight of those two groups. Right now that seems unlikely. A committee of the Association, headed by Chancellor William P. Tolley of Syracuse University, has drawn up a "Report on Minority Groups in the Colleges." When you compare it with either of the other two reports I have discussed, it is a musty document, belonging to the educational Middle Ages. It expresses great alarm at the prospect that there may be "coercive legislation" to deal with the discrimination problem. It raises the specter of "state or national dictatorship." It gives lip service to educational democracy, and to the "motives" of those who want to do something about it. But it ends by proposing that the Association appoint a commission of its own which will look into complaints and make annual reports.

Considering that it is the colleges themselves that have been the principal and inveterate offenders on the quota system, this proposal is like suggesting that the best way to deal with crime is to get the criminals to appoint a committee of their own number, and look into complaints against themselves, and publish annual reports.

JAN. 25, 31, 1946; DEC. 23, 1947; JAN. 14, 1948

The Double Price of Religious Freedom

1. "A Little Case Over Bus Fares"

AMIDST THE TURMOIL of other matters, Americans have made the mistake of almost ignoring a recent Supreme Court decision which deals with issues central to our freedom. It is the case of *Everson v. Bd. of Education.*[1] By a five-to-four vote the Court upholds a New Jersey state law (and also similar laws in New York, Massachusetts, Louisiana, Michigan, Indiana, and Illinois) by which public tax funds can be used to pay for school buses serving parochial schools as well as public schools.

There is no more essential doctrine in the American tradition than the separation of church and state. We have always recognized that this has a double meaning: the state must leave the churches free, but the churches must also be kept away from meddling with the state, and especially from using state funds. That doctrine has now been broken, under sufferance from a bare majority of the highest court in the land.

[1] Decided Feb. 10, 1947. 330 U. S. 1.

I want to say, in fairness to Justice Black's majority decision, that several times and in the strongest terms it reasserts the doctrine of the separation of state and church. But in its reasoning and its conclusion it legalizes an act whose essence is to give church education the support of the state. As Justice Jackson in his dissent wryly comments: "The undertones of the opinion ... seem utterly discordant with its conclusion. The case which irresistibly comes to mind as the most fitting precedent is that of Julia, who, according to Byron's reports, "whispering 'I will ne'er consent'—consented."

At once the deepest and most brilliant treatment of the whole issue is in Justice Rutledge's thirty-five page dissenting opinion. In the decade since Justice Brandeis' resignation from the Court, I do not recall an opinion which more satisfyingly combined historical thoroughness, legal acumen and logic, and moral passion. "This is not," writes Justice Rutledge, "just a little case over bus fares." I agree.

Americans suffer from having too easily forgotten how strenuous and costly was the early struggle to lash down the principle of the separation of church and state. The same year that saw the Declaration of Independence—1776—saw also the great Virginia Declaration of Rights, in which James Madison and George Mason joined to assert that religious freedom is not merely something to be *tolerated*, but an *inherent right* of the person. Ten years later, in 1786, Madison led a fight in the Virginia Assembly against a bill to tax Virginians for the support of religious education. In his campaign against it he wrote his famous *Remonstrance*, which deserves to be one of the great classics of the American credo. He beat the bill, and then succeeded in getting through the Assembly Jefferson's measure banning state support of any church. In 1789 Madison led the fight to add a Bill of Rights to the new United States Constitution, and the very first amendment in the present Bill of Rights reads as follows: "Congress shall make no law respecting an establishment of religion, or prohibiting the free exercise thereof."

Where does "the little case over bus fares" fit into this framework?

There is a new tide rising in American thought which ignores the tradition of Madison and Jefferson, and which is ready to surrender to an uncritical and mystical demand to bring the state back into religion and bring the church back into education. That movement has two facets. First, it is demanding the introduction of religious teaching into the public schools under the "released time" program. Second, it is looking around for state subsidies for church schools.

Back in 1925 there was an epochal Supreme Court decision, *Pierce v. Society of Sisters*, establishing the right of the Catholics or any other religious sect to maintain their own schools (if they so wish and at their own expense) outside the public school system. That was a weighty decision to make in a democracy founded on the community's stake in public education for all, but it was all to the good in the interests of religious freedom. The question now is whether freedom to run sectarian schools also involves the right to use general tax funds for that purpose.

Does the school bus issue involve the First Amendment, forbidding any "law respecting the establishment of a religion"? I think it does, and this is also strongly the view of the dissenting opinion in the Everson case. The purpose of all sectarian education, Justice Rutledge points out, is the propagation of a certain brand of religious belief. The means used are not only teachers and books and classrooms and school equipment, but also transportation. The transport item is, at least in the rural areas, as essential as the teaching item. For the public to pay that out of taxes is as much a support of sectarian education as for the public to pay the teachers.

But, argues Justice Black, the support of school buses by the township or state is like the support of any other measure for the public safety or the public welfare. And the state must be neutral in conferring these benefits on children of various religious groups.

This is the heart of the majority decision, and before Justice Rutledge gets through with it he leaves it a shambles. For, as he points out, the whole purpose of the First Amendment was to exclude religion and religious education from the public functions supported by the state. If it is a "public function" to provide religious schools with bus transport then why not also (he argues) provide them with school lunches, payment for teachers, and everything else?

Justice Black at this point assures us that he does not mean to go any further than bus transport, and that this "approaches the verge of the state's power." [2]

It will be a disaster if America yields any further to the drive for state support of religious establishments. That way lies social chaos and bigotry and tyranny. For, as Madison pointed out long ago in his *Remonstrance*, the whole point about separating church and state is to take the question of religious education out of politics. Once it is admitted, you get a competition between various sects for state funds and state support and, finally, for state power. Religious controversies are fatal to democracy.

[2] In the next important case involving education and the separation of church and state—*McCollum* v. *Illinois*, decided on March 8, 1948 (92 L. Ed. 451)—the Court majority (including Justice Black) dealt a blow to the "released time" program when it is an integral part of the school program.

The only way to avoid them is to stick to the rigid separation of church and state, and especially of church schools and state funds.

There is a double price, as Justice Rutledge points out, that we must pay for religious liberty. One is the immense effort to keep the state from interfering in the way a man worships his God. The other is the equally immense effort to keep the churches from using state strength to propagate one particular version of religious truth. Let us not forget that to assure religious freedom in the first sense, we must assure it in the second also. That the road away from one also leads away from the other has been amply shown not only by the religious despotisms in the Europe of Jefferson's day, but also by the even more terrible despotisms Europe has seen in the twentieth century.

2. *Federal Aid and the Church-State Separation*

THE BILLS NOW before Congress providing for Federal aid to education are first-rate in purpose. But they bring up one of the great questions of our time. It is this: When you move beyond giving Federal subsidies to public schools, and give them to parochial schools, are you not shattering the great tradition of the separation of church and state in America?

About the general merits of Federal aid to education it is too late in the day to argue. Only the most hopeless mossbacks would quarrel with it. Actually the nation has been roused to its importance for at least a decade. But for a decade Federal aid bills have been drawn up, sent to committee, discussed at hearings—and allowed to die without (except in one year) even reaching floor debate. Why? Partly because of the "states' rights" cry, and the fear of state and local administrators that a Federal bureaucracy would supplant them. Partly because there has never been enough urgency behind an aid-to-public-schools bill to get it over the hurdle of the opposition from the parochial schools.

If ever that urgency was felt, it is being felt now. If ever there was a chance to break the charmed spell in which the sleeping beauty of Federal aid has so long been held, this ought to be the time. For now, as never before, Americans have come to understand some facts about their school system.

They have come to understand that teachers need higher salaries and schools need better equipment; that the American teacher who makes a decent living will soon be as rare as the vanishing bison; that our teaching standards are too low; that a child who will grow into an ignorant and intolerant man is as much of a menace to his community as an unquarantined case of smallpox; that Federal aid means help and not control, and would not take education away from the localities, any more than the GI Bill has taken education away from the colleges.

The big question is no longer: Shall we have Federal aid? It has become: *What kind* of Federal aid?

There is a spate of Federal aid bills before both houses. The big differences between these bills may be reduced to three: whether they try to *equalize* the educational differentials between states; how much of a Federal program they take on; and finally, what they do about parochial schools.

A great to-do has been made, especially by Senator Aiken of Vermont, about the difference between the Taft Bill and his own in the first two respects. The Taft Bill sets a "floor" of forty dollars a year expenditure per child and helps the poorer states to reach that floor: it is thus an "equalizing" bill, and spends relatively little (150 million a year, later 250 million). The Aiken Bill, although not quite as ambitious as the Murray-Morse-Pepper Bill, starts with three times Taft's starting sum and ends with five times his closing sum. It does not stop at equalizing, but goes on to make sizable grants to rich as well as poor states on the basis of the numbers in the schools.

Aiken is right in feeling that his bill is more sweeping, and he has worked hard to get a "compromise bill" that steps up the Taft expenditures and no doubt will combine equalization with average grants.

The real question is that of church and state. Here the Taft Bill, whatever its other weaknesses, is the right one, and the Aiken Bill (like the Murray-Morse-Pepper Bill before it) the wrong one. For Taft would allow grants to "private" (i.e., parochial) schools only in the ratio that the particular state already provides aid to such schools. The Aiken Bill by-passes the states on this issue and grants direct Federal subsidies (which he estimates at sixty million dollars a year) to parochial schools in every state.

This is the big issue, and Aiken does no service by trivializing it and brushing it aside. Aiken tries to give the impression that a "compromise" is being reached on all issues. That can be done on the question of amounts for the public schools, but on the question of what the Constitution calls "an establishment of religion" under Federal funds, it cannot. That issue must be faced and decided one way or the other.

It is true that dangerous inroads have already been made on the principle of the separation of church and state. The first step was taken when the Supreme Court decided that a religious group could not be compelled to send its children to the public schools, and that it could run its own schools at its own expense. Two values conflicted here: the nation's stake in having a common democratic education for its children, and the principle of freedom of conscience in education. The latter won.

This should have meant the end, but the inroads have gone on. Every state except one has now allotted "released time" for religious education at public expense.[1] School lunch subsidies are given parochial and public schools alike. School bus transportation is being provided for both out of state and local tax funds, and in the fateful Everson case several months ago, by a five-to-four decision, the Supreme Court decided it was constitutional for the states to do so.

For each of these encroachments a specific reason was somehow found for getting around the general principle. But now the issue goes to the root of the principle, for what the parochial schools (mainly Catholic, but to some extent Protestant) are demanding is that while they keep their schools wholly to themselves and run them in their own way in order to indoctrinate their children with a particular religious and political creed, they be allowed to do so at Federal expense and share in all the Federal aid benefits given to schools run by the whole community.

This demand is breathtaking. The strategy has for years been to whittle away at the principle of separation of church and state unobtrusively, on the margins. Now with the defenders lulled and bemused and confused, the assault is directly on the citadel. Once that is taken, the rest of the city—the city of man, of secular democratic education—will not easily be defended.

What are the arguments used? They all follow the same pattern: that the parochial schools are not asking for subsidies as schools, but are asking only that there be no discrimination against Catholic children in the use of public funds. This is an appealing argument, and one hard to resist. I detest anti-Catholicism as I detest anti-Semitism or anti-Negro racism. There is no room in a democracy for discrimination on the basis of religion or color. All must be treated equally.

Yet the argument is none the less thoroughly fallacious. No one is proposing that Catholic children in the public schools be treated differently from others. That would be monstrous. The real point is that the *parochial schools are not part of the public school system in a democracy. They are part of a religious establishment.* A democracy goes as far as it can go in allowing them to break away from the public school system, and withdraw their children and indoctrinate them along lines determined not by the democratic community, but by a church. To deny public subsidies to

[1] See Footnote 2, page 135.

church schools is not to deny equality, but to insist that the granting of a special privilege must not carry in its wake the subsidizing of it.

Let me put it this way: Schools exist in a democracy in order to develop its civic ideals, to transmit its cultural heritage, to mingle youngsters of every race and religion so that they can learn to live together. When public funds are used they are used for these purposes. Any religious group that wants to secede from the public school system can do so—at its own expense. It can, if it wishes, develop not secular civic ideas, but supernatural. It can, if it wishes, transmit not the whole Western cultural heritage, but a small section of it devoted to certain "absolute truths." It can, if it wishes, refuse to contaminate its children by contact with the community's ideas. But if a church makes this choice it must stand by it. It can scarcely expect that the community will not only allow the secession to take place, but underwrite it with public money. That is not a demand for equality for the minority, but of suicide for the community itself.

In all honesty can we take any other position? The Catholic clerics accuse the Protestant leaders who oppose Federal subsidies for parochial schools as being "divisive." That is a curious argument from a group that has insisted on its right to split off from the general school system, and has at the same time kept up a continuous attack on the "irreligion" and "moral emptiness" of that school system.

They point out also that they spend many millions for education, thus making the community's school expenses less. True: but they spend those millions on their own decision, for their own church and educational purposes, not for those of the community.

Senator Aiken cites the GI Bill of Rights as proof that the separation of church and state no longer has meaning. "The United States," he says, "is paying today to educate priests, Protestant ministers, and rabbis." True: but those are grants we make not to keep the divinity schools going but to reward the veterans: they are grants to a particular group of persons to be used educationally as they wish. The Federal aid bills are bills to prop up the school system.

I sympathize with the plight of the parochial schools. They need more money, just as every school does. Under rising costs, they find it hard to compete with the publicly supported nonsectarian schools. They would like to shift part of the burden of cost to the community as a whole.

But if they do it will mean that all of us are supporting the schools of a particular religious group. It would mean that we are supporting "an establishment of religion." And nothing in the Constitution is clearer or wiser than that "Congress shall make no law respecting an establishment of religion." The framers of the Constitution knew that once the Government begins to tax people to support a church and its special ideas of sin and salvation and truth, it opens the door for infinite-religious strife, and democratic harmony becomes impossible. The encroachments on that principle have already proved its truth. To prove it further and more deeply would invite disaster for the religious freedom of all of us— Protestant, Catholic, Jewish, agnostic.

American teachers and schools and students need help badly. If the parochial schools cannot maintain their present burden, their children are always welcome in the public school system. It would be tragic if the insistence of one church group, however powerful politically, were to prevent a Federal aid bill from being passed.
FEB. 20, MAY 18, 1947

Toynbee: History as Poetry and Religion as Bulwark

THE CURRENT CULT of Arnold J. Toynbee is one of the signs of what may be called *the hunger for connections* that our generation shows. Feeling itself bewildered and adrift, it searches passionately for whatever may tie. it to what is fixed and divinely unchanging. Toynbee has proved to be the answer, for is he not a historian, and is not history an immovable fact? And is he not, by virtue of having found the laws of birth, growth, decay, and death in the history of societies, the seer who can pierce the future of our own? And is he not that wonder of all historians and social thinkers: the religious historian and social thinker?

All this is, of course, not meant as an aspersion on Toynbee but as casting light on ourselves. It is not Toynbee's fault that he has been made part of Henry Luce's gallery of secular saints and been canonized in both *Time* and *Life* and his writings treated as if they were a Koran of the American Century. The fact is that Luce and his editors, and the assortment of book-reviewers who have been bowled over by the one-volume edition of *A Study of History*, are as bewildered and as hungry for connections as the rest of us.

Toynbee simply happens to be there. He turned up just when he was most badly needed by an America which is entering on a power-adventure over a world whose moral and intellectual outlines it can barely glimpse. The reviews ought to be not about Toynbee but about us.

I find his books exciting, and I regard him as a figure of considerable importance in our intellectual history. But not in the roles in which he is generally cast. I do not find him a discoverer of the laws of history, nor do I find him a prophet who can pierce the future. Nor do I find in him, as some others seem to, the way of salvation for our time.

His laws of history seem to me not science but poetry: his projections into the future are at once romantic and fuzzy, and his final tendency to fall back on religion whenever he needs a solution seems to me only another expression of that hunger for connections of which I have already spoken and which marks him so distinctly as of our time.

I find in Toynbee a sort of poet of history,[1] a wonderful illuminator of the myths and beliefs by which men have lived and of the ups and downs of the psychic history of civilizations. This—along with a really first-rate literary style such as few political writers possess, at once lucid and evocative, graceful and yet capable of emphasis—is what is creative in him. Let us abandon the cult of Toynbee, which does him a harsh service and one which I am certain he does not relish, and single out what is genuinely creative in him.

If you do that, you find that his most crucial concepts are a kind of poetry of the collective psyche and that, while the framework of his thought may remind us of that heavy German, Oswald Spengler, his real masters (as he himself confesses in one of the essays in his new book) [2] are Aeschylus and Goethe and—obviously—Jung.

Take the Toynbee concepts that are now entering into the vocabulary of the civilized American: *challenge-and-response, time of troubles, schism in the soul, nemesis of creativity, creative minority and uncreative mass, dominant minority, internal and external proletariats, universal state and universal church, new ground, penalization, withdrawal and return, the mechanicalness of mimesis, the suicidalness of militarism, the sense of drift and the sense of sin, the savior with the sword, the savior with the time machine, rally-and-relapse.*

Merely to list these, and to follow the reverberations they set up in one's mind, is to understand how influential a part of our outlook Toynbee has already become and how deep is his preoccupation with the symbols and the poetic myths which do so much to shape history because they fire the imagination of men.

Toynbee's current book, *Civilization on Trial,* is not part of his great work, *A Study of History,* the last three of whose nine massive volumes still

---

[1] See the discussion of Toynbee in Emery Neff's *The Poetry of History* (1948), which I had not read when I wrote this. Neff quotes the phrase from an essay by G. M. Trevelyan.

[2] *Civilization on Trial.* Essays and lectures by Arnold J. Toynbee (Oxford University Press).

remain to be written. It is an incidental collection of essays and lectures, one of which goes back to 1926 and one to the thirties but most of which have been written in the past two years. They are, in the main, the product of the Toynbee who has become a VIP in America and has been asked to deliver lectures at American colleges and write for American magazines.

Given this origin, the fact that they stand up so amazingly well and are so substantial is due to Toynbee's having a philosophy on which he draws, within the framework of which the poetic symbols I have listed take on depth and meaning. It is the philosophy of a humanistic, Anglo-Catholic historian who sees the problems of today in a broader time-perspective than the rest of us and brings to bear on them a melange of mellow wisdom, genteel despair, and conventional hope.

Let me illustrate this by some of the things that stand out in my mind after reading these essays. Toynbee sees Europe (as in the essay, "The Dwarfing of Europe") as no longer the center of Western power and activity. Europe-as-a-radiating-center of the world's energies has been replaced by Europe-as-the-object-of-converging-forces-from-outside—that is, from Russia and America.

Europe has become "the arena of conflict of non-European forces." And what is likely to emerge for the present is not the United States of Europe, of which many have dreamt, but rather the Partition of Europe. In this situation (see the essay on "The International Outlook") the function of the Western Europeans is that of a sort of practical mediation in the field of social institutions: "to get the issue of free enterprise versus socialism off its ideological pedestal and to treat it, not as a matter of semireligious faith and fanaticism but as a common-sense, practical question of trial and error."

Toynbee does not seem to have many illusions about the extent of the danger to Western civilization today. He sees it being torn apart by war and class. "The institutions of War and Class," he writes in "The Present Point of History," "are social reflexions of the seamy side of human nature —or what the theologians call original sin—in the kind of society that we call civilization. . . . Class has now become capable of irrevocably disintegrating Society, and War of annihilating the entire human race." In fact, Toynbee's vision of the ravages of an atomic war is as grim as any I have noted, including that of the scientists.

In his title essay, "Civilization on Trial," he says that he once thought the Tibetans and the Eskimos would survive the next war and help rebuild civilization, but he now feels they will be directly in the north-south pathway of destruction between Russia and America. He finally settles on the people who alone may be left to take up the task of rebuilding: the Negrito

Pygmies of Central Africa. And it is lucky that it will be they, for "they have an unexpectedly pure and lofty conception of the nature of God and of God's relation to Man."

Which leads us to the question of salvation. "What shall we do to be saved?" Toynbee asks. His answer, given in the essay "Does History Repeat Itself?" and again in the concluding essays, "Christianity and Civilization" and "The Meaning of History for the Soul," is a triple one:

"In politics, establish a constitutional cooperative system of world government. In economics, find working compromises between free enterprise and socialism. In the life of the spirit, put the secular superstructure back onto religious foundations." The last he finds most enduringly important, but the first two—the secular tasks—he finds most urgently needed.

These are the utterances of a man of good will. But they might have been written by almost any humanistic, perplexed, sensitive man of good will today. They lack the magic of Toynbee when he is dealing with the old dynasties of China or the abstruse details of Middle Eastern history or the spiritual history of Sparta or the Greek myths. His strength lies in the new perspectives in which he sees the familiar patterns of history. These new perspectives are not sharply presented when he deals with today's problems.

I fear that those, like myself, who will continue to go to Toynbee for the almost inexhaustible imaginative recreation to be found in his historical volumes, will not be content with his conventional religious exhortations as the answer to the problems of our time. I think Toynbee does not quite understand the Challenge and is therefore not ready with the adequate Response.

MAY 2, 1948

On the Christian Idea

1. Jesus: The Battlefield Is Man

CHRISTMAS TIME is a good time for our minds to go, as Albert Schweitzer has put it, "in quest of the historical Jesus"—in quest of the personality and the quality of the man whose image has cast its spell over two thousand years of history.

By now Christmas has become a broader thing than a religious ritual; it has become a folk-holiday. Every year the agonized world tears itself away from its agonies, looks about ruefully to find what comfort and Christian spirit it can squeeze out of a comfortless and un-Christian time, talks of peace and good will where both are painfully lacking, exchanges gifts, and teaches the children to celebrate the now myth-laden version of the nativity of a child in the Middle East.

Poetic stories have been woven through the years about his birth—about its miraculous nature, about the manger in the stable, about the adoration and the gifts of the Magi, about the search instituted by Herod and the slaughter of the children, about the flight into Egypt and the return. They make great literature in the Gospels, and they have inspired great literature and art since. They arise out of the generous feelings of devotion that men have felt for his personality and his teachings, which are the things that count.

After several centuries of fierce debate about the "higher criticism," most scholars in the field of religion agree now that there was a historical Jesus, and that Christianity as an institution would not have much meaning unless it were the "lengthened shadow of a man."

What we can piece together about him is moving enough. The boy's father is a simple carpenter, his mother the distillation of all the mothers of the world—proud of her son, hurt when he is hurt, inseparable from him at his death. He grows up in the village of Nazareth—a sensitive, dreamy boy who absorbs his culture yet has a special quality about him that evidently sets him apart from it. He is a boy of probing mind who, without schooling, somehow knows enough to put questions to the scholars at the Temple. He is born among a people who, oppressed by the Romans, long passionately for their freedom from Rome. Yet his own thoughts turn not so much to politics as to religion. He lives in a time and place where the atmosphere is electric with religious discussion and religious excitement. It is an age filled with magic and myth, teeming with new Oriental religions. It is a creative age, filled with the all-important sense that anything is possible.

He is all compact of gentleness and idealism and love, yet he develops an inner firmness which he is to show in all the crises of a storm-tossed life. He feels called on to take part in the actions and passions of his time. He joins the movement of John the Baptist, takes over at John's death, and preaches and teaches in the synagogues. He has lived all his life among simple men, and it is to them that he turns with his teaching. He is a man with a mission in life, and with a gospel to spread at any cost.

In pursuit of his mission he grows resourceful, eloquent; people gather about him, he finds disciples and followers. He discovers in himself unsuspected powers, especially when he is dealing with people who want to believe. He feels himself the vessel of the Divine influence, the carrier of something much bigger than any human being. He comes finally to believe that he is the Messiah long bruited in Jewish teaching. The priests and scribes fear him as a dissenter, the Romans pursue him as a dangerous agitator and revolutionary who stirs up the masses. Thus his life ends, only to have his real influence begin.

What was it he sought to teach? He outlined a new ethic—or at least he gave an old ethic a new edge and a new intensity. He gave men a new personal and social conscience. So much of what he taught received its power from the impress of his gentle personality that we have almost forgotten how dangerous, how downright subversive, it must have seemed at his time—and must still seem. For he taught what was, in effect, a classless and raceless society. In that sense his teachings have as much cutting-edge today as they had almost two thousand years ago.

The words of *Isaiah* (Chapter 53), describing for the Jews the Messiah to come, apply to his life: "despised and rejected of men, a man of sorrows acquainted with grief." Being thus, Jesus spoke best and appealed best to the other men of sorrows in his community—and that has been, ever since, the dynamism by which the Christian idea has spread over the world. It is the ordinary people—often poverty-stricken, battered about by life, hopeless if the hope of an immortal life is not left to them—to whom Christianity has the greatest appeal.

Luke tells us that when Jesus arose for the first time to read the lesson in the synagogue, he read from *Isaiah*: "The Lord hath anointed me to teach glad tidings to the poor; he hath sent me to heal the brokenhearted, to preach deliverance to captives, and recovery of sight to the blind, to set the down-trodden free." You have in this incident the best fusion of the Jewish-Christian ethical tradition. In two thousand years it has humanized much in history that might perhaps have been more brutal. Yet in the end the tragic sense that vitiates the celebration of Christmas is that— judged in terms of Jesus' own ethic—his teachings have failed. Or, better put, the world has failed the teachings. They did not prevent the last two wars, and may be unable to prevent another.

The best hope we have is that in these two thousand years we should have learned that the real battlefield is man himself. It is the human mind and the human conscience across which the forces of self-aggrandizement and of brotherhood—of destructiveness and creativeness—march and wheel and fight it out. Nor is the battle wholly lost. There will be some hope as long as there are other boys being born of humble parents, growing up sensitive to their world and filled with a burning idealism. This recurrent process of life and growth is the true miracle, beside which all others pale.

2. The Gifts of the Magi

I THINK the gifts the Magi brought to the manger were the gifts of the Christian social teaching and the Christian conscience. The question is whether we have taken the gifts seriously.

Our world has need for an ethic of some kind that will prevent men from stifling and butchering each other for their own aggrandizement. We are working on the theory that the Christian ethic can carry that burden. If it cannot, the world will have to build another one that can. What is generally called the "crisis of Christianity" is, in effect, the test to see whether Christianity can seize the imagination of hard and grasping men with the image of human brotherhood.

We have been through a heartbreaking experience in our time, more heartbreaking than any in the world's history. We are beginning to come out of it with a slow numbed bewilderment. Have we saved anything out of the bitter darkness, carried anything of value out of the charnel-days of Hitler's era and the current sway of armament-politics and jungle-economics?

The only thing that will avail us at all is the conviction that human brotherhood is not a phrase for the pulpit but a program of action, not a luxury for the good but a necessity for the world's survival.

There are not enough people now who have this conviction. Those who mouth the slogans of the Christian doctrine are often those who have it least. Yet despite the ranters and the shouters, the baiters and the haters, there is something beginning to stir in our bone and blood that may in the end add up to an ethic.

Let me put it differently. The ice of hate, like a great glacial deposit, has for some years been moving down on the human spirit: hate, and anarchy, and arrogant power. But wherever it moves, it still finds men who manage to free their hearts from it—men who break the ice and make little clearings in it. The empire of hate is widespread, but it is never left alone in its sway: it is always being challenged by the reachings for human decency.

Much of this challenge has come from the Christian ethic, and for that the world is grateful to it. Yet there are few students of religion and society today who can escape the feeling that something has been lost out of the early dynamism of Christianity. The Catholic teaching of Church unity and of disciplined acceptance of dogma has held together a community of believers, but one gets from it rather a sense of the retention of past strength than of new beginnings. The Protestant teaching of the importance of the individual judgment and of salvation by faith was of enormous importance in laying the foundations of modern freedom. Yet one wonders whether this kind of individualism can meet the tragic social splits of our time.

What men are seeking is a rebirth of belief in which the central emphasis is on neither the discipline of the group nor the private judgment of the individual, but on the linking of all men in the bond of the human plight and the human opportunity. The world as a whole is abandoning the laissez-faire idea in economics. We shall have to move away from the laissez-faire idea also in social and religious belief.

This can no longer seriously be a matter for argument. The last two wars, and the annihilation camps in Germany and Poland, have proved it. The impending war, if it comes, will clinch it.

Democracy and socialism have sought to give a content to the new doctrine. Yet they have not by themselves been able to create a body of belief which has the kind of hold on men's imaginations that religions have. And the sad fact is that in the recent battles to establish a social basis for a democratic order, the slogans and energies of the churches have in many instances been invoked against such an order and not for it.

I find it disquieting that the phase of the Christmas message which is most stressed in these days is "Peace on earth." Peace is not a prime mover: it is an end-product. You may call for peace as loudly as you wish, but where there is no brotherhood there can in the end be no peace. It is the other part of the Christmas message, "Good will to men," which is the creative one. The road to peace leads through the creation of a new, less greedy and acquisitive, more decent social order. Either men will learn to live like brothers, or they will die like beasts.

3. Laissez-Faire in Social Justice

THE PERSISTENT question is, of course, that of the strength and weakness of the Christian idea. How did it happen that a religious and social idea with enough power in it to sweep and hold the greater part of the world has been so powerless to govern men's daily conduct and prevent chaos?

The fact to start from is that the Christian idea was, at the beginning, a revolutionary one. The historians have debated over and over again the issue of the extent to which our present picture of Jesus is actual history and the extent to which it is myth. But on one score there can scarcely be any debate. Georges Sorel has put it best by writing of Christianity itself as a great "revolutionary myth," which swept the Roman Empire because it told the poor and the wretched and the dispossessed that they would inherit the kingdom of heaven.

However true or false this promise was, it was a great force that moved the early Christians in the catacombs and in the Church Militant, fortified their firmness, steeled their collective will.

Let us look now at our own era. The doctrine that the meek will inherit the earth was once a flaming idea that burned through the foundations of the Roman world. That same doctrine has become in our time a complacent ground for social inaction, and for the acceptance of injustice and terrorism. Priests and pastors in high position have accepted the greeds of capitalism, the sway of imperialism, the pitiless acts of totalitarianism. At times they have even blessed them. In Germany it was possible for deeply believing Catholics and Protestants alike, with a few exceptions, to watch the annihilation of millions of their fellow men in furnaces which made the medieval burning of heretics seem the random play of infants.

These things are not pleasant to say, but they need saying. A great to-do has been made over the isolated acts of Christian protest in Germany, as in the case of Martin Niemoeller. But remember that even Niemoeller, in the midst of the war, volunteered for the Nazi submarine command. (He now explains that he felt he would be safer in the armed forces, and closer also to the anti-Hitler military movement.) And remember also that Niemoeller's first words to the Americans who released him were that he had no concern with Hitler's political doctrines, but only with his war against religion. Here we have the fateful heritage of Luther's famous pamphlet, On the Secular Power, with its command to the German people to submit to an injustice in the political realm, however oppressive.

It is this doctrine of passivism, or quietism, in the political realm that is the deepest weakness of the Christian idea. It is not humility in itself which is at fault: to be humble is excellent, when it means that you refuse to exercise a moral imperialism over the will of others. But when it leads you to an unconcern about what happens to others, to a laissez-faire let-each-shift-for-himself attitude in the sphere of social justice and injustice, then it means that the heart and fire which gave the Christian idea its strength at the beginning have all but gone out of it.

I am reminded here of Dante's picture, in the Inferno, of those "who lived without blame and without praise, who were not rebellious, nor were faithful to God; but were for themselves. Heaven chased them forth—and the deep Hell receives them not." They were the men who were above the battle. "Let us not speak of them; but look, and pass." That was the judgment of a good Christian who tried to seize and present poetically the whole Christian scheme of things, and who in his own life, in Florence and as an exile, was never above the battle. He is worth remembering.

I know, of course, that religion is far more than a system of social ethics. It is, and must be, a reverent sense of man's relation to the mystery of the universe and to something larger than himself and not wholly explainable in rational terms. Yet a religion which has lost its basic conviction about the inter-connection of men with men in their common struggles for the human, will never command belief in the realm of the superhuman.

Our modern era has not proved, during the past few centuries, a religion-creating era. New *political* religions have arisen, like communism, but they have not brought with them a new conception of the nature and destiny of man. Perhaps out of the travail of our present time something creative will arise, or the Christian idea may find new sources of vigor. For there is a great and untapped reservoir of religious feeling among men all over the world, for whom none of the existing religious creeds serve as a stirring and fulfilling answer.

DEC. 24, 1947; DEC. 24, 26, 1946

PART II

Movers and Shakers:
Notes on Economics and Politics

The Captains and the Kings

I GOT AN invitation to sit in at last night's Waldorf-Astoria banquet honoring the fifty biggest business barons of the United States.[1] It was a sore
temptation, since it isn't often that one sees fifty men together who are by
common acclaim the conquerors of the conquerors of the earth, and in
addition "a thousand heads of corporations in the audience," as the letter
of invitation put it. To cap it all, there was the chance to hear Governor
Dewey, whose job it was to convince these men that he could be trusted to
govern the American people starting in 1949, and at the same time convince the people that he could be trusted not to be governed by these
men. It was a chance, in short, to see power, glamour, and acrobatics. Unfortunately I had another date.

But the men are none the less worth writing about, because they are the
captains and the kings who more surely than any other group run America
today. Years ago, before people got so absorbed with picking the one hundred greatest books, they used to play the game of picking the fifty men
who ran America. Ambassador James W. Gerard once had a famous list,
and John Gunther revived the old practice in the magazine '47. Gunther
had a good list, but it suffered from being too representative, including
politics, business, labor, the churches, the minority groups. He picked the
men who, for one reason or another, have to be reckoned with. That is
different from picking the men whose power is decisive.

I fear that the fifty who were honored at the Waldorf comprise a more
realistic list, if a much narrower one. For they command the fulcrum of
power, which in our civilization is economic power. If they throw their
weight toward war, then war it is; if toward peace, then peace it is; they
don't run the political machines, but the machines are run at their bid-

[1] This banquet was given by *Forbes Magazine of Business* to celebrate its thirtieth an-
niversary. The list of the fifty was as follows: Winthrop W. Aldrich, Stanley C.
Allyn, John D. Biggers, Lewis H. Brown, Walter S. Carpenter, Jr., Martin W. Clement,
John L. Collyer, Charles D. Dallas, Richard R. Deupree, Donald W. Douglas, Willard
H. Dow, Benjamin F. Fairless, Harvey Firestone, Jr., Clarence Francis, Henry Ford
II, Lawrence M. Giannini, Walter S. Gifford, Bernard F. Gimbel, Samuel Goldwyn,
Eugene G. Grace, Paul G. Hoffman, Eugene Holman, Charles R. Hook, Eric A. John-
ston, W. Alton Jones, Henry J. Kaiser, K. T. Keller, James F. Lincoln, Leroy A. Lincoln,
Henry R. Luce, Charles Luckman, Glenn L. Martin, Thomas W. Martin, Richard
K. Mellon, Charles E. Merrill, Fowler McCormick, Ernest E. Norris, Edgar M. Queeny,
James H. Rand, Gordon S. Rentschler, Edward V. Rickenbacker, Nelson A. Rocke-
feller, David Sarnoff, Emil Schram, Thomas J. Watson, Charles Edward Wilson,
Charles Erwin Wilson, Gen. Robert E. Wood, Robert W. Woodruff, Robert R. Young.

ding; they may not be able to say who shall be President, but they can generally (not always, as the New Deal showed) say who shall not be President, and very often the man chosen is not far from their heart's desire. Above all, they are the mold in which, through press and radio, the national mind is formed. And they are the men around whom the dreams of the young men are woven.

America is a business civilization, and it is not surprising therefore that the businessmen run it and are its type-figures. They were once called "captains of industry," but that phrase is no longer used because it no longer applies. It is not they, but other men, who thought up the industrial inventions upon which their profits and power are built. It is not they, but other men, who have in their brains and hands the technological skill that runs the machines.

For the most part the fifty are neither inventors nor industrialists. They are the managers of production, the general staff of investment and finance, the promoters of new stock flotations and new corporate combinations, the dynamos behind high-powered salesmanship campaigns. They are the sellers, not the makers; the reapers, not the sowers; the decision-makers and the holders of power. In most instances they are not themselves the owners of the enterprise, but part of a small group which runs and controls things and acts for the owners. One of the new facts about these business giants that distinguishes them from the earlier inventors and industrialists is that a separation has taken place between owners and managers.

What kind of men are they, and what are the qualities that have given them success?

The first thing that strikes you as you compare them with their predecessors is that there are no longer any commanding figures among them. There are no business personalities now who can compare with "Jupiter" Morgan, James J. Hill, Commodore Vanderbilt, Jim Fiske, "Bet a Million" Gates, E. H. Harriman, Charles T. Yerkes, John D. Rockefeller, Henry Ford. The fact is that when you go through the list of the fifty, there will be a large proportion whose names will mean very little to you until you read what corporation they head up, and then you will say, "Oh, yes." The old captain of industry who conquered everyone has now himself been conquered by the vast impersonality of the giant corporation. He still wields massive power, but he wields it as the man behind the corporate name. In the earlier days it was the men who created the corporations. In our time it is the corporations that create the men.

The Thunderers, like Morgan, have passed. With them has also passed the age of what Matthew Josephson described so well as the "Robber Barons" in his book of that name. Business piracy no longer dare be as open or as swashbuckling as it used to be in the era of Vanderbilt and Fiske, Rockefeller and Hill. Things are done more smoothly now, more quietly, more impersonally.

All of which does not mean that they are done less effectively. The big corporation lawyers, the public relations men, the advertising agencies— all of them watch over their clients to see that they don't say foolish or vulnerable things out loud, such as "The public be damned," or "We are the trustees in whose hands God has placed the wealth and power of this country." But while the words have changed, I wonder how much the facts have changed. The consumer is still the goat, the small business- man is still crowded out, the competitor is still crushed, the worker still has to fight and fight hard for every penny of wage increase and every improvement in his working conditions.

Many of the qualities of the business giant have changed: his strain of magnificence, his flaring imagination, his gambler's instinct, or (as in the case of Rockefeller and Ford) his small-town Puritanism of spirit, about which Thorstein Veblen wrote so well in his essay on "The Country Town," in *Absentee Ownership*. But one quality has endured. I mean the tenacity of the business giant, his single-mindedness of purpose in the pursuit of profit and power. The socialists and radicals of Debs' time, the progressives of La Follette's time, the New Dealers of Franklin Roose- velt's time—all of them made the error of writing off the corporate barons of this country, and writing them off too early. Not only have they sur- vived, but they are back in power as firmly as ever, and are making some of the same mistakes they always made.

These men have always known how to make money and how to ex- tend American production and how to run their businesses. What they have not known is how to organize and plan an economy as a whole, in its inter-relations. And how to run a nation. Today they are going even further, and are dreaming of a power that will reach to the far corners of the world.

They are caught in a dream, but they are also caught in a fear—the fear of what they call "Communism," which is sometimes merely a ferment in the minds of distant people whom they cannot understand.

In their great dream, and in their great fear, much of the world's future may be written. The saving element is that not a few of the fifty have shown that, like the lowlier classes among the Americans, they do care about freedom and about peace. The job of the American people is to make sure that the dream of power and the fear of socialism will not **be** permitted to crush the tradition of freedom and the will to peace.

NOV. 6, 1947

Must We Choose Between Hunger and Serfdom?

I WANT TO TALK about something that is not an "event," but more powerful than an event—namely, an idea plus a slogan. The idea is that the greatest danger that confronts a democracy is government action to help shape full employment. The slogan is that such action is "the road to serfdom." The slogan comes from a book by an Austrian economist in England, Friedrich Hayek—a book called *The Road to Serfdom*, which gave an impetus to the idea in America and a battle-cry to its cohorts.

The propaganda drive based on the Hayek book, and in which some of America's most powerful publishers joined with the National Association of Manufacturers business bureaucracy, reached many millions of Americans. Both Hayek and some of the people involved in the drive agree that his book was distorted, and that what came out of the Big Business-Big Publisher mill bore little relation to what went in.[1] These men oversimplified what is at best a difficult and complex argument—and always in the direction of opposing government controls. One of them has admitted that the picture strip his magazine ran as a summary of the book was "deliberately" meant to shock, and was "painted in extreme black and white."

I cannot help finding it a distasteful story, and it comes with especially bad grace from those who take high moral ground in opposing government action.

Let me give three instances of the effect of the propaganda drive, of varying degrees of importance:

If living costs are not to zoom out of reach of workers and returning soldiers, we need to keep price-controls and rent-controls in effect. The fight to do so is a heartbreaking one, because it comes up against the argument that this would be the "road to serfdom."

The Tennessee Valley Authority is one of the most brilliant successes in

[1] This, along with the rest of the paragraph, was based on a series of interviews in a feature article by Croswell Bowen which ran in the same issue of *PM*, Oct. 14, 1945.

regional planning. It is the most creative social idea America has developed in a decade. To extend it to the Missouri Valley and the other river valleys would create new jobs and a new regional way of life. But the projected Missouri Valley Authority has come up against almost unbeatable opposition from the "road to serfdom" argument used by special interests, even though Hayek himself denies being against TVA.

Atomic energy used for industrial purposes may some day transform our world, just as atomic energy used for military purposes may some day destroy it. In both cases we are dealing with something too dangerous to be left for exploitation to private interests. Yet the fight to get effective civilian government control of it comes up against the fear that government action is the "road to serfdom."

It is not enough to argue, as many of the more progressive economists do, that only government action will give us full employment, and that otherwise we are faced with hunger. For the ordinary man, who loves freedom as much as he wants a job, the choice between hunger and serfdom is a cruel choice. What a tragic thing to say to him that he can have bread with chains; or he can starve, a free man.

I deny that this is the real choice before Americans. Here we get to the crucial fallacy in Hayek's argument (I refer now to what is really in the book, not to its distortions). Hayek says that once you start government planning (beyond certain minima) you move inevitably to the totalitarian state. Historically this is simply not true. What happened in Germany (as the classic case) and in Italy was *not* that a democratic government developed a plan which it had to force on its people, but that a democratic government *failed to plan democratically* and so gave way to a dictatorship that planned serfdom and death.

What happened, in other words, was a failure to plan when planning was most needed. The result was economic, political, and moral collapse, which created a vacuum into which tyranny and serfdom were able to enter.

Let me again make clear that planning *might* lead to dictatorship—if it is planning by a group that has fascist intentions and no real democratic will. But there can be *democratic planning for full employment*, if it is done within a tradition of freedom like the American, and if it is done with a moral passion to keep America free. That is what the creed of the new liberalism amounts to—not the nineteenth-century liberalism of Hayek, which has not moved from Adam Smith, but the liberalism that starts from Franklin D. Roosevelt and the New Deal and moves on to make their purposes real.

This liberalism is in the great tradition of American radical democracy.

But whatever you call it, it refuses to accept the alternatives of hunger and serfdom. It believes that the greatest enemy today is within the American mind: the danger of a failure of democratic will.

OCT. 14, 1945

The Battle of the River Valleys

1. *The History of a Dream* [1]

AMERICAN RIVERS have the greatest amount of potential power in the world.[2] Harness that power fully, and you get staggering figures of the machines that can be driven, the industrial and agricultural work that can be done, the lights and radios and refrigerators that can be used in households across the face of the land. Clearly this power will be worth billions. It can transform every region in the country, as the Tennessee River Valley has already been transformed by it. If private companies control it, it can mean staggering wealth and domination. It belongs in public hands. It belongs to the people. In the process of developing it, all sorts of other things can be done. River floods can be dammed. River navigation can be smoothed out. Flooded areas can be reclaimed and chronically dry areas can be irrigated.

There are two nightmares under which the utility companies live. One is that the power generated as a result of river valley development will not be turned over to them to do with as they please. The second is that the TVA, which has established itself so successfully not only in its own region, but in the minds of all Americans, will be used as a model for later river valley developments.

Given these incessant nightmares, the utility crowd got the scare of their lives when a movement developed in Missouri, Nebraska, the Dakotas, Montana, and Wyoming, for a unified set of flood-control and power projects in the great Missouri River Basin, covering the whole or

---

[1] At the risk of going back to what may seem a chapter of ancient history, I have included here a discussion of a program of river valley development which loomed large in the minds of the Roosevelt group. It will once more have to be considered when America faces the problems of a true peacetime economy.

[2] This was written some six months before the announcement about atomic energy.

part of nine states. It proposed One Big Plan for One Big Valley, and set out to put flood control and navigation and irrigation and land use and power generation where they all belonged—into a single package.

At the same time came the renewal of the President's old idea about seven river valley authorities—an idea he first put forward in 1937.

In 1928 Franklin D. Roosevelt became Governor of New York on a platform that included the principle that the power resources of the state belong to the people. He fought hard for the development of the St. Lawrence power, and appointed a New York State Power Authority to develop the project. He learned in this experience what tough fighters the utility companies are, but also how high the stakes are in the struggle for public control of hydroelectric power.

When he became President this experience was fused with the passionate persistence of Senator George W. Norris for the development of Muscle Shoals as a public project. The result is history—the history of the Tennessee Valley Authority. Whatever may have been the important role of the technicians and the administrators, TVA was one of Roosevelt's biggest flashes of insight as a political leader. He saw what it could mean both in transforming the face of the land, and as a symbol of democracy in action.

As early as 1936 the President was holding conversations with Senator Norris, David Lilienthal, and others about extending the TVA idea to other river valley regions. In 1937, encouraged by the overwhelming mandate in his re-election victory over Landon, he sent to Congress on June 3 his historic message recommending "legislation for national planning and development of natural resources through seven regional authorities." The message was a strong one. Roosevelt was obviously writing of something very close to his heart.

What were the famous "seven" river valley regions? As given in the President's message, and afterward embodied in a bill introduced by Senator Norris, they were:

One for the Atlantic Seaboard.

A second for the Great Lakes and the Ohio Valley.

A third to be added to the TVA—for the drainage basin of the Tennessee and Cumberland Rivers.

A fourth for the Missouri Basin, including the Red River of the north.

A fifth for the Arkansas Basin, including the Red Basin and Rio Grande.

A sixth for the Colorado Basin, and including the rivers flowing into the Pacific south of the California-Oregon line.

A seventh for the Columbia River Basin.

To these seven the President added the Mississippi River, which was to remain under the Mississippi River Commission, which represents a loose compact of the states affected.

The reception that the idea met, in the press and elsewhere, was a cold one. This was the year in which a campaign was being carried on against the TVA, on constitutional grounds, on tax grounds, on administrative grounds. The opponents of the President's plan immediately labeled it the "Seven Little TVAs," and the public utility crowd and their mercenaries in the press and on the radio had a field day with the phrase. So much so, that in a press conference on October 6 the President took occasion to repudiate the phrase, saying that all that Norris and he had in mind was planning agencies to develop the resources of the regions, whereas the TVA was an administrative agency as well. The President saw that people's minds had not been prepared for his idea. In this respect, at any rate, he was far ahead of the press and the nation. The idea was dropped, and Senator Norris's bill got nowhere.

But the intervening years saw the brilliant and enduring success of the TVA. Nothing that the New Deal did in the twelve years of its history has been so gleaming a pennant, signaling what Americans can do with their resources once they find the right plan, the right men, the right administrative setup.

On September 21, 1944, the President sent a message to Congress recommending the establishment of a unified plan for the development of the Missouri River Basin. Again Roosevelt was combining the skill of the politician with the insight of the social statesman. The message seemed to come out of the blue—just when people had written off any further domestic liberalism on FDR's part. But it followed also a remarkable movement that had developed in the Missouri Valley for a valley authority patterned after the TVA.

The movement sprang from the people, and was not a synthetic build-up by politicians. There are many interest-groups in the Missouri Valley Basin that wanted different things. The down-river people wanted flood control and navigation projects; the up-river people wanted irrigation for their agricultural and grazing land; other groups wanted new land-use policies. This would ordinarily have been a perfect situation in which, as elsewhere, the utility companies could have followed the traditional policies of "divide and rule." Yet they were met by one of the most vigilant grassroots movements it has been my privilege to study. The two great liberal St. Louis papers—the *Star-Times* and the *Post-Dispatch*—under the editorial direction of Ernest Kirschsten and Ralph Coghlan, placed themselves at the head of the Missouri Valley community. They put on a campaign of education and information. They met every one of the efforts to sabotage the MVA so effectively that lame-duck reactionary Senator Bennett C. Clark bitterly attacked both newspapers as the head and fount of the MVA movement.

He was right. But no newspapers, however enlightened or powerful, could by themselves have created the MVA movement. The material was there. The river and its basin were there. The valley was there. The resources were there. The TVA was there as a living instance of what other people had done in a similar situation. The people's desire was there.

The precipitating factor was the economic one. Various estimates have been made of the cost of the proposed Missouri Valley flood-control, irrigation, and power projects. One informed source in Washington gave me the estimate of $1,000,000,000. This is obviously guesswork, since no reliable survey has yet been made. But if you take anything like the billion-dollar estimate, or that of a half-billion for the St. Lawrence project, not only do they mean a considerable body of employment for that region, but the indirect employment that it will set in motion (as all public works projects do) will be even greater. The development of family-sized farms, the irrigation of land, the development of new industries in the valley basins will mean even more to the American economy than the direct and indirect employment resulting from the public works projects themselves.

I have given here what may seem to many the history of a dream. But it is the history of a dream that can be realized.

2. Missouri Valley

WHAT HAPPENED in the Tennessee Valley could happen in the Missouri Valley.

The Missouri River is in itself almost 2,500 miles long. With its tributaries—the Milk River, the Yellowstone, the Little Missouri, the Platte, the Kansas, the James, the Big Sioux, the Grand, the Osage, the Gasconade—it drains an area of over a half-million square miles, in nine states. This is about one-sixth of the area of the whole United States, with a population of only one-twentieth the whole American total. That population has been steadily declining, especially in the arid and mountain states, and has decreased steeply in the past few years. It is an area that suffers droughts in the highlands, and devastating floods in the lowlands. Some five million acres of land are now under irrigation; a Missouri Basin plan could add at least another five million. The power actually in use in the area is small. It is estimated that the Missouri Valley Project would generate additional hydroelectric power of anywhere from one million to three million kilowatts.

These are dry figures. But if you have the social imagination to translate them into terms of the life of all the communities in the Missouri Basin, you will understand why the thinking people of the Basin, farmers and city-dwellers alike, businessmen and intellectuals, are determined to make TVA live again in MVA.

In fact, among the initiators of the MVA plan, and among those who have given it the strongest support, have been the trade-unions of the region, particularly the United Electrical Workers. They have, of course, a direct interest in increasing the power resources and the electrification of the region. But beyond their immediate interest there is the larger fact that the health of trade-unionism is possible only in an expanding economy.

That is the meaning of the proposed MVA—an expanding economy for the whole Missouri Valley Basin. It may cost a billion dollars to set in motion the train of economic events that will serve as a physical basis for an expanding regional economy. It may cost two billion, or in the end, a good deal more. After all, the TVA will have cost three-quarters of a billion before its construction work is wholly finished; and the Missouri River is four times as long as the Tennessee, the expanse of the Missouri Basin thirteen times as great as that of the Tennessee Basin. But if the cost will be great, the stakes will also be high—nothing less than a new start in an integrated plan of regional economic development.

New land could be won back to irrigation and cultivation and grazing. The Great Plains area, from which came so many of the migrants when the droughts swept the Middle West, could become once more a place where a man and his family can put down their roots. The power generated from the fall of water could be used, as it is being used in the Tennessee Valley, in the manufacture of the ingredients needed to restore the soil's fertility. Those who hunger for family-size farms would be able, under effective land-disposal provisions, to realize their dream. Crops could become more varied and cash income for farmers more regular. The new purchasing power on the farms and in the small towns would be reflected in the growth of regional industries, and the navigation aspects of the Missouri River development would help in lowering freight rates for materials and goods. Power to run the machines could be generated at the dams at a drastically low cost, and the savings in cost could be passed along to manufacturers and householders through the building of transmission lines that would reach municipal power plants and rural co-operatives, as well as the established utility companies. A yardstick would be set up by which to measure the rates and service of the utilities, and in the end the people in the valley could buy out the big utility companies as they did in the Tennessee Valley. Low power rates and lower transport rates would mean that the industries of the region would not have to squeeze the wages of their workers in order to compete with the large producers of the East.

That this is a not impossible regional pattern the TVA has shown. Is there any reason to believe that the people of the Missouri Valley would not be able to do what their neighboring region did, if only the Federal Government and Congress would give them the chance? Is there any reason to believe that later the people of the Arkansas River Valley would not be able to follow their example? FDR projected a sort of instantaneous photo of seven river valleys. But they need not come at the same time. In fact, if they come in succession each will be an experimental chamber from which the next may learn, and each will dare more than its predecessor.

Not the least important part of the Missouri Valley Authority plan is the fact that it will help restore the balance between the regions of the nation. The industrial maturity of the East gives it a great advantage over the industrial immaturity of the South, the Great Lakes region, the Great Plains region, the Pacific Coast region. The development and distribution of war industries have served to remedy that to an extent, but after the war the regions are likely to revert to their former status. The MVA, like the TVA, will show the way to correcting the imbalance between regions. And within each of the regions themselves it will help to create that balance between industry and agriculture that any large community expanse needs.

3. *St. Lawrence Seaway*

WHAT APPLIES to the Tennessee and the Missouri applies also, although in a somewhat different way, to the St. Lawrence.

There is far more emphasis in the St. Lawrence project upon the construction of a navigable waterway which will open the Great Lakes ports to ocean commerce. There is no emphasis upon flood control, irrigation, or the prevention of soil erosion. There is great emphasis, however, on the generation and distribution of hydroelectric power. Navigation and power —these are the two main purposes of the St. Lawrence Seaway project. Since the project would have to be completed by a common agreement between the United States and Canada, there could be no single Federal Authority, as in the TVA and as contemplated in the MVA. Yet the ef-

fect on industry, trade, and the development of resources would be tremendous on both sides of the boundary line.

This is not the place to give the history and the scope of the St. Lawrence
project. If you are interested, you will find a wealth of material on this
subject, gathered together in 1941 in a survey covering thousands of pages
(*The St. Lawrence Survey, Parts I-VII*) made for the Department of
Commerce by N. R. Danelian. This is the only projected river development on which a thoroughly competent survey has thus far been made, in
economic as well as engineering terms.

The St. Lawrence Seaway idea has had a long and tortuous history ever
since 1895, when interest in it first began to show itself, and since 1914,
when President Wilson made the first approaches on it to the Canadian
Government. Hearings on it have been going on since the 1920s, and by
now every nook and cranny of the idea has been looked into, and every
aspect of it has been torn to tatters and reconstructed.

In 1941 the State Department negotiated an Executive agreement with
Canada. It is a good beginning, but it needs Congressional approval. But
it is foolish to argue that such approval must take the form of a two-thirds
Senate vote as in treaty ratification. There are ample precedents for putting the approval in the form of a joint resolution by a majority of both
Houses. It is significant that the same Senators who tried to use the
strategy of reaction to spike the MVA on the Senate floor have shown
their readiness for a bitter-end fight to apply the two-thirds rule to the St.
Lawrence project.

The St. Lawrence project will take from four to six years to build. It
will cost, according to the best estimates at postwar figures, about three-
quarters of a billion dollars. As an engineering project, the St. Lawrence
is one of the most challenging of our time—more exacting even than the
Panama Canal. As a navigation project, it will transform the commercial
and economic life of the Great Lakes area and beyond. As a power project,
it will generate more hydroelectric power than all the twenty TVA dams.
At a 300-mile transmission distance from the International Rapids sector,
it will take in every one of the New England states, the whole of New
York and New Jersey, and a large portion of Pennsylvania.

The crux of the St. Lawrence fight, as is true everywhere else in the
Battle of the Valleys, will be found in its power aspect. The real question
is: Who will distribute and control the power? Under President Hoover
the project was pushed hard because the utility interests confidently expected to get the gravy. In the 1920s, in fact, they almost succeeded. In
1920 Colonel Hugh Cooper, acting for the Aluminum Company of
America, the General Electric Company, and the du Pont interests, of-

fered to build the whole project at a cost to the companies of $1,300,000,-000, and to make a gift of the seaway and its navigation improvements to the two governments. In return the companies asked only that the license to develop the waterpower of the whole river—some 5,000,000 h.p.—be turned over to them. In 1926 they almost got away with it; the New York State Waterpower Commission gave them a preliminary license. But Al Smith carried the issue to the people and the license was revoked.

When FDR became President, the enthusiasm for the St. Lawrence project on the part of the big interests cooled off considerably. One can guess that their influence was felt in the failure of the Senate ratification vote in 1934. Their influence still is present. If the private utilities could be sure of building their own transmission lines to the dams, the powerful opposition to the St. Lawrence project would vanish overnight. Their fear is that either state or Federal agencies will transmit and sell it.

If the private interests win out in the end, it will be against the often-declared and reiterated policy of both houses in the New York State Legislature and both parties in the state government. In 1931, the legislature unanimously declared the St. Lawrence ownership and resources to be the inalienable possession of the people. It created a New York Power Authority, which is an independent government corporation, to survey, construct, and operate the project. In March, 1944, a unanimous legislature again indorsed the project. Governor Dewey and his Democratic predecessors have declared themselves unequivocally for it.

Nevertheless the St. Lawrence dams have not yet been built, nor the generators installed. Why? The answer is again the powerful corporate opposition of the utilities and their allies. "But you are so unreasonable," said an official of one of America's most powerful corporations, which covets the power of the St. Lawrence. He was speaking to a member of the Power Authority. "You are so unreasonable. Why don't you let us build the transmission lines?"

4. The Real Wealth of a Nation

IT IS IRONIC to think of how often it has been said that America's frontier is closed. Actually we are just on the threshold of the use of our potential resources. I do not intend here the ordinary glib repetition of the phrase "new industrial frontiers." Electronics, television, and other "new industries" will not be additions to the country's actual wealth. They are only new variants—new molds into which that wealth can be poured. Or, to change the figure, they are only part of the superstructure on a base which forms the real wealth of a nation. That real wealth is made up of natural and human resources—the land and water and energy resources of the community, and (most valuable of all) its human beings.

Even in America, which has developed its resources far beyond any other great continental expanse, we have only just begun to tap them. The American continent, with less than fifteen per cent of the water-power resources of the globe, has developed more hydroelectric energy than the rest of the world put together. Yet even our continent has developed less than one-fifth of its potential power. We are so rich in what Kirtley F. Mather (in his book *Enough and to Spare*) has called "nature's stored capital" that, giant-like as we are industrially, we are only a Lilliputian to the Gulliver that we could become.

I gave above some estimates of what it would cost us to develop these resources, both in the Missouri River Basin and in the St. Lawrence Valley. Taking the river valley picture for the nation as a whole, those figures are only a beginning.

I cite, for example, some of the estimates in the 1943 "Report on National Resources Development" put out by the National Resources Planning Board. That report was the swan song of the Board. The members of Congress were so frightened by the prospects it opened for an increase in the harnessed and usable natural wealth of the nation that they cut the Board's funds out of existence. Yet the promise of American life that the Board's report unfolded will be evocative and alive long after the Congressmen who sought to stifle it have become forgotten dust.

Two sections of the report deal with "Valley Development" and "Energy Resource Development." One learns in them that three billion dollars can well be spent for construction to take the run-off of our soil and convert it into irrigation, and that this would bring some twenty-two million new acres under cultivation; that a similar amount still needs to be spent for combating soil erosion; that two billions are needed for cleaning the polluted streams of the nation, especially in the coal and smelting districts; that two billions could be used to good effect in developing the Arkansas Valley project alone and similar sums for the other valley projects; that on the main stem of the Columbia River eleven major dams and reservoirs need to be built, of which only three have been thus far completed (the Bonneville, Grand Coulee, and Rock Island); that on the tributary rivers of the same basin, some seventy-five reservoirs will be needed.

The over-all NRPB estimates are that from twenty-five to fifty billion dollars will be necessary as a total investment fully to develop the water resources of the United States. This may seem a gigantic figure, but it is less than we spent on the war for a single year, and only a fraction of what America produces annually. With that expenditure or less, we could increase the installed hydroelectric power capacity of the nation from something like thirteen million kilowatts to seventy million—more than fivefold. The full development of the Columbia River Basin alone, which now has an installed capacity of three million kilowatts, could increase it from three million to forty-five million—an amount more than three times the total national capacity today.

These figures are benumbing. They must be translated into human terms to become intelligible.

They must be translated into terms of regions whose whole life has been transformed: whose cities and towns have received new lifeblood from the improvement of navigation, from cheaper transportation, from the new economic vigor of the surrounding areas; whose urban and rural slums have been wiped away and whose ghost towns have ceased to be ghosts; whose young people no longer leave the land because the land will not support them; whose polluted waters have been cleansed; whose floods have been dammed; whose eroded soil has had its strength restored and its phosphates put back; whose parched earth has drunk up the water from irrigation channels; whose power resources are the possession of the people, developed by the people, distributed over their transmission lines, sold to rural co-operatives.

I mean regions whose industry has been located in relation to the sources of power, of labor supply, of markets; whose businessmen make once more their own decisions in manageable business units instead of being the industrial helots of vast impersonal holding companies; whose trade-unions grow in health because of the health of the whole community of which they form a part; whose households are equipped with lights and radios, washing machines and refrigerators, because light and power have for the first time been made available to the farmer's wife and the worker's wife at a low cost; whose schools and hospitals and public health services have become accessible to the people, both in physical terms and in cost terms.

I have not been describing Utopia here. What I have given is a sketchy description of what has actually happened in the Tennessee River Valley. What I have given is an account of the real connection between the planned development of the water and power resources of a river valley and the transformation of its industry, agriculture, human resources, way of life.

DEC. 4–7, 1944.

The Power of a River

THEY ARE talking now about the mangled budget appropriations for Federal flood control in the Pacific Northwest states. Now that the floods have come, it is a bit late to talk of the money that was asked for and not granted—the money that might have saved tens of thousands from homelessness and scores from death.

We need a vacation from political cynicism. To the ordinary Congressman, as to the ordinary American, all public-works programs smell of the pork barrel. The Republicans have long been pounding away at the thesis that the Federal Government spends too much on humanitarian projects. The small voter and the big taxpayer both agree. As a result, a Republican-dominated House slashed away the budget estimates for dams and levees and spillways, and made even more drastic slashes of the Interior Department budget. The result is to be found in the homeless and dead of Vanport.[1]

Wherever, of course, there is a question of fighting the Russians, money is available—and plenty of it. The initial cost of adequate flood control in the Pacific Northwest, which Senator Morse estimates at $200,000,000, could have been met by what we appropriate for less than a single week for the armed forces. To turn living men into dead men seems somehow a noble project. But to keep living men alive is, one gathers, one of those humanitarian projects that can always be pared to the bone when the budgets are submitted.

But there is nothing namby-pamby about the Columbia River when the spring rains come, and the waters gather in its upper reaches and come rushing down upon the lowland cities. The disasters in Oregon will serve to recall to us that America is a nation of great rivers. When they get swollen with their power and their glory, they sweep everything out of their torrential path.

The engineers contrive dikes, which are makeshift affairs at best. They measure the strength of them against the strength of the river, they make calculations, they tell you how long you will be safe against disaster, how

[1] This was written just after the Columbia River floods had engulfed the small industrial city of Vanport, Oregon.

long you can take in finding a new home. They guess wrong. Disaster comes swiftly, and what was once a city, with factories and workers' homes and children playing in the streets, is now a shambles of cluttered wreckage covered by the waters.

It was especially ironic that the floods should have come right after the great political debates in Oregon. All the attention of the nation converged on Oregon, where two of the Republican masterminds were talking of the great things each would do if elected President[2]—how he would stop the Russians, how he would render the Communists harmless, how he would harness the power of the big rivers. They talked and talked, and then they left—and then the river talked. The big river has pushed out the little men and their little talk, and for the moment it is undisputed master.

There is something of grandeur as well as of terror in this, as there has been in all the great flood disasters of history. Floods can create civilizations and keep them alive, as the annual floods of the Nile have done for Egypt and its crops since the beginning of its history. But mostly they destroy. Americans are lucky, for we have never had the sort of floods the Chinese have had, nor have we been as helpless in the face of them. The "Sorrow of China" they called the flood some sixty years ago on the Hwang Ho. It killed millions of people. We Americans are luckier and cleverer—although still not clever enough.

We have come to think of ourselves as so secure against these elemental events that they no longer release our imaginations. In the Middle East, where great religions came from, the memories of flooded river valleys gripped people's minds and out of them came the myths, like that of Noah, about the floods as retribution for sin and as proof of the power of God. In America there are folksongs, especially among Southern Negroes, about the Mississippi—but very little else that has made great literature. On the Mississippi the periodic danger that the levees will burst is chiefly the signal for the gangs of convicts to be sent out from the state prison farms, to work without conviction at keeping alive a society that cares very little whether *they* are alive or dead.

The American approach to these disasters is not an imaginative approach, but an organizing one. Whatever our foolishness in having let them happen, as in Oregon, we whip every resource together to alleviate the victims when it does happen. All kinds of rescue squads are on the way to the Northwest now, the Army Engineers have taken charge, a Navy

[2] This refers to Harold E. Stassen and Thomas E. Dewey, who were campaigning in the 1948 Oregon Presidential primaries.

mosquito fleet has been mobilized, the Red Cross is on the spot, state and Federal forces are converging on the disaster area. That is the sort of thing we do well.

But when will we learn that grace resides not in rescue but in prevention? The problem of the rivers, for all their unbreakable power, is minor when compared with the big catastrophes that hang like a shadow over the world. They are not Nature-made catastrophes, but man-made. The little city of Vanport, which lies under the swirling waters, is a tiny thing compared to the whole City of Man which may some day lie in ruins because of man's stupidity. But it is a symbol.

JUNE 3, 1948

Brandeis and Lilienthal

1. Then and Now

IT'S ALWAYS dangerous to trace historical parallels, because history never repeats itself exactly. But there is a whopper of a parallel between the fight over confirming the Lilienthal nomination as chairman of the Atomic Energy Commission and the fight over confirming the nomination of another man, thirty years ago. His name was Louis D. Brandeis.

I take the story from A. T. Mason's recently published biography, *Brandeis: A Free Man's Life*. Brandeis was an astute and successful Boston lawyer, a conservative in the depth of his belief in capitalism, but a radical in thinking up methods for making it work. He had been known for many years as "the People's Attorney," a militant champion of liberal causes. He was close to President Wilson, and was a New Dealer a generation before the New Deal. He had made enemies aplenty as well as friends. When Wilson, on January 28, 1916, announced Brandeis' appointment to the Supreme Court, there followed one of the bitterest Senate fights over a confirmation in American history—a fight that showed up with terrifying nakedness the structure of power in our society, and the potential of evil in that power.

Brandeis' most sinister opponent—the Senator McKellar of that struggle—was Clarence Barron, later a figure in Wall Street journalism, but before that a propagandist for the New Haven Railroad. He had to work from behind the scenes in bringing up the heavy artillery against Brandeis: the Senate committee at that time didn't have the very convenient and monstrous role of "guest inquisitor" which McKellar is now filling.

First of all, Brandeis was accused of being a "radical," just as Lilienthal is now accused of being a "Left-Winger" and a "New Dealer." The men who made the accusations were the men who smarted under the defeats he had administered to them during the course of his career. Brandeis had fought for lower railroad rates, for public control over traction franchises, for low-cost savings-bank insurance, for scientific management and greater efficiency in public utilities, for control of the Money Trust which built its power on "other people's money." He didn't use kid gloves, and he fought for keeps.

Brandeis, like Lilienthal, was accused of having the wrong "temperament" for his job. McKellar's cohorts say that Lilienthal is "domineering." Barron's cohorts said Brandeis was "unjudicial." The meaning in each case is simple: Here is a man who believes in what he is doing, and doesn't just go through the motions as in a shadow-play.

In the Brandeis case, as in that of Lilienthal, the accusers didn't come up with a scintilla of real evidence. So they fell back on the argument that, whether the charges were true or not, the very fact that the suspicions had been raised was enough to damn a Supreme Court appointee. "The scheme," wrote a Brandeis supporter at the time, "is to arouse dust, and then argue that because there is dust, the confirmation should be denied." Which is a perfect way of describing the antics today of men like Senator Wherry, who know they can't back up the McKellar charges but are willing to hide their real motives behind them.

Against Brandeis, as against Lilienthal, the most fantastic lies were permitted to masquerade as "charges." Typical was the charge that President Wilson had used Brandeis' services in buying the now well-known courtship letters to Mrs. Peck, that Brandeis had paid $75,000 for them, and had received his Court appointment as a reward. This was, as Brandeis called it, a "vile slander." Another charge was that Brandeis did not believe in a written Constitution. None of these fantasies was voiced publicly. They circulated only in the malicious whispers of cloakroom gossip.

Then, as now, there was talk of the Jewish issue. No one at the Brandeis hearings asked the kind of racist questions about the nominee's parents and their birthplace that McKellar asked Lilienthal. (Incidentally, in both instances the parents came from what is now Czechoslovakia.) But the fact that Brandeis was a Jew was part of the Senate cloakroom talk, just as

—for the first time in Lilienthal's career—the issue of his religious affiliation is being dragged into the Washington discussion.

Then, as now, the Senate hearings seemed interminable. They stretched out for three months, and covered thousands of pages of transcript.

But I don't mean to suggest that the parallel goes all the way. The storm of protest against Brandeis came immediately after his appointment was announced. In the Lilienthal case there was almost unanimous approval of the appointment from all over the country. Not until someone decided that a campaign of abuse might possibly break down even the highest and most widespread prestige did the money start flowing to beat Lilienthal. In Brandeis' case there was a petition against him signed by fifty-five Boston lawyers, and another signed by seven former presidents of the American Bar Association, including William H. Taft and Elihu Root. In Lilienthal's case every person of competence in his profession of government administrator is for him; and added to that the entire group of atomic scientists, the power of whose brainchild has now to be controlled.

Yet, for all these differences, the fact is that the men and the groups aligned against these two men have been much the same. They are the men and the groups who do not intend to relinquish any jot of their power to public control. They fought Woodrow Wilson's New Freedom in 1918 and FDR's New Deal in 1932. They fought the TVA. They fought the McMahon Act for public control of atomic power under civilians. They are now making a last-ditch fight against the one man who is obviously qualified to organize that public civilian control. In Brandeis' time they felt that the crucial fight would have to be made on the Supreme Court. Today they feel that the crucial fight will be on the Atomic Energy Commission.

In each case they were unlucky enough to pick men of stature to destroy. And men with the same kind of faith in democracy. Both men were basically engineer-minded, thinking in terms of a good life for all the people. Both men were lawyers. Both of them turned to the craggy question of concentrated economic power and how it can be organized for the people themselves. Both of them were so effective because, as the servants of the people, they mastered their craft better than the highly-paid servants of the corporations. Both were independent progressives who never had any roots in the Marxian tradition and were more concerned with the arts of conciliation and creation than with the arts of the popular conquest of power through the logic of class interest. Both believed in democracy with a passion which had become a secular religion for them. Both distrusted the concentration of power, whether in the hands of a governmental bureaucracy or of a private corporation. Both believed that the smaller units are the manageable ones and that bigness bears a curse. Both had moral passion in their belief in freedom.

My postscript is cheerful. After months of the bitterest wrangling, the Brandeis nomination finally came to the Senate floor, and he won, 47 to 22. He proved to be not only one of the greatest of our Supreme Court judges, but one of our greatest Americans.[1]

2. The Hero as Administrator

AMERICAN HEROES are of two types. There is the man or the girl who is the symbol-object of our daydreams: the King of Swat, with hefty muscles and the ability to swing gracefully and powerfully at a baseball; the young man with a cornet, who can set the kids swooning; or the small-town girl who made good as Hollywood's image of desire and whose face and figure are infinitely provocative. There is also the man of whom we are proud, even if we can't see ourselves in his place: the general or President or scientist who, by the fact of his achievement, gives us an enlarged sense of collective stature.

David E. Lilienthal belongs to the second group. Can he, one may ask, properly be called an American hero? I think so. It took the Senate hearings on his Atomic Energy Commission appointment to show how tenacious a feeling the people of the Tennessee Valley had for him, how unanimous was the agreement among scientists, technicians, businessmen and the saner newspaper publishers, and even Senators, that they were standing at Armageddon and battling for a man of quality. Rarely has a public hearing brought so spontaneous a rallying of forces behind a man —especially when that man was the lowliest of God's creatures, a governmental administrator.

Willson Whitman, who has written about the TVA in an earlier book, God's Valley, tells in a new book[2] the story of the man who carried through the New Deal TVA idea and is now the key figure in atomic energy administration, and who is thus a symbolic bridge between a crisis with which we dealt creatively and a greater crisis through whose darkness no candle of ours has yet pierced.

Miss Whitman tells the story without the usual gushing and padding

---

[1] As it turned out after this piece was written, Lilienthal also was confirmed.

[2] *David Lilienthal. Public Servant in a Power Age.* By Willson Whitman (Henry Holt and Co., $3).

and romanticizing that corrupt so many biographers who try to bedazzle with the wares they peddle. She tells it sparely, and with dignity—perhaps with too much dignity, as if she were a bit frozen by her subject and were terribly careful lest she write anything that might be distorted by the inevitable McKellar at the inevitable next battle against Lilienthal's reappointment. Which is a pity, because the subject might have profited from a more robust and somewhat less reverent handling.

The Lilienthal success-story is played down in this book, for which I am grateful. It seems to follow the usual American pattern—the Indiana boy, born of an immigrant Jewish family from a village in Austria (now in Czechoslovakia), whose father had learned English and become a small-town storekeeper; the years of high school and college in the Middle West, the skill as a debater, the youthful essays full of fervor and idealism; the course at Harvard Law School, the immersion of the young lawyer in railroad and utility rates and state public-service-commission law and economics; the emergence of a skillful and workmanlike mind which threw fear into the barons of the utility paper-empires and which proved useful to reforming governors like Phil La Follette of Wisconsin.

And then the long spell (1933–47) on the TVA, and now the beginnings on the AEC, with world-wide attention focused on him and a name that has come to stand in the minds of hundreds of millions—foreigners as well as Americans—for the exploits of peace, not war, of which America has shown itself capable.

I have discussed in the section above the obvious parallels between Lilienthal and Justice Brandeis. The differences between the two men are also important. Brandeis became a judge, Lilienthal an administrator. I think this was more than chance and more than temperament. For in Brandeis' generation the crux of governmental control was in the Supreme Court: "government by judiciary" had a grim meaning. In our generation, the crux of government is in the administrative process.

The other big difference is that Brandeis aroused far more hostility throughout his whole career than Lilienthal has done. In fact, Lilienthal has handled his enemies as well as his friends with such consummate skill that—as Miss Whitman recognizes—one gets the picture of an intolerable perfection. "There must be somebody," she writes, "besides Dr. Arthur Morgan and Senator McKellar, who doesn't like him." I am sure there are plenty, yet it is true that Lilienthal lacks the gift for making enemies which plagues most great public figures. He does make the enemies, but he knows how to curb their strength against him. His latest warning to the American people is to study atomic energy for themselves so that they will not "permit science and scientists to be kicked around by the organized forces of ignorance and demagogy and petty politics."

He is, by instinct and by honesty, a master diplomatist. When he came to the Tennessee Valley, a young man of thirty-four fresh on his first Federal job, he said the exactly right thing: "I am greatly interested in two things: people and facts. The purpose of this project, as far as I am concerned, is to make the people happier. I am terribly interested now in finding out more facts about the Tennessee Valley."

In the businessmen of the Valley he faced a potential wall of hostility: yet, by convincing them that he was there not to pursue a theory but to get things done for their common interest, he prevented the wall from ever coming into being. Those businessmen became his staunch supporters through the whole turbulent history of the TVA and when he faced McKellar's fire in the 1947 Senate fight over his appointment.

The TVA is now an accomplished fact—so much so that one forgets the time when it was deemed a dangerous adventure. Wendell Willkie made it the butt of his raillery in the struggle between Commonwealth & Southern and the TVA. Senator Bridges tried to destroy it. Yet the adventure has become reality. Most students of government now consider it the most creative idea of the New Deal. Behind that creativeness is Lilienthal's basic thinking.

I would put it thus: that people are part of a natural universe but that nature must be harnessed for human ends; that there is a cyclical flow and return between nature and human beings—a seamless web of relationships—in which men apply their energy to nature and take renewed energy from it; that science—and particularly the new science of atomic energy—makes possible not only an expanding universe of knowledge but also new frontiers of social opportunity; that men are also part of a moral universe which alone can give meaning to their mastery; that, except in this moral universe, all our vaunted science loses its meaning; that men can do their best work when they work together for common purposes; that the expert can do little more than give direction to the experience of ordinary men at the grassroots; that power must be centralized but its administration must be decentralized, in the region, the university, the operating unit of any project; that planning is not a set of blueprints but a developing job within a framework of purpose and vision.

Lilienthal has managed to get this basic thinking across to people. You will find it best expressed in his own book, *TVA—Democracy on the March* (available in a 25-cent Pocket Book edition). The famous credo, which he spoke in answer to the obscene prodding of McKellar at the hearings on his recent appointment, caught people's imagination, yet the enduring meaning lies rather in the broader philosophy I have discussed.[3]

Somehow he is a public servant whom most of us trust. The sense of relief we felt when his nomination as head of the Atomic Energy Commission was finally confirmed was the deepest tribute we could have paid him. For we live in an age of anxiety, and it is good to know there are at least a few men to whom the explosive power at our command can be entrusted. Without being a plaster saint or a pedant or a fanatic, he is a moral person; and—what may in this case amount to the same thing—a creative one.

As Lilienthal has himself put it: "Beyond this night's darkness lies neither destruction nor slavery for the Children of God, but instead that City of freedom and of peace toward which it is man's destiny to strive." When any man has lit a flame, however small, in this night's darkness, the people can tell.

FEB. 18, 1947; JAN. 18, 1948

The Inflation Crisis: Anarchy, Scapegoats, and Magic

1. Anarchy

EVER SINCE the war Americans have been living in fear of a runaway inflation, with its skyrocketing prices and its destruction of values. Up to the end of the war the fear was kept under control because prices were kept under control. When price controls were swept away, the fear mounted as the prices mounted.

There is the immediate high-price crisis that you read about in every paper and hear about in every radio broadcast—the shortages and the price leaps in meats, eggs, fish, grains. But what marks an inflationary period is the pervasive psychological sense that the dams are down, that no price is too fantastic to ask or to pay, since the whole world of prices has lost touch with the old realities and has become a fantasy world. The prevailing mood among wholesalers, shopkeepers, small-enterprisers, workers, consumers, is becoming one of outrage, resentment, and revenge. You never

[3] For a lucid and moving recent statement of Lilienthal's thinking on atomic energy development, both military and peaceful, see the interview in the form of a "dialogue" between him and Archibald MacLeish, in the Sept. 27, 1948, issue of *Life*.

know from purchase to purchase what the price will be. Finally you say to yourself: "If that's the game, then I can play it as well as the next fellow." When the prices of the goods and services you buy are jacked up, then you in turn jack up the prices of the goods and services you sell.

If this isn't price anarchy, it's so close to it that the term will have to do. For anarchy is the breakdown of order. In that sense what we have now is a price anarchy. It is not only controlled and planned economies that require a framework of order. Capitalism requires it just as much. You have to know from day to day what you are going to be able to count on the next day. Capitalism, exactly because it *is* a system that tries to get along with the barest minimum of governmental controls, depends on a sense of economic stability and economic security even more than do the other systems. The ironic fact is that in their anxiety to scrap all controls, and in their greed for quick and big profits, the men of power in the business world have gone a long way toward destroying the psychological bolstering of their own system—the essential stability it must have in order to function.

What we are witnessing is the preliminary stage of price anarchy and the inflationary psychology. A study of the historic experience of runaway inflations—in Germany after World War I, or in China today—indicates what the later stages of the disease might become. As insecurity grows, men give up hopelessly on prices, and concentrate on the dwindling value of the money unit. They spend recklessly, because it is better to consume things than to hold on to money whose value slips through your hands while you hold it. They turn whatever money they have into tangibles— land, durable goods, jewelry—because those remain firm while money values dwindle. Those are the panic stages of inflation, after anarchy has become widespread and inveterate. Still in the "creeping" stage of inflation, we obviously have not reached those later "runaway" stages. But the smell of them is in the air, and the fear that they will come cannot be erased until we act in a planned fashion to do away with the present initial phase of price anarchy and bring back price order.

To shape such a program of action, we must first understand the nature of the crisis. It is being called widely a crisis of shortages. That is, of course, one element. Not shortages from a strictly American viewpoint, but from a world viewpoint. What America is producing is not enough to take care of its own needs—including a sixteen per cent per capita increase of food consumption among the American people today as compared with 1939 —plus the needs of Europe as well. And the shortage of commodities, along with the increase of money in circulation, is one way of explaining the price runaway.

But it is only one element. There have been crop failures in past years that have not led to price anarchy, for the simple reason that they did not come as part of an inflationary cycle that was already under way before the crop failures. There were shortages during World War II, when we had to export not only food but an immense portion of our entire national production; yet those shortages did not mean price anarchy, because they took place inside a framework of price control.

This brings us to the real nature of the inflationary crisis. It is a price-and-control crisis primarily, made more serious by shortages, changing consumption-habits, and the burden of Europe. Unless we keep our attention on the central element, the rest will either lose their meaning or take on a disproportionate meaning.

2. Scapegoats

ONE OF THE most shameless and cynical aspects of the American crisis is the current campaign to blame all our ills on Europe. The hungry mouths of the European people, we are being told, are responsible for American food scarcities and price-rocketing. The argument is that we are "giving food away" to Europe (as the *Daily News* editorial writer puts it), sending it "down the drain, and in addition paying through the nose for what is left here." The inference is that if we stopped the shipments, our own price problem would be solved.

Like all effective wrong positions, this argument contains enough truth to give sharpness to its falsity. There is no question that we are exporting more food to Europe than we did in 1939, just before the war. The increase in grain exports, while large, is a different case from the even larger increase in the export of meat and dairy products. While our corn crop is poor, we have a bumper wheat crop. For the world as a whole there need be no immediate shortage of grains.

The increased export of meat and dairy products is a different matter. It is the result not only of Europe's great need, but also of a little-noticed revolution which has taken place in the agricultural production of both Europe and America as a result of the war, and which is described in the excellent study on American foreign trade, *Rebuilding the World Economy*, by the Twentieth Century Fund. Cut off from the rest of the world, the countries of Europe had to go slow on the production of meat animals which needed feed grains, and they concentrated on food grain and potatoes. America, on the other hand, with enormous commitments to its allies during the war, as to its large Army and to a working population with a new war purchasing power, expanded its capacity in both grains and meats. It is true that we are eating more than in 1939, and that we are sending far more abroad. But it is also true that we are producing far more foodstuffs, and any comparative figures which leave that out of account give a false emphasis. Actually the authors of the Twentieth Century Fund report are worried that in later years we may not find the foreign markets for our own food production.

What then is the present answer on the question of food exports to Europe?

Is it to cut them drastically, and tell the hungry mouths of Europe that they can be even hungrier for all we care, because ours must be filled? That seems to be part of the policy the Administration is starting to adopt, in its recoil of fear when confronted by the widespread campaign to make Europe shoulder the blame for our high prices. The Agriculture Department has announced cuts in grain exports running to thirty and forty per cent, in order to "put the squeeze" on the European governments and force them to supply more of their own grain. One is reminded of the man who fed his horse less every day in order to see how little he could get along on—until one day the horse failed to get up at all. The cut in grain exports comes with special irony after the news that Perón's Argentinian Government is extorting from its European buyers grain prices that are twice as high as ours, and that Perón is using the extra money to build up armaments for his fascist state. The only result of further cuts on our part will be to leave Europe even more at the mercy of Perón's extortions.

I doubt that we will go on with this insane policy of cuts. Aside from humanitarian feelings, we don't dare to politically. We can't stop exporting food to Europe because aid to Europe is the crucial element in our foreign policy, and our only constructive one.

Will export cuts lower prices for the American consumer? No one dare assert that they will. *Time* magazine reports, from unnamed "Washington economists," that "the index of food prices rises seventeen points every time the United States sends $500,000,000 worth of food abroad." Does *Time* mean that there is a direct causal relationship between the two? The fact is that billions of dollars' worth of food was sent abroad during the war without any rise in the food index at home. The fact is also that the food index has gone right on rising, *not since we started sending food to Europe, but since we did away with price controls.* Even if the exports were cut drastically, it is a safe guess that domestic food prices would fall very little, if at all. For the governing fact about our prices is that there is no framework of control, and there is therefore a price anarchy.

Is the answer, then, for the American people to eat less? As Senator Taft puts this remedy it is a shocking one, for it involves an unplanned and uncontrolled decrease which would be bound to hit the low-income groups the hardest. It would mean less meat and less milk for the children of the poor, while the rich went on stuffing themselves. But to decrease food consumption in America by a program of shared sacrifices—a program enforced by law, on rich as well as poor—makes sense. If prices go high enough, they will automatically eliminate the low-income consumer. A program of rationing, in order to let Europe live and to let America share the sacrifice, would go a long way toward justice by equalizing scarcities.

3. Magic

AMERICA, which by common opinion carried through between 1941 and 1945 the best wartime price-control job in its history, is now by common opinion doing the worst peacetime price job in its history. Who is to bear the political blame for this price anarchy? To most Americans the argument may be futile and wearisome. What they want is not so much to fix the blame as to do away with the price bulge. The great danger is that the Battle of the Bulge will end, as it has begun, by the exchange of political insults, and the price anarchy will remain.

But to the politicians these insults are the breath of life, and the political battle to fix responsibility is the important one. The politicians remember that the last Congressional election, in 1946, was lost and won because meat was scarce and its price was high, and because the Republicans managed to place the political blame on the Administration and on price controls. When the issue of living costs comes in at the door, most other issues go out by the window.

The question is no longer one of high living costs but one of a price anarchy that can become a runaway inflation and destroy the whole economy. Senator Taft has sensed the change in political climate. He now attacks President Truman not for holding on to price controls too long, but for scrapping them too quickly. This is a curious reversal of Republican strategy. As I understand Taft's point, the Republicans should have had the right not only to kill the Office of Price Administration in their own way, but also to kill it at their own pace. Taft's present indictment against the President is that after the Republicans had killed the OPA ninety per cent, Truman proceeded to wipe out the remaining ten per cent.

If price controls were the enemy—as·they were to the Republicans in 1945 and 1946 and still are to them in 1947—it is a curious position to blame the Administration for finishing the job of destroying them. If you shoot to kill, and empty six bullets into your enemy's stomach, and then settle down comfortably to wait for his last gasp, it is scarcely a defense to say that someone came along and gave him the finishing kick to put the victim out of his agony.

If Taft is wholly wrong, that does not mean that Truman was wholly right. It isn't for the Republicans to say it, but it's true that in the eyes of the liberals of both parties the President acted with indecent haste in taking up from where Taft left off. Why did he do it? Partly because the two contending positions were waging a battle in his own mind, and he was himself almost half won over to the Republican arguments against the OPA. Partly also because he had been on a spot politically for so long that he had a sense of relief in putting the whole political burden back on the Republicans. He did not want the issue confused by the remaining price controls, knowing as a politician that the Republicans had left those controls to give themselves an out. He wanted a clear test and clear responsibility, and as a political tactician he was right.

The President's real fault lay elsewhere. It lay not in what he did at the end of the price control fight, but in what he failed to do at the beginning. A President with vision would have seen that the OPA would be needed for a long transition period after the war, but that all the impulses would be to get rid of it. Instead of waiting for the Republicans to attack, he should have taken the offensive from the start and launched a campaign of education to show the people that their choice was control or chaos.

President Truman's weakness was a failure of foresight, but the Republican crime was a willful and calculated campaign to destroy price controls. Behind their calculation were two main motives. One was the cynical desire to serve the National Association of Manufacturers. The second was the conviction that while prices might rise a bit after the controls were removed, the inevitable postwar prosperity would wipe out the memory of the increases, and the Republicans could claim the credit for that prosperity.[1]

More important than either of these motives was the fact that the Republicans were caught in the grip of a system of economic magic, and could no longer reason about economic processes. They stuck to the theory that a peacetime economy could operate only if the "laws of supply

[1] As the 1948 Presidential campaign finally turned out, this proved to be a futile tactic, but it looked good at the time.

and demand" were left unhampered by price control. Every deviation from this uncontrolled operation of supply and demand they considered a blunder, and every governmental interference with it a crime. They never explained, either to the nation or to themselves, why a system that worked so well and so automatically in peacetime should have to be scrapped in wartime—exactly when an effective economy was most needed. They did not have to explain it. They were content with the mumbo jumbo of "free enterprise" and the abracadabra of "supply and demand." Now that their magic has failed them, they are in anguish. The nation accepted their witch-doctor potion, and President Truman even insisted on draining it to the last drop. Yet the disease of scarcities and high prices, instead of being better, is infinitely worse.

Dollar-a-pound meat, dollar-a-dozen eggs, dollar-a-pound butter—these are the harsh realities of the Battle of the Bulge. The confused statements by Taft, the silence of Dewey, the embarrassment of the Republican National Committee—all these are proof that the magic of supply and demand has no power left in it. The pious advice about voluntary cuts in eating, while they would make sense within a new framework of control, make no sense without it.

More is involved here than political advantage. Prices, figures, index numbers, scarcities, are in themselves cold things. But when they are translated into less food and less milk for children, into dwindling family savings, into constant scrimping and constant anxiety, they take on a living meaning.

SEPT. 18, 19, 23, 1947

Big Management, Big Unionism, Big Government

1. Civilization by Combat

IN THE MIDDLE AGES, when two men had conflicting claims against each other, the authorities would sometimes order a trial by combat, to determine the question of justice by the performance of prowess. The idea was that if your heart was pure, a providential vigor would be added to your good right arm, and your strength would be as the strength of ten. We have abandoned the theory that prowess is justice in our law, and civilized men are striving to abandon it even in international affairs. But within our own economy we seem to be going back to the law of the jungle, where the prime question is: Can I kill you, or can you kill me? We are trying to run a civilization by combat.

In one sense, industrial combat is an inherent part of a capitalist economy, with its unequal distribution of economic power. Take the three big industries that are soon to be involved in warfare—autos, steel, electric power and products. They are the heart of our whole economy. Do the American people own them? They do not. Do the American people control them? They do not. They are owned and controlled by a handful of men. A single family, the du Ponts, owns a quarter of the far-flung empire of General Motors, and its shadow falls over the whole empire. One hundred and eighty-five thousand workers are at the mercy of the decisions these men make. The only way the many can balance the power of the few is by banding together and acting together. Their final weapon is the strike.

This ought to be elementary. But we forget it all the time. The strike is a weapon that a responsible trade-union does not invoke except as a final resort in an unequal struggle. The unions and the union leaders in these three industries have shown themselves repeatedly to be responsible. The ordinary newspaper reader learns that "they" have called a strike again, and for him it is the workers who are the aggressors in the combat. All that he sees is the end product.

What he does not see, and what he is not told, is what precedes the decision of the men and the leaders to strike. He is not told that when 700,000 men in the steel industry decide to brave hunger and idleness in a cold winter, it is not because of a whim on their part or because of their lust for power. It is because of the decisions of a few men who control the steel plants and resources and processes—a few men who choose to sit on their heap of power, secure in the knowledge that they cannot be budged except by a costly and agonizing strike.

In our kind of economy, how do you avoid strikes? By collective bargaining. What has happened to collective bargaining? Many answers are currently being given to this question. The cry of the big corporations, and of their paid advertisements that scream at you from every newspaper, and of their mercenaries on the radio and in the financial columns and on the editorial pages, is that the unions scorn collective bargaining because they want the power of decision over management. This has become one of the Big Lies of our time, and the fact that it is a fantastic lie does not make it any the less powerful.

Anyone who knows the conditions inside the unions in these industries knows that the function of the leaders has been not to make the strike decisions but to register them. The decisions have been made by the men. Even if they wished to, the leaders could not hold the men back. And what are the men's motives? To believe that the steel worker or the auto worker or the electric worker wants to run management, or that he wants to overthrow capitalism, is to betray the bleakest ignorance about the mind of the American worker. What he wants is better pay and more security.

He is not interested in the abstraction of power or of capitalism. It is not for an abstraction that he is willing to go idle for weeks or perhaps for months; nor is it for an abstraction that he is willing to stand in the cold on the picket-line, and tangle with police and National Guard. It is not for an abstraction that he is willing to use up his small savings, and cut down on meat and milk and clothing for his children. In the name of primitive common sense, consider this man and his motives; and don't let the ad-writers and the propagandists and the mercenaries sell you on the fantastic idea that he is doing what he is doing because he wants to take over the power of the capitalists.

JAN. 7, 1946

2. *A Look at the Books and a Share of the Pie*

To MOST PEOPLE the demand of the General Motors workers for a thirty per cent increase, or of the steel workers for an increase of two dollars a day, will seem pretty steep. Since it is collective bargaining that is involved, these must be seen as starting points for bargaining, not as final sticking points. The unions defend them on two grounds. The first is that with the overtime of the war period gone, the take-home pay has dropped steeply; and with the rising price levels, their living standards must drop even more. Hence, if the take-home pay and its ability to buy are to be kept at the war level, this can be done only by steep increases in wage rates. The second ground is that the national economy as a whole will not function unless the large mass of people (which means centrally the workers) have the capacity to buy the products that the factories make. Otherwise, there will be great breakdown and unemployment.

Thus the two bases of the union's wage claims, in principle, are the need for sustaining the take-home pay and the need for maintaining purchasing power in the economy as a whole. Where, then, does the much-mooted question of the company's capacity to pay come in? It comes in as a rebuttal to the refusal of the companies to take the wage claims seriously in collective bargaining. What labor is, in effect, saying to the companies is this: "If you don't meet our wage claims, then what are your grounds? They must be, in all common sense, that you cannot afford to meet our claims without raising prices. Well, if that is your position, let us look at your profit figures or let a public board look at your profit figures. And let us argue it out on that basis and submit our arguments to the people." That makes sense to me—good, hard, common sense. The unions say that if there is to be an argument on wage increases without price increases, *the profit figures have to be part of that argument*. Otherwise it becomes an argument in a vacuum.

One answer to this argument is that, whatever may be the relevance of profit figures in collective bargaining, no corporation can afford to disclose them in detail, else it gives away all its plans. General Motors, for example, says in its ads that its profit figures are already public, in its periodical reports and its tax figures. That is true. The current profit figures show how steep the corporate profits have been not only in the richest corporation in the world, but throughout the economy.

But here is the rub. What the unions want to see is not only profit figures in the large. They need a breakdown of them. They need to know the profit per unit of production. If the company says, "No, we can't pay you this wage increase you ask without increasing the price of each car we make," then the union can't help answering, "Show us your production costs on each unit, and how much of that is labor cost, and what our wage increase will do to labor cost per unit." And that's where the blood pressure of the company officials shoots up to the boiling point. "Even if we showed you that for past years," they answer, "it wouldn't do any good in wage discussions for the coming year. And our cost figures for the coming year are related to our production plans, our promotion plans, our reserve plans, our pricing plans, our material quality. If we tell that to you we tell it to our competitors."

I have put the company argument as cogently as it can be put. Actually, the answer that the General Motors executives gave Walter Reuther, President of United Automobile Workers, was that they price their cars "on hope." It was a flip and arrogant answer, and the company deserves a better statement of its case. Having given it, I must go on to say that it fails to convince me. The fact is that the auto industry is what economists call an "oligopoly"—a division of a monopoly field among a few big competitors. There are only three big ones, with a fourth coming up now. There is no price competition; at certain levels prices are roughly the same. The competition is in model, looks, promotion, performance. There is plenty of espionage in the industry. To submit the cost figures to fact-finding boards would not tell the competitors what they do not already know. It might tell the public some things; but who can object to that?

General Motors is not sparing its money in this propaganda fight. One of its full-page ads asks in bold headlines: A "LOOK AT THE BOOKS" or "A FINGER IN THE PIE"? It concludes: "A 'look at the books' is a clever catch phrase. . . . It leads surely to the day when union bosses, under threat of strike, will demand the right to tell *what* we can make, *when* we can make it, *where* we can make it, and how much we must charge you . . . this threatens all business."

In an attempt to conceal their own power-tenacity, the companies accuse the unions of a power-lust. They figure that the best defense is to take the offensive. By shifting the argument to the charge that the union is trying to grab capitalist power, they shift attention away from their own power-behavior in refusing to bargain collectively.

Is it true that the union position "leads surely to the day" when the unions must take over control from the companies? This sounds to me like the sort of argument that Thomas Reed Powell used to call "the parade of the imaginary horribles." It was the argument made a century ago when the fight for collective bargaining was started, the argument that was used when the National Labor Relations Board was proposed, the argument that was used every time a social advance was discussed. It was the argument made against every move taken by the Roosevelt Administration. And yet the net effect of those steps has been not to destroy our economic system but stabilize it, not to undermine it but to make it responsible to the people.

If you mean by capitalism the God-given right of a few big corporations to make all the decisions that will affect millions of workers and consumers and to exclude everyone else from discussing and examining those decisions, then the unions are threatening capitalism. But if you mean that the owners of corporate property and its managers have an immense economic power, in the discharge of which they are responsible to the people as a whole, including the workers, then the survival of capitalism is not endangered by the union demands.

The champions of capitalism have long boasted that only through capitalism can the nation get prosperity, and only through capitalism can the workers get high wages. The nation, including the workers, is now seeking to test the genuineness of their claims. They do not want to put their "finger in the pie"—except as the making of the pie is a public concern. They want to watch how that pie is made, they want a fair share of it when it is made. And if they are not given a fair share, they want to know how the rest of the pie is being divided up, and why so large a portion of it somehow gets spirited away.

JAN. 8–9, 1946

3. *How Not to Settle a Railway Strike*

HARD-PRESSED AS President Truman was, it was not necessary for him to resort to extreme measures to settle the railway strike. It could have been settled by the give-and-take of compromise. I am forced to the conclusion that at a certain point in the proceedings, the President became more interested in settling the strike his way than in settling the strike. It had become with him a crisis of prestige, even more than a crisis of economic paralysis. He could have had a settlement finally on his own terms, leaving only the loophole (and a fair one) of continued negotiations about the rule-changes while the men returned to work. But no, he would not have it thus. He had already called Congress into joint session, he had a speech to make and a bill to propose—and he meant to go through with them. The patient was showing every sign of getting well, but the funeral oration had been written and the pallbearers had been called together—and the burial went on even though it meant burying the victim alive.

The President's apologists will say at this point that, even granting the truth of what I have written above, the President was dealing with more than the railway strike: he was dealing with coal as well, and with the strikes still to come. I suspect that the President got tired of being pushed around by labor and management and Congress and the press, and decided once and for all to end his difficulties. He saw his chance in the railway strike, and instead of trying to settle the strike he used the strike to show he was a strong man and to get the blank-check power he wanted. You may applaud him or damn him for this strategy, but at least be fair enough to recognize that this was his strategy, and that at some point the two railway brotherhoods became the pawns of that strategy and not the monsters they have been pictured.

Now let us take a hard look at the cure the President has proposed. Its main provisions are:

The President is given the power to declare a national (war) emergency in any industry, in the interests of the transition from war to peace.

Once that is done, there are criminal penalties against any union leader who "conducts or permits" a strike or who does not take action to end it.

The President (through his Attorney General) is given the power to ask the Federal courts for an injunction against the strike.

In addition to judicial penalties, economic penalties are provided: any worker who doesn't return to work loses his job, and if he is later re-employed he loses his seniority rights anyway.

The President is given the power to draft the workers into the Army, and to run the industry not by turning soldiers into workers, but by turning workers into soldiers.

This is the proposal which the two Houses of Congress cheered, which the House of Representatives passed in a few hours, which the reactionary press is hailing as the salvation of America. Does it in all reason deserve these plaudits?

I think not. I commend to President Truman a sentence from President Roosevelt's Labor Day message in 1941: "We know that a free labor system is the very foundation of our functioning democracy." This was no empty rhetoric. Three months later we were at war with German and Italian and Japanese fascism, whose first step, in setting up fascist power, had been to crush their labor movements and place them under military rule. In all reason, is it not an ironic thing for the American people, a year after their victory, to be adopting the fascist principle they fought?

I seem to remember an old myth about the victor eating the heart of the vanquished, so that his strength will be transferred. But what a hideous strength it is—this fascist strength we are seeking to take over.

The free labor system in America does not mean and has never meant complete freedom from government control. Labor has been hedged about by all sorts of legal restrictions in the past—and also by all sorts of safeguards. But always the right of organizing, the right of collective bargaining, and the right to strike have been crucial to a free labor system. What President Truman's proposal does is to leave the first intact, place limits on the second, depending on the President's own will, and wipe out the third.

The difference between a free labor system and a compulsory labor system has always been that in the latter the Government could give commands to a worker under penalty of losing his job. When that power has been sought by the employers—through the lockout and the blacklist—labor has fought it, and fought it successfully. Now the Government wishes to assume that power, and to hold over the head of every American worker the threat of depriving him of his job or his seniority rights if he strikes.

The American tradition has always been anti-militarist. In wartime we have mobilized our strength under Army leadership, when it was a question of national survival. In peacetime we have always put the Army back in its place. Whenever the National Guard or the Regular Army has been used in strikes, it has been a black day in labor history and in the history of American democracy. Yet now the President proposes as his final weapon that any worker who does not follow his orders be drafted and become a soldier. This means putting labor under military discipline and military law. It means what happened when Hitler came into power and drafted workers into the labor battalions of the army.

At this point the defenders of the President's proposal may say that his is an emergency measure, and therefore temporary. The experience of history shows that every temporary measure tends to become a permanent measure. Once a President finds this convenient military way of resolving his labor headaches, he will continue using it and every President will use it. President Truman asks us to trust his good will and his prolabor record. In the same way every dictator assures his people that he knows best what is best for them, and they must trust him not to abuse his unlimited powers. The President's hysterical performance is no happy augury of how he could be trusted to keep his head in the future. When a man is where (to paraphrase the famous sentence of former Chief Justice Harlan Stone) the only restraint he has is his self-restraint, he is no longer an officer of government. He has set himself up as God.

The President will find that he can't run a nation in peacetime by laying hold of a military remedy every time he finds it hard to solve a civilian problem. I know how sorely he has been beset by every kind of trouble, by the locust-plague of crises that bedevil a President in our crisis democracy. But the lazy way of solving these problems—by placing them under a military dictatorship—is the fascist way. Democratic government is hard, but its stakes of freedom are high.

Of course he has become a hero—to the wrong people—to those who have wanted to crack down on labor all along, and who are delighted to use him as an instrument. It is easy to win the applause of these men. He has only to betray the people and keep betraying them—and he will have the reactionaries of both parties hailing him as the nation's savior. The medicine the President proposes and the House of Representatives has underwritten is bad medicine. It will cure the ills of labor troubles only by killing the patient, democracy.

Walter Lippmann and others have said that there is no longer a moral right to strike in crucial industries that affect the whole economy. If that is true, then let us place those crucial industries under public management —not only their labor aspect but their property aspect as well. It is time to end the farce in which the Government pretends to seize an industry, holds it just long enough to break the strike in it, then hands it politely back to the corporations.

It may be that we can no longer afford to take any chances of interruption of coal production or steel production or railway transportation. But if that is true, the logical course is to nationalize those industries. If the free labor system is too dangerous in our great industries, then the free-enterprise system is also too dangerous. If there is no longer a moral right to strike in these industries in order to get a living wage and decent health and safety conditions, then there is no longer a moral right to run these industries as part of the private profit system and give a handful of men the power to deny their workers a decent living wage.

Give the American people a chance to decide their own destiny in their industrial life. Let it not be said of our democracy that it has one logic for the masters and another for the men, one system of justice for the workers and another for the possessors.

MAY 28, 1946

4. *Government by Injunction in Coal*

I. LABOR'S DRED SCOTT CASE

CHIEF JUSTICE VINSON and his Supreme Court majority [1] no doubt slept quietly last night with the sense that they had vindicated the sovereign power of the United States Government against the threat of paralysis by strikes. But I think history will show that in smashing at John L. Lewis and the coal miners, their blow reached beyond Lewis and the coal miners and landed at the heart of the American labor movement.

What the Supreme Court majority decided was not only that Lewis and the coal miners would have to pay through the nose in fines, and would have to eat crow publicly. What makes it a decision that will cast its shadow over decades to come is the Court's holding that when the Government enters the industrial picture, either as an actual or as an ostensible employer, it does not have to live up to any of the obligations imposed on a private employer.

Do I express this too sweepingly? I wish such a charge could hold against me, but I submit that my statement is not too sweeping. What Chief Justice Vinson and his colleagues decided was that the Norris-La Guardia Anti-Injunction Act does not apply to the Government as employer because it does not mention the Government as employer,

[1] This was written as a comment on the Supreme Court decision in *U. S. v. United Mine Workers of America*, 330 U. S. 258 (1947).

and because there is no clear proof in the legislative history of the bill that the motive of Congress was to include it. By the same token, all other labor legislation enacted during the past half-century of struggle for labor's rights—and enacted with the private and corporate employer primarily in mind—has no meaning when the Government is employer. Which means that if labor wants to build up a body of protections against the Government itself, it must start its heartbreaking struggle all over again—a struggle which may again take a generation or two.

Let us get one further fact clear. Not only does the Vinson decision strip labor of its protections when the Government is the actual employer, as when an industry has been nationalized, or placed under a Government corporation. It does the same when the Government is a phony employer—when Congress has empowered the President to "seize" a factory or industry for some real or fancied emergency reason. To speak of the Government as the employer in the coal industry today is, in objective terms, nonsense. The managers are the same as under private ownership, the profits go to the private owners. The whole thing is staged as part of an elaborate legal *as if*. Yet even this *as if*, this transparent fiction of Government employment without any of the substance, is also held to invalidate the ordinary protections that have been built up over a long period in order to make a reality of collective bargaining.

Now add one further fact to this—although it may seem irrelevant to talk about social facts to a Court majority that is so obsessed with legal fictions. Add the fact that all over the world the irreversible movement is toward the socialization of industry. For the moment America is keeping itself an island in this sea of tendency, but it will not continue for long. In America, too, the trend will increasingly be toward the Government as employer—if the economy is to be kept from periodic collapse. Or, if emergencies are allowed to pile up, the Government will increasingly be vested with the power of temporary seizure of industries.

Add these facts together, and the conclusion is that the Supreme Court majority decision is calculated to leave labor powerless in the coming generation. It ties the unions hand and foot with regard to the one force they will have to deal with increasingly, and it hands them over to any unscrupulous Congress and Administration which may wish to use the "sovereign" power for reactionary ends.

Granted that Lewis' legal case on the interpretation of his contract with Krug was shaky. Granted that he should never have tried to cut a legal corner by reopening the wage clauses. Granted that his conduct throughout was characteristic of his illusion-of-grandeur neurosis. Granted that he was stupid to flout the Court arrogantly, and to refuse to abide by judicial process until the Supreme Court had interpreted the injunction power as applied to the Government. Granted that he needed to be taken down a cut or two.

But all these things added together do not give the Supreme Court the moral right to hand down a decision which in essence is political. I go along with the courageous and farsighted analysis of it made in the dissents by Justices Rutledge and Murphy. I find the middle position taken by Justices Frankfurter and Jackson at least tenable and judicious. But the position taken by Justices Vinson, Black, Reed, Douglas, and Burton is far more a political coup than a constitutional defense of freedom.

What makes the whole thing sadder still is the use by the majority opinion of the kind of static and arid reasoning which Justices Black and Douglas, at least, have in other cases always rejected. Any student of Supreme Court history knows the dismal feeling of reading the reactionary opinions at the turn of the century, when the Court majority refused to apply the commerce power of Congress to modern conditions because there were no railroads or telegraphs when the Constitution was framed. Yet today the Court says in effect that the Norris-La Guardia Act must be construed narrowly because the Government did not fill an important role as employer fifteen years ago.

The Norris-La Guardia Act was intended to be part of labor's charter of freedom. The present decision will go down as labor's Dred Scott case.

II. THE NOD OR WINK DOCTRINE

WHAT WOULD you think of engineers or technicians who brushed aside a half-century of experience with the problems of production and insisted on starting from scratch? And what would you think of a military general staff which proposed to return to the war technology of the 1890s as the principal method of national defense? Both of them would be greeted by mountainous waves of disbelief and ridicule.

Yet this reversion to the past is exactly what is now happening in the area of labor relations. Justice Alan Goldsborough's conviction of John L. Lewis and the Mine Workers is notable chiefly because it flouts the national experience of half a century. When I look at it against the background of American labor history, the decision strikes me as one of those grotesque tableaux of mummery and buffoonery you might expect to see at a Gay Nineties ball. Except that it is in dead earnest, and is a symbol of the way American labor relations are moving toward disaster.

The Assistant Attorney General, representing the Justice Department, spread a lot of damning evidence on the record against John L. Lewis. He showed pretty well that there was no strike trouble in the coal fields before Lewis proclaimed that the operators had voided their contract. He made a good, if obvious, point that it was difficult to imagine 400,000 men making individual decisions to stop work. And Justice Goldsborough was right in ridiculing the now classic Lewis telegram to the miners: "Your voluntary cessation of work should now be terminated." In short, it would be hard for any sensible and realistic person to take seriously Lewis' contention that he is not linked with the walkout in coal. I don't quarrel with any of these facts. And I don't defend Lewis as a labor leader. On the pension question he managed in the end to get from Senator Bridges, as impartial arbitrator, terms not quite as good as he could have got in the beginning, without a work stoppage, from Thomas E. Murray as arbitrator. That is not exactly brilliant labor leadership.

But the question is not John L. Lewis' skill as a leader. It is not even, except in a very narrow sense, John L. Lewis' deeds and misdeeds. It is the question of how you best organize labor relations, not only in coal but in all crucial industries, at a time as dangerous and anguished as ours. The method used under the Taft-Hartley Act, of which the Lewis case and the Goldsborough decision are the most dramatic instance, stands out as an extraordinarily stupid and wasteful method. It shows an arrogant contempt for both social principle and social experience at a time when to ignore the principles and the experience of a democracy is to court disaster.

Consider the record on American experience with the labor injunction. The Norris-La Guardia Act of 1932 was passed because of the overwhelming tide of resentment against "government by injunction"—the use of the court injunction method to break strikes and settle labor disputes. The resentment came from all sides, from Republicans as well as Democrats, from decent conservatives as well as from labor and the liberals. It mounted for the simple reason that over decades of experience the method of the labor injunction had proved a dismal failure, had increased disputes instead of settling them, had embittered labor rather than served to introduce order into labor relations. Now we have this same system of blundering by injunction back again. Whatever Justice Goldsborough's own sense of judicial integrity—and no doubt it is high—he is starting again the old process of building up bitterness against the arbitrary power of the courts in labor disputes. It looks as if we never learn anything and never forget anything.

The Taft-Hartley Act brought back the system of the labor injunction, and I can understand Justice Goldsborough saying that he is there to enforce it. He probably feels pretty cocky because the United States Supreme Court backed him up last March on the earlier contempt case involving Lewis. And he also feels that the entire majesty of the law is involved, and that he can make no compromises with that majesty. That is exactly the most deadly fact about the labor injunction. It relies on the courts, and the courts have their dignity to maintain and their face to save, and so they dare not be flexible. They must compel the union and its leaders to drain the cup of wormwood, lest someone accuse the courts of opportunism.

This shows the kind of instrument of labor order we have in the court injunction and the contempt proceedings. The great advance in labor relations in the past half-century has been in the substitution of administrative agencies in the place of the courts. The system of collective bargaining, under administrative supervision, is flexible and informal enough to get results. The courts are concerned not with results but with face. Note that Lewis had already settled the pension problem: in effect, he was being tried *because he had settled it in an unorthodox* way. Justice Goldsborough felt the whole world, and all the "lawless forces" in it, were watching him. Which makes fine dramatics, but is no way to settle labor disputes. We need to get back to the administrative system, which has worked so well under the NLRB, and get away from the system of blundering by injunction.

Not content with following the established lines of the law, Justice Goldsborough has struck out on new paths, and has announced two rather novel doctrines of law:

The first is the doctrine that a union leader, to be guilty of violating the Taft-Hartley Act, need not have called a strike in defiance of the Act. In fact, he need not have made any sort of utterance—provided that "a nod, or a wink, or a code was used in place of the word *strike*." This is my favorite grotesque quotation from the whole grotesque episode. I shall call it, in my own meditations, the "Nod or Wink Doctrine" of labor guilt. Up to now the labor agencies and the courts have had job enough trying to interpret verbal language used in labor disputes—and there has been plenty of it. Now I suppose they will have to become experts in the more primitive language of nonverbal signs. Why not set up a special division of the Department of Justice to concentrate on the interpretation of nods, winks, and codes? It could be called the Division of Labor Thought Control—which is indeed what we seem to be moving toward.

As if this were not enough new law for one decision, Justice Goldsborough adds another novel doctrine for good measure. It is the doctrine that a trade-union is responsible for everything its members do, whatever the source of the conduct. There may, of course, be a work-stoppage which is against the wishes of the leaders and beyond their control: if so, the union leaders have the burden of proving it. This means that unions must become self-policing for the punitive provisions of the Taft-Hartley Act and the contempt procedures. It means you are guilty not only for what you do as a union leader, but what you fail to prevent your men from doing. I suppose that if the coal miners stay away from work as a protest against the conviction of Lewis, that will involve further punishment of Lewis and the union. This is an interesting way of making the unions part of the Government's Labor Front.

The fact is, of course, that this whole fantastic pyramid of injunction blundering, nod-and-wink espionage, and collective guilt for negative actions is so monstrously unworkable that it is bound to fall of its own weight. But until it does, what a mess it will have made. I cannot see how you can mine coal by injunction, or by the nod-and-wink doctrine. If I were a coal miner I could not imagine a surer way of getting my dander up, of making me stay away from the pits, and of making John L. Lewis a labor martyr in my eyes, than the way that has now been adopted. I don't see how a jailful of labor leaders, and a succession of whopping fines on the unions, will achieve anything but smoldering resentment and industrial chaos. Nor do I see how this new form of crackdown on labor by the Truman Administration—so reminiscent of the hapless adventure in military fascism in the railway strike—will help to create the orderly war economy for which the military men today have so passionate a desire.

MARCH 7, 1947; APRIL 20, 1948

5. New Frontiers for Labor

I

THERE IS no one today who does not sense that American labor is living in a new era, and it must find its survival and direction and strength under new conditions. I am referring now to something more than the regular pattern of an anti-labor drive. These attacks have been repulsed in the past, when labor has been able to count on the strong support of large sections of middle-class opinion. Something new has been added to the situation.

The dismaying fact about the just-ended coal strike has been the fairly wide acceptance of the methods the Government used in breaking it. Except for some of the labor leaders, there was no vigorous protest against the use of the court injunction by a single judge to decide a great economic issue by a legal technicality.

Partly, no doubt, this must be set down to the account of John L. Lewis himself, and the vast gamble he took with the livelihoods of the coal miners and the very life of American labor. So intense was the popular resentment against Lewis that it swept aside whatever scruples many Americans may have felt about invading the basic rights of labor.

But let us not delude ourselves. It was not all a question of Lewis. There is also a more generalized feeling that labor has come to the end of its era of gains, and that it must now accept an era of restrictions.

There are too many people who are all too ready to throw all of labor's achievements and freedoms to the anti-labor wolves. They forget that the rising living costs which make necessary the negotiation of new wage contracts are the result of a deliberately created inflation which the unions fought with all their strength. They forget that Congress has not passed a measure to help American labor for almost a decade; that the most blatant fact of our economic system is the continuation of fantastic corporate profits; that the real threat to America is from concentrated corporate power, not from labor power.

I hear it said all around that labor will now have to adopt defensive measures, and make concessions to its enemies lest they destroy the whole of trade-unionism. I do not agree with the premise—that labor's cause is a selfish one, to be defended selfishly. Labor's gains in the past half-century have been gains not only for workers, but for the welfare of all the people. They have helped not only the unions, but the nation. For labor to beat a strategic retreat now will be an admission that it has made an unsuccessful bid for total power—which is not true. It will mean that labor will brand itself with the very stigma its enemies seek to place on it.

American labor as a whole has nothing to be ashamed of and nothing to recant. The problem is not how far to retreat, but how best to carry on this fight—in what areas, toward what goals, by what methods.

Up to now labor's great reliance has been on purely economic action, to build a trade-union organization whose strength could counterbalance the strength of the big corporations. That balance in the economic area is now pretty well achieved. Up to now labor has fought to win a recognized place for itself in the American economy, so that it could not be trodden under foot. That too is pretty well achieved, although labor's freedom—like all other freedoms—must continue to be defended with as much vigor as it was won.

Labor must now become completely responsible in the way it uses its economic strength. It must stay within its contract obligations while it fights to make the contracts decent. It must stay within the framework of law while it fights to make the laws fair. It must use every instrument of collective bargaining, and resort to the strike weapon only as a last and desperate measure when the employers refuse. For the big fact of our time is that our economy has become incredibly delicate and easily disrupted. The group which can hit at the economic nerve centers is the group which will have to assume in the public mind the responsibility for paralyzing everyday economic life.

From now on the vital area of social action will be the power of the Government. In its hands will lie the instruments for controlling both labor and industry. More and more it will bring the public utilities and other key industries under its management and operation.

Which means that from now on labor will have to turn its main energies into political action as the base for its continued economic existence. It will have to achieve unity in its own ranks. It will have to form an alliance with those groups outside its ranks which have the same basic ideas about economic and political democracy.

This is labor's new frontier, one in which it can prove as creative and militant as it has been for half a century on the frontier of straight economic action.

II

THE MAY DAY present from the Republicans to American workers is the Taft victory in a Senate test vote on the anti-labor legislation. The May Day present from the Administration is a generally lip-serving and lifeless "defense" of collective bargaining, and a willingness to accept a bill that mangles the unions provided only it doesn't kill them wholly dead. The May Day present from the unions themselves is the continuance in the old rutted tradition that the unions do their whole duty by fighting for wages and hours and against anti-union Congressmen. And the May Day present from the Left-Wing parties (including Communists and Socialists alike) is the old traditional May Day parade, but without the old revolutionary fervor, without the old passionate hopes for a new world, and with nothing to replace them.

Is this too harsh on everyone concerned? I think not. The fact that anything as barbarous as the Hartley Bill has passed the House, and anything as primitive as the Taft Bill will pass the Senate, is one of the most damning things about American political life today. But even more damning is the fact that with fifteen million Americans in trade-unions today, there have been protests only from the trade-union leaders: there has been no spontaneous outburst of feeling 'and will in every American community that would make the Tafts and the Hartleys and their cohorts in Congress too scared ever to go back again to the folks at home.

Something is undoubtedly wrong with an America whose lawgivers on the question of labor are willing to turn us back to the primeval ooze. But something is also wrong with a labor movement that knows only how to function on wage-bargaining and in lobbies, and—failing those—has no other resources left.

A young Washington friend of mine who follows the labor scene closely and shrewdly describes the House Labor Bill as a solution of the labor problem very similar to former Governor Earle's solution of the Russian problem—annihilation via the atom bomb. It torpedoes more than a decade of precedent-building in labor law. The House bill was drawn by representatives of companies that have obstructed and sabotaged the Wagner Act from the beginning. But the important fact is that the sponsors and supporters of both bills have felt pretty sure they could get away with it. On what do they base their hope that they can cripple the labor movement, and make what remains of it operate as a Labor Front for the employers, and still get re-elected? Their calculation, with all its cynicism, is one of the most acid commentaries on the whole labor movement as a cultural pattern.

Which leads me to some harsh thoughts about the aspects of labor failure in America.

One aspect is that economically and politically labor has allowed itself to be estranged from the rest of the nation. Forced to rely for its immediate gains on its own unaided strike-and-boycott strength, it has never basically departed from the narrow patterns set by Gomperism. It is true that Sidney Hillman for a brief spell tried to teach labor the meaning of political action, and that Walter Reuther has recently broken away from the "higher-wages-at-any-cost" tradition by publicly linking wages with prices and living-costs.

But these are exceptions. The American people have the impression that labor is a pressure-group, and by and large that has been true. What follows is logical: if labor is a pressure-group, then let it fight its own battles. That is what Hartley, Taft, Ball, and the others are banking on: that labor will be isolated.

I have an even more serious charge: that while the trade-unions have allowed themselves to be isolated economically and politically, they have allowed their members to become the captives of their enemies culturally. They read reactionary papers, listen to reactionary radio programs, lap up the standardized mental products of an anti-labor culture. The unions have never taken seriously the prime tasks of converting themselves into powerful educational and cultural instruments.

The American worker must become a full human being in his own right —not as a placid sheet on which the capitalist culture places its rubber-stamp, and not as a member of a narrow pressure-group. All the May Day marching and speechifying will not hide the hollowness of a labor move-ment that does not develop men who lead full lives, who can handle ideas, who know about history and politics, and who can make themselves into centers of democratic contagion for the whole nation.

DEC. 10, 1946; MAY 1; 1947

Jacques Duclos and Earl Browder

THESE ARE some notes on the now famous Jacques Duclos article, in the *Cahiers du Communisme*, about Earl Browder and his Communist line. Judged purely in aesthetic terms, as Thomas De Quincey might have judged it with his interest in murder as a fine art, it is a beautiful job of annihilation and dissection. By the time Duclos gets through, Earl Brow-der has not only been publicly chastised: he has been pitilessly cut to pieces.

How does Browder take it all? Whether from a morbid love of punish-ment or from the faith of a zealot baring his neck to the divine knife ("though he slay me, still shall I believe in him"), he not only reprints the whole article in Thursday's *Daily Worker*, but runs along with it an abject foreword. He has been hacked into bits; but, as with the night-crawler worms, each of the hacked-up pieces still wriggles and squirms and crawls on the ground, and will continue to do so until fed to the fishes.

But the real issues go beyond the personal question of Browder and his suffering. What light does the Duclos criticism shed on Communist policy in America, and on its future?

Duclos flays the policy on two basic grounds. First, because it "deforms in a radical way the meaning of the Teheran declaration." What Brow-der's line did, he says, was to "transform the Teheran declaration, which is a document of a diplomatic character, into a political platform of class peace in the United States in the postwar period." The second charge is that the line was "a notorious revision of Marxism on the part of Browder and his supporters," expressing itself in the doctrine of "the suppression of the class struggle in the postwar period and the establishment of harmony between labor and capital."

It will be clear to anyone who has read the long Duclos document—"sharply expressed," as Browder himself puts it—that this is not simply another doctrinal raft launched on the tempestuous Communist sea. It is a statement of American Communist failure, an expression of the wide gap between the outlook of the European Communists and that of the Americans, a manifesto of the new prestige of European Communist movements, a sharp posing of the issue of the class struggle in a world still moving in the twilight between capitalist and socialist power structures, and an augury of a coming change in the orientation of American Communists.

Let me consider each of these in sequence. Browder warns his followers in the foreword to Duclos's article: "Some will shout that it marks the disintegration of the Communists, others that it is the re-emergence of the Communist International." The fact is that both accusations have a core of truth in them. "Disintegration" is certainly too strong a word, but it is hard to challenge the use of "failure." What is the failure of the American Communists? Duclos mentions some figures that were published in the *Daily Worker* itself, showing that between February and July, 1944, when the Communist party was dissolved and reorganized in the Communist Political Association, membership was cut from eighty thousand to forty-five thousand. One may hazard that this was only partially due to the disappointment that many Communists felt at being asked to embrace the House of Morgan with a fraternal ardor. It was at least partially due also to the unwillingness of many to assume again the burdens and contumely of Communist membership once they had been given a chance to get out from under without disgrace or betrayal. "They must conquer or die who have no retreat," a poet once wrote. But in this case a retreat was offered, and both death and conquest were removed as alternatives.

Yet the big fact remains clear to any outside observer that at the most favorable time in world history the American Communists were losing rather than gaining ground. This was the moment of the great test of Russian socialism: the greatest prestige of Russians arms, the most dynamic sweep of socialist ideas over Europe. Yet this was also the moment that Browder and his ruling party group chose for retreating from the socialist positions and abandoning labor militancy. They may have purchased thereby the good will of a few industrialists and the local co-operation of a few politicians. But if they hoped to build a mass movement, their efforts were a fiasco. They lost the militant elements without winning over any moderate elements. They paid a price without getting anything in return. Nor is it easy to see how they could have won the moderates. For always it was clear that, whatever the policy they adopted, there was a basic insincerity and unscrupulousness behind it. These leaders who long ago had lost their moral authority now had stripped themselves of their passion as well.

I know that much of this is a matter of intramural interest for Communists, in which people like myself have no concern. The Communists may adopt whatever line they wish, abandon it, readopt it, play hide-and-go-seek with it. But even the outsider has a stake in these matters in so far as they affect the material with which a genuine American movement for a socialized democratic society must work. Even without numbers, the Communists, because of their organization, have influence—especially in the trade-unions. Their lightning-like shifts in line bewilder men who might otherwise have had clarity. Their class-harmony pap weakens the stomach that men might otherwise have had for fighting the people's battles. Their obvious sailing by the polestar of Russian foreign policy, and that alone, makes things terribly difficult for those who care deeply about Russian-American friendship, yet who insist on being independent of Russian policy. Their moral cynicism corrupts the whole atmosphere within which each new generation of American youth grows up.

The most heartening thing about the Duclos statement is the proof it offers of the continuing militancy of the European resistance movements. Browder says in his foreword that the Duclos attack "reflects the general trend of opinion of European Marxists in relation to America." That is important. It may mean that the brief flirtation of the French Communists with the policy of supporting De Gaulle at any cost is now over, that class-peace harmonies were as much of an anodyne in France as in America. The Duclos statement must therefore be regarded as an apologia for the temporary French Communist "error" almost as much as an attack on the major American Communist "error."

This pushes the question further, beyond the role of Europe's labor and resistance movements to the role of Russia. The obvious interpretation of the new move is that the Russians may intend it as a warning that they can always use again the weapon of internal class struggle and world revolution. Browder himself suggests this in a tone of mockery and repudiation. I am not interested in his histrionics. The fact is that American Communist policy has all along been shaped by the interests of Russian foreign policy. Even without direct instructions from a Comintern, when you take a group as accustomed to command as the Communists have been, it is natural for them to watch every straw in the winds of Russian doctrine and policy. Since Roosevelt's death, the relations between the Russian and American Governments have suffered a sharp worsening. There has been reckless talk among our power-groups of war with Russia. What more natural than for the Russians—and the French Communists as well—to hint that if it comes to a showdown they can always make a delicately poised capitalist structure reckon with the internal forces of class struggle?

So much for Communist perspectives, European perspectives, Russian perspectives. How about American democratic perspectives? Speaking in terms of a radical democratic creed, I shall be as little influenced by the newly emerging Communist policy as I was by the old one of last year, or as I shall be by the super-new one of five years from now. Last year's Candide policy of acting as if all were for the best in the best of all possible capitalist worlds seemed silly. If the new policy means indiscriminate attacks on the Truman Administration, on Great Britain, and on all liberals and conservatives, it will be just as silly.

The American future lies in the militant democratic energies of its labor and progressive groups, allied with similar energies throughout the world. America cannot establish economic justice and abundance overnight, but we must not flinch from the tasks of the transition period. The American promise lies in waging a two-front struggle. One is the home struggle for an adequately planned economy that leaves the traditional freedoms intact and creates new ones as well. The other is the struggle to build a structure of world peace and order, within which all peoples can shape their destiny.

MAY 28, 1945

Communists, Liberals, and the Unions

1.

THE CENTRAL PROBLEM of the next decade for liberals will be that of building a trade-union and political progressive movement which is clearly non-Communist but does not spend its best energies in Communist-hunting.

The CIO Convention at Atlantic City [1] had a chance to face up to that

[1] November, 1946.

task. Philip Murray and the other CIO leaders have of necessity gone at it warily. They "resent and reject"—so the convention declaration says— "efforts of the Communist party and other political parties and their adherents to interfere in the affairs of the CIO." Note that while this is more strongly worded than any similar CIO declaration since 1940, it hits only at interference from the outside, not at Communist activity from the inside. Note also that three of the six CIO leaders who drafted it—Gold, Quill, and Flaxer—have generally been reckoned as Left-Wingers, and Gold is a recognized Communist party member. Note finally that while the resolution solves nothing, anything more drastic might well have split the CIO wide open exactly at the time when it needs most to be united. The CIO doctors have applied a poultice and not a remedy—mainly, I think, because the remedy must be sought and applied outside of a convention.

To speak of a remedy means there is a disease. I think there is. Let me put it this way: the Communists have only a handful of adherents in the United States, mainly because Communist solutions and Communist tactics are alien even to the native radical tradition in America. Yet because of their cohesiveness, their energy, and their militancy, the Communists and their sympathizers have won an influential, if minority, place in the CIO, and dominate some of the unions. They do not represent the thinking of the large majority of the workers, yet they make the whole CIO— and even the whole labor movement—vulnerable to unscrupulous attacks on the "Red" issue. America is still a middle-class country, and its basic thinking is middle-class thinking. As long as the remedy is not found, American trade-unions will take a beating in the public-opinion battle in strikes, and American progressives will take a beating in elections.

This is not to say that Communism is a big danger in America today, whether in the trade-unions or outside. It is not. Philip Murray was right in his speech when he said that a far greater threat than Communism is "the boom-or-bust profiteering of the exploiters." And, he might have added, the potential fascism that the exploiters will not flinch from if they find their power slipping. This is to put the matter in its true perspective.

Yet one big reason why the new Congress majority may, in Murray's phrase, try to "put a cross on the back of labor" is that the Republicans were able to win the 1946 elections largely on the basis of a Red scare. The CIO will fight its trade-union battles with one hand tied behind its back so long as it has not resolved its internal problems. The Communists in the trade-unions—like the Old Man of the Sea in the Sindbad tale—are not the prime danger, but they are the prime burden, deterrent, and nuisance.

I have said that a CIO convention cannot find the remedy. Consider the proposals that have been made. There has been talk of a "purge"—a phrase perilously reminiscent of the Russian *chistka*, or party purge. But at the most only a few nonelected staff-members could be purged, and even they would be non-Communists, although sympathetic to Communist policies. Once you start a purge for political opinions—and a purge from on top—you are on the road to the direst ideological reign of terror.

The long-range remedy lies inside the individual unions. As long as Philip Murray, in the top leadership, finds himself heading a group of unions so balanced between Left-Wingers and Right-Wingers that he must walk a tightrope, then walk a tightrope he must. The way to give him greater decisiveness is to give him greater backing.

And no way to do that in trade-unions has ever been invented which can by-pass the need for fighting the Communists day after day on specific issues, and winning away from them the vast trade-union membership which is non-Communist but in many cases has at present no other militant leadership to turn to. The fight will be hard because the Communists form, in Harold Laski's phrase, a "secret battalion." But you cannot purge a union of the leaders whom the men have elected. You can only move into the vacuum and offer a rival militant non-Communist leadership. You cannot purge them by edict. But the trade-union members can vote them out of power in democratic union elections.

This is a policy that goes beyond harmless convention statements. It is part of the blood and tissue of trade-union democracy.

2.

WE HAVE COME to the stage in American history when a trade-union movement is more than a technical instrument for wage-and-hour bargaining. It is a social and political whole—which means that it is also a base for political education and action. The kind of political education and action it will undertake will be largely determined by the internal controls within the unions. Hence the CIO need for facing the problem of "interference" by the Communists and other political parties which I have discussed above.

Only when you recognize how crucial the trade-unions are in any progressive political movement in America do you come to grips with the real problem. Since as far back as Andrew Jackson's time the newly emerging working class has been the crux of any American progressive democracy.

That was true again in Lincoln's campaigns, and again in Bryan's. It was true in Wilson's, and it was supremely true in Franklin Roosevelt's. In every one of these movements the core of progressive strength has been located in the alliance between the labor groups and the liberal middle-class (including farmers) groups.

That is still true of American politics. In the recent Congressional elections the alliance was broken for the first time since 1932, and there was a break also internally within the labor movement and among the independent liberals. That break came for a number of reasons. But basically it came because the labor-liberal coalition was leaderless; because it had not worked out a dramatic and recognizable program of its own; and finally—and mainly—because the Republicans succeeded in labeling the labor part of the coalition as "Communist."

The nation is probably slated for a period of Republican domination until the next major depression. Even when that depression comes, the question whether we shall have another New Deal depends upon how cohesively the labor-liberal coalition can be rebuilt. Merely to wait for it solves nothing. We need to rethink the whole basis of progressive political action. If we fail in doing that, the next major depression may lead to a fascist era rather than to another New Deal.

I suggest we can learn something from the experience of Britain, where a Labor Government has come into power with the support of the liberal middle class. The British have had a unified trade-union movement. We have not had it for a decade, and it may take another decade before we get it again. The unity of British trade-unions has not been prevented by the existence of Communist-led unions. But the militant work of the non-Communist Left in Britain has kept the Communist union strength more closely proportionate to Communist membership and consequently held it to a subordinate place in the larger movement.

The British have also found a way of linking the economic strength of their trade-unions with the political strength of the Labor party. The British scheme of trade-union affiliation with the Labor party is not perfect; the Canadian Commonwealth Federation with its more decentralized plan has, I think, a better scheme. But both of them point the way, and both need to be studied here.

The British allow Communists to hold whatever posts they have legitimately won in the trade-unions, but restrict their political activities to their own Communist party. This is, I think, what Philip Murray and other CIO leaders are aiming at now. The trouble is that they put it in terms of "resenting and rejecting" political interference in the CIO. Obviously that is impossible. It ignores the fact that any trade-union movement these days has immense political importance, and to keep political activity out of it is like trying to discourage drinking at a bar. The British solution has been to create a Labor party whose local units have the right to demand a single political allegiance from their members, and to oust anyone who introduces a double political allegiance. Until the American trade-union movement has clearly found its place in politics, it cannot face up to this problem.

This brings us to the most important lesson of the British experience. By creating their own type of native labor progressivism in the Labor party, the British have offered the workers a practical alternative to the militancy of the Communists. We in America had such an alternative as long as the New Deal lasted, and had it lasted longer the problem of competing with the Communists for trade-union leadership would have ceased to be a problem. It is a problem today because the workable alternative no longer exists within the Democratic party.

Can it be re-created? Or can we afford to withdraw while we build another party, meanwhile (perhaps for a decade or even longer) leaving the field to a battle between the Republican-Democratic reactionaries and the Communists? My own answer is that we must continue in a coalition with the Democrats while we try to build—inside the trade-unions especially—a new base for a new non-Communist labor-liberal party.

3.

MY TWO PIECES on trade-union and progressive strategy have roused the *Daily Worker* to its characteristically laborious irony, invective, and argument.

For the irony let me cite the titles of the two-article attack by Milton Howard, the associate editor of the *Daily Worker*: "Politics and Bargain Basements," and "Dr. Lerner's Painless Extraction." For the invective: it seems I am a "Red-baiter," "witch-hunter," perpetrator of "the cruelest and most deceitful of frauds"; it seems that my philosophy is "the mirror image of the tory viewpoint," besides being "infantile logic-chopping"; it seems that I am a "slanderer" and "calumniator"; it seems that I "repeat the basic falsehoods of the tories," and that all I could fall back on in a debate with the Communists is "the familiar tripe manufactured by the tories, the fascists, for use against democracy itself."

But I leave these rather mild specimens of Communist rhetorical art and stylistic grace. What is more important is the reasoning that leads to them. This is not the first time the *Daily Worker* has attacked me; nor—if I understand the Communists at all—will it be the last. I have no intention of engaging in a running debate with a group that is so marginal to American life and thought as the Communists. But I welcome this chance —which the *Daily Worker* attack gives me—to restate my position on the Communists and on progressive strategy, sharpen the issues, assess again the high stakes involved in building a genuinely free and liberal movement in the American trade-unions and in American politics. What are the main *Daily Worker* arguments against my position?

The first one is the charge that I accept "the reactionary philosophy that democracy does not apply to Communists." This is unusually willful distortion of what I wrote. I called for "a trade-union and political progressive movement which is clearly non-Communist but does not spend its best energies in Communist-hunting."

Let me make this clear again beyond the possibility of distortion. I believe in the American tradition of civil liberties—the tradition the Communists cannot believe in because it is alien to their whole conception and technique. Not for the sake of the Communists, but for the sake of America, I stand ready to defend their civil rights: whether it is their right to exist as an avowed political party, or their right to keep their jobs and to belong to trade-unions without persecution because of political opinion, or their right to hold offices in the trade-unions if they are chosen in democratic elections.

But to defend the civil rights of Communists does not mean to refrain from opposing them for their philosophy and attacking them for their tactics where they deserve attack. When they seek to infiltrate political parties and movements not their own, we have the right to oppose and expose them. I know the Communists have for years sought to build up the impression that their right to civil liberties gives them immunity from criticism and opposition by liberals. It is time to break that false logic once and for all—break it in the minds of Communists and in the minds of liberals.

Let me again say that I do not intend to divert my energies into Communist-hunting. I believe that the great enemy of American democracy is boom-and-bust reaction and its potential fascist sequel—an enemy with a far greater hold on the American mind than the Communists have. But that enemy can be fought effectively only by a liberal-labor coalition which has replaced Communist influence by a militant non-Communist leadership.

The second *Daily Worker* argument is that I want the American trade-union and liberal movement to be non-Communist in order to "make it-self respectable in the eyes of its enemies." This again is a characteristic distortion. It is not the enemies of democracy whom we want to win over to a liberal program, but its friends; not the bigots and fanatics whose minds are closed, but the large labor and middle classes whose minds are still open. The problem is that of giving these groups a genuine liberal non-Communist leadership and direction.

This is a question not of form but of substance, not of seeming but of being. I want people to be what they are, and not something else. I want Communists to be what they are—Communists—and not to masquerade as "progressives." I want them to stay inside the Communist party, and let the liberals build their own political organizations. I have no hope of converting either reactionaries or Communists to liberalism. But I do think that the large majority of Americans are potential recruits for a genuine liberal movement that will go on with the work of the New Deal. We can win the struggle against reaction only when we can convince this majority that their liberal movement has its own native roots, its own ideas, its own independence; that when they organize for a fight, it is for their own stakes; and that when they win the fight, it is their own victory.

I come now to the final *Daily Worker* argument. "In the end," says the *Daily Worker*, "Mr. Lerner would have to join with the Communists against the common enemy, or go over to the reactionary enemy. History knows no other choices." This is again a characteristic Communist argu-ment, and it poses a thoroughly false choice. I suppose that "in the end" means in a fascist America. The whole point is that the liberals don't in-tend the American nation to be brought to that pass. And brought to it we most certainly will be if the liberals swallow the Communist idea that we have no choice except the choice between an uncritical alliance with the Communists and the deathly embrace of fascism.

No, there is another choice for liberals. It is the choice of a democracy which does away with private corporate monopolies but does not put in their place the monopoly of a single Communist party; a democracy which saves the ordinary American from the pathos of being a victim of the ups and downs of planless economy, but which saves him also from the pathos of being the victim of a police state. It is the choice of a democ-racy which is both economic and political. We have not gone far enough or fast enough. But the job of finishing the unfinished business of democ-racy must be done by passionate believers in the democratic credo and in the potentials of American life.

"How," asks the *Daily Worker*, referring to the fight I propose for de-mocracy on the floor of every trade-union meeting, "how could Mr.

Lerner be so sure that the opinion of the membership would support him and not the Communists?" "Sure" is an overstrong word. But we have the right to expect ultimate victory—because of everything we know about how Americans think within the framework of their history and their institutions, because of everything we know about their proud refusal to wear the shackles of any single-party system. The real failure would be our failure to offer them, in strengthened form, the kind of militant progressive leadership America has produced from Andrew Jackson to Franklin D. Roosevelt.

This serves as a clue to the question of why the *Daily Worker* so bitterly and so consistently attacks the liberals. It is not because we are "tories," "Red-baiters," "witch-hunters." The fact is that the *Daily Worker* fears us exactly because we are *not* tories and *not* Red-baiters; exactly because we do *not* believe in diverting our energies into the sterile and unsavory channels of obsessive anti-Communism. They fear us even more than they fear the tories and the Red-baiters. For they know that what we are working to create is a free and liberal non-Communist movement, close to the mainstream of the American progressive tradition, with a philosophy that can attract the overwhelming number of decent ordinary Americans. Such a movement would most decidedly leave the Communists out in the cold, with only their few immediate partisans for company, and only their epithets for warmth.

NOV. 19–20, 25, 1946

FDR: The People Remember

A FEW DAYS AGO, when it had become clear that the whole nation would observe the first anniversary of FDR's death, the spearhead paper of the group whose hate for him had been most festering—the New York *Daily News*—published a griping editorial. Why, it asked, should Americans be observing both Roosevelt's birthday and his death-day? Even for Washington and Lincoln one observance day was enough. Why should this fellow rate two?

The answer is, of course, that the people remember in their own way. Their remembrance does not take the shape of the *Daily News*'s politics or anyone else's. A year after FDR's death the grief is still fresh in their hearts, their sense of emptiness is great. His political enemies cannot detract from the people's remembrance, nor can political friends add to it. As by some surging tropism, deeper than thought, the people are drawn to the man who for so long was the symbol of American strength and American humanity.

In the end, that is all history is: the collective memory of people who have endured great things together, have fashioned great things. Many large generalizations have been made about Roosevelt's qualities: his flexibility of tactic combined with his long-range planning of goals; his consummate political generalship; his dramatic flair; his sense of history; his adroitness in finding the broad common ground for a coalition of groups or of nations. All these are true, and always we must come back to them. But today they are stilted things—today when the occasion renews our sharp sense of a personal loss.

When soldiers gather to renew old times and memories, they remember the one who fell after leading them through the most dangerous battles. Their minds go back to the trials and the triumphs they shared. So with the American people when they think back to the man who led them through the greatest crisis of their history. . . .

They remember the collapse of an economy in 1929, the pathetic inaction of the men who boasted themselves the leaders of America, the Hoovervilles, the bread lines, the farmers' riots, the bonus march, the battle of Anacostia Flats, the blank and fearful despair of the world's greatest nation.

They remember the crippled man to whom they then turned for leadership, the man all the days of whose years up to then seem now to have been a preparation for that crisis. They remember his words: "The only thing we have to fear is fear itself," the succession of crisis measures —bank deposit guarantee, farm bill, WPA, NRA—that came with the staccato authority of communiqués from a battlefield. They remember the hope that began surging back into their hearts, the sense that whatever mistakes might be made, America had found its greatness again.

They remember how the devastation was slowly repaired . . . the effort to restore strength to the corroded land and lives of sharecroppers, the legislation to give workers the measure of unity and protection without which collective bargaining is a farce, the controls over stock speculation and security issues, the building of power dams that transformed the life of whole valleys.

They remember the buoyant voice as it talked to them over the radio about their common problems, the smiling face of the man who rode among them on his campaign trips, and his checking-up tours when he wanted to learn what Americans were thinking. They remember the charges and countercharges, the hatred and love he inspired, the enemies he made and fought, the blunders, the improvisations—but always the sense that "this generation of Americans has a rendezvous with destiny."

They remember the looming shadow of fascist power; the man who recognized the enemy for what it was, and sought against heartbreaking odds to educate a whole people out of their dream of peace and security to an awareness of danger. They remember the preliminary rumblings of war, the destroyers and materials that were sent, the anxiety to see whether there would be any allies left to join. They remember the news of Pearl Harbor, the nation that overnight found itself knit together, the grave man who kept vigil in the White House.

They remember the civilian who was their Commander-in-Chief and picked the generals who held in their hands the destinies of all the young Americans. They remember the globe-circling missions of an increasingly tired man. They remember the day when the Continental wall was breached, and we knew victory would be ours. They remember the gray-looking man with a cape at Yalta. They remember the spring day when the news came that he would no longer be with them to lead their victories and shoulder part of their burdens. . . .

These are not utilitarian memories. We cannot use them to clothe the nakedness of our present discontents. But just as refugees in their wanderings will clutch some keepsake that recalls a more secure time, so the American people in their dark night cherish these fragments of a memory.

APRIL 12, 1946

The Waste of History

I WONDER whether the sweating Democratic delegates at Philadelphia have a book, or whether they will let me recommend one for those long dreary stretches while the orators are droning on. It is by Dixon Wecter; it is called *The Age of the Great Depression.*

Wecter has written a social analysis of America during the history-laden decade of the 1930s, when the Democrats were united, and when the President of the United States was a fighting tribune of the people. It was the period when the New Dealer was still the new type of American man and not (like a man named Douglas) one of the few survivors of an almost extinct species, to be hunted for avidly in the fastnesses of the Pacific Northwest by the White House boys hoping to offer him up as a Vice-Presidential sacrifice.[1]

Perhaps the delegates will be repelled by chapter-headings like "New Design for Living," "Change of Command," "Unions on the March," "Old Sections and New Regions," "Youth in Search of a Chance," "Age in Quest of Security," and—most disquieting of all—"Reading, Writing and Revolution." But maybe I can sell them the book as escape-reading—escape from the miasmic doldrums of an unheroic convention, back into the heroic swashbuckling age when Democrat, New Deal, and dynamism were synonymous terms.

The real hero of the book is not FDR. It is the American people during one of those decades, rare even in a democracy, when the people take the direction of things into their own hands.

That was the outstanding fact of the 1930s. Wecter is, I think, wrong in calling it *The Age of the Great Depression*—even more wrong than Milton Crane was in calling the excellent compilation he edited some months back *The Roosevelt Era*. For the depression was the negative phase of the era, just as FDR's personality and élan were the leadership phase. They were parts of something bigger.

The depression, brought on by the reckless forces of capitalist anarchy and myopic faith in the planless decisions of Big Business, left the ruling group incapable any longer of ruling. The people took over—the hungry people, the bonus-marching veterans, the unemployed and insecure, the workers who organized a new vertical brand of industry-wide unions, the farmers who were sick of "farm relief" and wanted markets for their crops and crop-control to fit the market, the "Okies" and "Arkies" on their trek from the Dust Bowl, the scientists who wanted their science used for the strategy of abundance, the youngsters who didn't want to be cast on the dump-heap unused—whose passion was that they "wanted to be wanted."

The New Deal was an idea and a movement. Roosevelt, who was a reader of Mark Twain, remembered the sentence in *A Connecticut Yankee* saying that when six men out of a thousand crack the whip over their fellows' backs, "it seemed to me that what the 994 other dupes needed was a new deal." As an idea, the New Deal meant recapturing the democratic revolutionary tradition of America. As a movement, the New Deal was a fighting coalition of the productive groups in America, headed toward a socialized community, using the techniques of democratic planning.

[1] The reference is to the efforts of President Truman's advisers to persuade Justice William O. Douglas to run on the Truman ticket as Vice-President.

Most of the New Deal agencies are gone, along with the New Deal administrators and idea-men. The core gains will go on—techniques like the Tennessee Valley Authority and the Securities and Exchange Commission, the basic idea of social security benefits, the wage-and-hour controls, the control of giant power, the concept of regions as administrative units, the idea that workers in their unions must have a hand in shaping their destiny instead of being commodities on a labor market.

But these are residues from the past, not new creations. The creative capacity itself seems to have gone out of American political life. The Republicans have only a passion for power. The Democrats don't seem to have even that. The Progressives, who do have vitality, have cut themselves off from American life by embracing a political parochialism.

What strikes me hardest about all this is the terrible waste of history it involves. We had a creative decade, followed by a decade of war and postwar tensions. Now we are in for the dry season. Most of the energies that Wecter so well describes in his book were recklessly flung away in the trivial Truman years, and what remains of them will be destroyed in the deadly Dewey years.[2]

The worst part of it is that most liberals seem to feel hopeless unless a new Great Depression comes. Can it be true that the greatness of the American people can be evoked only in adversity, and that liberalism is a plant that flowers only among the ruins?

That is not my reading of the moral of the New Deal era. What I see is different. I see that for a gleaming interval American life had direction, that it was moving away from the economic and social jungle: that it was becoming a genuine *society*. What we did once we can resume. The tragedy lies in the waste of our experience, in the waiting while all the old blunders are committed over again.

JULY 13, 1948

A Wreath for Harry Hopkins

A wit and philosopher once defined democratic government as "just one damned crisis after another." No one knew this truth better or embodied it more completely in his public life than Harry Hopkins. History will set

[2] The election results four months later, in Nov., 1948, proved how poor a prophet I was.

him down primarily as Franklin Roosevelt's confidant and emissary, the man who was FDR's second personality. But if they are wise, the historians will not be content to give him a footnote as the shadow of a great man. They will remember that one of the things linking Roosevelt and Hopkins so closely was that each, in his own way, knew life as a succession of crises. That is what made it possible for them as a team to play so historic a part in the life-and-death struggles of democracy.

It is an easy thing, oh, so easy, to pillory a man because he belongs to a President's "kitchen Cabinet" and lives in the White House and goes and comes through the back door. Harry Hopkins occupied that place, and for years he suffered a martyrdom for it. When the press wolves lusted for their daily banquet of political blood, here was a ready victim. When the mercenaries of economic power, to earn their money, needed a butt for their ignorance and malevolence, here was one ready made.

For was he not the man of the shadows who slipped in and out of the President's room? Was he not the captain of the janissaries, the "Rasputin of the New Deal"? Was he not the center of palace intrigues, the man who made and broke careers, and carried policies through or blasted them? And was he not (oh, most scurrilous crime of all!) a social-worker and do-gooder who had dared invade the portals of the temple that in previous administrations had been the sacred monopoly of professional politicians and bankers?

It is part of the weakness of our governmental system that we pick a man for President, and then hand over to him the biggest single executive and administrative job in the world, without providing him with an adequate and recognized public staff to perform that job. Every President has a kitchen Cabinet; and when a President has a tough campaign mapped out for fighting the great privileged interests of the nation—as Andrew Jackson did, and Woodrow Wilson—he has a special need for men who are committed to him and not to privilege. Harry Hopkins was one of those men, one of the defamed "brain-trusters." For all my hatred of political secrecy, I would give a good deal to have men like Hopkins still filling the inevitable confidential posts, instead of the sort of men who have taken his place under President Truman.

But why—the question keeps recurring—why did this fellow last so long? I think the answer must be sought not in the political structure of the Government but in the nature of the human heart. We are apt to forget that the American Presidency, for all its democratic trappings, is a position of immense power; and that every man in power, for all the public fanfare and handshaking and hysteria that surround him, is essentially a lonely man. Put a man into the Presidency, and you cut him off from being a normal man, with normal friendships and amusements. A great democracy, like the gods of Carthage, must have its human victims. And when you have a man with as much love of life as Roosevelt had, and cut him off, and build a wall of hostility around him, he must find friendship or die.

Franklin Roosevelt found Harry Hopkins. The greatness and resoluteness were Roosevelt's; but because Hopkins offered the integrity of a complete political and personal partnership, the qualities of greatness in Roosevelt could be fully evoked. Hopkins was Roosevelt's angle of refraction. This son of a landed aristocrat and this son of a harness-maker were able, in the greatest crisis of our national life, to make democratic history together.

Why did they hit it off? Ever since Hopkins first came to New York from Iowa and became a settlement-worker, he dreamt of a larger arena for his talents. He found that arena in Roosevelt's power as Governor and then as President. He had an immense interest in ideas and personalities—and Roosevelt liked to explore both, especially late at night, after the visitors had gone and the business had been dispatched. He had political dexterity, and Roosevelt—who had that quality to the full—sorely needed men around him who also had it. He was without personal ambition,[1] a man who not only was willing to be anonymous and let others take the credit, but preferred it, and that was another reason why he survived all the factional wars.

But I have left the big link for the last. The two men supplemented each other beautifully. Hopkins was a social-worker with a deeply ingrained sense of the politically possible. Roosevelt was a master-politician with a deeply ingrained sense of social welfare. That was why they made a historic partnership of it.

Hopkins's career, along with Roosevelt's, fell into two parts. The first was the New Deal, the second was the fashioning of the great war coalition. In the first period—the New Deal—Hopkins was the whipping-boy of the economic reactionaries: and necessarily, for the area in which he operated best was in the public expenditures necessary to keep a crisis capitalism from going wholly to pieces. In the second period—the war—he was something of a whipping-boy for the liberals; and again necessarily, for in his single-minded concentration on the war itself, he was willing to help Roosevelt scrap the New Deal agencies and measures and ideas.

[1] Robert E. Sherwood reveals, in his *Roosevelt and Hopkins* (1948), that Hopkins had hopes for the Presidency in 1940, and that Roosevelt was confident he could swing it, and also that his sickness would not stand in the way. This is the only respect in which I would want to correct my basic analysis of the relationship of the two men in the light of Sherwood's great book.

He had his weaknesses. How could any man with his background fail to have, through the first period, a sense of great power from the vast expenditures for which he was responsible? And in the second period, he tended—being a social-worker—to lean too far backward, to show that even a social-worker could be as tough and ruthless as the movers and shakers with whom he associated.

He had his weaknesses, yes. But he served his country and world democracy well. He belongs with perhaps a half-dozen men of his time who fought the crisis battles of democracy.

For almost a decade before he died, he had been a man whose every year was snatched from death. But as long as FDR was alive, and as long as there was still the war to be fought, he managed miraculously to live on. For there was in him the demonic will to live, not to break the partnership. When Roosevelt died, the partnership was broken, and the will ebbed away. The man who died yesterday had really died nine months ago, and his heart and will were buried at Hyde Park.

JAN. 30, 1946

Ike

A MAN NAMED Dwight D. Eisenhower has become a civilian and a resident of our city, and will soon start on his job as president of Columbia University. I know that all New Yorkers will welcome Ike to the rather large fellowship of New Yorkers. They will also watch eagerly to see what happens when the winds of the Presidential campaign blow even more intensely than they do now.

This talk of the Presidency is part of America's tribute to Eisenhower. In the myths and fairy stories a man who has performed valorous deeds is rewarded by being made king. The Americans act much the same way when they take a man to their heart, except that they want to make him President.[1] I suspect that even if Eisenhower does not accept the nomination this year, he will be talked about again in 1952. It is not only because

[1] This was written between the two 1948 booms for Eisenhower as President—the Republican boom in the winter and the Democratic boom in the summer. Eisenhower ended each with a statement refusing to be a candidate.

of his valorous deeds. It is because of the kind of man he seems to be—his traits of personality and ways of doing and saying things which for the most part awaken the right responses in Americans. The psychologist Jung has a theory that some women have an *anima* or soul-image, as he puts it, which stirs most men because it recalls the condensed sexual experience of the race. Perhaps Eisenhower's *persona* stirs some kind of national memory in us, and comes close to the image we have built up of the American. That is what I have meant in writing of Eisenhower's "political sex appeal."

There is a timely new book, *Eisenhower Speaks, A Selection of his Speeches and Messages*, edited by Rudolph L. Treuenfels (Farrar, Straus). Don't start it with any false hopes that it will solve the great Eisenhower enigma, or that it will give you the map of his political and social beliefs. It does no such thing, and the publishers should stand in the corner for hinting on the jacket that in the speeches and reports in this book Eisenhower has "expressed himself on many vital issues." They are vital enough, but we don't learn very much from them about the things we are anxious to know: how Eisenhower stands on subjects like Jim Crow, civil rights, Russia and the chances of a meeting of minds with her, west-European socialism, trade-unions and their struggle in our own country, housing and health legislation, business controls and economic planning.

The reason we don't learn much is a simple reason. Eisenhower has been a general, and a good general doesn't talk out of turn. He doesn't talk about the issues I have listed above because they don't come within his province. Actually Eisenhower, as a returning national hero, has spread himself more than most generals. This book, covering the three years of his utterances since his Victory Order of the Day on May 8, 1945, includes a toast to Marshal Zhukov and a press-conference statement at Moscow, a statement on UNRRA aid, a speech to disabled veterans, a speech to the CIO convention and one to the business moguls assembled at the Economic Club on the same day, a speech for the United Jewish Appeal and one for the Daughters of the American Revolution, Congressional testimony on the bill to arm the Latin-American governments, several speeches on education, the famous letter withdrawing from the Republican presidential race, and the long final report as Chief of Staff.

Eisenhower's speeches and statements are tied together by a single theme. It is not how we shall build a liberal America, or a conservative one, or what we shall do to be saved. It is, quite simply, *how we can unify our America to pursue common purposes in peace as in war*. When you approach the book from this angle, not asking questions which it cannot answer but letting Eisenhower speak on the topics that have come his way, he reveals not the political hopeful or the reluctant candidate but the lineaments of a man. What you get is the quality of his mind and the character of his leadership.

The one big thing he stresses is national unity and the sense of *together-ness*. The amazing fact about Eisenhower is that when he says these things they don't sound either stale or platitudinous. His sense of inner convic-tion gives them freshness. When he was in command of the European theater he always expected and exacted the subordination of the part to the whole. This applied inside the American armed forces, and it also applied as between the Americans and the French and the British and the others. It still applies to his thinking on world affairs. "I am a zealot in the cause of democracy," he told the members of the Economic Club, "and I believe that democracy—if we have to define it in one word—must be grasped in the word 'co-operation.' " And in another speech he defines democracy as "the volunteer method of solving vital common problems, no matter what the cost or how great the individual sacrifice."

He must be the most literate of our great army commanders, and the one most interested in general ideas. He cares about the structure and the finish of a sentence. No matter what the occasion, he manages to say something at once graceful and simple about it—as witness the opening sentence of his speech on the City Hall steps when the New Yorkers gave him their rousing welcome. "New York," he warned, "simply can-not do this to a Kansas farmer boy and keep its reputation for sophistica-tion." But always, beneath the banter, we get the sense of a mind work-ing away at the central problem of our time: How can we apply the best elements of our democratic thinking to the problems of power in a world of power?

The answers given are often those of a military man: be strong; prepare; train your young men; don't stand off from the world; be ready, if need be, to make the final test of your principles in war. But for Eisenhower these routine military attitudes are never the end, always only the beginning. He reaches beyond them as another soldier whom he quotes with approval —Justice Oliver Wendell Holmes—reached beyond them, to human values so basic that they wipe out the differences between soldier and civilian. When he says at a university dinner: "Why doesn't the presi-dent of every great university throughout the world teach his people to put the people of my profession permanently out of a job?", you feel the conviction by which he was himself moved to become a university presi-dent and put the professional soldiers permanently out of jobs.

I differ with Eisenhower on some important issues, Jim Crow in the armed services being the one that bothers me most. But, Presidency or no Presidency, I would trust him in whatever post he might occupy. For he has the restless mind, the capacity for self-criticism, the buoyant vitality, and the integrity which make a great leader. Given these, even big mistakes can be remedied. Without them, even small mistakes are a canker that corrupts everything.

I have been reading about some new doctrines that are cropping up. In Latin America a colonel called Perón offers the workers a new brand of thinking based on his own political potency plus strong-arm squads. In France a man named de Gaulle (also an ex-general) talks mystically of the French nation, and his admirers in France and America are enraptured by what they call his "decisiveness" and his steel will which can break any opposition.

It is in the light of this that one turns with relief to a modern American who can be strong without being a bully and adroit without being a hypocrite, who has as passionate a belief in a united democratic nation as de Gaulle or Perón has in an authoritarian one, and who knows that the only thing that is ever "decisive" is what the people have willed. "Even Lincoln," he writes after recounting his qualities as a leader, "could not have achieved success unless these great qualities of his had accurately mirrored similar traits implicit in the great mass of all the people." It is this understanding which makes the quality of leadership.

The almost incredible thing about it is that it should come from a Kansas boy who spent his lifetime in the Army, and who had to endure not only the impact of authority but also the corrosive effect of immense power. It is the fact that America creates this kind of figure which makes us so blasted proud of her.

MAY 4, 1948

Harry S. Truman: A Miniature Portrait

1.

IT IS BY ONE of those wild accidents of history that at the world's greatest crisis we find in the world's biggest job today a man who has said repeatedly that he never wanted the job, that he hates it, and that he would

rather be anywhere than in the White House, where he is.[1] There have
been leaders in the past who have had greatness thrust on them by cir-
cumstance, but never surely one who wore the mantle of great office
so uneasily.

For a time this reluctance and the accompanying humility had a certain attractiveness, especially for the men and the press who for twelve
years had fumed about Roosevelt's "arrogance" and "grand manner."
Now it has outworn its welcome. The Republican strategists, always
shrewd at exploiting a weakness—however blind they may be to the larger
reaches of policy—have exploited this one to the hilt. Wherever you go
the air is thick with stories, jokes, and legendry—some genial and some
vicious—but all having for their common theme the inadequacy for his
office of the insecure and wistful man who would rather be piano-player
than President. In FDR's day the whispered stories made him out to be
a sick dictator, arbitrary to the point of insanity. The whispering campaign
against Truman is less dramatic, but no less dangerous.

What is the truth about Truman as leader, about his ideas and abilities?
It is always said that the clue to them must be sought in Missouri, where
Truman had and still has the roots of his being. It was from Missouri
that I first wrote, in the spring of 1944, my conviction that Truman
would be the Democratic candidate for Vice-President. I have returned
to Missouri three times this year, the last time several weeks ago, and have
talked with politicians, newspapermen, and friends among whom Truman
lived.

It was in Missouri that I came to understand the Truman qualities—
and the defects of those qualities. In the terrible tensions that beset a
man in the American Presidency, in the white light that beats down on
him, in the crucifixions that he must undergo and in how he responds
to them, a President first reveals his essential nature. But the qualities he
shows have been long in the making.

Truman's first quality is personal honesty. This is striking in a man
all of whose political life has been spent within one of the toughest
political machines in the country. If any of the boys in Missouri politics
thought that the happy days of the Harding Gang would now return to
Washington, Truman quickly and sharply disabused them. Truman is,
moreover, a hard worker who gets up early and works late and goes at
the business of being President with business-like dispatch.

He is a loyal friend who gives his friends loyalty and expects it of them

---

[1] This was written after six months of Truman's tenure as President. He later
changed his mood and manner, showed satisfaction with his job, and confidence that he
would get it again.

in return. He nurses a long memory of an affront: to be sure, he wiped all slates clean when he came into the White House, and invited into it men who had not visited it for years; but remember that the people he thus invited had quarreled not with him, but with the previous President. Yet he can pursue an enemy of his friend, as witness the short shrift he gave to Maurice Milligan, the United States District Attorney who had prosecuted Pendergast. He surrounds himself with men (as George Allen, John W. Snyder, and John C. Collet) whom he picks not because they are big men for big jobs, but because he knows them and feels he can count on them. His first approach to a problem is to be friendly and handshaky (as with Congress) and call for co-operation. Truman feels to his bone that the crux of government lies not in social forces, but in personal factors, not in historic and class relations, but in man-to-man contacts.

These are weighty virtues—honesty, hard work, loyalty, a direct personal approach, a sense of detachment from the fighting issues and a feeling that they will somehow yield to manipulation. But they are not adequate for the American Presidency in a crisis period. Loyalty to friends is an excellent quality in a private citizen, and a useful one in a local politician: and we need more of the emphasis of the Middle Ages on honor. But you can't run a government on the loyalty of mediocre advisers. And there is more in the heaven and earth of national policies than is dreamt of in a fraternal club or a political one.

The truth about Truman is that his virtues are those of the middle class in a Middle Western community, and his liberalism has the same social soil. His is a middle-class mentality, which has met its first great crisis now. There is no record of a great personal crisis that deepened and tempered him before he came to the Presidency, as there was in Lincoln's life and in Roosevelt's. There is no lifetime of intellectual discipline, as with Wilson. Moving to the men of our own day, there is no sense of intense social and religious conviction, as with Wallace. There is no story of a self-education to social militancy, as with Justice Black.

I do not say that the material for a very substantial stature is not to be found in Truman. I do say that he has not yet risen to the crisis, and that his social conditionings in the middle-class mind are against him. In a crisis the middle-class mind falls back on personal virtues and personal relations. In a crisis the middle-class mind shows itself more fearful of labor and strikes and labor's political power than of anything else. In a crisis the middle-class mind tries to assume a lofty detachment from the deep issues of the day, and tries to blink the real social cleavages and struggles.

These struggles are not reconcilable by a personal appeal for co-operation. In the end you have to choose your side and fight on it. It is the nature of American Presidential government that the President is the only champion the people as a whole can look to. All the weights of American capitalism and of the Congress and the press are thrown against them. Only a militant popular leader in the Presidency can balance the struggle and give the people as a whole a fighting chance.

In the end, President Truman's basic weakness lies in his failure to understand imaginatively the nature and the greatness of the office he holds.

2.

IN THE PAST two years Truman has changed from a man who seemed to despise himself and loathe his job into a man who seems to trust himself and enjoy his job with at least a little of the jauntiness that FDR used to show. To understand the nature of this change and how deep it has been is to get an insight into the personality and politics of Harry Truman—for the two are pretty well related.

You have to start with Harry Truman's misery. His big problem after Roosevelt's death was how to be as unlike Roosevelt as possible and yet not fall too ludicrously short of Roosevelt's achievement. He botched it. The people, stunned by FDR's death, strained for some sort of father-image to replace him. This scared Harry Truman half out of his wits. He knew that he could not be a political father to anyone—that his role was rather that of the small-town politician who is one of the folks. The only way he knew how to avoid assuming the burden of what was expected of him was to speak of his incapacity and dislike for the job that had been thrust on him. The people took him at his word. The newspapers —in order to give him a good scare and show their power—ridiculed him. To quiet them he started firing his Roosevelt holdovers from office, and those he did not fire left of their own disgust. He also got rid of most of the wartime controls. He had strike trouble. There were rumblings about Yalta and Potsdam and the appeasement of Stalin, that threatened to grow into a thunder of criticism. The Republicans were getting ready to use the tried and true technique of baiting the Democrats as Leftists, and did use it in the 1946 campaign. But they didn't have to use it much, because of the ease with which they won the Congressional elections on the meat-shortage issue.

That was Truman's low point. What saved him politically, gave him a new confidence, and molded what may be called the "Truman line" was the convergence of two events.

The first was that the Russians pushed their diplomatic policy too hard —or at least hard enough for Byrnes, under Churchill's tutelage, to start a "get-tough" policy. It paid off in good dividends, getting an almost complete support from the press, serving as the basis for a "bipartisan" foreign policy which called off the Republican dogs, and—most important —getting Truman out from under the "brave Allies" spirit of Yalta and Potsdam and away from the shadow of FDR. Here finally was the formula Truman had been looking for—how not to be FDR and yet seem to be a strong crisis leader. The Russians supplied him with the chance, and Churchill and Byrnes supplied him with the "no appeasement," "anti-Iron-Curtain," "get-tough" policy. But it was Truman's own political shrewdness which sensed that this was his political meat and the answer to his prayer. And he was ruthless enough to scrap Byrnes when he saw that Byrnes might not be strong enough to hold the bipartisan policy together, and that a military man with General Marshall's prestige could give him the support he needed in Congress and the press almost forever.

Throughout this analysis I have dealt not with the merit or validity of Truman's policies as policies, but with their effect as tactics, both on the people and on Truman himself. The policies themselves seem to me dangerous and self-defeating. The "get-tough" program was America's contribution to the current cold war, and, while Russia made a strong enough contribution of its own, it was the conduct of a struggle for power on the American plane of "high principle" which froze the cold war. The Russians would have compromised, and would still compromise, but by this time the Truman-Marshall policies have grown so rigid that a compromise might break them—and at the same time break Truman politically. The policy has also had the dangerous effect of starting an "anti-Red hysteria" throughout the nation. And—not least—of delivering many of the strategic civilian posts and policies to the generals, and of keeping the national economy on a brink-of-war basis.

If this were all, one could say that Truman had sought to outsmart the Republicans and ended by adopting their policies, that he had beaten them only by joining them. Yet this did not turn out to be wholly true. For, while Truman was burying the corpse of FDR's foreign policies, the Republicans were trying to work out some domestic policies of their own in Congress. Under Taft and Wherry, Halleck and Taber and Knutson, they worked out a labor-prices-taxes program that stank in the nostrils of the people and was a Heaven-sent delight to Harry Truman.

For here was exactly the second element he needed. His foreign policy made him a not-Roosevelt man-of-his-own, but too dangerously close to the Republicans. But what Taft and his cohorts did in Congress saved Truman by giving him exactly the margin of distance from the Republicans that he needed. *To be not-Roosevelt yet not-Republican: that has* turned out to be the Truman formula. From the standpoint of genuine liberalism this combination of a brink-of-war economy and brink-of-war psychology with a liberal program on inflation, taxes, and labor, makes Truman a Mr. Facing-Both-Ways. But from Truman's own standpoint it is a way of integrating himself into the image he wants to present to the people and himself: tough on the Russians, tough on the pro-Russian American Left, tough on the Republicans.

The trouble is that we have seen this sort of combination before, and it can be a dangerous one. The haters of Truman call him a Hitler without a mustache—which is fantastically wrong. He is much closer to a Daladier, and his position is not far from that of the French Radical Socialists before 1940. Yet comparisons with other cultures miss the point. Truman is an American phenomenon, with deep roots in the lower middle-class mind of the Middle West small town. He is the small tradesman who became a politician who became a President. He has the respect for generals that a soldier might have who never got further than a minor officer in the artillery. He has the respect for Wall Street men that a man might have who once failed in a haberdashery shop. His formative thinking was shaped under Wilson and FDR, so that he has a pro-labor outlook; yet underneath this there is the middle-class fear of labor which Truman betrayed in the way he tried to handle the railway strike. He allows men into his Administration who wield too much economic and military power for the nation's safety; yet he also surrounds himself with mediocre minds with whom he feels at home and toward whom he displays a tenacious loyalty.

In short, we have here one of the biggest paradoxes of American life today. For America is a big world empire being run by the standards and the philosophy that come out of a Middle Western small town. It is a small-town mind which is overimpressed by military brass and by business success, and which is fearful of the revolutionary ferment in the world. But it still clings to many of the ideals of the American liberal past.

DEC. 17, 1945; JAN. 28, 1948

Henry Wallace: A Portrait in Symbols

EVERYONE IS SHOUTING either against Henry Wallace or for him. What is needed is an effort to understand him, and to understand the sources of his strength and his conduct. More than any other man in politics today Wallace is more than a politician—or rather, not at all a politician. He is called a demagogue, yet the real demagogy today is in the stirring up of popular passions by the hysterical anti-Russian and the hysterical pro-Russian groups. Whatever Wallace's faults, they are not faults of the demagogue. Nor is he, as he is so often called, a "dreamer." Whatever his virtues, they are not the virtues of the visionary or saint. Henry Wallace, like other men, must be understood as a whole man, in terms of his origins, his growth, his beliefs. The elements in him hang together. The contradictions, of which there are many on the surface, are those which flow from a mind that has been in constant change, groping for a philosophy which will fit America in the twentieth century. But in this change there have been several fixed points that delimit his personality and his mind.

The first is *insurgency*. Wallace comes, as Bryan and La Follette came, out of the Populist tradition of the Middle West. It is the tradition which glorifies rebellion and dissent, and is not fearful of being in a minority. There is an obstinate, hard cast to his jaw. The friends who tried to dissuade him from running on a third party ticket found the same obstinacy in his will. Some of his critics like Dwight Macdonald have charged him with a lack of moral courage. And it is true that Wallace cut some passages out of his famous Madison Square Garden speech when the Left-Wing audience booed his criticisms of Russian policy. Yet whatever be the explanation for this flabbiness, it is hard to accuse Wallace of running away from unpopular causes. The flaw in him is not that of the time-server, or the trimmer, or the opportunist wooer of whatever is orthodox. His fault is rather that he has so identified his image of himself with insurgent and unpopular causes that he cannot stand being thought a traitor to that insurgency.

It is this, I think, which has made him the political ally of the Communists—not any kinship with them, but this sense of conscience on his part, this fear of being thought to be fearful. Actually he is, in his basic thinking, as far from the Communists as was Bryan or La Follette. His thinking is Populist—agin' the trusts, agin' imperialism, agin' Wall Street. He is no intellectual, and his roots are in the rural Middle West rather than in the big Eastern cities. He came of a family which expected you to do your own thinking and stand by your own conscience. He came to the New Deal as an insurgent Republican who wanted to do something about the farmers' income. He remained to out-New Deal the New Dealers. He has shifted the base of his popular support from the farm group to the workers, the intellectuals, and the minority groups. But through all ais changes he has remained the Great Insurgent, unhappy unless he feels a ferment in his mind and unless he is leading his little band of Gideonites.

The second fixed symbol in Wallace's thinking is his work on *hybrid corn*. So much has been said about Wallace's "mysticism" that we are in danger of forgetting that this mystic is also a man of science who has done first-rate work as an agronomist. I do not say this to diminish his importance as a political leader, but to suggest that as an agronomist he approaches politics experimentally, with the practical purpose of improving the breed of political man and social institutions. Such a man could not be caught up in a holy war against Russia, for the simple reason that he sees the Russians as a scientist might—sees them as adapting their political forms to their historical needs. To his view the Russians are not the wicked monsters they are pictured: they are possessed of a portion of the political truth, just as we are possessed of another portion. His only vision—if indeed he is a visionary—is of a day when a political amalgam will emerge in the world, with the economic planning and the racial justice of the Russians added to the political freedom of the Americans. For a man who has thought about hybrid corn without any ethical qualms, it is natural to think about hybrid social forms without working himself into a lather about the differences of ideologies.

It is as a scientist also, rather than as a dogmatist, that Wallace has approached the economic problems of America. I have seen him in a group of intellectuals, baffled by their dogmas, indifferent to their abstractions. He is no socialist, and I suspect he knows little about the history of socialist schools of thought and their conflicts. He is himself a successful businessman and when, after his 1944 defeat, he was told he could have any Cabinet post, the one he chose was that of Secretary of Commerce. Unlike his capitalist friends, he believes capitalism makes no sense unless it builds an economy of abundance. Unlike his Communist friends, he believes abundance can be achieved under capitalism. But while his purposes have been clear, his economic methods have often been vague and blundering. Under the Agricultural Adjustment Administration in the New Deal he allowed himself to be saddled with an agricultural program of plowing-under which belonged to the economics of restriction, not of abundance. For any other man that might have been possible, but in Wallace's case it made no sense at all. At the same time he was also groping toward a philosophy of economic nationalism which seems a macabre phase for a man who was to become the symbol of internationalism. Wallace's development is full of such contradictions. It is because he has the mind of an experimenter, ready to abandon an idea if it no longer makes sense to him, and take up another that does.

I come now to the third fixed symbol in his thinking: He is deeply a *Christian*. He is a profoundly religious man for whom the teachings of Christian ethics have a living meaning, and for whom God is not simply a word to be put into the closing paragraph of an opportunist politician's speech. He has himself spoken about his long quest for a theology that would satisfy him. For a time he was attracted by Catholicism, for a time he flirted with theosophy. But his deepest roots are in the tradition of Protestant dissent, in which both his individualism and his militancy can be satisfied. He takes the teachings of Christianity seriously—on social justice, on racial discrimination, on peace—so seriously that he insists on applying them. Obviously this makes him a dangerous man to the corporation presidents and the generals and the newspaper publishers—and even to some churchmen. But to people who have felt the lash of injustice and glimpsed the promise of equality—to Negroes and Jews, workers and sharecroppers—he has been a leader. To many of the youngsters who fought a war to achieve a lasting peace, he is with all his weaknesses a symbol that evokes intense loyalties. And to many simple people, young and old, who are weary of the war talk and frightened at its ugliness, Wallace's passionate belief in peace transcends everything else.

This is my evaluation of Wallace. I see no reason for changing it merely because I disagree sharply with him on the question of the political tactics of a third party today. He is to me none the less a great political figure of our time and a profoundly moving democrat with a small d. On some issues, particularly economic, I find myself on the left of Wallace. I think there will have to be a greater degree of socialism mixed with capitalism before the American economy can iron out the depression cycle. I also find him somewhat naïve about the Russians and the nature of their foreign policy; he does not recognize the extent to which the ruthlessness of the police-state has led to a Communist imperialism, just as with us the power of the monopolies has led to a capitalist imperialism. Finally I do not admire his flirtation with the isolationists and with isolationism. It is a dangerous business to join forces with a philosophy that starts from a belief in the possibility of an isolated America in a changing and shrinking world.

But these differences do not wipe out the major areas of agreement I have with Wallace. Why then do I differ with him on the crucial question of a third party today?

Because I do not think it will help the drive for peace. Because its immediate effect will be the election of a reactionary Republican President and Congress.[1] Because whatever beginnings are made now toward a third party will be wiped out in such a catastrophe.

My belief in Wallace as an insurgent liberal leader with an almost religious commitment to democracy does not carry with it a belief in Wallace as an infallible tactician. If my readers insist on believing him infallible, they are free to do so. I cannot. In fact, his whole career in national politics has shown him to be a wretched tactician, from the plowing-under program to the ill-fated Madison Square Garden speech and the European trip that left him so vulnerable to attack. He is equally a faulty tactician today. He is a poor judge of men. He is the easy victim of a clique. He does not choose well the ground to fight on, or the time for marshaling all his forces. These are his faults. I thought much less of Roosevelt as a democratic fighter than I do of Wallace. But I thought much more of Roosevelt's sure sense of strategy, his immense resourcefulness, his understanding of the American mind. On all these scores Wallace rates low.

The most tragic fact about him since 1944 has been the way he has allowed himself to become isolated from the main currents of the labor movement, the farm organizations, the middle-of-the-road liberalism. I think of the Chicago Convention, and of the way in which the true liberal strength of the party was behind him, and almost nominated him despite the party bosses and despite FDR's own coolness. In less than four years he has dissipated much of that strength, allowed himself to be cut off from the liberal middle-ground that counts in America. His campaign will be a futile insurgent gesture, with the main organizational strength provided by the Communists, whose prize victim and trophy Wallace has become. And the movement he leads will go down in history as a valiant but mistaken fringe-movement, instead of part of the central current of American liberalism.

FEB. 1, 1948

[1] This proved untrue—but mainly because of the surprisingly effective campaign by Truman, and because most of Wallace's own supporters grew so frightened at the prospect of a Republican victory that they switched to Truman.

Sketches at a Series of Conventions: Philadelphia, 1948

1. *The Hungry Well-Fed Men*

WHEN YOU CALL Republican Convention Headquarters here at Philadelphia the telephone exchange is Locust. I find that appropriate. The delegates milling around in hotel lobbies and on the convention floor are hungry men. Not, of course, in the ordinary sense, like Chinese peasants or the squatting figures in Bombay or the Arab fellaheen. The Philadelphia hunger story is of a very different sort. The politicians, lawyers, shrewd-faced editors, hard-faced men of substance, have most of what are deemed the good things of life. They are the men who, in their combined wealth and power and community position, own and dominate this country. That being so, they don't see why they should not run it, as well.

They have waited for sixteen long years. These have been for them the years of the locust. They see a board groaning with national political power, almost within their grasp. A benign Republican providence has prepared a table before them in the presence of their faltering enemy—a table with some 250 billion dollars of national income a year. He has anointed their heads with oil and other profitable products. They want to dwell in the House of the Lord forever—but as its masters.

These men—or the bosses whose puppets they are—own everything in America worth owning. They own the factories and the fields, the machines, the big press, the mass movies, the chain radio and television stations, the transport and communication, the heavy industry, the banks, and even—one comes to think—many of the universities and churches. Everything but the people and their suffrage, their political power, their national apparatus, their public treasury, their armies, their young men.

The rankling injustice of this is what has filled the Republican leaders with bitterness throughout the long years of the locust. For to those who own the country, the divine right of running it ought to be clear enough for even a dumbbell New Dealer to grasp. Success has no room for even partial failure. In a country where Success is the reigning goddess, the failure to capture national power is intolerable. They have power already in both Houses of Congress, but in the American system what counts is

229

not Congressional government but Presidential government—the Presidency and everything that goes with it.

They want the Presidency so badly that nothing else seems to matter right now. That is why there is so terrible a sense of unreality about all the gaudy and tawdry trappings of this convention. The acts don't mean anything. The speeches are phonies, even the clever ones, especially the clever ones. The phrases are hollow. Even the anti-Communist ranting is like brackish ditchwater. The battle over the platform was a bloodless battle of contrived phrases, because no one here believes the issues mean very much to these men, and everyone knows that when the Republicans get into power they will do what they will do. There are no issues at this convention, not even the highly touted ones between the beatific Senator from Michigan and the ineffable Colonel from Chicago.[1] There are only hungry men.

The hunger of the candidates themselves is real enough. I wish Dürer were alive, or Goya, or Hogarth, to draw what the smiling faces of the candidates seek to conceal—the lust for power eating away at their insides, like the fox under the jumper of the Spartan boy. The naked appetite for power shows most clearly, of course, with Stassen and Dewey, whose youth is so quickly gray because the flames of hunger have licked at it. But this goes for the others too, old as well as young, internationalist as well as nationalist, Senator or Speaker or Governor or General. Each carries within him a burning passion for a Presidency, so long denied to him, now so tantalizingly close.

Behind the candidates are the delegates and the bosses, who have also a single-minded passion. The big question with them is not whether a particular candidate would make a great president, or even whether they like him. The question is only whether he will be able to win handily, and how much power they will be able to exercise with him and under him. What jobs they will get, how important they will be, what prestige they can count on: those are the things that move them.

They are not really king-makers, these little people: for a Warwick must have a sense of grandeur, which they lack. Nor are they "imperialists," as the Communists would have it. They are uneasy with the bigness of the new American world power. They would feel more comfortable with a garden-variety Republican like Martin or Bricker than with the world perspectives of a Vandenberg. They have always been thus, and they change hard.

As for Dewey, who glows with the certainty that the coveted prize will

[1] The reference was to the interventionist-isolationist fight between Sen. Vandenberg and Col. McCormick.

finally be his, they have no real affection for him. They would as soon choose someone else, if they were sure he would win, if they were sure he would be regular. That is what their lives are bounded by—success and regularity. They want to round out what they have, to hold more securely what they hold, to cut a figure in their home town.

They are not here to make history. They are here only to make good.

2. "*A Dead Kitten, an Egg Shell . . .*"

THE BEST-HATED, most lukewarmly loved man in the convention walked down the platform toward the microphone to receive the acclaim of the multitude. The confident party, rampaging toward victory, had picked its man, and for a moment you might have thought that a real spark had been struck between him as a human being and the sweating, cheering people. But the moment passed, and you knew it was no go, and would always be no go. The audience continued to cheer, but the force of emotion ebbed out of it as out of a spent bullet, and it was now formally applauding its formal candidate.

The candidate wore his candidate's smile. It was deliberately gentle and bland, fixed there with exactly the correct degree of gratitude toward the delegates, firmness toward the Democratic opposition and the Russian enemy, chivalry toward the defeated Republican hopefuls. He spoke honeyed words of conciliation, of unity, of the world crisis of freedom. The smile, too gentle and too self-deprecatory to be believed, seemed frozen on his face by the force of an iron will. I mumbled to myself, murdering T. S. Eliot:

> *This is the way the world ends*
> *Not with a bang but a simper. . . .*

He stood there, with the whole apparatus of camera, radio, newsreel, television grinding away. This was the culminating moment. This is what everything had been building up to—the struggle and polemics, the millions of words poured out and the millions of dollars, the people coming from every corner of the United States and its possessions, the hopped-up excitement, the straining multitudes. Upon this moment converged all the emotions and energies of a great nation, and from this moment there stretched out into the future strands of destiny for the whole world.

I sought in my mind for the image that would express the terrible anticlimax of this hollow little man and the hollowness we all felt about him.

Then the image came to me. It was from the famous passage in H. G. Wells's waspish book, *Boon*, describing a Henry James novel: "It is like a church lit . . . with every light and line focused on the high altar. And on the altar, very reverently placed, intensely there, is a dead kitten, an egg-shell, a bit of string." It came to me that the klieg lights and television cameras were focused on the Republican altar.

How then did he win? His victory at Philadelphia was a triumph of technics over civilization. He won not because he had principles, or even appeal, but because he had a machine. The machine was ruthless and well oiled, run by a group of slick and modern operators. It combined the age-old methods of power politics with the newest strategies of blitz warfare and the precision tools of American industry and administration. He employed technical means in a technical age in a technical nation. He had tested his machine over a period of ten years, for he has been running for President since 1938. All the bugs had been taken out. It was a beautiful thing to watch—provided you were not one of its victims.

This was the victory of a faceless machine man in a depersonalized machine culture. Yet there this man stood, deploring materialism and mechanism, appealing for higher spiritual values.

It was when he spoke of God, with an unbreakable assurance, that I suddenly understood. Now nominated, he counted on God just as confidently as he had counted during the convention upon the Pennsylvania and Indiana delegations. It was, I suppose, all settled. God was like Joe Grundy and Charlie Halleck. Maybe He might even trade for a vague implied promise of the vice-presidential spot on the ticket. It was a deal.

3. *"Out of the Cradle Endlessly Rocking . . ."*

IT WAS TWO in the morning, the hour when vitality is at its lowest. The sweating delegates, correspondents, cameramen, and assorted campfollowers waited grimly for the Presidential candidate to appear. After the drama of the Civil Rights fight, everyone figured the final Presidential speech would be anticlimax. And the convention managers, evidently fearing only a half-hearted reception for their candidate, tried to forestall a flop by asking that there be no demonstration.

Both the audience and the managers were wrong. The last act went over big. He spoke too rapidly, too jerkily, too emotionally. But he was caught up in what he was saying. It was a harangue, I suppose, and it was what the polite people call "demagogic." But it carried conviction, because it was the truth, and had been waiting to be said for a long time. It had no taste. The candidate used un-Deweylike words like "lousy" and called the Republicans the "enemy." But the Republicans richly deserved both the adjective and the noun.

Somehow a rapport was built up between this stumbling, fumbling little man and an audience which neither loved nor admired him. They sensed that this was the most militant Presidential acceptance speech in either major party since Bryan. They liked the fact that he came out of his corner fighting.

I had mixed emotions as I listened. I knew he had not grown a new skin or sprouted wings. He was still the Truman of the Truman Doctrine, of the Palestine switches. The natty clothes, the jaunty step, the eyes sparkling clearly through steel-rimmed glasses, the set of the jaw gave a squarish look to the insignificant face. The whole appearance bespoke not a great man but a stubborn mediocre man whose mediocrity was straining to fill out the large outlines of his great office.

At the moment the enemy were the Republicans, the real-estate lobby, the money changers in the temple. But I remembered when the enemy had been the Russians, the railway labor chiefs, the CIO, the Zionist pressure group, Henry Wallace, John L. Lewis, the anti-Truman opposition within the Democratic party. The enemy changed, but always the burning intensity was unflaggingly personal.

It was a great speech for a great occasion, and as I listened I found myself applauding. I thought how different this speech was from Dewey's acceptance speech. Dewey was stilted and frozen inside, and his stilted words froze his audience. Truman's words, tumbling out, released the fighting energies of his audience. Yet I could not help remembering that the administration managers had that afternoon fought against the ADA civil rights amendment; that Missouri, the President's own state, had voted against it; that the group of conservatives who make administration policy, and use the President as a puppet, had been pushed for the moment into the background, but were still there; that the President's new-found militancy was a campaign militancy; that he justly blamed the Republicans for the domestic policy, but foreign policy was the area of his own Presidential power, and in that area his policy was Republican policy.

I came away from the convention with few illusions about the candidate and his managers, much as I welcome their militancy. But I came away with a sense of respect for the vitality of the Democratic party itself, and the way in which its great tradition of progressivism defies the stifling forces of an era of fear.

In these closing sessions of the convention, something very like a miracle had happened. The battered liberals, who had lost every preconvention fight, came back under ADA leadership to win the crucial battle for civil rights. The Southern reactionaries were beaten, and the fight for the soul of the South will now have to be fought out where it belongs—in the Southern communities themselves, rather than in the councils of the party. A convention which had until that day been an inert collection of empty men came to life under the leadership of a group of new young men whose faces will be seen and whose names will be heard in the next four years.

Truman will, in all probability, be beaten; but Democratic progressivism is not dead. Its aliveness is underlined by the fact that in this hour of its great crisis its candidate knows he must assume the mantle and militancy of FDR if he is to stand even a chance of winning.

As I watched the climax of the convention—the sloughing off of the old and tired, the secession of the rotten, the new vitality of the mediocre, the beginning of the new—I thought of Walt Whitman's line: "Out of the cradle endlessly rocking . . ." He had written it about himself, he had meant it for America. The processes of birth and death and agony and rebirth are as real in politics as in organic life.

4. The Ordeal of Henry Wallace

I WATCHED Henry Wallace holding his press conference at the Progressive Convention. Everyone expected that the questions hurled at him would fall into three groups: How about the Communists in your outfit? How about the Guru letters? [1] How about freedom in Russia and Eastern Europe?

On none of these were his answers adequate. He read an earlier statement refusing either to disown or embrace the Communists. On the Guru letters (which are an idiot issue swollen into headlines by Pegler-Hearst venom), he refused to make the candid answer which would have deflated the whole business. And on Russia and Eastern Europe, he might have said sharply and simply: "Look, their notion of freedom isn't mine or that of our party. We reject it utterly and passionately. But that is no reason for the war-making gibberish which fills our nation today." But he didn't.

[1] Letters that Wallace was charged with having written to one of the leaders of a mystical religious cult.

I felt a tragedy about the whole thing, as I had felt it about the exchange the day before between the ADA and the New party people. The ADA has good principles but no leader and no mass following. The New party has a leader who engages the devotion of his followers. But he and they are caught in muddled thinking on the great issues of Communism, freedom, and the nature of liberalism.

The ordeal of Henry Wallace, like the ordeal of all the liberal groups in America, will not be resolved until a clear body of genuinely liberal principles and tactics—Democratic, non-Communist, militant—has been worked out. And until the gap has been bridged between those principles and the felt needs and emotions of the mass of people who have long been duped and doped by propaganda.

The big story of the convention is not that of the Wallace press conference, however, nor of the ADA invasion of the platform hearings; nor of the formal speeches. It is the story of the tensions between the Wallace progressives and those members of the New party who are seeking to use it for the purposes outside American progressivism—of tensions which never developed to the breaking point or even to the breaking-out point. And that fact too is part of the ordeal of Henry Wallace and of American liberalism.

One misses here the smell of power that one sensed at the other conventions. The delegates are a better sort—writers, intellectuals, workers, preachers, housewives, doctors. They know they have no chance, but they think in big terms. As I listened to the platform hearings, with each speaker outdoing the other at militancy, I got a feeling of the pathos of it. There was an expenditure of issues, phrases, dedicated intensities, with no chance of their becoming actualities. It was like one of those fantastic card games between a group of men on a desert island, conducted for fabulous stakes, and carefully recorded on slips of paper which would never be honored.

Or will they? At this founding convention it is the delegates and not the Peglers who have the last word. The elements of birth and vitality are present here in abundance.

This may not be the party which will continue to carry those elements. My own conviction is that it is not, and that something a good deal different will in time have to take its place—something less confused on the issue of an unequivocal democratic liberalism whose passion for liberalism does not stop at the borders of America. It will have a different leadership, different direction, less of a chip-on-the-shoulder belligerency, a deeper sense of the American grain, a greater maturity. But the kind of people who rescued the Democratic Convention from emptiness, and the kind who give this one its sense of strength and dedication, will have to find themselves and fuse themselves.

5. *The Independent Left*

THE THREE MAJOR conventions being over, now is the time for all good men to come to the aid of their sanity and their intellect, and do some hard thinking before they jump into a voting booth.

I hereby serve notice that I intend to continue thinking out loud in this column, weighing arguments pro and con as I have done. This may not satisfy the bands of the faithful, but it is not for the faithful I am writing, but for the rational. And they—critical liberals of every variety, who are the salt of this American earth—want not so much manifestoes as day-by-day analysis of issues, programs, tactics, personalities, ideas.

I am open-minded as to the merits of Henry Wallace, Norman Thomas, Harry Truman—the three candidates among whom the critical liberals will have to choose. I could not possibly have a 100%, or even a 75%, feeling about any of them. But I want to watch them in action and comment on them as the campaign develops. When the time comes to hold my own convention and to strike a trial-balance, I shall do so and add up my reasons.

But when I do that, I shall do it not as one of the Progressive-party faithful, nor of the faithful of the Socialist party or the Democratic party. I shall do it as a member of what seems to me the last best hope of America—the group that I call the critical and independent Left.

I've read and listened to a lot of talk about the sad fragmented plight of the American liberal. It is true that the times have dealt harshly with the people who will not plump for the NAM, who are unimpressed by Dewey and Grundy, who don't like the war lords of Washington grown so powerful in the Administration today, who cannot whip up enthusiasm about an ineffectual Socialist party, and who have their eyes open as to the role the Communists are playing in the inner controls of the Progressive party. Our age has dealt harshly with such people in the sense that it has not presented them with anything like a clean-cut, wholehearted choice.

But in one sense the times have dealt most generously with them: it is they whom every party (except the secessionist Dixiecrats) must look to for decisive support. The polls show how large and crucial the group of independent voters is this year. Most of those voters are liberals—liberal

Republicans of the Willkie variety, liberal Democrats who wanted Douglas, the liberal antiwar and internationalist group to whom none of the existing choices gives an adequate answer.

These people together make up the most important political force in America today. They are, if you will, the real Fourth Party in American politics.

I call them the independent *Left*, partly because they are all left of center, but mainly because their experience and social position demand of them drastic attitudes and thoroughgoing measures. Take the Negroes for example, whom all the parties are bidding for now: the experience of being a Negro in America is a radical experience and puts you necessarily on the Left. Take the young veteran, who doesn't want to go through the hell of war again. Take the thinking worker, who knows that only democratic socialization of industry can keep him from the agony of depression. Take the young scientist, or the college student, who knows that only a world authority stronger than either Russia or America can assure him that his world will not be shivered into fragments.

These are, by their intrinsic outlook and their intrinsic social position, part of the Left. They are, in a genuine sense, radicals.

This group has no party and candidate of its own. If the Democrats could have ditched Truman, and chosen Douglas, all these people would have rallied around him. If Wallace had been able either to fight it out inside the Democratic party or to make an early alliance with the main body of the CIO, which would have given him an independent political machine, there would again have been a clear rallying center. But all that is over the dam.

And so the critical and independent Left has no clear choice. It will have to wait another four years before it has its own candidate and its own party. Meanwhile it must play to the hilt the role of what has been well called the nonautomatic voter. And it must keep alive the spirit of critical intelligent action, and the passion for freedom and tolerance under whatever political sky, which all the groups of the faithful seem to be conspiring to snuff out.[1]

JUNE 24, 26, JULY 18, 25, 27, 1948

[1] Even with the Truman victory in the 1948 elections, I still feel that the progressive political force of the future will have to be an independent Left which will work through the Democratic party if possible, as it will also work through the trade-unions and the other groups in the "Great Coalition."

Love and Hate in Politics

AN AMERICAN ELECTION campaign is usually a good emotional show, with fierce partisan passions of love and hate. That was true of the campaigns of FDR, of Al Smith in 1928, of Wilson, Teddy Roosevelt, Cleveland, Blaine, Lincoln, Jackson, Jefferson, and—above all—of William Jennings Bryan.

I was reminded of this again the other day, reading Vachel Lindsay's "Bryan, Bryan," the great chant in which he recalls how he felt as a boy when Bryan turned up in his home town to make a campaign speech. The poem is a battle hymn of radical democracy, almost Joycean in its symbolic equating of the big Western rivers and plains with the young orator who, out of an elemental strength, dared to challenge the gods of gold and power.

By comparison the current campaign is loveless. It recalls the dreary years when Cox ran against Harding in 1920 and when Davis ran against Coolidge in 1924. Who trembles with emotion for Truman? Who would delight to die for Dewey?

It is different, of course, with Wallace. If he were the candidate of one of the major parties, we should have another Bryan campaign. The cheering, snake-dancing crowd at Shibe Park was filled with adoration of its Magus. For he was the symbol that released their energies, made them feel at one, like martyrs and crusaders.

But while Bryan and La Follette were in the mainstream of native American radicalism, Wallace has made the mistake of being caught in a rivulet, cut off from the great and deep currents of traditional American progressive thought and feeling. His appeal for a small group—perhaps 10 per cent of the people—is intense. In the case of another small group, perhaps 10 per cent more, there is an equally intense hatred of him. But most of the rest—which means four out of five Americans—feel confused, divided, and sullen about him, as if they had hungered for water in the parched desert of American leadership and, when they caught up with it, found the spring tainted.

In one sense the dreariness of the current campaign was inevitable. Our era is one in which so much emotion has been used up in the American-Russian cold war, and in the Communist and anti-Communist feuds, that

238

little is left for such sideshows as elections. Truman and Dewey can't really pretend to any gargantuan hatreds of each other when both feel they have to huddle in the same spite corner every time Stalin sneezes or Molotov scowls. The fake Montagues and fake Capulets of the Washington scene, whatever their grimaces over inflation and housing, are obviously hamming their roles with less conviction than the most amateur summer stock actors.

The fact is that our invective is used up. In the last two years of the great verbal war on Communism, we have overdrawn on our invective account. When you use words like "rats," "spies," "fifth-columnists," "traitors," day after day, then all political cuss words get squeezed dry of their meaning and become as tasteless and bedraggled as orange pulp in a waste can. The result is that invective becomes ever more hysterical with ever less effect. Try the punishing experiment sometime of reading Pegler or O'Donnell for a week running. They now find it necessary to call Truman a "little squealer" and Wallace wholly insane, yet in every column you get the feeling of emotionally exhausted men trying to find new thrills in a vocabulary that no longer responds to their hate.

Yet newspapermen have proved sensitive plants. They were deeply hurt when Henry Wallace, in his now classic press conference, blunderingly called some of them stooges. There is a double standard of etiquette in political invective. A politician wouldn't dream of being allowed to call a columnist the things a columnist is allowed to call a politician. No one imagines that political figures are capable of being insulted. Since they are (as our folklore has it) by nature vile and by choice vulnerable, it follows that no one could stoop so low as to be below them.

Pegler and O'Donnell, as if drawn by a suction-force to the world of pathology, use the vocabulary of pathology. But it was left to Rebecca West, an Englishwoman, writing of the Wallace convention, to focus on the physiognomy of the young people present, and describe the angle of the jaw, the shape of the features, as an index to their democracy or their fascism. One can only hail this introduction of political anthropology, or political anthropometry, into a campaign which is bogging down in repeated spy revelations. Not since an Italian criminologist claimed you could tell a crook or murderer by the shape of his profile has anyone come up with so epochal a discovery in social science.

AUG. 8, 1948

On Building a People's Party

I HAVE FELT that the Third party is a bad tactic because it will elect a Republican, because it will not help much toward achieving peace, because it may help bring in an even less liberal rather than a more liberal Congress. But I can understand someone saying that all these matters are expendable, and that the big problem is to make a start toward a new party because the two we have now are worn out, worthless, and almost interchangeable. You have to start sometime (the argument runs), so why not now? You'll be licked this year, and you'll probably be licked four years from now. But in time you will build a new party like Britain's Labor party—one that starts as a third party and becomes a first party.

Sometimes I can't tell how clear Wallace is in his mind about his real purposes. Sometimes he talks as if his purpose is to use the Third party in every way possible, come hell or high water: use it to smash Truman and the Democrats, use it to scare the bosses, use it to show he is not himself a scary-cat—one of the "faint-hearted liberals" he is so fond of deriding—use it to show the world how many Americans are willing to stand up and be counted for peace. But sometimes he talks seriously about making a start in building a real long-range people's party. It is this latter Wallace I want to discuss now.

For a Third party text to study, I have gone right to the horse's mouth—Wallace's own column in the *New Republic* for January 19, 1948. It is called "Third Parties and the American Tradition," and it is learned, historical, and detailed.

I agree with Wallace that third parties are not new in American history, and that they form a long and honorable chapter in it. We have always been a nation of joiners, disjoiners, unjoiners; political animals who love to rear up and kick over the traces; rebels, insurgents, and dissidents who hate to be fenced in. If we were not that kind of people, we wouldn't be worth our salt, and we would lose our savor.

Wallace also argues that even when the Third parties have failed (which has been practically always) they have left their imprint on our history. The big example, of course, is the way Bryanism absorbed the teachings of the Populist party in 1896, and the way the regular Democrats and Republicans in turn took over Bryan's planks every time he got beaten for the Presidency. But there have been other examples too. If what you want is a political picnic, with a lot of ferment and a rattling good time had by all, and the victory of the worse of the major parties along with the hope that some day you'll be embalmed in an also-ran footnote in the history books, and all the risks and consequences be damned—then this is undoubtedly your dish.

But suppose you feel that building a real people's party is a serious business, that you are not interested in a one-election stand, that you are not interested in political soliloquies in which you are alone with God and a few choice souls, that if you play you want it to be for keeps, that if you make a start on a new party you want it to be the real enduring stuff that will some day sweep the country and win elections. What then? Then you have to draw your lessons not from the fly-by-night parties that failed and left a memory behind, but from the parties that succeeded and became major parties.

Of these there have been two: the party Jefferson founded, later rebuilt by Jackson, which became the present Democratic party; and the party Fremont and his associates founded in 1854, which in 1860 captured the Presidency for Lincoln as the Republican party.

The big fact about Jefferson's party was that there was only one other in the field at the time—the Federalists, the reactionaries of that day. Jefferson had everything wide open (for a people's party), and he formed the broadest possible combination of liberals, radicals, and agrarians; of Virginia planters, city mechanics, frontier farmers, and intellectuals. When the combination got thin and stale, Jackson renewed its strength by injecting the vigor of the Western frontier and the new workingmen's groups. But he did it inside Jefferson's framework, and he did it by capturing the party organization. Wallace seems to forget that in his article.

The big fact about Lincoln's party was also its realistic economic and social base. Wallace stresses Lincoln's liberal utterances on labor, and implies that this was a labor party to start with. That's stretching things. Lincoln was a pretty hard-headed lawyer not averse to playing machine-politics. He was no Left Winger: he was hated by the abolitionists, and he despised them. But he held them in a party that contained also the new working class *and the new business class as well*. The forces of free labor and the forces of Northern and Western business combined against the slave plantation system. If there is any lesson to be drawn from the origins of the Republican party, it is that you have to hold together some pretty strange companion groups in a successful party.

I don't think the Wallace party has any resemblance to Jefferson's, which was a major party from the start; or Jackson's, which took over the party organization; or Fremont's and Lincoln's, which ushered in the era of industrial power under the slogans of free labor.

Now let us look at the parties that failed. The big examples are the Populists of 1892, under James B. Weaver; Theodore Roosevelt's Bull Moose party of 1912; and Bob La Follette's 1924 Third party venture. Each of them started well. At the Populist Convention of 1892, to quote a contemporary report, "the great stage, brilliant and vivid with the national colors, was filled with the leaders of the Alliance, the Knights of Labor, the single-tax people, the Prohibitionists, the Anti-Monopolists, the People's party, the Reform party, and the Woman's Alliance." The roundup covered a lot of territory. In 1912, T.R. did not announce his candidacy until the governors of seven states had appealed to him to run. In 1924, La Follette had labor strength, farm strength, middle-class, radical and Populist strength.

Compared with these, Wallace's announcement seemed pretty much a one-man, one-group affair. Not counting the Communists, he had only the Progressive Citizens of America with him, and the Left-Wing minority segment of the CIO. He does not have the farm-groups the Populists had. He does not have the civic-reform groups that T.R. had. He does not have the large labor-farmer coalition that La Follette had. While he says of the Bull Moose 1912 venture that it was a one-man affair, built only around the personality of T.R., that is almost as true of the current Third party. Subtract Wallace and his personality and his dynamic appeal from it—and what do you have left?

The other groups, starting stronger than Wallace, failed. Will Wallace, who starts with less of a mass organizational base, succeed? The other groups were all one-election, fly-by-night affairs. Can we hope this one will be different, given its start? The Wallace supporters are gleeful because the Gallup Poll shows his strength in New York—his best state—as thirteen to eighteen per cent. But the Populists pulled eighteen per cent nationally in 1892. La Follette had seventeen per cent in 1924, and T.R. ran second in popular vote. Where are their parties now?

I have given some factual history and some sober analysis. I have not dealt in easy slogans or even easier appeals to the despairing sense of frustration that all liberals and all decent people have today. I am not arguing now against a Third party adventure, but only that we should recognize how much of an adventure it is, and not kid ourselves about its being the beginning of a new party that will sweep the country at some future time.

Can such a new party be built? I think it can, if it makes its appeal to the same groups that FDR appealed to. I think it can if it bases itself squarely on the labor movement—not a fragmented one, but one containing all the progressive segments of labor; if it succeeds in not frightening the farmers off; if it appeals to liberals and internationalists in the middle class; if it is, in short, genuinely a people's party, not the instrument of one wing of the progressives.

The great pitfall of Wallace's movement is that, with so many extreme and fanatic hopes placed on it, its failure will disillusion many who might otherwise join a people's party in 1952. The bitterness it will necessarily engender in the ranks of progressives will further split, not further unite, the elements of a possible combination. The pity of it is that instead of being an advance toward a future victory, it may prove a setback.

FEB. 8, 1948

A Long-Term Program for America

A GROUP of British rebel Labor M.P.s, headed by Richard Crossman, Michael Foot, and Ian Mikardo, have put out a remarkable pamphlet on British domestic and foreign policy called *Keep Left*. They have quarrels to pick with their party leadership on the question of the pace of socialization, and on the extreme British dependence upon America. But what is most striking about the pamphlet is what its authors—and everyone else in Britain except a few Tory diehards—*take for granted*.

They take the fact of nationalization of all the basic industries for granted, and quarrel only about how fast. They take it for granted that if a public utility is going to be a private monopoly anyway, it had better be a public monopoly. They take it for granted that the banking and credit and insurance systems belong to the people and should be run for them. They take it for granted that the industry of the nation, partly in the hands of public corporations and partly of private, should all be administered as part of an over-all national plan. They take it for granted that first things come first: that nationalization of coal, power, transport, communications, is a first thing; that milk for children poor and rich alike, and a postponed age at which children leave school, are first things; that health and housing and social insurance programs are first things. They take it for granted, finally, that a democracy cannot survive unless it maintains a system of free trade-unions, a network of co-operatives, and a press and radio which refuse to give to a single class a monopoly of the spread of ideas.

We Americans can learn a good deal from what the British are doing at home with their run-down economy and their limited resources. Our own economy is still modern and our resources are huge, our national income (except during major depressions) is staggering, our living-standards are high at the same time that the inequalities in them are steep. The British have a deficit economy to cope with, while we have a surplus economy to set in order. We have so much more to start with than the British that the American potential—once we decided to put first things first—would be unparalleled in history. Then truly could we fulfill the promise of American life. What long-term program would be required to achieve a genuine economic as well as a political democracy in America?

I place first the problem of monopoly. For close to sixty years we have led a double life, keeping an antimonopoly law on our statute books but doing little at any time—and nothing most of the time—to enforce it. It is time this sort of masquerade stopped. Obviously there are areas of industry in which the impulses toward corporate monopoly are too powerful to be restrained by lip-service legislation. The only answer in these areas of industry is to turn a private monopoly into a public monopoly. If, for example, the aluminum industry cannot operate on the competitive principle, and price-and-production policies are to be shaped by a small group of men, let it be done by men responsible to the people—that is to say, by the Government.

Another area in which private enterprise makes no sense is the public utilities. If the post office is properly within the domain of being run by the people themselves, then why not the railroads, the telegraph and telephone lines, the companies furnishing water and light? To run these by competition would mean infinite duplication and waste. To give a single company a monopoly over the country, as we do with American Telephone and Telegraph Company, or over an area, as we do largely with railways, or over cities and states, as we do with "public service" utilities, is to give fat profits to men who take little risk and carry through no innovations. "Public" utilities must indeed become *public*.

In the power-industries, including electric power as well as atomic power, the stakes are too big to entrust them to a private group. We have recognized that, at least in principle, about atomic power, and about hydroelectric power in communities like the Tennesse Valley. That recognition must be made clear for all the power-industries.

The sort of development that took place in the Tennessee Valley can and must take place in the other great river valleys of the nation. The Columbia Valley has shown what can be done as a start under very different conditions. The St. Lawrence Seaway and the Missouri Valley are next, and after them the others. This will mean covering the nation with a network of public power developments that make power accessible to all the people at low rates, that give small businesses a chance against the big, and that create a new community way of life.

In the case of sick industries—and the coal industry is the outstanding example—where generally only the profitable units are brought into production, where the greed for profits makes safety-expenditures a luxury, and where chaos is king, the answer is public ownership and operation. What the Navy showed it could do with the coal mines could be done even better by a national coal authority.

Where industries are publicly administered, this must be done not by politicians but by administrators trained in business, engineering, law, labor relations, public service. It should be done by public corporations, each of them operating to pay for itself, to put the profits into the public treasury, and to lower prices and improve quality whenever the profits threaten to be too high. It should be done not from Washington or New York, but from local centers all over the country. While power must be centralized, administration can be decentralized.

The largest portion of American industry must be left under private ownership and operation, but under public regulation. Large sections of it, however, should be organized as co-operatives. Thus we shall achieve a mixed economy, divided into the public domain, the private and competitive domain, the co-operative domain. That is where the British economy will be, five years from now. The Americans, who have in most governmental matters been a generation behind the British, should be able to achieve it in twenty or twenty-five years.

But whether any particular industry is under private operation or governmental or co-operative, it must fit into a national economic plan. This will not mean a rigid blueprint, but it will mean that we shall have our economic goals constantly in mind and we shall be constantly watching and reappraising our economic activity to see whether and how we must shift our course in order to reach the goals.

The principal instruments of such economic planning are clear enough. The banking system, which came to grief so badly in 1933 and had to be rescued by the Government and whose risks are at present partially assumed by the Government, will make much more sense when nationalized. When the social services have been drastically extended, much of our insurance system will also be governmental. Together this will mean a large leverage of control over the volume and flow of credit. Add to this a tax system which must become thoroughly progressive, and which must also be used not only for revenue but as a leverage to control the pace and direction and channeling of economic activity as a whole. Add to this finally the sort of system that Stafford Cripps has inaugurated in the privately owned British industries, where the larger policies are shaped by "working parties" representing industry, labor, and the Government. Through banking and credit control, tax control, and such "working parties," economic planning can be carried on flexibly and without assuming a constant plague of bureaucratic red tape.

There remains the crucial question of freedom. Will not this degree of socialization crush the individual's freedom? For a long time American democrats have been scared by such bugbears, and books like Hayek's *The Road to Serfdom* have stoutly maintained that when you socialize any major industries and try to plan the operations of an economy, you cannot remain free. The example of Russia is constantly held up to us as clinching proof.

In answer, American believers in economic democracy have always insisted that you can have a rational economy without crushing freedom. The British experience bears us out to the hilt. No one's freedom in Britain has been crushed or even impaired by the socialization program. There are, of course, cries of bureaucracy, but they come from a few Tory journals only, and the people themselves are only amused when they think back to Winston Churchill's warning cries about the coming Gestapo.

In fact, the real point about having a rational economy is that you remove the chief threats to freedom because you remove the constant fear of depressions, you thin out the concentrated power of a single, small corporate group, you give the trade-unions a chance to function without the continued need for large-scale paralyzing strikes and without a constant sense of pressure from their enemies. Above all, you restore the conditions of free economic opportunity for all, under which every man can show the stuff he is made of.

In this sense a rational economic system will give us a chance, for the first time since the days of Jefferson and Jackson, for a rounded American democracy.

MAY 22, 1947

The Risen Phoenix

THEY ARE SINGING the requiem for American liberalism. Too soon, I think.

The *Herald Tribune* yesterday, in a ring-out-the-old-year mood, pointed to the splint₂ring of the liberals on the Wallace candidacy and concluded that American liberalism is dead. Wallace's vague liberal attitudes, says the *Tribune* editorial writer, his lack of a program, mark "the bankruptcy of the liberal insurgent tradition in America." "There is," the *Tribune* intones—and I cannot tell whether its mood is mournful or joyful—"no liberal view, no really self-consistent and logical body of principle and policy responding to any basic concept of purpose and interest."

I am afraid our Republican contemporary is keening over the liberal corpse before it is dead. True, the sprawling labor and professional group that is generally called "the liberals" is disunited today, but disunity is not by any means a sign of death: it is a far more certain sign of ferment and vitality than is the boss-ridden "unity" of the Republicans. Except for a few stray mavericks like Morse and Tobey and Aiken, the Republicans are not bothered much with insurgency because the difference between Dewey and Vandenberg, McCormick and Luce, even Taft and Stassen, is the difference between varying degrees of dry rot.

Even the Wallace incident does more to disprove than prove the death of liberalism. A dying creed does not move one of the great men of our time to break with the party under whose banner he had so long served, and stake so much on a Third party plunge. Nor is it a dying creed which moves at least several million of his admirers and former followers to depart from him when they believe he has made the wrong move. If anything, the intensity that animates both Henry Wallace's camp of liberals and those who have broken with him on this issue, shows the reach and depth of the liberal conviction on both sides. The fact is far different from the *Herald Tribune's* lament that liberalism has no body of principles. The trouble is that it has two, and the battle between them is so sharp that it gives aid and comfort to the enemies of both.

What is that battle? The significant split between liberals today is one of intellectual outlook.

247

One camp of liberals—or "Left Wingers"—has its attention fixed on the main current of world revolutionary striving, which still flows through a channel first given shape by the Russians. They are not Communists, and would be incapable of Communist discipline or hardships. Some of them may be fellow-travelers, who—like a sunflower—turn by a tropism to the Russian sun. More likely they are not even that, but independent liberals who feel they must put first things first. They may be genuinely troubled, in their more private moments, by the ethical flaws of a totalitarian Russia. But they keep their eyes averted from these flaws, and have ceased to make any deliberate analysis of them. Their eyes are fixed in a different direction. They see decay and breakdown in the world's economies, rottenness in the world's still feudal social systems, blindness in the conduct of foreign affairs, no real efforts at world peace. They find capitalist and fascist regimes collaborating in order to hem in the Left Wing regimes. They see a hysterical fear of Russia riding mankind.

There is another liberal camp. These liberals have their attention wholly fixed on the ruthlessness by which the Russian ruling group reached and has maintained its power, and on the police-states of Eastern Europe that have come up in the wake of that power. They are obsessed with the symbol of the commissar, with the fact of forced labor in Russia. They spend much of their emotional energy speculating on the millions in the prison camps. So fixed are they on this that they give only minor attention to the main social forces in the world at large. The fact that there is a revolutionary energy in the world which must find some sort of expression, and that a negative anti-Communism will not give it expression—that fact they are largely blind to. They are troubled because American capitalism is making alliances with the most reactionary regimes in order to fight the Communist influence, but they push this flaw of American policy into the back of their consciousness.

Thus liberals are caught, like Dante in the midpassage of his life, at the foot of the Delectable Mountain, with a decent world in view. But one path that leads to the top is guarded by the leopard of the totalitarian police-state. The other path is guarded by the she-wolf of capitalist avarice and its social blindness. And each group of liberals is so horror-struck by one of these animal death's-heads that it rushes along the other path to embrace whatever it finds.

That is, I am convinced, the double flaw of the liberal attitude today. That is what splits the liberals into two camps, makes it impossible for them to unite to achieve either an orderly economy or an orderly world. The weakness, I repeat, is not that the liberals have no principles. The weakness is that they have two sets. The revolutionary liberals want to see social changes carried through, even at a deadly risk to personality. The ethical liberals have grown so embittered over Russian police methods that they run the danger of preparing their minds for a war that may destroy the world.

This defines the task of our generation. We must make what Louis Fischer has called the "double rejection"—both of totalitarian power and of capitalist avarice. But a double rejection is too negative. We must also make a prime affirmation—that Americans, with their immense resources and their economic margin, have the plastic opportunity to build a new kind of economic and political commonwealth on this continent, and still leave room elsewhere in the world for other peoples to build their own kind.

We do not have to start from scratch. One of our biggest resources is the continuous tradition of American insurgent liberals and radicals. William Lloyd Garrison and Wendell Phillips, Edward Bellamy and Henry George, Thorstein Veblen and Randolph Bourne, John P. Altgeld and Lincoln Steffens, "Old Bob" La Follette and George Norris, Daniel De Leon and Gene Debs—these are only a few of the stars in the rich galaxy.

Building from their thought, we can move on to a synthesis of our own. It must reject Russian totalitarianism without rejecting Russian friendship or world peace. It must reject the Communist philosophy without depriving Communists of their rights and protections under the law. It must take over the technical and managerial advances made under capitalism, and use them for the collective welfare under new social forms. It must count as the big enemy fascist reaction, whether it appears in feudal regimes abroad or in our own hearts.

In this way liberalism can get a new unity, and it must have such a unity before it can start out on independent political adventures. As the year's end turns into year's beginning, let us remember that if liberalism is dying it is dying only as the phoenix dies. Out of its own ashes comes, even if dimly and afar, the figure of the risen phoenix.

JAN. 1, 1948

PART III

Empire, Chaos, or Law: Notes on America among the Powers

On Living in a Great Time

IT IS EASY to say that we live in a time of world-shattering events. It is not so easy to probe into what truth this truism expresses.

Consider the events and their pace. Do you remember when, only a few years ago, the landing of Rudolf Hess's airplane in England captured the headlines and our imagination for days and weeks? Or what a sensation was caused by the assassination of a second-rate French politician called Darlan?

Compare that with what has assaulted our eyes and minds in these closing weeks of the war in Europe. The steel and concrete of the most-vaunted army in history, the German Army, has been shattered. The Nazi will which Hitler took two decades to build has collapsed. The greatest democratic leader of our time died in the death of President Roosevelt. The two big fascist leaders in whose shadow our whole generation has lived—Mussolini and Hitler—are now lying dead amidst the ruins of their empires, one following the other in the space of a few days.

Berlin, the citadel of Nazi power, has fallen to the Russians. The men around Mussolini are dead, and the men around Hitler soon will have a similar fate. The French fascist leaders are scurrying about to find some safe exit off the stage of history: Pétain has given himself up to the French; Laval has sought the shelter of Franco's lingering fascist power in Madrid. The whole Nazi Army in north Italy and western Austria has quit, a million men. The von Rundstedt whose drive through the Ardennes Forest made military history this winter is now a prisoner. The long-awaited meeting of the American and Russian armies has taken place. New governments have been formed in Poland and in Austria. The complete surrender of the Germans is expected every day. A constitutional convention for a new world security organization is meeting at San Francisco.

Any one of these events would be grist for headlines, analysis, speculation, day after day. Together they make a newspaper office at once paradise, because of the richness of the events, and Heartbreak House, because of the ruthless, wasteful pace of events.

This is, in Thomas Hardy's phrase, a "time of the breaking of nations." What happens to the individual who is living in so great a time, whose senses and imagination are battered by such events? Hardy in his poem

253

describes the European peasant in World War I "harrowing clods . . . though Dynasties pass." That is the poet's view of life's continuity whether the events are small or big, and it is a valid view. But Hardy's peasant was the material the dynasts used, the anvil on which the hammers beat. If we are all to be only that, the new Hitlers of this world will arise and triumph.

The dangerous thing about living in a great time is that the events outrun the imagination, and finally both our senses and our imaginations are dulled. When events are small the individual gets no feeling of the heroic quality of history, when they become big he does, but when they become too big he is overwhelmed. And this is almost as true in the times of victory when the events are on our side as in the times of catastrophe when they are against us. It is almost as easy to be enervated by triumph as by defeat.

The individual always measures himself against the bigness of the things outside himself. A man can feel big in a village, he feels dwarfed by skyscrapers—unless he owns them. A man can feel big with a rifle, he feels dwarfed by a tank—unless he is running it. A man can feel big in an ordinary time, he feels dwarfed in a time of huge events—unless he has a sense of having a hand in them. André Malraux has said, in *Man's Fate*, that "we hear the voice of others with our ears, and our own with our throats." All the time that we are watching the immensity of events with our eyes and mind, something is happening inside our will which is an appraisal of how big or small we are in the face of them.

And here the great danger is that we feel that the events are taking place without the individual. That is not true. Berlin did not fall, like the walls of Jericho, at the blast of seven rams' horns by seven priests. The Russians took Berlin at the end of an incredibly costly three-year march from Moscow. The expenditure of millions of lives was the cost of Berlin's fall, and the fusion of millions of wills was its means.

The same is true of Hitler's death. It was not just a bullet that did it, nor a blood clot in the brain, nor a random impulse to suicide. The collapse of Hitler and his power comes as the climax of a long war waged by a three-power coalition that we were able to build only after a decade of blindness.

We are part of these events—every one among us. If we remember that, the events will not bewilder or dwarf us.

MAY 3, 1945

The Consequences of the Atom

1. The Stakes of Power

WHAT THE RELEASE of atomic energy does is to create an utterly new landscape of politics and power. Unless we recognize that fact we shall lose our bearings, and blunder about in the increasing darkness of the world.

The revolution in energy power is bound to produce a revolution in political power. The power to outkill and outproduce others has always meant the power to dominate others. But in the case of atomic energy you have an instrument which widens the margin infinitely between those who have it and those who have it not, those who strike and those who do not. It means the end of what an English historian, J. Holland Rose, once called "the indecisiveness of modern war." And, by the same token, it means that power is raised to the superlative degree; that those nations who are powerful become almost absolutely powerful.

Note that we cannot yet tell who those nations will be. You cannot judge wholly by the present distribution of power. For atomic energy makes many of the present war and industrial weapons a part of the historical record rather than the living present.

In our own age the countries that have had coal and oil resources and hydroelectric energy have been the powerful ones. That will not necessarily be so in the future. Russia and America are the two richest countries in the world in these resources: yet if Germany or Japan had possessed the secret of the atomic bomb, even the Russian-American combination could have been beaten. It happens that America, which was richest in the old sources of energy power, is also the possessor of the new. It has used its immense resources, its mass-production techniques, its great engineering skill, in solving the problem of creating the new energy. But the old energy, once it has been used to create the new, has to recede into the background.

Obviously I am not talking of this year or next. I don't expect the coal and steel and electric power shares to go toppling in the security market right away because of the atomic bomb—and in watching Wall Street quotations I have not yet noted any such tendency. And in immediate

255

terms Wall Street is right. For some years atomic energy, even when developed for peacetime uses, will supplement rather than supplant the present sources of power. But I am talking in long-range terms. In the span of history, the change from the combustion engine and the dynamo to the explosive universe within the atom may prove as far-reaching as the change from hand power to the machine.

Until now it has been true that power belonged to the countries with mass-population as well as natural resources. But atomic energy shrinks the importance of large numbers, as it shrinks seas and sea-lanes, armies and land-mass. The few people who thought up, made, and dropped the atomic bomb did more to bring Japan to its knees than the American fleets and (despite *Izvestia's* recent denial) the massed Russian armies. For the atomic bomb is packed terror, an irresistible assault on the human will.

In war and peace alike, it can become a minority instrument. You may like this or dislike it. I dislike it. But it is none the less a fact we must face.

The outlook for a rough democracy in power—for power as belonging to the largest number of people, the largest heap of resources—is thus not a cheerful one. The world of which the fascists have been long dreaming, in which a small pitiless elite could hold the power of life and death over the large mass of mankind, has become a not impossible world.

Today America holds the secret of this power, and for the present it is safe. But for how long? Other nations will discover it. And even America may in time become the prey of its own internal fascists, who now have a bigger stake than ever in capturing America and its immense world strength.

2. World State and World Society

IF YOU MEAN by sovereignty the freedom of a nation to decide whether it will use war as the instrument of its national policy, then sovereignty was the first casualty of the atomic bomb. If you think of the United Nations as an organization of sovereign states, an *international* organization, then it, too, was a casualty.

In the brief period between San Francisco and Hiroshima, the United Nations as an idea in the minds of the world's people was transformed, even if it was not transformed as a charter. The question now is no longer *whether* we shall have a world state, but *how* we shall achieve it. We have moved from arguing about it to the point where we must plan it. The bomb at Hiroshima was the bell that tolled for us all. Its message rang out clearly: world state or world doom.

There is, of course, still another choice. It is world empire—an imperium over the world by a single nation, a single people, a single armed might, a single economic and military power. What are its chances?

The single world empire would, as things stand now, be American. If any one people is to rule the world, as Rome once ruled the then known world, it would be the American people. For the bomb is our secret. Canadian Munitions Minister C. D. Howe has revealed that while the British and the Canadians helped in the scientific research, they do not actually know how to put the bomb together. Only the Americans know.

Eventually other nations will know. For the next few years world history may become in truth a secret history—not just the battle of the chancelleries, but the race of the laboratories. But there is bound to be an interval, perhaps of years, when America alone will know the secret. In that interval a more ruthless people, bent on world dominion, might possibly achieve it. "Speak softly, but carry a big stick," Theodore Roosevelt used to say. Well, we have a far bigger stick to wield now than any people in history has ever had. Whether we choose to speak softly or loudly, our voice can carry command—if what we want is world empire.

I don't think world empire is what the American people want. Our soldiers have been all over the world and they want none of it, to conquer or to occupy, to have or to hold. The world outside America remains for most of them, after their enforced travels, still an outlandish space full of foreigners. What they want is a job and a competence and a piece of the American earth into which they can sink their strength and their dreams. Never before has so much power to destroy been given to a people so deeply unmilitaristic. Never before has such a chance to conquer the world by terror been given to a people so unwilling to use it.

For all of which we must be profoundly thankful.

Does this mean that the American ruling groups have no interest in empire? It does not. Imperialism and empire-building will continue for some time to absorb the energies of American statesmen, as of others. Note, for example, that after President Truman had said on his German trip that we wanted no foreign soil for ourselves, he had to amend it later by admitting that we might want to keep (either outright or by United Nations mandate) the naval and air island-bases that our military leaders feel we must have. The British—even the Labor Government—show no inclination to turn Hong Kong back to China. The French intend to hold on to French Indo-China. The Russians will not easily relinquish their new power in eastern Europe, and in the Far East their armies march implacably onward into Manchuria.

Thus we have the crazy fact that in a world which must in our time choose between becoming a world state or being ruled by a single empire, statesmen are still behaving as if it could be parceled out among empires. They may pull up in time, or they may go on playing with the map until they start the game of dropping a few atom bombs.

Meanwhile, though we may act as if everything is as it was before the atomic bomb was made, the fact is that everything is different. The Russians, for example, are far more uneasy than they were. The vast land-mass, the natural resources, and the population they control had more meaning once for world power than they have now. Power belongs now to minorities, not majorities. What matter if the greater part of the world is moving toward socialism? The secret of the atomic bomb is in the hands of a capitalist power. We hold it, we say, as trustee for the world. But then, the rich have always said they hold their wealth in trusteeship. That has not helped the poor. It is more blessed to be guardian than ward.

In the end, however, we shall find that if the world survives it will survive not only as a world state, with a world monopoly of the ultimate force, but also as a world society. Atomic energy may prove to have undercut the basis of private ownership of the essentials of power and life. How absurd, in the face of the peacetime uses of atomic energy, seems now the Hayek stuff about government economic control as serfdom.

Just as men cannot now escape taking on collective responsibility for peace, neither can they escape taking on collective responsibility for economic plenty. The bomb dropped on Hiroshima can spell either death and anarchy or peace and socialism.

AUG. 19–20, 1945

Ms. to Be Put in a Bottle

THERE IS a tradition in literature that the mariner on a sinking ship sometimes sets his last thoughts down in a manuscript, which he places in a bottle and sets afloat on the sea, in the hope that somewhere a curious eye will read there the message of his ship's plight and the record of its fate. Since ours seems now to be an idiot world bent on its own destruction, a similar expedient may not be out of place. Perhaps in some not distant future one of the straggling survivors of our era will read these notes on how a whole civilization sought to commit suicide.

The second World War ended in a victory for us, but at its end we ingeniously discovered how to release the energy of the atom. The discovery might have made of us (and may still make, if we survive) a race of men like gods, sitting on a heap of abundance, masters of the sun's strength, capable of using it to spread plenty and destroy poverty. But thus far we have used it instead to spread fear among the nations and destroy their hard-won confidence in each other.

Millions of lives were laid down not only to defeat the enemy, but to build that confidence among the Allied peoples. Young men died at Coventry, at Stalingrad, at Iwo Jima; and those who mourned them found some solace in hoping against hope that the wormwood taste of death might some day give place to the clean sense of a common human cause. For a flashing moment in world history a great American President, Franklin Roosevelt, gave us a glimpse of the possibility of that common cause. Through darkness and blunders he clung to the idea that the Great Powers could cement their war coalition into a permanent peace coalition.

But he died, and the atom bomb came, and under its gray spell the coalition fell apart. Today little remains of it except a bitter memory of brave words spoken on a rostrum at San Francisco, and some already musty signatures on a document. Even the formal beginnings of the United Nations which that document set up have passed almost unnoticed; for ordinary people know enough to distinguish rhetoric from reality. And the atom bomb is today the big reality of the world, as well as the big symbol of men's plight.

The nations have fallen to quarreling over the atom bomb. The

Americans want it for their own. The British are at once in on the secret and not in on it: they were partners in its development, but have neither the engineering facilities nor the experience that we have. The Russians say cryptically that they will have it soon. Everyone affirms at once that there is no secret—and quarrels about whether the secret will be kept or shared. The only thing certain is that the world is now launched on the most lethal weapons-race in its history. For the weapons are little eggs, each of which (as General Arnold tells us in his report on the American air forces) will soon be carried by rockets faster than the speed of sound, and a few of which will be able to wipe out everything alive in a city and reduce it to its original components of water and earth and fire.

To be sure, men of good will are protesting. They are writing and speaking, holding conferences and sending petitions. You can take scarcely a step without stumbling over an atom-bomb conference. I do not mean to underrate their importance, and the importance especially of the almost miraculous clarity with which the atom-bomb scientists are thinking about the social and political consequences of what they created. But it is a bitter thing to report that thus far all the meetings and resolutions have not been able to budge the narrow tenacity of the President and the Secretary of State and the Congressional and military leaders in whose hands the decision lies.

These men, with a ghastly travesty on what is called "realism," are committing the blunder of making two worlds out of what could have been one world. The Russians have helped in that blunder: they have used our failure to internationalize the control of the bomb as the excuse for a course which is half-aggressive, half-isolationist. To the Russians our attitude on the control of the bomb was the symbol that seemed to prove all their fears and suspicions of encirclement by a world leagued against them.

The world is in the grip of big forces and little men. We are led by men who mistake stubbornness in holding to a mistaken position for strength, and who think it is wisdom to practice balance-of-power politics in an atomic-power age. In the engulfing wave of their "realism," they have missed out on most of the great moral issues of our time. With an eye on everything else they forget the one thing that alone can save us in a world of savage atomic terror—that sense of the common plight of all mortals which is the ultimate morality.

Is it a wonder that so many Americans have been filled with dismay? Is it a wonder that they have lost their sense of having leadership, that our internationalism now appears to them a sham, our diplomacy a naked Big Stick; and that the world seems once more to be reverting to the jungle? With all their love for their country, they cannot believe that there is a special destiny which sets Americans apart from the rest of humanity, and which will spare America and its civilization from the consequence of atomic warfare.

The odds are strongly against the human race and its chances of avoiding a suicidal war. But we still remember the cry of the greatest humanist of all, in another time of great despair: "Work . . . while it is day: the night cometh, when no man can work."

NOV. 14, 1945

Nuremberg and the Dream of Law

WHEN THE NUREMBERG trials were first discussed and planned, the atom bomb did not yet exist. What was outlined therefore as a matter of international law has now had added to it the stakes of human survival. For the world will surely go to pieces in an age of atomic warfare unless it is held together by the thongs not only of a rudimentary world government, but of a rudimentary world law: and the Nuremberg trials offer the first instance of such world law in action.[1]

The duty of the reporters at Nuremberg is evidently to report the dramatic tidbits about Hess and Göring and Streicher and how they behave: that is the stuff of human interest, and that is what most newspaper readers eat up. But if you are concerned with the long range you will not be deflected by these personalities, nor by considerations of hatred or pity or revenge for them. Long after they are mold and their memory but a dim stench in history, the real meaning of Nuremberg may still live.

That meaning is best summed up in one of the sentences from the opening statement by the American prosecutor, Robert H. Jackson: "I cannot subscribe to the perverted reasoning that society may advance . . . by the expenditure of morally innocent lives, but that progress in law may never be made at the price of morally guilty lives."

This drives straight at the heart of Nuremberg's importance for the world's future. We have had in the past a few fragments here and there

[1] This piece was written at the opening of the trials.

of a body of international law. We have had laws of warfare, more often defied than honored. We have had covenants and treaties for peaceful relations between nations, but the history of diplomacy is also the history of their flouting. There can be no question that the German defendants at Nuremberg violated both the laws of war and the agreements of peace. But what a pitifully trivial way that is of putting the enormity of their acts. We cannot measure how truly monstrous they were unless we measure them not only against the written agreements but against the most elementary conscience of human beings.

That is why the task which the American prosecution has taken over—that of presenting the Nazi deeds as crimes against humanity—is the key task of the trial. Its failure or success will determine whether we simply get vengeance out of the trial, or whether we get out of it the first big advance in international law since the seventeenth century, when a Dutch lawyer called Hugo Grotius first sought to map out a body of standards of conduct binding on nations.

We must get clear in our minds why we seek to punish the twenty-odd broken and bedraggled men who sit at the bar at Nuremberg.

It is not out of a sadistic desire for revenge or even a measured belief in retribution. Either in terms of personal revenge or historic retribution, their death will be but the paltriest sort of repayment for what they and their fellows have done. It will not wipe out their acts; neither will it add to our own moral stature if we act from such motives.

Nor should we punish them in order to rid the world of them and make sure they will not again commit such crimes. As political forces these men are through. No millions will ever again cheer them; no armies will march at their orders.

Nor do I see much in the idea that the punishment of these men may be a healing and reforming principle for the rest of the German people. Most Germans have been so denuded morally, and they are now so sunk in the desperate struggle for sheer physical survival, that one doubts whether the trials will mean very much to them, one way or another.

The idea of punishment as a deterrent is more in point. To establish the precedent that the leaders of armies and states cannot hide behind the screen of being simply the instruments of state policy may be a big step in warning other states and army leaders who may plan aggressive and in-human war in the future. It is time to remove the impersonal state as a screen behind which the worst crimes can be committed. It may be a healthy thing to make statesmanship a dangerous profession, and to get the idea across that the leaders of states do not necessarily die in bed.

Yet none of these four conventional theories of punishment—retribution, prevention, reform, deterrent—really gets at the meaning of Nuremberg. You get much closer to it when you see it as an immense and revolutionary effort to give utterance to a collective human conscience, to bring into being a collective standard by which the gross violations of that conscience can be punished.

For centuries men have dreamed of the time when crimes could be punished on a world scale as well as between states; when the fact that a criminal had magnified his crimes a million fold would not make him immune while the petty criminal who took only one human life was punished. Always there stood in the way the fact that there is no clear body of statute law for the world, and that nations recognize only the law they have themselves made.

It is better to punish with a clear statute than without it. But in this case of the Nuremberg trials the act of punishment can, like any great forward-moving act in history, help create a new consciousness which may. lead us to set down some day as clear law the things that are now only part of the human conscience. If we do this at Nuremberg it will be an act so crucial that it could have been produced only by the most violent revulsion of the moral sense of men. It is possible that we needed something as monstrous as Nazism to produce that revulsion.

There are those who will argue, as the German defendants do, that this dream is all very pretty; but that you cannot punish men unless they have violated explicit law by an explicit government, and that this must wait until we have set up a world government which will codify a world law. I do not think that will be the sequence. The statute will be, if at all, the end product. It cannot come into being unless we have a world government; but the world government cannot come into being unless we have a collective conscience and a collective will to punish the violations of it. Thus the conscience and the moral sense come first. Once we have them, and once we are aware we have them, the rest will follow.

Some may gibe that I am speaking of a "human conscience" and a "moral sense" that are vague and formless, things on which no body of law can be built. I submit they are the only things that a body of law ever rests on. The surest basis of a future world society lies in the sense of our common plight. When a Negro is lynched, all of us are strung up on that rope. When the Jews were burned in the Nazi furnaces, all of us were burned. When Hitler told his generals and his party leaders about his plans for exterminating the Polish people, and when Göring—on hearing the plans—jumped up and down on the table in sadistic glee, he was jumping on the bodies not only of the Poles, but of us all.

If we never saw this clearly before, we must see it now in the age of the atom bomb. Some of our commentators are talking of making the laws against the use of the atom bomb binding directly on individuals, rather than on nations only. I am all for it. But it will be hopeless ever to make the human conscience binding in the future on the men of the atom bomb unless we make it binding now at Nuremberg on the men of the human furnaces.

NOV. 26, 1945

Germany and the Giants

1. The Key Problems

THERE HAS BEEN endless talk about the German problem ever since it was clear that Hitler's insane gamble had failed. All the big questions about Germany remain: whether political power in it will be centralized or decentralized; whether Germany will have to pay reparations to Russia and its other European victims; whether German industry will be rebuilt, and to what extent, and by whom; and most of all, who will control the great industrial potential of the Ruhr.

In themselves these questions are not insoluble. The Russians are talking loudly of a centralized German government, partly because that is the popular thing among the Germans, partly because it would give their trained Communist leadership a chance to spread itself. Yet no one believes that the Russians would make this a sticking-point in peace negotiations.

The question of reparations is more difficult, especially since these would have to come out of a German industry revived by American capital. Yet on moral grounds who can question the right of the Russians—and the other European nations as well—to be repaid (how pitifully small the repayment will be at best!) for the unutterable damage the Germans have done to their industrial life? Nor can anyone doubt that, once the reparations principle is accepted, the Russians would be willing to postpone the actual payments, to give the German people a breathing spell until they are back on their feet in meeting the immediate problems of economic survival, and to make German imports of foods and raw materials a first charge against current German production.

But the key problem of all is neither the German central government, nor reparations, nor the rebuilding of a German economy. From the very start the problem has been, and still remains, a question of who will supervise the rebuilding of German industry, who will control the vast industrial potential of the Ruhr. American authorities are now handing the Ruhr coal mines back to private German management. Which means back into the hands of the men who not only worked with Hitler but created Hitler. There has been no evidence that they have suffered a change of either mind or heart. They cannot be the nucleus of the "democratic Germany" about which there is so much pious and piffling talk. Their only use can be to make them the nucleus for a bitterly anti-Russian economic force in the heart of Europe. And what applies to the coal industry applies also to steel, chemicals, machinery.

What this adds up to is the conviction that the German problem today is not primarily a German problem. It is a Russian-American problem. Germany is the principal weapon in the battle between the two giant Powers; it is the principal stumbling-block to a lasting peace between them. By the same fact the German problem—once a compromise on it has been struck between America and Russia—can lead to a whole series of other compromises on the other issues that divide Russia and America.

There are two big facts about Russia that all our State Department diplomats and planners ought to know. One is that we cannot deal with Russia wishfully, in the hope that if we apply pressures all along the line her power will crumble and her people will revolt. The other is that the Russians have even less desire for a holy war than we have, and that their leaders will compromise if they are given a chance to.

The London Conference offers a chance to test the Russian willingness to compromise. In former Secretary Byrnes's memoirs, *Speaking Frankly,* there is the flat statement that the key to peace with Russia is a German peace, and that the Russians would make a horse-trade on a German peace if they were given reparations and a hand in the four-power control of the Ruhr industry. Byrnes dismisses this as impossible. Will Secretary Marshall also dismiss it as impossible, even as a basis for negotiations?

Of these two key questions, I have already discussed that of reparations. The four-power control of the Ruhr opens wide horizons of possibility. I can see why the Russians want it so badly: it would give them at least the power of watching and vetoing the uses to which Germany's rebuilt industrial potential might be put. It would mean that German power could not be used against Russia itself. I can see also why the American delegation at London will feel that such a setup is impossible: for it takes away from us our free hand in the disposition of Germany's potential strength, and

Russian veto power could also mean the power of bringing German industry to a standstill.

Yet in the end there can be no worse solution to the key problem of Germany than to use Germany as the battleground of another war. There are, as Harold Laski says, two ways by which Europe can unify itself economically and survive. One is the "civilized way"—by American aid without political strings and by a basic American agreement with Russia. The other is the "hard way"—the path of socialism for Europe without America's aid, with all the attendant dangers of hunger and civil war. If America and Russia do not resolve the central problem of Germany at London, the chances of ever getting back to the "civilized way" will be pitifully dim.

2. *A Mad World, My Masters*

THE GREAT PANJANDRUMS of the Big Four at London have broken up and gone home to take back to their people the happy Christmas tidings of *No Peace on Earth, No Good Will Toward Men*. The air will be filled for some days with blast and counterblast by Russian and American spokesmen alike. But by this time the routine cries from the panjandrums have become so hollow that they will convince only those who have scrapped their thinking-machinery and surrendered their minds and consciences to the official line.

I could not help feeling disgust as I read the statements with which the London Conference broke up. Listen to Bevin: "My country has been falsely accused . . . of taking things out of Germany. This is untrue. . . . Our people have gone without food to feed Germany, all because the unity of Germany has not been established." Now listen to Molotov: He said that the other three had rejected Russia's demand for a German central government and for the abolition of the zonal governments. "That shows the others want Germany divided." He said Russia could not consent to the efforts of America and Britain to hamper Germany's peacetime industrial development. And now listen to Marshall: Russia's demand for reparations, he said, "implies the establishment of an economic power so comprehensive that it would in reality be a power of life and death over any German government . . . and enslave the German people. . . ."

It must be clear enough that these statements were not directed to the world conscience or even to domestic opinion. They were directed to the Germans as the new audience which, even in defeat, is able to dictate the relations between the victors. The best commentary on the state of our world in this Christmas season of 1947 is that the German people (unchanged in heart and mind) have replaced the United Nations as the "Parliament of Man, the Federation of the World"—at least, so far as the London Conference was concerned. As Thomas Carlyle used to put it: "It is a mad world, my masters."

These appeals to German opinion reveal that the whole point of the London Conference was not an effort to establish peace in Europe, but a jockeying for position in the struggle for Germany. It was pretty well known before the conference began that neither side expected it to reach agreement. Yet both sides went through the motions—to leave as good a record as possible of good intentions. If we are spared a separate peace for the time being, either by the Western Powers with western Germany or by Russia with eastern Germany, it is because neither side wants to take on the onus of splitting Germany and thus suffering the hostility of German nationalism.

Actually the difference between a separate peace and the present situation is technical rather than real. Secretary Marshall has already announced that the three western zones will be merged, and we may well expect that the German industrialists of the Ruhr and the Rhineland, even though denied formal political sovereignty, will more and more exercise economic sovereignty. On the Russian side, eastern Germany is already being run as a unit within the larger zone of Russian economic power in eastern Europe, and while the Communist-trained Germans have no economic sovereignty they are effectively the political commissars of the Russians. A mad world, my masters.

Yet even this analysis does not express the full extent of the moral bankruptcy shown in the breakup at London. If the struggle for Germany were all that was involved, an agreement could have been reached on reparations and on German industry and government. Neither issue need be insuperable unless the panjandrums of the Big Four make it so. You could rebuild German industry safely if you kept it under UN control. And, rebuilding German industry, there would be quite enough production from it to allow for taking care of the German people plus the payment of reparations over a twenty-year period, not only to Russia but to all the peoples of Europe whose lands and lives the Germans ravaged. And if reparations came out of German industry, they would not have to come—as is so speciously argued—out of American pockets. Finally, if the German economy is run by a sort of Tennessee Valley Authority under the UN, it can be done—as the TVA is done—through decentralized power in Germany itself, and there is no need for the kind of strong central German government the Russians want.

All this must be clear enough—unless you have made up your mind in advance that *for other reasons than Germany itself* no settlement in Germany is possible. Let us look at what those other reasons might be, on both sides of the struggle.

What made the London Conference impossible from the start was the fact that a German agreement was the key to the ending of the cold war between Russia and America, yet the agreement could not be reached so long as the basic premises of the cold war were still held on both sides.

The American premise is that whatever strength Russia has she will use in aggressive expansion of her power. It follows, therefore, that Russia must be kept as weak as possible. Despite the skill with which the Russians have handled their inflation problem, they still suffer from critical weaknesses in both heavy industry and consumers' goods. To fulfill their Five Year Plan they need as much machinery and manufactured goods from abroad as they can get. Their demand for reparations from Germany is therefore not a perverse whim, but flows from the internal Russian economic position as well as from a sense of justice. American policy, on the other hand, still seems determined to press Russia as hard as possible, in the hope that its own internal weaknesses will force it to give up the struggle. Hence the adamant refusal by Secretary Marshall even to discuss reparations—a refusal that is best illumined within this framework.

The Russians are as determined to wreck the Marshall Plan as the Americans are determined to squeeze Russia. The Russians know that under American management German economic strength might be used as a center for consolidating western Europe into an anti-Russian bloc. They will therefore have nothing to do with a German settlement which leaves America free to make an economic alliance with Germany and give large subventions to German industry under the Marshall Plan. The Russian desire for Four-Power control of the Ruhr industries is less motivated by the fear that private control will mean the restoration of German war potential, than it is by the desire to prevent the German economy from fitting into American plans for Europe.

That is how the German problem is tangled in the cold war. Agreement did not come at London because neither side wanted agreement. That is as true of Marshall as it is of Molotov. Both worlds prefer to wait it out, because each believes that time is on its side. The Americans believe that time will show up the internal weaknesses of a police-state which started the industrialization of its economy too late to afford a world-wide challenge to the world-wide American economic empire. The Russians believe that time will show up the internal contradictions of capitalism, as the

Marxians put it, and bring a greater, rather than lesser, revolutionary ferment in the world.

Meanwhile both sides have postponed peace indefinitely, and are callously taking the "calculated risk" of war. While they wait they also push and squeeze. But the victim that is caught in between them is the human spirit and the human future. A mad world, my masters.

NOV. 25, DEC. 17, 1947

On Britain: Ashes, Shame, and Hope

As AN ANTIDOTE to the recent unhappy outbreak of *furor patrioticus* against an American traveler who made some speeches,[1] it is worth your while to read Henry Wallace's "Report from Britain" in the *New Republic*. Its greatest value is not that it says anything new about the lamented Truman Doctrine, but that it says some mellow and true things about Britain today. As an American, when he is talking of his own country's blindness and neuroses, Wallace's temper is bristling, militant, immediate; as an outsider in Britain he sees the subject in depth and extension.

I have recently had a chance to talk to several of the younger and more rebellious Labor M.P.s. They have a fighting faith in the prospects of a new democratic socialism within Great Britain. But on the foreign policy of their Government they have as astringent a view as Wallace has on the foreign policy of his Government. Which is as it should be.

Take their testimony on Britain, add it to Wallace's in his *New Republic* report, and then add to both the brutal British policy of treachery and repression in Palestine along with the very different British policy of withdrawal from India and Burma—and you get the material for a total profile of Britain today. The ingredients for drawing that profile are ashes, shame, and hope.

It has always been a mistake to equate British greatness with the British colonial empire. The empire will go, but the greatness will remain. There will always be an England, but why can't it be a socialist England which

---

[1] The reference is to the turmoil occasioned by Henry Wallace's speeches in Europe in the spring of 1947, attacking American foreign policy.

has found its true greatness in social construction at home, rather than with its proconsuls and its "White Man's Burden" in the far corners of the earth? Looking at the British, the new American proconsuls may well ask themselves what doth it profit a people if it gain half the world and lose its own soul? We speak fondly and nostalgically of the glories of British Empire, and how it kept the world stabilized. We forget the slave trade and the Opium War and the massacre at Amritsar. I am happy that the British are beginning to win back their soul even in the midst of the Palestine shame and the Jewish agony. I hope that Russia and America, which are building their own kinds of empire and dreaming of further empire beyond that, can learn something from the British lesson.

What is the lesson? That the power of empire is hollowness, and the glories of empire are dust. Here are the British at the end of their imperial road. What has empire done for the ordinary Englishman and his wife and children? What can it do for them? Can it give them the coal they need, or the steel, or the new machinery, or the missing industrial manpower, or the goods for export, or the dollar credits? No, what it does is to continue to drain manpower for the divisions in the Middle East, and the Navy, and the armament industries that must maintain them. The British have for so long, under their Tory statesmen, been absorbed with the demands of empire that they have let the march of technology pass them by. That is the bitter heritage the British Labor Government has received from the Tory imperialists.

It is just as well for the British to face their crucial problem now. It is not the problem of how to maintain their empire. It is the problem of how to feed their people and rebuild their sinews of industrial strength. Above all, it is the problem of how to carve out a democratic socialist domestic policy. No nation can afford to be a Dr. Jekyll at home and a Mr. Hyde abroad. Ever since the Labor Government came into power it has had a fault-line between its domestic and foreign policy. The new titans of Downing Street have tried to hold on to past imperial greatness on a shrunken economic base. They didn't get away with it. There is a growing understanding among the rank and file of Labor M.P.s that their job is to build socialism in Britain, that it is more important to take care of their coal mines at home than to rule with an iron hand the lands in the Middle East which hold the oil they may need to fuel another war.

Actually, if we ask not about Britain as a colonial empire, but about Britain as a world force, Britain's future is healthier than its past. I believe in what the British people will be able to do under planners and administrators like Cripps, Aneurin Bevan, Strachey. It will take a decade before they can get a new economic base under way, but they can do it, especially if their economic and moral energies are not frittered away on fruitless foreign adventures. Given this base, the British can become a first-rate world force. For they are shaping at home a way of life that combines the techniques of economic socialism with the tradition of political democracy and freedom.

On one thing Henry Wallace is right beyond all cavil. The real choice for the peoples of the world is not the choice between Russian communism and American unplanned capitalism. If that were the choice, it would be a desperate plight for the world. There is another path, and it is the path the British people are clearing for themselves—the path of democratic socialization, of a mixed company which is organized and run by the people's representatives for the people's good. And the curious irony is that this is exactly what the Jews of Palestine are doing, with a passion and buoyancy far greater than any the British can show.

That is why I say Hail to both British and Palestinian democratic socialism, at the same time that I say Farewell to British colonial empire.

APRIL 24, 1947

The Jew and the Western Conscience

1. Nowhere to Lay His Head

IT IS TIME to do some basic thinking and some plain speaking about the homeless, stateless Jews of Europe and the need for opening the gates of Palestine to them.

Americans have finally had the problem about the displaced persons dramatized for them. The ugly picture it draws raises the question of what will happen to these hundreds of thousands of homeless people. And beyond that, the bigger question of what will happen to the Jews of Europe as a whole.

The basic thing to remember here is that this is not merely—not even primarily—a Jewish problem. It is a problem of all the peoples of the Western world. It is a problem of Western humanity, and it goes to the roots of the survival of that humanity.

In this shrunken world of ours where we have all perforce become members one of another, no people can become the victims of injustice and fascist terror and democratic cowardice without dragging all other peoples along with it in its fall. That was proved true by what happened in Spain. It was proved true by what happened in China. It has proved abundantly true by what has happened to the Jews.

It goes deepest of all in the case of the Jews. That's why the pity of those who pity the Jews is as dangerous as the indifference of those who find the whole business too wearisome to think about. This is not a case for pity of a defenseless minority. It is not a case for the broad-mindedness of "tolerance." It is not a case for making a generous gesture—political or otherwise—toward a hapless people that has suffered so much. The suffering of the Jews has been—and still is—of such a staggering magnitude and intensity that it reaches further and deeper than tolerance can ever go, and it makes pity seem a puny emotion.

Think back to the early 1930s, when Nazism first came into the open in its systematic slaughter of the Jews. How broad-minded the Western world was at that time—with the Nazis. How judicious it was in weighing a few hundred thousand Jewish lives, a few million even, against the danger that Hitler might be offended, that his military force might be unloosed against western Europe. How prudent, how terribly prudent we were, how "realistic," as we wondered whether action to stop Hitler might not upset the delicate power balance in Europe.

The fact that was staring us in the face all the time was that Hitler's assault on the Jews went far beyond the Jews, and was an assault on the whole of Western civilization. The Western democracies waited and waited, hoping somehow to disentangle their own fate from the fate of the Jews. They could not. They waited until it was terribly late, almost too late. Then they acted.

We have passed through that first phase, and the war against fascism is won. Now we are in the second phase of the same continuing historical process. It is a different phase, because we are no longer dealing with an active fascist terrorism. Jews are no longer being slugged with truncheons, dragged naked through the streets, flung into mass graves, burned in furnaces.

But the same forces are still at work, passively but no less really. The Jews are still the despised, the rejected, the homeless. Even if they are let out of the concentration camps, and tents or attics are found for them in the German villages, it is unthinkable that they should want to remain for good in the Germany that tortured and killed their children, their wives, their parents. And not only Germany. Everywhere in Europe the fascism of Hitler and Goebbels has left behind a monstrous residue of anti-Jewish feeling and practice.

But once again the old familiar voices are heard. It would not be prudent, say the British, to admit more than fifteen hundred Jews a month to Palestine. It would be better, we hear, not to inflame the terrorism of the Arab League. It might possibly happen, we are told, that the delicate balance of power will be upset in the Near East. This is, they say, a problem not for Britain and Palestine, but a problem for the United Nations. There must be conferences, agenda, memoranda. And meanwhile the homeless wait.

Nor are the British alone in this guilt. The Americans too must share it. We have not shown any tendency to open our doors to those refugees who may wish to come to this land of freedom. No one pushes the idea because it might stir up the primitive Rankins in Congress, just as Clement Attlee fears to stir up the Arabs, just as Neville Chamberlain once feared to stir up Hitler.

What we do not see is that the big question is not the suffering of the homeless Jews, big as that is. The bigger question is the paralysis of the Western conscience when faced with the plight of a people who have borne the brunt of the struggle against fascism longer and more brutally than any other—a people who have become in the deepest sense the symbols of that struggle.

Palestine is not the only issue in Jewish survival. It is the emergency issue now, because no other country will admit the homeless Jews in large numbers, no other people will welcome and care for those who have borne the most terrible battle in world history. There are other Jews, millions of them, in Britain, France, America, and elsewhere, who want to stay where they are in the countries they love, and whose fate will depend on the battle for democracy and liberty in those countries. But if the Western peoples do not face up to the meaning of Palestine for the world today, the same forces of apathy that will doom the homeless Jews of Europe will also doom the Western democracies, and the Jews and Christians in them alike.

Victor Gollancz, the British Laborite, has written a brilliant pamphlet about the Jews of Europe. He takes as his text the parable of Jesus: "The foxes have holes, and the birds of the air have nests; but the Son of man hath not where to lay his head." That parable has a tragic truth today that applies to millions of the sons of man. As long as it remains true the Western peoples will not find a moral base on which to build their world after battle. The fate and survival of the Jews have become the crucial index of the fate and survival of Western civilization.

2. *Two Men and a Mission*

WE ARE BEGINNING to get from the inside the story of one of the most remarkable and most futile missions in history, the Anglo-American Committee of Inquiry, whose job was to study the problem of Palestine and
of the Jews in Europe. It was appointed in October, 1945, and finished its
report in April, 1946. It is now clear that the whole project was conceived
by the British Foreign Office in the hope that an inquiry could win a six-
month delay for the British. But when Bevin and Attlee found that the
report was not the one they had expected, they scrapped it and started
instead on the policy of military repression.

I don't know how many of the twelve members of the Committee kept
diaries. One who did was Richard H. S. Crossman, the young British
Labor M.P. Another was Bartley Crum, a liberal Republican lawyer.

Crossman will be remembered as the young Labor M.P. who led a revolt of his colleagues against the Bevin foreign policy. His book, *Palestine Mission: a Personal Record* (Harper), sheds a good deal of light on
the making of a Labor rebel.

Crossman comes from a conservative British family. He had a British
public school education at Winchester, studied philosophy and the classics
at Oxford, and was all set to write on Aristotle's doctrine of the soul and
settle down as an Oxford don. Hitler's rise to power jolted him out of his
dream of scholarly peace and made him a Socialist. The war gave him a
chance to show his brilliance in psychological warfare. The Labor victory
made him an M.P. The Palestine mission turned him into the sharpest
and most effective critic of the Bevin foreign policy inside Labor's ranks.
When that policy changes, as change it must, Crossman is one of the
younger men logically slated to organize that change.

Like the other members of the Committee, Crossman was chosen not
because he had studied the Jewish problem but because he had not studied it. The idea was to bring fresh viewpoints to an old problem. But
Crossman had something far more important to start with than factual
knowledge. He had the intellectual discipline for canvassing every boundary and corner of an assignment, the sensitiveness for opening his mind
to new impressions, the imagination to follow his problem wherever it
led him, the honesty to come out with a different conclusion from the
one expected of him and the one he started with. Such men are rare and
precious, and I would not exchange a whole carload of Foreign Office experts and State Department Machiavellis for one of them.

You can read the book as an "inside" story of a mission that failed; you can read it for its delightful and acid verbal portraits of Jewish and Arab spokesmen, of American and British actors in the Palestinian tragedy; or you can read it as an analysis of the problem of the Jew in a world criss-crossed by hatreds and power-politics. Any way you read it, it has the al-most intolerable brilliance that has made Crossman suspect among the small men who distrust sharp insights and verbal deftness.

But I prefer to read it as an education that took the form of a journey— an intellectual exploration that moved as the Committee's hearings moved from Washington to London to Vienna to Cairo to Jerusalem to Lausanne. Crossman started his journey (as he puts it) "very pro-Arab." He ended with the realist's conviction that the existence of a Jewish nation in Palestine is no longer a subject for argument but a fact to accept, and that to betray the Jewish cause to considerations of oil or aviation imperi-alism and anti-Russian power-politics is to be callous not only to a peo-ple's existence but to world peace itself. Looking at it from the standpoint of a Bevin, he must seem someone who let the team down. But from the standpoint of a Weizmann or a Ben-Gurion, and of liberals and socialists in Britain, Palestine, and America, he came to mock and remained to pray.

The intellectual and moral journey that Crossman and Crum and their colleagues took I can only describe, shamelessly transposing Céline's fa-mous phrase, as a journey to the end of the night. For, as they found out, the problem of the Jew's place in the modern world is one to test the very foundations of that world. I have no hesitation in saying that it is the deepest political, psychological, and moral problem of our time. You can-not probe it half-way. Before you are through, you find that you have traveled into the darkest recesses of the human heart, and into deep and none-too-slumbering passions which (as Crossman puts it) are like vol-canic forces erupting below the thin crust of Western civilization.

The outlines of Crossman's present thinking on the Jewish problem are worth summary. In the first place, he insists it *is* a problem, not to be thought or wished out of existence: by killing six million Jews and creating more than a million homeless ones, Hitler made it a problem. For the homeless Jews of Europe the solution he sees is immigration not only into Palestine but into America and the other Western countries as well. Crossman draws a sharp line between the Jews of Palestine and those of the Dispersal. The former (and, unlike Koestler,[1] he leans to the moderates among them and advocates partition) he regards as already a nation, standing on its own feet. ("While the rest of the world was argu-

[1] For a discussion of Arthur Koestler's *Thieves in the Night*, see above, p. 51.

ing, the Jewish nation had been born.") About the Jews in other countries he is not wholly clear: sometimes he talks as if American Jews, for example, will find their fulfilment wholly as Americans, sometimes he sees anti-Semitism engulfing them as the world turns to a reactionary crusade.

Of one thing he is certain: that the problem cannot be settled except as part of a larger settlement of the American-Russian conflict, and within the United Nations. On that he is dead right.

What Bartley Crum learned about Palestine and the Jews of Europe and the Arab rulers and the British rulers is not different in essentials from what Crossman learned. Crum has set down his impressions in *Behind the Silken Curtain* (Simon and Schuster). There are, of course, differences in emphasis, for Crossman's method is reflective and scholarly, and Crum's is direct and sharp. Yet the larger pattern is the same.

The reason is that for any mind not wholly closed to them, the facts are overwhelming. To be sure, the psychological tangles around the position of the Jew in the modern world have grown complex, and the paths of solution are thorny. But the big facts are simple enough: that the original Balfour commitment looked forward to continued Jewish immigration and—when the Jews were a majority—the creation of a politically free homeland; that the stream of immigration was stopped by the 1939 White Paper exactly when the need for it was tragically deepest; that the constructive achievements of Palestine's Jews have been undeniable, and have lifted Arab as well as Jewish living-standards; that the Jews are in Palestine to stay, and have carved out a new way of life.

If anyone has ever made these and other facts persuasive beyond cavil and moving even to the most obdurate heart, it is Bartley Crum, setting down not pleas but experiences, not rhetoric but a series of episodes that enclose you like panels in a house of death.

But to what avail? The big question, as I have said, is not what arguments and facts there are, but whether those who make the decisions are open to arguments and facts.

Thus far they have not been. The British Foreign Office expert on Palestine, Harold Beeley, explained to Crum that the United States would do well to join Britain in establishing a *cordon sanitaire* of Arab states to resist Russian power. Loy Henderson, of our own State Department, also briefed Crum, urging on him that the crucial angle from which to view the Palestine problem was Russia. The official mind not only in Britain but in America as well is deeply impressed by Arab control over Middle East oil. It also is—or professes to be—frightened by the possibility of an

Arab-Russian alliance if Jewish immigration is resumed or the Jews are given their freedom.

It is these fears and stakes, rather than logic and history and justice and compassion, that will shape the UN decision on Palestine. They are worth examining.

First of all, the oil question. The British need their Middle East oil desperately in the event of a war with Russia; we do not. We have our own oil here in our country, the British don't. They have helped, not hindered, the American oil companies in getting the forty per cent of the oil reserves of the Middle East that are now under concession to our oil giants. Their effort has been to link us in partnership with their own oil power in the Middle East, tangle us in their own guilty oil politics. The facts are, of course, that we can get along on what we have; that in the event of war it would not be hard for Russia to overrun the Middle East oil fields; and that the Arab oil lords have more at stake in keeping good relations with us and our capital and technical skill than we have in keeping them appeased.

As for the Russian question, the prospect of the reactionary Arab feudal lords' striking an alliance with Russian state socialism is fantastic. It is one of those arguments that can survive only in the kingdom of fear, where every value is turned topsy-turvy.

America will have immense influence in the UN sessions on Palestine. If we give a decisive lead, most of the smaller nations of Europe and all the nations of Latin America will go along with us. The decision will be that of the UN, the responsibility for it will be that of the United States of America. If the Jews of Palestine and of Europe are once more betrayed, as they were by Bevin's breaking of his promise to accept the report of the Anglo-American Committee, the betrayal will be ours.

On that too there is a story in the Crum book—the story of the State Department "secret file" on Palestine, showing that every time the American Government made a public promise on Palestine, the State Department sent the Arab rulers a private message discounting it and reassuring them. The time is long overdue for honesty and for action.

America must in all honesty throw its prestige in the UN toward a partition plan under which Jews and Arabs can carve out their own destinies.[2] If we do not, it will be because we have shut our minds to every consideration of reason and decency and world peace—to everything except the dis-

[2] The American delegation did, and the UN resolution for the partition of Palestine was passed. Then some of the people in the State Department and in National Defense became apprehensive; the U. S. delegation backtracked on partition, leading the UN to reverse itself; a civil war broke out in Palestine, and out of the Jewish military successes the new State of Israel emerged. See pp. 280-84.

torted images of our fears. And if we shut our minds to reason, we are in a poor position to condemn the current outbreaks of the Irgun groups in Palestine. For they too have lost their faith in reason, and have moved beyond it to the naked fact of violence. Theirs is the cynical belief that the sound of dynamite is the only sound the world will heed. It is up to us to determine whether they are wrong.

3. *The Battle of the* Runnymede Park

THE BRITISH brought them on three caged ships into the port of Hamburg—onto the soil of Germany that was soaked with the blood of their brothers, into the murderous German air where the ashes of their brothers had been scattered. They were the people of the Exodus, some 4,500 of them, and they had spent fifty-five days in their "floating concentration-camp." They were weakened from their hunger strike. In the first of the three vessels that landed, there was some stiff fighting before they could be carried off. The men and women and children of the second came off peacefully, much to the bewilderment of the British until they discovered a time bomb had been left behind. But it was the third ship, the *Runnymede Park*, that gave the British their real trouble.

No one came off that ship. The British soldiers had to go in to get them. High-powered fire-hoses with Elbe River water were turned upon them, massed in the hold of the vessel. Then the soldiers went into the hold with rubber truncheons and clubs. When they brought the Jews out, many of them with battered heads and with blood streaming down their faces, five British soldiers carried each Jew. They took them past lines of German police, and flung them bodily into German freight cars, while their women wept and their children shouted "German beasts" at the soldiers. The freight cars were sealed up, and the people who had lived through a decade of Hitler's hell were sent off to camps near Lübeck.

That is the story of the battle of the *Runnymede Park*. The story began long before the episode at Hamburg, nor does that episode end it. The people who have survived Hitler will not surrender to Bevin. Their fear was stifled in the gas-chambers, it went up in the smoke of the human furnaces: nothing the British can do will suffice to revive that fear. The real questions to be raised are not about the Jews of the Exodus, 1947, or the Jews in Palestine, or the Jews still left in Central Europe. The real questions are about the British.

We keep asking: Why do these men do it? Obviously one can call them

"Nazi beasts" only out of the unreason of embittered hearts. The British are not the Germans, and they are not Nazis. Yet their crime against these refugees, whom they fling like animals from caged vessels into sealed freight cars, is a moral crime monstrous enough in its own terms not to need any added inflating by invective. The men who have ordered this action—and all the other actions that make up the whole British Palestine policy of which this forms part of a pattern—are people who belong to a labor government, who talk about socialism and human dignity, who spent themselves fighting the Nazis, who are trying to create a new economic democracy in Britain itself. How can such men commit this moral crime, and the others like it?

They do it, I think, because while they call themselves Laborites and Socialists, they have never disengaged themselves from the spell of empire. True, they have withdrawn from the least tenable of their imperial possessions—India. But what remains of their empire, scattered over the twelve corners of the world, is still the largest and most motley imperial aggregate of peoples in history. Remember: the British don't have much with which to hold down these peoples—yellow, black, and white, heathen and Christian, ignorant and "Westernized." Their troops are dwindling, and are having to be husbanded more and more carefully. Their economy is weak. All that they have is the spell of empire. Let that spell once be broken—and let the breakers of the spell get away with it—and the whole empire crumbles.

The British are weak, yes: in fact, they are too weak to be generous. Only a strong empire can afford to be generous. A weak empire must govern either by the method of freedom or the method of terror. The British made the initial mistake of not applying the method of freedom in postwar Palestine. The episode of Hamburg is the logical result of the method of terror.

If it be asked how the British can square this with their socialism, the answer must be that for the present ruling group within the Labor party the idea of socialism is not a living conviction. It is the slogan on which these men came to power, and it is the slogan which even Bevin still parrots, although decreasingly. But it is not a moral passion within the hearts of the men of Downing Street, in any degree comparable with the moral passion of the Haganah "agitators" in the hold of the Runnymede Park. Since the socialism of Attlee and Bevin has become an empty phrase, a moral vacuum has been left. The only thing left to fill that vacuum is the old imperial consciousness.

It won't work. It will neither hold the empire together nor build socialism within Britain. Something epochal happened in the battle at the

Hamburg docks. A dying empire was fighting a living idea. In that battle there can be only one outcome.

OCT. 2, 1945; MARCH 26, APRIL 23, SEPT. 10, 1947

History Is Being Made in Palestine

1. What the Jews Fight For

BEFORE YOU CAN say much about the prospects of the civil war in Palestine you have to know about the long struggle for a Jewish homeland which has preceded that civil war. The headlines about the Palestine bombings have little meaning unless you ask: What is it the Jews are fighting and dying for?

The answer falls into three parts: a homeland they can call their own; a place where they can stand up as free men at peace with other men; a new way of life for themselves.

The winning of the first objective—the homeland—came with the United Nations decision on the partition of Palestine. Behind that stretches a long history of Jewish striving which we are now in danger of forgetting or taking for granted. Back in 1882, amidst a wave of Russian pogroms, an Odessa doctor called Leo Pinsker published a book called *Auto-emancipation.* Pinsker saw that as long as the Jews had no homeland they could be the butt of every fanatic. "To the living," he wrote prophetically, "the Jew is a corpse, to the native a foreigner, to the homesteader a vagrant, to the proprietor a beggar, to the poor an exploiter and millionaire, to the patriot a man without a country, to all a hated rival." The technique of Goebbels, fifty years later, was to prove how right he was. A few young Russian Jews, stirred by Pinsker, went off to Palestine to start the movement for agricultural colonization.

The other great pioneer of the Jewish national idea was Theodor Herzl, whose pamphlet *The Jewish State,* published in 1896, became the Bible of political Zionism. It is easy now to look back at this journalist, at home in the intellectual circles of both Vienna and Paris, and point out flaws in his thinking: he was no great liberal, he had little knowledge of Jewish history or culture, he was not aware of social forces aside from international politics. But the fact remains that Herzl was one of those one-idea men who by their driving will give history a nudge in one direction or another. He died young, in 1904, but not until he had brought together the first international Zionist Congress at Basle (1897), and lit a flame in the minds and hearts of Jews from every country of Europe and from the United States as well.

That flame was fed from two sources: what anti-Semitic hatred did to the Jews dispersed throughout the world; and what the increasing number of Jews in Palestine did in reviving the eroded soil and sending down into it the cultural roots that had not flourished since Biblical times. Herzl had had a dream. He was an intense young Jew, with eyes that drew men to him, and an egocentric sense of mission (he wrote in his diary: "At Basle I founded the Jewish state"). But to convert a dream into reality takes blood and sweat, and the Jews poured out plenty of both in the two generations after Herzl's death. The United Nations partition decision was paid for by the blood of at least six million martyrs in Europe, and the sweat of hundreds of thousands of pioneers in Palestine.

Against this background it should be clear even to the Arab leaders that the Jews will not allow themselves to be frightened away from Palestine, or killed off in it. They recognize that the Arabs too have a historic claim to Palestine—a claim that the partition decision makes ample allowance for, giving the Jews the smaller part of the territory, and even then only the soil they have themselves brought to fruition and the cities they have themselves built. There have been nationalist movements in the past— the Italian, the Polish, the Irish notably—in which men have fought bitterly to redeem their unredeemed native country from foreign sway. But this is the first nationalist movement in history in which the strivers for nationhood had first—quite literally—to create the soil and cities they were to redeem.

The Jews of Palestine want peace, but they are ready to fight for it. Not even the most fanatical Arab leader can claim that the Jews started the civil war. It was started by the clique around the Mufti of Jerusalem, which hopes—by inflaming the Arab masses against the Jews—to use the stirred-up mass passions as a weapon against the moderates among the Arab leaders. The Jews in Palestine and in the displaced persons camps of Europe have faced death before, and they can face it again. The thing to remember is that many of the Palestine Jews, and almost all the Jewish DPs, are the sole survivors of families the rest of whom have been exterminated by the Nazis. Their passion is for the dignity of living out their lives among their own kind, as free men, and not as a tolerated minority. But if they cannot have that, their passion is for the dignity of dying not like cattle in boxcars, but with weapons in their hands, fighting for their homeland and their freedom.

I said above the Jews are fighting for three things: a homeland, freedom, and a way of life. It is the third which looms most important in the future, and which gives a new meaning to the first two. From the start there were Jewish leaders who saw that political Zionism was the means and not the end—the means toward a cultural and social rebirth. Ahad Ha'am ("One of the People," as he called himself), who died twenty years ago, saw the task of Palestine as the rebuilding of a Jewish cultural center in the spirit of the Hebrew prophets. A. D. Gordon, a Tolstoyan figure, preached the creative effect of productive labor on the soil, and set in motion the Chalutzim—the pioneers in the agricultural collectives. Justice Louis D. Brandeis, of the United States Supreme Court, brought to the Zionist movement not only the kind of talent for diplomacy that Weizmann had but also the passion for an economic democracy which could operate in small units and would not be destroyed by the "curse of bigness"—the modern worship of gigantism.

The problem the Palestine Jews are trying to solve is that of building an economic democracy without totalitarianism, and without a top-heavy state bureaucracy; and that of maintaining political freedom without the curse of concentrated corporate power in private hands; and finally that of welding both economic and political democracy together by a sense of society—of togetherness. This is the problem that all peoples face today. If the Jews face it freshly, it is because they have come to it along a hard way, through suffering. The right to solve this problem in their own way is what they are fighting for.

2. Triple Armor

OUT OF THE AGONY and bloodshed in Palestine, a big fact is emerging. It is the fact of a Jewish Palestinian nation which is showing itself as impressive in war as it has been creative in peace. Everyone expected that the Haganah would give a good reckoning of itself in defending the Jewish settlements. But what has come as a surprise even to the friends of the Jews— and as a sharp shock to their enemies—is the demonstration at Haifa that the Jewish forces could move swiftly in large-scale operations on the offensive.

The Jews have shown themselves to be not just a militia but an army, and not just an army but a nation-in-arms. What accounts for their strength, and the weakness of the Arab forces thus far?

The fact is that the Arab states have finally found their real level of power. They are economically weak, socially backward, poverty-stricken, feudal in structure and thought. States like that can make trouble, can manage massacres, can carry on vendettas—but they cannot win a decision under the conditions of modern war. The outlook of the Arab leaders has been the outlook of a feudal fascism. Even more important, the Arab masses have not had their heart in the war which was not of their making but a conspiracy of a few leaders.

The Jews, on the other hand, have known what they are fighting for, and this knowledge is still—even in our highly complex age of war technology—the most crucial thing about fighting. They are making history in Palestine because they know their own place in the long-drawn campaign of history. They may still lose battles, but they will win the war because they are encased in a triple armor.

What is that triple armor?

The first layer of armor is the fact that in the deepest sense they are a nation. They did not wait to have the United Nations send forces into Palestine to make them one. While commissions of inquiry were inquiring, while gentlemen were debating, while power-politicians were power-politicking, the Jews created the materials of a going national concern: a going economy, a functioning machinery of trade-unions and co-operatives, an administrative system, a policy-forming body, an army, and—above all else—a community of people who could face dying together because they were in process of creating a new way of living together.

The second layer is the fact that, along with their religious tradition of the East, the Jews of Palestine are the heirs of the modern science and technology and administration of the West. The modern Palestinians are a striking fusion of Western techniques with the prophetic passion and the moral depth that comes from their own religious tradition.

The third layer is the fact that the Palestinian Jews are the end product of the agonies through which the Jews have been put in the era of the fascist shadow. Men and women and children who have survived the annihilation camps of Europe will not quail before the Mufti's hirelings and will not even quail before Britain's Abdullah. They have met worse and are still there. And the boys and girls of the Haganah who are fighting do so in the knowledge that they must survive to build something which will make up for all the suffering and the indignities of the dead.

The Jews are fighting well, but they do not make a cult of holy war as the Mohammedans do. They are fighting to establish a livable peace. They mean peace, and they mean it when they say they want to live in the same communities with the Arabs. It was not the Jews who compelled the Arab civilians to evacuate Haifa after the city was taken. It was the Arabs themselves, under the spur of their leaders, who insisted on evacuation. The Jews believe in civil liberties for minorities, since they have themselves been minorities for so long in so many parts of the world. And they believe in an economic union between their state and the Arab state, whatever it may turn out to be.

As for American policy, the reasons of several months ago which presumably caused the Administration to back-track on the partition decision no longer exist. If the Forrestal crowd once thought that the Arabs had the decisive military strength in the Middle East, they must now feel disabused of that illusion. It is the Jews and not the Arabs who have the decisive military strength. In the light of that fact, the last obstacle in the path of a policy of American honor should be considered removed.

The Jews have confirmed their nationhood. Let the Americans redeem their own honor.[1]

JAN. 6, APRIL 28, 1948

Byrnes: Tragic Peacemaker

WHEN A Secretary of State who has been in the thick of peacemaking turns writer, and lets down his hair, you can expect a startling book. That is exactly what former Secretary Byrnes has given us in his memoirs, *Speaking Frankly* (Harper).

It is a book that will make headlines, and is obviously intended to. Its biggest disclosure is the news—from German sources—that as late as October, 1940, more than a year after the Nazi-Soviet Pact of 1939, Molotov and Hitler came close to concluding a pact for the division of the world, and that if Molotov had not demanded too much, Russia might have fought the war on Germany's side.

There are also lesser disclosures: that Roosevelt and Stalin had had some bitter exchanges of correspondence before FDR died; that Stalin showed only perfunctory interest when President Truman told him

[1] Two weeks later, when the Jews of Palestine proclaimed their new State of Israel, President Truman at least partially repaired the mistakes of American policy and helped redeem American honor. The United States was the first government to recognize the new state de facto.

about the atom bomb at Potsdam; that Admiral Leahy thought the bomb was overrated; that Leahy and the White House gang around Truman were hostile to Byrnes and (the book hints) forced him out; that Byrnes had earlier forced Wallace out of the Cabinet by threatening to resign after the Madison Square Garden speech.

All these disclosures will be discussed in the press for many days to come. But I assume the real purpose of the book is not to titillate a sensation-hungry public but to help in finishing the process of peacemaking that Byrnes began. The real question about the book is not how candid it is, but how deep it is in its analysis—how close it comes to cutting to the heart of the Russian-American question with which primarily it deals.

Here I feel that with all his good will, his diplomatic adroitness, and his genius for a politics of maneuver, Byrnes has little to contribute that searches out the dark places of the Russian-American problem. His book is, of course—as any such book must be by its nature—an apologia for his course of action as Secretary. Byrnes convinces the reader that he genuinely and passionately wanted to build an enduring peace, get the treaties signed, get the occupying forces home; that he met with endless and exhausting talk by the Russians, delaying maneuvers, obstructions, conferences protracted until the early morning hours, heartbreaking disillusionments. No one who reads the book can fail to come away with the sense that this man meant well, gave of his mind and his health to bring peace to the world. The real doubts I have are doubts about whether Byrnes ever saw the Russian problem clearly and whole—in all its dimensions: historical, psychological, and economic, as well as political.

One thing that troubles me is that never once—so far as I can make out from the book—was Byrnes wrong. And very rarely were the Russians right. That's too black-and-white a picture for me. Any historian will tell you that in studying similar epochal struggles between great powers in the past, there were usually some mistakes on both sides and some sins on both sides. I refuse to believe that even FDR was right all the time, and that goes double and triple for the lesser men. Byrnes seems to believe that Stalin has been fairly reasonable—when you could get access to him. The real villain of the piece is Molotov. As the book is written, it is really about Byrnes and Molotov—their maneuvers, collisions, compromises, advances, retreats, impasses. It is a depressing epic (sometimes with comic interludes that make the gloom all the starker) of how the good will built up during the war between the world's two greatest peoples quickly went down the drain afterward, and how their coalition war against a common enemy became a cold war against each other.

It is easy enough to say where the Russians went wrong. The defeat of

the German power created a vacuum in Europe, and the Russian diplomats and commissars saw a chance to move relentlessly into it and fill
it up before the Western Powers had the chance. They started with
Poland and Rumania, and as hardened revolutionists who had been
taught to use every resource at their command, they kept it up until
what had begun as negotiation quickly and unmistakably became expansion. Byrnes is quite right in saying that the Russians are aiming chiefly
at training Communist leaders in Europe who will not themselves run
the governments but will be able by trade-union and propaganda strength
to set limits to what the governments can do. This is a big order, and
the world will not have peace until the Russians know it is too big.

But where did the Americans go wrong? Byrnes's answer seems to be:
nowhere. I don't believe that the historians will accept it. For Byrnes is
relating a more tragic history than he knows—a history in which wrong
moves were made not only by Jacobins overconfident of their revolutionary
mission and power, but also by Downing Street and State Department
titans overconfident that America with its strength and wealth could sit
on the lid of world ferment and act as if a revolutionary war had not taken
place and a revolutionary era did not exist.

Curiously Byrnes can see the humor of this position as it applies to
others: his shorthand notes of Churchill's apoplectic speeches at Yalta,
when he thought that any part of the British Empire might be subjected
to trusteeship, are revealing; and also his acid little story of the Englishwoman who heard Bevin make a speech and remarked that Anthony
Eden was speaking well, but had gotten somewhat fat. Yet it never
occurs to him that an American foreign policy which would receive the
unqualified approval of Dulles and Vandenberg might be wholly out of
accord with the reconstruction of a world moving toward socialism—a
world whose very foundations had been shaken by two decades of Hitlerism and six years of world war.

I find no understanding in the book that the solution of the Russian-
American impasse might possibly lie in an economic approach, such as
FDR had in mind when he talked of credits to Russia. I find no real
analysis of Russian attitudes, other than an equating of them with the old
Czarist attitudes of expansionism, in an overclever quotation from one of
Marx's articles. I find no effort to trace the roots of Russian revolutionary
history—or of the Russian fear of encirclement by the capitalist powers. I
find no effort to assess how it is possible that the Russians, who have suffered so from two wars, should be willing to venture a third. Most of all
I find no effort of the bold moral imagination comparable to the sharp
workings of Byrnes's shrewd legalistic mind. The big quality that Byrnes

seems to lack—and President Truman as well—is the big quality Roosevelt had.

It is pretty clear that Molotov approached Byrnes several times with an offer for a general "horse-trading" settlement. Byrnes refused to compromise—"on principle." He is to be commended for his stoic strength—unless possibly the compromises might have been tolerable ones, and achieved world peace. He still seems to think a compromise is possible, from the Russian side. He says he is convinced that Germany is the heart of the peace problem, and that the Russians would settle the German question if they could get ten billions in reparations, and a voice in the Four Power control of the Ruhr. Having said this, he quickly and sternly dismisses it as impossible. Is it really impossible as a basis for discussion, with reparations whittled down? Is it so wrong that Russia should have a share in the control of what was formerly Big Nazi industry, with the United Nations maintaining general supervision?

What is the alternative that Byrnes offers? It is to make "bigger and better atom bombs" until a solution is reached, to use the UN to order Russian troops out of eastern Germany and—if the Russians refuse to comply—a third World War. This will be treated by the press as a big headline. It seems to me a headline to end all headlines, and a solution to end all solutions.

JAN. 8, OCT. 15, 1947

The Burnham Crusade

THE NEW HERO of the war-with-Russia forces in America is James Burnham, a philosophy professor, a former Communist, later a Trotskyist, now (by his own account) a modern Machiavellian. His book, *The Struggle for the World* (John Day), has received the final accolade from Henry Luce—condensation in an eight-page spread in the current issue of *Life*. The results of the Burnham-Luce crusade will be felt further as time marches on, as life gets more dangerous.

Let us look at Burnham's premises and take them to pieces. Burnham says the Russians are aiming at world conquest and at the destruction of America. If this were true, it would be so grievous a truth that only the preventive atom-bomb war advocated by ex-Governor Earle and

Congressman Crawford would make much sense as a defense policy. The Nazis aimed to conquer the world and to destroy us, and therefore the only possible answer to them (once their power had grown so monstrously) was to enter the war they had started. Burnham's reasoning is that, like the Nazis, the Russians are totalitarian; that, like the Nazis, they have a dynamism in their system; that, like the Nazis, they have organized a group of satellite nations; that, like the Nazis, their leaders have at times said that either their system or its rival system must triumph in a struggle for the world.

While the Russians would not be averse to a world empire if they could get it, Burnham gives no compelling evidence that the present rulers of Russia are resolved to rule the world or ruin it. He views them—quite naturally, given the habituations of a former world-revolutionist which it is difficult for an individual thinker to shake off—as still bent on rule or ruin. But are they? Their tactics of compromise since the United Nations showdown on Iran are hard to reconcile with such a view. Their doctrinal hatred of militarism—as deep a hatred as the American—is also hard to reconcile with it. The stability of their economic system (a stability which the Nazis did not have, and even we do not have) makes it unnecessary for them to expand in order to create jobs. The Russian rulers have a going nation which has weathered some crucial storms, and would be insane to drive on to world conquest at the risk of very probable destruction. My premise that they will be content to share a partnership of world power inside a UN organization is fully as good as Burnham's premise that they must conquer or die; that is, each is a premise to be put to the test of action. Of the two, the premise to be tested is the one that will lead to peace, not the one that will lead to war.

What I have written above undermines another Burnham premise: that of the inevitability of a Russian-American war. Or rather, I should call this a part-time premise: half the time he assumes it, the other half he assumes its opposite. When he is arguing that we should keep the monopoly of the atom bomb, suppress the Communist party and the liberals suspected of "appeasement" views in our country (his proposal does add up to this), and join hands with every anti-Russian force in the world regardless of how reactionary or fascist, he is working on the part-time premise that a war is inevitable. When he argues that the best way to avoid war with Russia is to back her up against the wall by confronting her with an American empire, he is working on the premise that it is not.

I believe that his second part-time premise here is more valid than his first. Most of his talk about an inevitable war seems to be based on his misreading of Arnold Toynbee's Study of History. Actually Toynbee rejects any kind of fatalism or determinism with horror—including the fatalism of believing that our world must now enter the stage of being ruled by either a Russian or an American empire. Why must it be either, unless we have the suicide-impulse in us? Why cannot it be a co-operative concert of nations?

War is inevitable only if either we or the Russians act to make it inevitable. Burnham's proposals would make it so. He recalls to my mind the astrologer who predicted his own death on a certain day, and when that day came killed himself so that he would not falsify his horoscope.

Burnham's premise is that a balance-of-power, in which the variants of capitalism, democratic socialism, and communism live in the same world, can no longer work. He would be right if we tried to make it work outside of a world organization. The conflicts for power would then be bound to result in sparks that would light up the flames of war. But inside our own community, as Professor Quincy Wright has pointed out, we have opposing forces like capital and labor living by a balance-of-power. The point is that they carry their fights on within the framework of law and consent. By strengthening the UN, we can have a similar framework. Burnham's doctrine reminds me of the fiery speeches of the old Wobblies (IWW) who insisted that all government was a fake, and that it was a fight to the death between workers and capitalists. What he has done has been to transpose the "inevitable" class-struggle into a similar world-struggle.

If we adopt his program for forming a "non-Communist world federation"—that is, as Senator Byrd has suggested, a UN of our own excluding Russia and the nations in its orbit—Burnham's premise is that we can keep it from becoming a totalitarian American empire. He admits that we alone will have the power. He admits that we alone will have the atom bomb and the economic strength. It is hard to see how, once launched on a "dynamism" in which we take the view that only force counts, we shall (after defeating Russia) stop short of making a bid for our own totalitarian empire.

Which brings me to another Burnham premise: that America—or any other power—is capable of running the world as it is today. That is a form of megalomania about which it would be interesting to have the comments of our British, French, Scandinavian, Latin-American, Chinese, Indian friends. I say that the effort would land us in totalitarianism, but even then it would not work.

The final Burnham premise is that the world can survive an atom-bomb war. At one point he expresses doubt about this himself. "Both of the present antagonists may be destroyed. But one of them must be." The "must be" as a moral imperative is, as I have said, unproved. The "may be" as a technological guess seems a grim understatement.

I do not agree with the hysterical anti-Burnham contingent which thinks that because the Burnham book is a war book it should not have been published. I think it is a fuzzy book—strong in its appearance of logic, but muddled in its premises and therefore wrong in its conclusions. I am glad it was published because finally we know what the war-with-Russia argument is like in the hands of able intellectuals and how hollow it is.

I am depressed by those who call the Burnham thesis a "bold" one. To call it that betrays either an intellectual confusion or a moral exhaustion or both. What is "bold" about a fatalist militarism? What is "bold" about a program of scrapping the new concept of the UN and going back to the old one of a world divided into two alliance-systems? What is "bold" about seeing in atomic energy not its possibilities for transforming the work-lives of men, but only a chance for a military monopoly? What is "bold" about the technique of internal suppression as a way of internal order? What is "bold" about a program so negative that it abandons every method of winning the peoples of the world over to democracy except favors, concessions, and naked force, and turns its back on every reform proposal, with the plea that we must fight and reconstruct afterwards?

This is an old and weary and futile book. It is as old as the blood-rusted history of warfare and its provocations, as weary as the effort of talking about democracy when you have lost all but a verbal belief in it, as futile as the talk of war and power and empire when what people hunger for is peace and bread and a world order.

APRIL 3, 1947

Phases of the Marshall Plan

1. *The Original Plan and Its Problems*

DURING THE NEXT YEAR, perhaps longer, the great subject of world debate will be the Marshall Plan. Whether the plan for over-all economic aid to Europe came from Secretary Marshall or from some other source, the Secretary's name is likely to remain attached to it, to distinguish it from that other and lamented line of American foreign policy—the Truman Doctrine.

Its basic approach makes sense: that only a Europe which has been rebuilt economically can be politically healthy and have free governments. That is the emphasis that Secretary Marshall, Under Secretary Acheson, and Counselor Benjamin V. Cohen of the State Department have given to the new approach in their recent speeches.

How does the Marshall Plan differ from the Truman Doctrine? The Marshall Plan contains no provisions for military aid: it is wholly economic. It does not, as the Truman Doctrine does, wait for danger-spots of Communist infiltration to show up on the world's map and then move in with American power: it tries to sum up the economic needs of a whole continent, and offers help to meet those needs. Unlike the Truman Doctrine which, explicitly and by definition, excluded from aid any of the countries in Russia's sphere of influence, the Marshall Plan is careful to include even Russia itself as the possible recipient of aid. It is not accompanied, as the Truman Doctrine was, by emotional anti-Communist face-making and name-calling. Its basic assumption is not that we must make desperate alliances for a coming war against Russia, but that such a war can be avoided by positive economic measures applied to Europe as a whole.

When you analyze the two doctrines in this way, there can be no doubt of the differences between them, both in their substance and their philosophy and in their accompanying emotional overtones. This is important for American liberals to understand, especially in the light of recurring *Pravda* articles and editorials in the *Daily Worker* attacking the Marshall Plan as simply a new front for the Truman Doctrine. I have questions of my own to raise about the new American proposal, and I know that a policy must be judged by its operation and not by the way it is dressed up. But I regard it as shockingly irresponsible to brush aside, at this point in the development of the Marshall Plan, the obvious and crucial differences between it and the Truman Doctrine.

The real question is whether Secretary Marshall and, of course, President Truman as well have seriously measured what the new policy will involve if it is to be a genuine attempt to build a democratic Europe on new economic foundations. That, and also whether they have the strength to go through with it on that basis.

I don't mean only how much the plan will cost in dollars, and in the goods behind the dollars. That is in itself a big question, not because it will break the American economy (which is Herbert Hoover's argument) but because it is terribly hard to see a Republican "economy Congress" appropriating the needed funds.[1] The State Department current estimate, as given in Benjamin Cohen's recent California speech, runs as high as six billion dollars a year for the next four years. Although that is less than four per cent of our national income, it is a tremendous sum to add to our present budgetary burden, and to the average Congressman it will seem a fantastic Santa Claus role for us to assume.

But these are questions touching on the political acceptance of the plan when it comes before Congress. My own questions have to do with the plan itself and its implications.

Are Secretary Marshall and his aides thinking of economic help to Europe on the basis of an *over-all European economic plan*, or are they thinking of rushing aid to countries like France and Italy which they regard as most immediately in danger of Communist infiltration? The problems of increasing productive capacity, of allocating food and coal and electric power, of rebuilding and relocating factories, of stabilizing currencies, are problems of the European economy as a whole. Much as we dislike the concept of planning, we must understand that these problems can be met only by a European plan.

Gearing our aid to an over-all economic plan for Europe means that we must not allow political considerations to enter. Coal and food and electric energy are coal and food and electric energy, whatever the politics of the national governments involved. If Poland and Czechoslovakia and Yugoslavia want to come in on the reconstruction plan for Europe, they must be included.[2] There will be a lot of talk about *priorities*, but priorities (if they are economic, not political) have nothing to do with governments, only with aspects of a national plan that cuts across national boundaries.

If Europe is to be rebuilt, it can be so only along the lines of the European economic philosophy, not along the lines of our own. Harold Stassen, in a speech yesterday, talked of a "people's capitalism" for Europe. He must know that no two American political or economic leaders would agree on what the phrase means, and he must also know that to Europeans it will be wholly meaningless. It may well be that whatever money Congress grants will be granted on the proviso that we will not help out any socialist shenanigans in Europe.[3] But the fact is that capitalism is no longer a viable choice for Europe. The real choices are socialism under democratic political controls and socialism under totalitarian con-

[1] As the event turned out, I was wrong. A Republican Congress did appropriate the necessary funds, after almost a year of debate.

[2] See Section 2 of this article, p. 294.

[3] This proved true, in the actual operation of the European Recovery Program, under Paul G. Hoffman as Administrator.

trols. Rebuilding the European economy will be hard enough even in European terms, without our adding the extra burden of trying to remake Europe in the image of the National Association of Manufacturers.

It is hard to talk of a European economic plan without talking of where it will be centered. Outside of the Russian economy, there are three big economic plants in Europe—that of England, that of France, that of Germany. I assume that the French economy will seem too dangerous for us to use as the base for the new plan, since the Communists are so strong in France, and especially in the labor movement. I assume also that many of our State Department and War Department people, and many of the Wall Street bankers, would feel safest if a rebuilt German economy were made the base of the new plan. But that way lies the madness of a new Nazi Europe and a new world war.

Secretary Marshall must be more candid in discussing just where the rebuilding of the Ruhr industry comes into his plan. The signs point to its being an important item. This raises the question of whether the Ruhr will be rebuilt as part of a general German settlement with Russia or outside of it; and whether the Ruhr industries will be geared into the British socialist economy or handed back to the Nazi industrialists and geared into the old prewar Anglo-German-American cartel arrangement.

Secretary Marshall must decide whether we shall again by-pass the United Nations, as we did with the Truman Doctrine, or whether we shall use it and strengthen it in the most crucial decisions of our time. This is not an abstract or empty question. It will have to be decided soon in very concrete terms. Right now there are meetings going on between the foreign ministers and economic experts of the western European nations to map out Europe's needs. But there is already in existence a UN agency that could take over a large part of this task—the UN Economic Commission for Europe, whose secretary is the famous economist, Gunnar Myrdal of Sweden. The Commission has for some time been working on a plan for economic co-operation in meeting Europe's problems.[4]

These are some of the crucial questions that the Marshall Plan will have to face. If it fumbles, if it tries to play politics with Europe's economic destinies, if it tries to use the rhetoric of democracy to rebuild a cartel economy in Germany, if it tries to remake Europe in the image of American capitalism, then it will die of its own futility as the Truman Doctrine has done.

If, however, we hold to the basic spirit with which Secretary Marshall seems to have started, we will have for the first time a good chance for a

---

[4] As it turned out, the United Nations was not used. An American administrative staff was used instead.

healthy Europe and a peaceful world. This will mean a Europe divided between a strong democratic socialist movement and a Communist movement—both of them balancing American capitalism in a world big enough to include all three.

It will also mean a Europe whose economic needs will keep American machines and workers busy, and act as a safeguard against an otherwise certain American depression. Which in itself is not the least merit of the Marshall Plan.

2. The Russians and the Marshall Plan

MOLOTOV'S OBDURATE POSITION at Paris [1] raises the question of the nature of the larger Russian strategy of which his present tactics form a part.

He is not, as diplomats go, a stupid diplomat. He must know that the course he is taking is exactly the course which will turn the Marshall Plan into a plan for western Europe only, and will split Europe in two even more sharply than it is split at present. What larger strategy does he have in mind which leads him to risk such a result?

He is not stupid. He must know that, given the most cynical view of Secretary Marshall's motives, the Russians have now played into Marshall's hands. What is the most cynical view possible of the Marshall Plan? That from the start it was only the Truman Doctrine hiding behind false whiskers; that the State Department would greatly prefer to help only western Europe and exclude Russia and its friends; that the Truman Doctrine has been such a failure in Europe that it had to be dressed up in more acceptable terms. Assume this extreme cynical view, and the only conclusion possible from it is that the Russians have given the State Department exactly the out it needed. With Molotov flatly opposing any all-European economic plan on the ground that it would be an "interference with sovereignty," American economic aid to western Europe can no longer be viewed as part of an anti-Russian program. It has become the only remaining course open to us.

Molotov is not a stupid man. He must know that there is a struggle going on within the State Department itself. Some of the people around Marshall quite genuinely feel that only a Europe which is economically

[1] Molotov, after bringing a Russian delegation to the Paris Conference on the Marshall Plan, walked out of it with a statement that the Plan was an infringement on the national sovereignty of the participants, that its aim was intervention in their internal affairs, that there was a satisfactory rate of economic recovery in Europe, and that the rest could be done under the United Nations. Later the Czechs and the Poles were also either persuaded or compelled to withdraw.

strengthened—including a Russia economically strengthened—can be a base for peace. Others feel it is suicidal for America to give any sort of aid to the police-states. Molotov must know that his sharp refusal to have anything to do with an all-European economic plan strengthens the reactionary group in the State Department at the expense of the liberal group.

Molotov is not a stupid man. He must know that, in terms of immediate tactics, Russia had little to lose by going along with the Marshall Plan at Paris. For the final say will be with an American Congress which would be most unlikely to hand out billions to a European economic plan which included the Russian sphere of influence. If the Russians were to go along with the Marshall idea, and if Congress were at the end to smash it, the result would be disastrous for American prestige in Europe. The blame for the failure of aid would be on America, not on Russia.

If Molotov knows all these things—as he must—why does he act as he does? What are the Russians driving at?

I am forced to several conclusions about the whole Russian world-outlook which may shed light on their current moves. Here they are:

The Russians are a proud people, and the whole idea of the Marshall Plan would make them lose face with the nations of Europe. For the Marshall Plan puts Europe in the position of getting together to estimate its needs and hold out its hand to America for aid. It puts America into the position of the prosperous and generous uncle helping his poor relations. And it lumps Russia along with the other countries needing aid. The Russians don't want to be thus lumped. Hence their emphasis on "national sovereignty," hence their insistence that each nation in Europe deal separately with America. I think this is a foolish insistence, where the need is desperate. I think the opposition to a general European plan comes with special irony from the nation which has been so responsible for spreading the idea of planning.

The Russians know that if they discuss a general European plan, the question of rebuilding German industry will be crucial. In the context of the Marshall Plan, it would be hard to raise any strong objections to the revival of coal and steel production in the Ruhr.

The Russians fear that, even if the Marshall Plan were in the end smashed by Congress, the whole process of discussing it would make countries like Poland and Czechoslovakia, in their eagerness for aid, turn in the direction of New York rather than of Moscow. The Russians don't want any such ideas planted in the minds of the Poles and the Czechs.

The Russians consider the exclusion of American capitalist influence from Europe to be more important than the economic rebuilding of Europe. They fear that the Marshall Plan *might* succeed. How else can we interpret Molotov's statement at Paris that a "quite satisfactory and normal postwar European recovery is in progress"? If we were not so accustomed to diplomatic distortions, this would be a monstrous statement. It can only mean that Molotov prefers to have economic hardship in Europe with Russia as the Great Helper, rather than a speedy reconstruction with America as the Great Helper. This is a callous attitude, but no more callous than our earlier attitude in cutting off UNRRA supplies when we saw them going to countries in the Russian zone.

The Russians feel that chaos and time are on their side. They want to help eastern Europe, but they want the help to be theirs. They feel confident that under Communist leadership the nations of eastern Europe can ride out the economic storms of the next decade much better than the nations of western Europe can under their Centrist and Socialist leadership. They know that a Communist country is more cohesive and learns to endure hardship and get along with less. They also know that even American dollars will not benefit France or Italy much so long as Communist-dominated trade-union movements place obstacles in the path of economic recovery. They feel that there is little that America can do even for western Europe, and that the Communists will be the residual legatees of economic breakdown.

I give these as my conclusions about what is behind Russian policy at present. That policy can change. Our job at Paris, and in Washington, is to refuse to accept the fatalism of a belief that no agreement between America and Russia is possible. Our job is to give economic help, without political strings, to whatever nations of Europe are willing to come in on a European plan. Our job, in short, is to salvage as much as possible of the Marshall Plan, and to work on the sound proposition that wherever in the world you lift living standards you strike a blow for freedom and democracy.

JUNE 17, JULY 1, 1947

The Era of Economic Empires

IF YOU LOOK at facts, and not at conferences, reports, and projects, the most striking outcome of the Battle of the Marshall Plan thus far is the emergence of a new economic empire covering Russia and eastern Europe. In Paris the delegates are drawing up reports; in Washington everyone seems content to wait until next year before asking Congress for money to carry out the Marshall Plan; but in Moscow there is intense action. The Russians have sewed up trade treaties with Czechoslovakia and Bulgaria, and set in motion other treaties which intermesh the national economic plans of the nations of eastern Europe with each other and with the Russian plan. Whatever happens to the Marshall Plan, the Molotov Plan is already in operation.

Let me put it differently. If you take the long and clear view, and don't get bogged down by diplomatic talk, you will see that the nations of eastern Europe no longer form merely a "bloc." They have moved beyond being a "sphere of influence" for their Russian neighbor and mentor. Together with Russia they now form a new and increasingly consolidated pan-Russian economic empire. The important fact about this area is not the political "iron curtain." It is rather the consolidation of a new and vast economic empire by men trained to think in hard economic terms and in terms of the integration of plans.

I am convinced this would have happened even if the Marshall Plan had never been broached. What the Marshall proposal did was to give the Russians the occasion they wanted. It gave them the chance to make their own Molotov Plan sharper, clearer, bolder, more open. I don't say this was calculated by the Russians from the start. There can be little doubt that the members of the Politburo were split in their attitude toward the Marshall Plan right up to the time Molotov arrived at Paris with a large economic delegation. At some point during the first Paris Conference, the Politburo must have made its decision for a boycott, and Molotov carried it out. It reached this decision, among other reasons, because the Russia-plus-eastern-Europe economic area had already moved so far toward becoming a reality. The Russians were unwilling to take a chance at having this work undone by American dollars, at having their emerging economic empire broken up. Rather than let us drive a wedge in it, they decided to make the split in Europe a final one.

It is well for Americans to understand the logic of these events. We live in an era of economic empires. The Number One economic empire in the world is our own—the American. Our economic strength is unparalleled in history, and has thus far not been matched anywhere else in the world in our own time. The Russian move is a natural and logical move to build up an economic empire on the vast Eurasian land-mass which can parallel and balance the American.

Where does the Marshall Plan fit into this picture? It is not, I think, an effort to add the economic strength of western Europe to our own. Partly because the scope of our empire is already vast enough, partly because western Europe is today, from the American viewpoint, more of an economic liability than an asset. The real point is that we dare not risk an economic collapse of western Europe because it would mean that Russian power would be the inheritor. Hence, after all our pathetic fumbling with the Truman Doctrine, we finally took the only sensible course of action open to us—the effort to consolidate Europe into a *third* big economic area, under our economic leadership. The big question now, for us and for mankind, is what kind of Third Economic Empire this will turn out to be.

Let me again put it as starkly as I can. An economic empire must have an economic center. The center of the Eurasian empire is the Russian economy. That of the American empire is the American economy. What will be the center of the west-European economic empire?

The great danger is that we will be tempted to make it the German economy. The big pressures inside the State Department are in that direction, and also the big pressures among the military men and the Wall Street men who are today shaping American policy. The American military government people in Germany have announced that "the products of German industry are indispensable for the reconstruction of Continental Europe."

Again let me make a simple and self-evident statement. An economic empire takes its character from its economic center. If we make the German economy the center of a rebuilt western Europe, Germany will once more—it will only be a question of time—become the master of western Europe. Which will mean that two World Wars will have been fought in vain.

You may say that Germany with its resources is the natural economic center of Europe. But this is not true. The core of German power in the twentieth century was not its resources—which were relatively poor—but its ruthless system of economic controls and its ruthless military policy. The Germans borrowed the techniques of industrialism from the English, but developed them with greater ruthlessness. Even before Hitler, the German cartel-kings established a set of restrictions which gave them the monopoly of Europe's economic plant, and reduced the rest of Europe to their tributaries. When Hitler came into power he carried this one step further, and built a vast fascist economic empire. If we use our money to rebuild German heavy industry we will do so at the expense of the rest of Europe. We will thus be freezing the results of the German industrial conquest of Europe.

What is the alternative? It is to hold German heavy-industry strength down to a minimum, and to place even that under the control of some

Allied council. And, even more important, it is to make the Anglo-French economy the center of the new economic empire of western Europe, with the emphasis on England. The British are unlikely to go fascist, as they are unlikely to go Communist. They stand the best chance of developing a democratic control of a socialist mixed economoy. They are today the natural political and moral leaders of western Europe. With our aid this potential economic leadership can become a fact.

Our choice is clear. We can so arrange things that Europe will be run for the benefit of Germany and the future war-lords of Germany. Or we can so arrange things that Germany will be run for the benefit of Europe and the future democratic socialism of Europe. Let us have no illusions that there is any third course.

JULY 15, 1947

How Grateful Should Europe Be?

MANY AMERICANS SEEM to think that the people of western Europe are not grateful enough to us. Here is how the argument runs: They used our UNRRA supplies without gratitude; they are lazy and shiftless ingrates anyway, and the Marshall Plan dollars will only mean they will work still less; they are counting on our need for them—the need of markets to stave off depression—being as great as their need for us; their governments don't tell them that the food and dollars which are saving them come from America. So why should we stint ourselves and go short in order to help them?

Every one of these arguments seems silly and irrelevant, yet all of them are calculated to touch to the quick one of the sure-fire emotions of all human beings—the rancorous feeling that whatever we do is not appreciated.

This is especially true of the way Americans feel, because of the peculiar relation in which we stand to Europe. We were descended out of Europe. Our institutions came out of Europe, and at some point in our families' history we ourselves did. But most Americans reject that fact, and would like to forget it. With a sense of our overwhelming superiority to the people and the places from which we have derived, we have throughout our history enacted what I have called elsewhere the ritual of "the slaying of the European father." Just as a child in growing up comes inevitably to the point where he has to reject his parents, so we have rejected Europe. The same child, grown to be a man, may also find that he must help his parents, else they will die before their time and die in abject misery. He does help them, but at the same time he demands that they crawl on their bellies and lick the dust to show their gratitude. If they don't he feels that he has somehow been taken for a sucker—and there is no crime in the cynical American calendar more humiliating than to be a sucker.

I was reminded of this psychological fact the other night in the course of a debate on the Marshall Plan with Henry J. Taylor, on "America's Town Meeting of the Air." "Our free food," says Taylor, "should be plastered with the American flag—every package. Every box, every bag, every bale should be stenciled in indelible ink: 'Free from the U. S. A.' . . . Hungry people getting our wonderful help could and should be reading their government's full page ads saying: 'Thank you, America, for this food. Thank you for saving it. Thank you for sending it. You are the friend of the people of this country—the helper—the true helper.' "

If this were not so adolescent, it would be pathetic—this insatiable desire to be thanked for what we ought to do not out of a desire for gratitude but out of common sense and out of the impulse of humanity. There is an almost obscene insistence, which so many Americans have, that the people of Europe must rattle their tin cups in the unmistakable fashion of beggars, and then bow and scrape and cringe in gratitude to us who deign to give them a pittance out of our plenty.

And it is a plenty that we are enjoying. No people in history has ever lived so sumptuously amidst the poverty and desolation of the rest of the world. The whole of our proposed commitment under the Marshall Plan would mean something under two and one-half per cent of our national income. It would mean one week's work out of the entire year for Americans. We need to get the picture into an economic perspective.

And into a moral perspective as well. I am fed up with this talk of exacting "Thank you's" and of measuring gratitude. I am fed up with the bleak immorality of those who want us to stand in our high mightiness over the prostrate men and women and children of Europe, requiring them to say "Thank you, Uncle," before we lift them up a bit and stand them on their feet. Let's have less talk about what they owe in gratitude, and more honesty about what we owe to them and to ourselves as moral human beings.

If we act as moral beings we will also—as a sort of lagniappe—find that it pays us political dividends as well. Actually this is secondary, for we should be aiming chiefly at the economic reconstruction of Europe, rather than at its political allegiance to us. But if we want its political allegiance and alliance, the surest way *not* to get it is to plaster every package of food with the American flag, and exact a "Thank you" between every mouthful. The surest way to get it is to treat the people of Europe for what they are—people fully as good as ourselves, whom the miseries of war have hit far harder than we have been hit. Some of the more fatuous flag-waving Americans are in danger of forgetting that you can't extract gratitude as you would extract a tooth; that unless friendship is freely given, it means nothing and less than nothing; and that friendship— whether political or personal—is a mutual exchange between free men who are equals in their moral dignity if not in their economic strength.

OCT. 16, 1947

Mr. X., Mr. L., and Mr. S.

ONE OF THE MOST remarkable and most important intellectual controversies in our time is contained in the now classic article in the magazine *Foreign Affairs* by the not-so-mysterious Mr. X., and the equally classic answer to it by Walter Lippmann in his series of fourteen columns. The reader who missed both sides of the controversy can now find them within two books that have just appeared. X.'s article, "The Sources of Soviet Conduct," is one of some thirty that are reprinted from the files of the same magazine in *The Foreign Affairs Reader*, gathered together by the magazine's editor, Hamilton Fish Armstrong (Harpers). Lippmann's series is contained in his tidy, compact 62-page little book, *The Cold War: A Study in U. S. Foreign Policy* (Harpers).

What makes the controversy so important is that while Armstrong, in his editorial note, still clings to the myth of the anonymity of Mr. X., everyone has known since the article appeared that Mr. X. is George F. Kennan, the head of the Planning Division of the United States State Department. His analysis of the components of Soviet conduct is therefore, however thinly veiled, the official American analysis; and his program for an American policy of "containing" the Soviet power is the official American program.

Lippmann himself is, moreover, not simply a columnist, but without doubt the best-informed, most responsible, and most influential American commentator on world affairs. I have had my intellectual quarrels with him in the past, and no doubt there will be others in the future. But I have always believed him to possess the most brilliant and lucid expository gift in American political journalism. Even when he is wrong he is dangerously persuasive. A friend of mine once said that Lippmann's style is terribly clear—in fact, clearer than the truth. This gibe is sometimes deserved. It is true that Lippmann has shed his former militant progressivism and become a somewhat cynical conservative, skeptical of idealism, immersed in the realities of power and of power-politics.

Yet that is exactly what makes his little book so forceful an attack on State Department policy and the philosophy underlying it. Here is no Henry Wallace, nor an all-out United Nations enthusiast, nor a World Federalist stalwart—all of whom have their own quarrels with State Department policy. Here is, rather, a man who takes the State Department's own premise about our deep rivalry with Russia and the need for meeting Russian power by American power, and who shows how the State Department policy is confused and blind and must defeat its own purposes.

What both Mr. X. and Mr. L. are talking about, to start with, is Mr. S. —that is to say, about Stalin as the shaper and symbol of Soviet policy. X.'s article about the Soviet is concerned almost wholly with the Soviet ideology and the conditions under which the ruling group holds power. Considering that it has become, in effect, a State paper, it is a remarkably intellectual document, showing a considerable study of Communist doctrine and Soviet history, written with a certain literary grace, and decorated by quotations from Gibbon's *Decline and Fall* and from Thomas Mann's *Buddenbrooks*. Its treatment of the Soviet Trinity—the infallibility of the Kremlin, the iron discipline of the party, and the unquestioning obedience to a constantly shifting body of truth contained in the party "line"—is well-done and valid. But its emphasis is almost wholly on the argument that "Soviet power bears within it the seeds of its own decay," that Soviet economic strength is uneven and vulnerable, that the Russian people are physically and spiritually exhausted, that at the first chance they would rise up against their masters—in short, that the internal power of the men of the Kremlin is ripe for overthrow. X.'s program for American foreign policy—to "contain" and "frustrate" the Russians in every sector and segment of the world where they threaten to expand— is thus, as Lippmann points out, based on the hope and expectation that Communism in Russia can be overthrown and chaos replace it.

Quite aside from the question of how proper it is for an American official to admit we are working toward the internal overthrow of Soviet power, there are two further questions about X.'s argument. Even on his own assumptions, the bitterly anti-Soviet drive in our "cold war" is exactly what the rulers of the Kremlin need in order to maintain their power —an enemy-symbol to unite their own exhausted people, the chance to bolster their authority by pointing to the forces of "imperialist" encirclement. The second question is the one Lippmann's book raises: Hasn't American policy been wasting our strength and resources by exerting pressure on Russia exactly where she is strongest—in China, Iran, Turkey, Greece, and the nations of eastern Europe?

What is most powerful in Lippmann's reasoning is that the key to peace is not intervention in the perimeter of feudal countries surrounding Russia, but the withdrawal of all occupation armies from Europe, the economic reconstruction of Europe, and the resumption of trade between its western and eastern sections. The pressure on the perimeter countries, like Greece in the West and China in the East, was the essence of the Truman Doctrine. The reconstruction of Europe, and the alliance between America and the democracies of Europe, is the essence of the Marshall Plan. What Lippmann is pleading for is the complete scrapping of the Truman Doctrine and the wholehearted adoption of the Marshall Plan.

This is not easy. For George Kennan, the man who wrote the underlying philosophy and strategy of the Truman Doctrine, is still head of the State Department planning group which is guiding the Marshall Plan. The difficulty, however, goes beyond persons. The fact is that while we have shifted our emphasis from the Truman Doctrine, with its anti-Russian drive, to the Marshall Plan, with its reconstruction aspects, we have not shifted the underlying philosophy itself. We are trying to apply to the Marshall Plan the philosophy originally framed for the Truman Doctrine. We have not one foreign policy, but two foreign policies. We are trying to apply the mood and methods of the cold war to a plan which —if it is to succeed at all—requires not the splitting of Germany and of Europe, but the making of a common peace with Germany and the resumption of trade-relations between the two parts of Europe.

Which one of the two foreign policies will win out? The emphasis that the State Department continues to place on rebuilding German industry, on renewed aid to Greece and China, shows that the Truman Doctrine is still very much alive. The continued struggle between Russia and America inside the United Nations shows that we are, in Lippmann's phrase, making the UN "expendable" in our struggle with Russia, and "devouring the seed-corn" of a possible new world order.

I don't see how anyone can escape the rigor of Lippmann's logic. Western Germany cannot survive without eastern Germany. Neither can western Europe survive—even less rebuild itself—without economic relations with eastern Europe. Every further step we take in the "cold war" means that we are splitting Europe ever more deeply. The Russians, in their turn, have also adopted a belligerent position that has sharpened the split. Given this split, all the billions we will pour into western Europe will be stopgap relief, but cannot rebuild the economic strength of our natural allies.

America must choose between continuing a cold war which Lippmann says we have already won, and which is based on the hope of a pretty hopeless internal overturn in Russia, and on the other hand a policy of democratic reconstruction in a reunited Europe. We cannot have both. To follow the constructive path does not mean that we cease to regard the Russians as rivals, or cease to oppose their expansion. It means that we believe that even among rival powers there can be a working agreement to disagree, that you need not make war against your opponent simply because you do not like each other.

NOV. 13, 1947

An Interview at the Kremlin

I REGARD the account of the Stassen-Stalin interview as one of the most revealing documents of our time on the clash of the American and Russian systems—revealing as to the strengths and the weaknesses of both systems. What follows is a running series of reflections on it.

On the Nature and Diseases of the Systems: After Stassen put his prime question—whether the American and Russian systems "can exist together in the same modern world in harmony with each other"—Stalin moved quickly to the offensive. The crucial problem, he insisted, is whether the two systems want peace, not whether they are different, or similar. Germany and America, he pointed out, had the same system, yet they fought a war.

Stassen was slow in meeting this. Only three exchanges later did he come back and point out the obvious fact that the Nazi economy was a closed economy for capitalists and workers alike, while the American was free. Here Stalin with some fancy footwork slipped away with "let us not criticize mutually our systems," and tried to reduce the whole problem to name-calling and careless use of the words "totalitarian" and "monopolist." And Stassen let him get away with it.

I wish they had kept at each other on this score. For before you can talk about long-range peace between two systems, you must examine the nature of each, and the diseases that are organic to it. The Russian system is socialist, with state operation of enterprise, state planning, and the old class-structure destroyed. The American system is capitalist, with corporate operation of enterprise, profit as the prime mover, and a government of limited powers but democratically chosen. Between two such systems there need be no question of war so long as each stays healthy.

The trouble comes when each develops its own peculiar disease. The disease of the Russian system lies in one-party jitters, when a single party organized as the state gets frightened at opposition within or without the nation: at that point it becomes totalitarian. The disease of the American system might be called the corporate jitters, when the big corporations and their allies in press, army, and church get frightened at liberalism inside the nation and socialism outside: at that point it moves toward a corporate fascism.

Thus Stalin's remark about America and Germany having similar systems was not true as of 1939, because America under Roosevelt had not gone fascist. It *might become true* in the next five or ten years, but only if our ruling groups become frightened enough. If that happens we will become a war threat not only to Russia but to the world. Similarly Russia today, for all its unfreedom, is no war threat to America—so long as its rulers don't get the jitters, so long as Stalin's relative calm prevails in the Politburo, so long as the Russian economy remains adequate for its people's elementary needs. Failing these conditions in the next five or ten years, *it would become a threat*, not only to America but to the whole world.

Thus the question of the health and disease, the stability and jitters of each system is the crucial one. And that in turn leads to the question of depression.

On Depressions—American and Russian: The most interesting part of the interview came *after* what Stassen planned as the end of it. Stassen was ready to leave, but Stalin wanted to go on. From that point on Stassen no longer had his prepared questions nor Stalin his prepared answers. The talk became more random, more informal—and more revealing.

Inevitably the conversation turned to the question of whether we can prevent the next depression in America. Stassen insisted we could. Stalin was politely skeptical. The one "favorable" factor he conceded was expanded world trade for America. Stassen insisted rightly that the real burden would have to be borne by the home market. It could be done with the right controls, said Stassen. That would require a very strong government, said Stalin. The strength of a democracy lies in popular support, Stassen shot back. Yes, said Stalin, but would the businessmen go along?

The trouble with this exchange was that each man was talking about a different set of facts. Stalin, as a Marxist, believes that a capitalist system cannot avert a major depression. The Russians know little, if anything, about Keynesian doctrines, and how capitalism can be kept going if the corporations are prevented from tying up savings, drying up investment, and choking off mass purchasing-power. Stalin was wrong, and Stassen right, on the question of the *economic possibility* of averting a depression. But on the question of *political probability*—whether an American Congress and its corporate masters are likely to take the necessary action in the next few years—I suspect Stalin was close to being right.

But how about Russia? It too has economic problems, if not of depressions then of living standards. Perhaps Stassen did not want to touch on them because it would have led him to the problem of an American loan, which is a leprous question right now. Yet Stassen told a group of Congressmen on his return that Russia is terribly weak economically. Surely this is important to the question of war and peace. A weak Russia becomes a frightened Russia—and a frightened Russia is no help to peace, although incapable of starting a war.

Peace: Possible and Desirable: A good many commentators have singled out for attack Stalin's optimistic sentences on the possibility of controlling the atom bomb. If Stalin really means it, they say, why doesn't he tell it to Gromyko? It is a fair barb, and Stalin opened himself to it. Yet it fails to take account of Stalin's basic thinking. There are, as he sees it, two questions about long-range peace with the United States. First, is it possible? Second, is it desirable? His answer on the first is "Yes," and he spells it out in the interview in his remarks about controlling the bomb. On the second his answer is also "Yes"—with a proviso: provided that the American ruling groups also think peace desirable. Considering the current hysteria in America, he has the right to raise the issue. But we in turn have the right to press him hard on atom bomb control by the UN as a crucial test of Russian good faith on the question of peace.

MAY 6, 1947

The Battle of the Secret Files

Wʜᴀᴛ ᴋɪɴᴅ of mentality does it take to hold down a State Department post? Three weeks ago the propaganda specialists in General Marshall's office fired a blast at the Russians, publishing documents that showed the cynical Nazi-Soviet plans to divide the world. Did it never occur to any of the Talleyrand and Machiavelli master-minds that they were starting an exchange in which the United States and other Western Powers were terribly vulnerable? Diplomats who live in glass houses ought to be careful before they open fire in a documentary war.

The reader need not be bewildered by the cross-fire of the American-Russian battle of the Nazi files. Here is what it amounts to. The Americans say that the Russians planned to carve up not only Europe but also the British and French empires between themselves and the Nazis. Whereupon the Russians answer that it was the United States which financed Hitler's war preparations and it was Britain and France which gave Hitler a chance to strike by appeasing him and by smashing the Russian campaign for collective security under the League of Nations. The Americans are saying that the Russians planned to divvy up the swag with the murderer. The Russians answer that the Americans gave the murderer his death-weapons, and the French and British ran interference for him, hoping that his victim would be Russia and not they.

Which is right?

The bitter fact is that both are right—the Americans *and* the Russians. Each strips from the other the mantle of virtue, and each leaves exposed the nakedness of his own corruption and cynicism. Add it together, and it is a far from pretty sight.

If you put the Russian charges and the American charges together—and only then—you get a pretty good picture of how the ground was prepared for the Nazi thrust at the world's heart. Hitler would have amounted to nothing if he had not been financed by the Western Powers. He would have been nothing without the long-term loans and investments of American banking houses which rebuilt German heavy industry, and which were the basis for German rearmament. He would have been nothing without—to use a damning phrase used by the Russians—"the golden rain of American dollars that fertilized the heavy industry of Hit-

307

ler Germany." He would have been nothing without the cartel agreements between American and German monopolies, and without the
British-German cartel agreement that spread such a stench through the
Düsseldorf air. He would have been nothing without Chamberlain and
the spirit of the Munich Pact.

It was the Munich Pact which created the setting for the Nazi-Soviet
Pact. But it is silly to call the Stalin-Hitler plan for dividing the swag—as
the cringing *Daily Worker* calls it—"Stalin's correct and wise answer to
the treacherous Munich Pact." Stalin had provocation, yes. But the Nazi
documents the State Department has published (which the *Daily
Worker* calls with a wild irrelevance "these moth-eaten private Nazi
files") show that the Russian rulers had an almost obscene desire to benefit from the plight of Britain and France, to grab while the grabbing was
good, and as "realists" to close their nostrils to the stink that came from
the plunder. Byrnes's book, in fact, shows that Molotov was so anxious
for concrete plunder—instead of the golden promises Hitler was offering
him—that he overplayed his hand. What followed was Hitler's attack on
Russia.

Put these two pictures together and you get a pretty tableau of the
state of political morality in the Western and Russian worlds during the
two deadly decades from 1920 to 1940.

At present writing, the State Department giants are still preparing their
answer to the Russians. It is hard to see what it can honestly be except
a confession that both sides come away from the bedraggled story without honor. Of the various foreign offices, only the British seem to have
the courage to say that there is plenty of blame to share all around. After
all, the Labor party leaders have reason to remember ruefully the appeasement practiced by the Tory governments. The British now propose, very
wisely, a joint Four Power publication of all the Nazi documents as *historical* documents—that is, without any one of the Four Powers having
the right to censor or veto the parts where it comes off badly. It would be
a chastening experience for each.

But alas, it won't happen. Because it won't be useful in intensifying the
cold war. Obviously what both the Americans and the Russians are aiming at is not "the highest standards of historical objectivity" (the phrase,
ironically enough, is Secretary Marshall's), but the capturing of the
European mind. Europe, not truth, is the target.

One can guess fairly well what the State Department line may be. The
Associated Press correspondent, John M. Hightower, gives us a preview
of their arguments. First, say the State Department titans, the appeasement "was carried out in the fullest publicity." Second, "most of the

Western leaders responsible for it have long since passed from view."

That wouldn't look so good even in a high-school debating contest. It isn't a question of who can match whose secret documents, but of the responsibility before history of the acts that were done, whether secret or public. Actually much of what the cartels did was done secretly, not openly; and the cold-blooded secrecy of the Hitler-Stalin agreements to divide up the *political* world is almost matched by the cold-blooded secrecy of the plans to arm Hitler and divide up the *economic* power of the world with him. And as for the old faces being gone, it is a disquieting thought that men named Dulles and Forrestal, whose firms were so active in the twenties and thirties in this whole venture, are not only still around, but are exercising a strategic power in our councils.

The pity of it is that during the twenties and thirties, while the Western Powers and the Russians were each maneuvering to place the other on the spot, the only one who profited from it was Hitler. The great realistic statesmen and diplomats of Russia and the West were only pawns in Hitler's big sucker game. I think the Western powers proved to be the bigger suckers, because as capitalist powers they had the innocent feeling that they could somehow trust their Nazi cousins. Stalin, who trusted no one, rarely made that kind of mistake. Yet when you look at the picture in the large, the twenty million Russian dead show that even the realistic Stalin, for all his smartness, was a fantastic sucker—the victim of his "realism," as Chamberlain and Daladier were the victims of theirs.

The final pity of it is that the same sucker game is going on today. The cold war of the 1940s is the sucker game counterpart of the appeasement-and-treachery diplomacy of the 1920s and 1930s. Again only death and fascism can emerge the winners. I wonder what the battle of the secret files will be like after World War III.

FEB. 11, 1948

The Grandeurs and Miseries of Russian History

THE BRITISH have a genius for understanding the national character of other peoples whom their scholars set out to study. It is well-known that, aside from De Tocqueville, they have done the best studies of the American commonwealth and the American mind—those by Dickens, Bryce,

Brogan, Gorer, and Laski. Now they are showing the same capacity to get into the Russian mind and character.

Edward Crankshaw is a newspaperman, a novelist and a non-Marxian. He has written a boldly conceived, impassioned, swift, and yet just analysis of *Russia and the Russians*.[1] Sir John Maynard, who died a year or two ago, was one of the rare but great type of British civil servant who is at the opposite pole from the *sahib*—a quiet and scholarly man who spent most of his life on his job in India but traveled extensively both in Czarist Russia and in Soviet Russia, a democratic Marxian, a Labor party socialist who wrote what are beyond any question the greatest contemporary interpretative studies of Russia, now gathered together for American readers in a single volume, *Russia in Flux*.[2]

Crankshaw's is an impressionistic book, the work of an artist in words and ideas who paints his picture in swift, symbolic strokes but who has evidently given close and careful thought to his subject before he started to paint it. You can read his book in two or three evenings, and you will not easily forget it.

Maynard's book, on the other hand, will occupy you for the evenings of two or three weeks, working at it pretty steadily. Its structure leaves a good deal to be desired, partly because it was originally published in England, some seven or eight years ago, as two separate works that have now been telescoped together. It is a vast, sprawling affair, written by a great man who poured a lifetime of reading, study, research and reflection into it.

Scarcely anything is missing. It is a brilliant history of Russia, very much foreshortened up to the nineteenth century but done in painstaking detail from then on. It is a profound analysis of the Russian character and the spirit of Russian development. It is a close-up, slow-motion account of the Russian Revolution and the various stages of the Soviet regime. It is a history of Russian social and religious thought. It is a study of the great role of the peasantry in Russian life. It is a study of the revolutionary mind and the revolutionary will in action. It is a shrewd sifting of what is fact and what is fable about the Russian people and their rulers and an always searching differentiation between the rhetoric and the reality of this portentous, old-and-new thing that is Russian civilization.

There are two themes that Maynard and Crankshaw have in common.

First: that there is a deep continuity in the stream of Russian history —that there is far less difference between the pre-Revolutionary and the

---

[1] *Russia and the Russians*, by Edward Crankshaw (The Viking Press).
[2] *Russia in Flux*, by Sir John Maynard. With a foreword by Sir Bernard Pares (The Macmillan Company).

post-Revolutionary Russian mind than either the Communists or the anti-Communists are willing to admit. This is not to underplay the importance of the 1917 Revolution, which was a convulsive, far-reaching shake-up in Russian life and in world history. But the Revolution would have been impossible had not the materials for it already existed in the Russian mind, in the Russian land and people, in Russian institutions.

The best way I can put this is to say that Lenin and his little band made world history, but they made it as Russians, out of Russian material and in the context of Russian conditions. The Soviet regime is a *transformation of phase*, one phase of Russian development passing into another, however convulsive the change and however much an act of collective will.

This is important for us, in our time and with our prejudices, to understand. The ignorant and the hysterical among us assume that Communism is, and always has been, a diabolical conspiracy to overthrow the established democracies and impose a police state on unwilling victims. They should read these books, although it is hopeless to ask them to, because they cherish their ignorance and hug their hysteria to their breasts.

They would see the slow, centuries-old growth of the Russian mind, the tradition of persistent revolutions, the attraction-and-repulsion attitude toward autocracy which has been the Russian form of government—in one phase or another—from the beginning. They would see the curious melange in the Russian of the anarchist who can brook no bonds except those he has a yearning for, and the collectivist who does not feel himself complete unless he prostrates himself with his fellows before a community of love—the fierce, messianic love that is the obverse of ruthlessness.

The Russian regime is the product of what the Russians have been—not just a conspiracy. The Americans who fear Communism in our own country do not understand how different in every respect we have been—how different in our history and institutions and national character.

The Communists, too, would do well to read these books with an open mind, if that is possible for them. They would see that the triumph of Leninism and Stalinism in Russia was the end product of what we must call an *organic* process—that Lenin was great exactly because he understood the Russian mind and the forces of Russian history and knew how to adapt Marxism until it became the powerful, revolutionary engine he made it for the Russians. Where Leninism becomes most doubtful is when it gets away from the mechanics of revolution in a national revolutionary situation and makes vast generalizations about imperialism and world conditions and the inevitable downfall of capitalism and democracy and the triumph of communism on a world scale.

Those generalizations may or may not prove true, but thus far they are only dubious abstractions—poetic myths which explain some things and don't explain others, very much like the very different abstractions and poetic myths in (let us say) Arnold Toynbee. Or, equally, the abstractions and poetic myths of Henry Luce's "American Century" or James Forrestal's "Pax Americana," to be achieved by the atom bomb and biological warfare.

In dealing with the continuity of Russian history, from the earliest Kiev period to the new power of the Kremlin, Crankshaw and Maynard stress different elements. Crankshaw is obsessed (there is no other word for it) with the Russian plain. He presents a theory of Russian history which runs almost wholly in terms of geography—land, sky, climate, and the characteristics of the people that flow from this environment. What he says, in effect, is that because the plain and the sky are monolithic and the climate is one of immoderate extremes, the Russian, too, is monolithic and immoderate in his character and his institutions.

This is the kind of environmental theory that Buckle applied, in his famous *History of Civilization*, to the minds of the French, Spanish, English and Scottish peoples, and Crankshaw is not quite a Buckle. With Crankshaw it gives the reader a sharp, clear, sudden illumination, but, instead of treating it as such, he works it to death as a theory. The result is an essay that must be read but has only a partial and imperfect value. It is poetry rather than social science.

What Crankshaw misses, Maynard supplies. He, too, says a good deal about environment, and his phrase for the Russians as "land-sailors" on the plains is an unforgettable touch. But his real stress is on other factors.

His obsession is with the Russian peasant and his long, slow, turbulent history—the peasant with whom every ruling group in Russia has had to deal as the primary, intractable material. He does not, however, make the mistake of omitting the other big elements. I have seen nowhere a better analysis of the growth of the intellectual tradition in Russia and the role of intellectuals, on which Maynard does a sort of Vernon Parrington job.

Building on Berdyaev's work, he also stresses the religious element in Russian thought, insisting that the basic element of the Orthodox Church in Russia—that of a mystical communion in the congregation as a whole—is also the basic element in Russian Communism and that the Iron Men of the Communist party are another messianic priesthood. But, being a sane man and a deep student of history, he does not work any of these themes to death. He weaves them all together, along with much else, into a difficult, complex but profoundly true symphony.

The second thesis that both authors have in common is that the Russians are neither devils nor angels and that, just as the Western democracics have hold of a portion of the truth about what is needed for men to be free and lead a fulfilled life in a meaningful community, the Russians have hold of the other portion—and just as substantial a portion.

This will be the hardest feature of both books for the American reader to accept—the reader who is obsessed with electoral and intellectual freedom as the whole of freedom.

Neither Crankshaw nor Maynard plays down the harsh aspects of totalitarianism. Crankshaw's best section is a brilliantly written account of what he himself saw in Russia when he was there during the war as part of the British Military Mission—what he saw of the terror, the inefficiency, the stupidity, the prison labor camps, the sheer human waste and human expendability. He also saw the grandeurs as well as the miseries of the Russian collective spirit.

Maynard, in turn, tells of the man-created famine, which killed off millions of peasants, as part of the Bolshevik effort to industrialize and collectivize Russian economic life by an almost superhuman act of will, and in telling it, he does not pull his punches. He gives the best account I have read of the purge trials and the secret police system—an account that makes the starry-eyed book by the Webbs read like a naïve adventure of two innocents among people they did not understand.

But both Crankshaw and Maynard have the capacity to see that, despite these harshnesses, the Russian Revolution was the great historical event of our time and that the Soviet regime has added a new dimension to the human effort—that of economic planning and new social forms. It is a dimension that will never be expunged.

MARCH 21, 1948

Trotsky and Stalin: Violence Devours Its Children

CONTROVERSIES DON'T STOP at the grave, and the Great Debate between Leon Trotsky and Joseph Stalin has broken out again six years after Trotsky's death. The man who was killed with a pickaxe at Coyoacan, in his Mexican fortress, had left partly finished a book on his hated adversary; and Charles Malamuth has finished, translated, and edited it.

As a work either of analysis or of art, Trotsky's last book—*Stalin: An Appraisal of the Man and His Influence* [1] falls a good way below his great *History of the Russian Revolution* and his *Literature and Revolution*. As a hymn of hate and as a lethal weapon it is unequaled in its intensity by even the most frenzied of his other writings.

"Revolution," we have been told time and again, "devours its children." It also devours morals, and in extreme cases it may devour sanity itself. The clogged details of Trotsky's book will not be of much interest to the general reader. They will be absorbing to the student of the Russian Revolution and the Soviet state. And they belong just as much to the student of the conspiratorial mind.

After you have finished it, you will find yourself reaching for your chair, your table, your desk, to make certain you have not dreamt it all. You will want to take a few breaths of cool air to cleanse yourself of the fetid atmosphere which is the internal climate of the book and of the whole world of the Trotsky-Stalin vendetta. You will want to break the nightmare.

In Trotsky's version the present head of the Russian state was a dull-witted, unpleasant boy who grew up in Georgia in an atmosphere of Asiatic cunning and ruthlessness; became a revolutionary only out of hatred for the ruling powers and not out of a passion for justice; bungled every assignment, often placing his fellow-revolutionaries in jeopardy; played only a third-rate role in an outlying province of Russia; was only a minor participant even in the famed "Tiflis expropriation," when the revolutionaries got 341,000 rubles in a hold-up in 1907.

In Trotsky's version, Stalin pretended later to having sided with Lenin in the early factional struggles, when he was actually against him; was third-rate in council, a nonentity in doctrine, and unheroic when heroism was needed; got even his key-ideas on the "national problem" from Lenin; played no important role in the Revolution, was never a soldier or a strategist despite his claims, and botched his missions in the Civil War.

In Trotsky's version, Stalin became a key bureaucrat because he was cautious, cunning, knew men's weaknesses and how to play on them, and the value of a party machine; was envious of the more brilliant men and hated them with the hatred of an inferior; was treacherous to his leader, Lenin, undermined his authority at every step, and aimed to oust him from power; poisoned Lenin in his last illness because he knew it was a life-and-death struggle between them; then proceeded ruthlessly to plan and carry out the death of all his former associates and his potential rivals;

[1] Harper (1946).

manufactured all the evidence against them, and manufactured also a whole lying biography for himself.

In Trotsky's version, Stalin is a Nero in sadism and a Borgia in craft—in fact, out-Neros Nero and out-Borgias Borgia so that their crimes seem pallid and modest by comparison.

Is any of this true? Are there, at least, half-truths and quarter-truths in it? I cannot say. I know only that the various charges are held together by an inner unity—a hatred of Stalin so intense that, even if the whole structure is utter fabrication, it is a fabrication of genius.

It happens that I have spent this past week reading Trotsky's book alongside of another work by a Russian genius—Dostoievsky's *Brothers Karamazov*. In each of them I found a nightmare world that merged with the other, so that at times I thought I was reading Dostoievsky when actually it was Trotsky.

Take, for example, the passage toward the end when (according to Trotsky) Stalin told Trotsky and two other members of the Politburo—a year before Lenin's death—that Lenin had asked him for poison.

"I recall (writes Trotsky) how extraordinary, enigmatic, and out of tune with the circumstances Stalin's face seemed to me. The request he was transmitting to us was tragic; yet a sickly smile was transfixed on his face, as on a mask. We were not unfamiliar with discrepancy between his facial expression and his speech. But this time it was utterly insufferable. The horror of it was enhanced by Stalin's failure to express any opinion about Lenin's request, as if he were waiting to see what others would say: did he want to catch the overtones of our reaction to it, without committing himself? Or did he have some hidden thoughts of his own? . . .

"Ever since, each time I mentally review this scene, I cannot help repeating to myself: Stalin's behavior, his whole manner, was baffling and sinister. What does the man want? And why doesn't he take that insidious smile off his mask? . . . A mere month before he made this request of Stalin, Lenin had written his pitiless postscript to the Testament. Several days after making this request, he broke off all personal relations with him.

"Stalin himself could not fail to ask himself the question: why did Lenin turn to him of all people? The answer is simple: Lenin saw in Stalin the only man who would grant his tragic request, since he was directly interested in doing so. With his faultless instinct the sick man guessed what was going on in the Kremlin and outside its walls and how Stalin really felt about him. . . . No one but Stalin would do him this 'favor.' At the same time it is possible that he wanted to test Stalin: just how eager would the chef of the peppery dishes be to take advantage of this opportunity? In those days Lenin thought not only of death but of the fate of the party."

And when Lenin did die a year later, Stalin (says Trotsky) deliberately changed the day of Lenin's funeral and kept the news of the change from Trotsky, who was away on vacation, so that he could not return in time. "He might have feared that I would connect Lenin's death with last year's conversation about poison, would ask the doctors whether poisoning was involved, and demand a special autopsy. It was, therefore, safer in all respects to keep me away until after the body had been embalmed, the viscera cremated and a post-mortem examination inspired by such suspicions no longer feasible."

This, I submit, is neither biography nor history, but literature. It is the literature of a phantom pathology that can build an accusation of political murder on a "sickly smile" and a failure to notify a rival of the change in date of the master's funeral.

Trotsky and Stalin: it seems hard to think back to the time, only a few years ago, when intellectual circles all over the world were split between them, and everyone had to take sides or risk being called a straddler. Without question Trotsky had more brains, more eloquence, more passion, more dynamic power to attract, a more conscious sense of history and its forces. Stalin's talents were different, but Trotsky was only fleeing from reality when he sought to diminish those talents to the third-rate.

The historian will find in Stalin a more massive will than in Trotsky, a less intellectual but more accurate appraisal of men and forces, a steadier purpose, a more tenacious leadership of a whole people in the great crises of its life. If we are to believe in Trotsky's Stalin, it is impossible to see how either Stalin or Russia survived those crises. According to every rule of Trotsky's logic they should not have. They did.

But to say that Stalin's qualities, whatever they are, are first-rate does not mean that we must clothe him with virtues he does not own or strip him of the crimes he may have committed. It is hard to read the history of the past twenty years without being convinced that Stalin has been not only astute but cunning, not only strong but ruthless. But I prefer to take my evidence from other sources than Trotsky, who wrote his book after he had himself been accused of plotting not only the overthrow of his enemy but also of his people.

One should read Trotsky's book along with the records of the evidence at the Moscow Trials. If this is Trotsky's biography of Stalin, then those records are in a sense Stalin's biography of Trotsky. All through his book, Trotsky accuses Stalin of having falsified his own life. I think that in many respects he is right.

But it is hard to see how so many witnesses could together have falsified Trotsky's life. Any one—or even a group—of the confessions might have been faked, or extorted, or self-induced after the manner of the one described in Koestler's *Darkness at Noon*. But it is hard to believe that all of them were. They interlock, and between them the evidence is impressive of a conspiracy, headed by Trotsky, which involved foreign aid and did not even stop at negotiations with the Germans.

Trotsky has elsewhere (in his speeches to the John Dewey Commission) sought to answer these charges. Yet I think he may have intended the present book (for him every book was a polemical weapon in the struggle with Stalin) as the final answer. "You accuse me of all those things," he says, in effect, to Stalin. "Well, here are the things I accuse you of. You are a tyrant, a betrayer, a poisoner."

But however dark Stalin's record may be, that does not wipe out Trotsky's. In fact, what the book does most effectively—in a way Trotsky never intended—is to make even more real the atmosphere of mutual hate and desperate mutual struggle which makes the charges against Trotsky more credible. One can see how, in the struggle for power with a man whom he believed to be a Nero and a Borgia, he would have stopped short of nothing.

As for myself, I find each set of charges playing upon and re-enforcing the other. I find it possible to believe a substantial part of what each accuses the other of being and doing. I don't believe that Stalin poisoned Lenin and I don't believe that Trotsky was a fascist. But I do find it possible to believe that Stalin's ruthless bid for power forced Trotsky into ruthless opposition; that, once there, Trotsky went all the way over to conspiracy and treason; that to crush tl is treason, Stalin not only had to wipe out the enemies of his State but also took the occasion to wipe out the enemies of his power.

But I find myself also concluding that the victim of both has been the dream of a socialist humanism. And the forces which tortured and stifled that dream are not only Trotsky and Stalin. They are the one-party totalitarian state, which Lenin and his comrades in the Russian Revolution never willed, but which came out of it nevertheless. Push further back, and you will find the conspiratorial tradition which filled the whole atmosphere with an unhealthy moral fog. Push back still further, and you will find the rottenness and tyranny of the Czarist system—political, economic, religious—which made the Revolution necessary. For this is what happens when injustice is so deeply rooted that it can only be wrenched loose by violence and a moral overturn.

And don't forget that we, too, the Western world, have had a hand in the mortal unprincipled struggle of Trotsky and Stalin. For Lenin's Russia might have achieved Lenin's hopes of recasting humanity in a brighter and freer mold if it had not from the start had to face our hostility.

This is what happens when you surround a new socialist regime with a ring of hostile fire; when you call—as Clemenceau did as early as 1918 and as Churchill has repeatedly done—for a *cordon sanitaire* around it; when you intervene to embitter the Civil War; when, out of fear of socialism, you wink at the building of a hostile fascist power against it, encourage anti-Comintern pacts, "nonintervene" in fascist rebellions, and desperately flourish even the threat of the atom bomb. Partly, at least, the story is not only about Trotsky and Stalin, but about us too. We have a complicity in it.

But the deepest roots of it lie in the inevitable cycle of a one-party state. In such a state, when opposition is not allowed to be freely voiced, power must become tyranny, tyranny must provoke treason, and treason must in turn redouble the tyranny. Trotsky became what he did because the opposition of a fierce and ruthless mind was driven underground and turned to treason. Stalin became what he did because a fierce and ruthless will could, under such a system, remove every obstacle to itself.

Thus the book touches, in its blind way, on one of the great tragic themes of our age. Trotsky's story will be one of the great ironic stories of history—the story of magnificent gifts which played a big historic role and then turned to frustration, of a mind so powerful that it left the spirit sterile, of a tortured human being who hungered to share events but had to eat out his heart in exile.

And Stalin's story has an irony of a different sort: that one of whom so little was expected should have survived and snuffed out his more brilliant colleagues, that a state born of an intellectual dream should have come into the hands of a party organizer, and that the whole anti-fascist world should owe so much of its victory over the Nazis to a man whose slow patience and flexible tactic were matured in a ruthless internal struggle for power.

These are some reflections on Trotsky's book. I don't see why we should either hail it or damn it because it seeks to damn Stalin for eternity. To be sure, it will be used by the Soviet-baiters the world over. But that is no reason why one should flinch from the book.

If you care only for sifting the evidence and seek only the truth, whatever the consequences, you lay your mind open to bitter truths and dangerous ones. But in the end it is the only safe way. I have long contended that ideas are weapons, but much as I care for Russian-American unity I will not narrow the use of the idea-weapon by that test. If peace depends on what we think of the Trotsky-Stalin feud, then we may as well burrow into the ground right now, like Hamlet's mole.

MAY 5, 1946

Reflections on the Russian Economy

THE NEW SOVIET decisions on the ruble devaluation, and on prices and rationing, are not the good news that the Russian-haters had awaited from the Soviet economy. The build-up which the State Department broadcasts had given to the reports of price and currency chaos from Russia had led to the revival of some of the old hopes that the "Russian problem" might get itself settled at long last by the simple process of internal economic collapse. There seems now little reason to believe that such a collapse is near. The sober verdict must be that the Russians have handled a rather messy postwar economic situation with skill and decisiveness.

It is true, as American official sources point out, that no great nation in modern times has ever repudiated its own currency as drastically as the Russians have done by turning ten of the old rubles into one of the new ones. But it is ignorance to conclude, as one of the news accounts has done, that this means prices must drop to one-tenth of their former level before the ordinary Russian comes out even. One may note some rather obvious things about how the deflat·onary move will work within the framework of the Soviet economy.

First, the deflation of the ruble was accompanied by several other moves for which the Russian people had been waiting. One was the end of the rationing system, originally scheduled for 1946, but postponed because of the bad harvests that year. Everyone who has been in Russia recently testifies to how wretched the scarcities of food and consumers' goods still are. But the decision to end rationing means that, with this year's good harvest, the scarcities are not as bad as they have been.

Another move which most Russians will welcome is the scrapping of the multiple-price system—one set of prices in the government stores and a set of much higher prices on the "free market"—prices that brought big incomes to some groups and offered additional amenities to the new Soviet middle class, but were wholly out of the reach of the large mass of people.

Add to this the fact that bank deposits in the government banks were affected far less severely than the hoarded paper ruble notes, and the smaller bank deposits were treated best of all. Add finally the central fact that wages will be paid by the state to the workers in the new ruble at the old rates, so that on the whole the Soviet Government is right in pointing out that the ordinary worker comes out pretty well. He has a stronger and more stable currency, a single set of prices for his food and other goods, and probably slightly higher real wages than he had before.

Who, then, has suffered? The Soviet Government says "the hoarders" of currency, and the "speculators" in prices on the free market. That is one way of putting it, and true enough. For it is true that during the war and since the war's end the inflationary gap between available civilian goods and available money in circulation had grown serious. This was true of every economy, but especially true of the Russian, where so much industry and goods had been destroyed by the Germans and where so much money had been issued. The free market and the multiple-price system had not been retreats from socialism back toward capitalism, but suction-forces to get the surplus money out of circulation—modes of severe governmental levies on the higher incomes. Yet they had not been enough, nor had the Government pleas to turn rubles into Government bonds. The severe ten-into-one penalty for outstanding ruble notes is thus a sort of executioner's axe for lopping off the problem of the inflationary gap.

Another way of putting it is that the sufferers are the new middle class that has grown up on the edges of what was meant to be a proletarian class-economy. Russia, even before the 1917 Revolution, had not developed much of a middle class in the American sense of small businessmen, prosperous independent farmers, workers with property holdings, professional groups, and the distributive occupations. Since the Revolution a new middle class has shaped itself. It falls into two groups: one consists of the highly skilled workers, the actors and writers, the engineers and technicians, and the Government bureaucracy; the second consists of the peasants and artisans who sold their surplus goods on the free market, and the small merchants who drove a good trade there. From the Russian standpoint the first still has a great economic function to perform; the second has performed its function. To the extent that both had ready cash and bank savings, both will, however, be hard hit.

Which means, in effect, that the new Russian move in the internal economy is a move not toward compromise with elements of internal "capitalism," but a militant move away from them. It is a cutting to the bone of the Russian economy—cutting away the surplus inflationary tissue at the expense of those best able to bear it, without hurting the workers themselves and the peasants on the collective farms on whom Russian strength, for better or worse, depends.

One might interpret this as meaning that the Russians are worried about the morale of their workers—perhaps they are—and are thus moving to strengthen that morale. Yet the State Department group around George Kennan, who are staking a good deal in American foreign policy on the idea that the Soviet Government, when hard-pressed, can be overthrown from within, cannot get much comfort from this move. For the very boldness and extent of the devaluation are proof not of the sense of weakness but of the sense of strength the masters of the Kremlin still have as a governing group. There is the same quality of militancy about this internal decision as there has been about many of the Russian actions and pronouncements recently in foreign policy.

Yet when I say this I do not mean to minimize the larger weaknesses of the Soviet economy. Those who have followed the figures on the current postwar Five Year Plan know how desperately stretched the economic goals of the Plan were, how shattered the Russian economy was after the experience of World War II, and how far the results of the first year of the Plan have been from meeting the developing needs of the Russian state and the Russian people. Compared with the economic strength and prosperity of America, the Russian economy does not loom very powerful. Thirty years ago the Communist leaders took over a largely preindustrial economy, in which what industry existed was dominated largely by foreign capital. The Revolution included within itself the industrialization of Russia, at a pace unequaled in all of history. The process was, however, broken and set back by the war. The Russians have not recovered from it, and even their most heroic economic efforts today still leave them far from American standards, either in heavy industry, technological skill, consumers' goods, or living standards.

That is the larger framework to remember in assessing what the Russians are doing. They feel themselves threatened. They are trying to carry through an almost incredible program of economic reconstruction and further construction, almost without foreign capital, and with a weary people. They have done this in the past too, largely by appealing to the sense of capitalist encirclement, and to a brink-of-war psychology. Those are the appeals that they are again making. Their willingness to sacrifice some of their marginal groups in order to consolidate the morale of their working masses is another proof that the Russian ruling group is tough in purpose and realistic in method.

DEC. 16, 1947

The Return of the Comintern

HERE WE ARE AGAIN. After a five-year spell during which the Communist International was at least formally dissolved, it is now back again as an open and declared weapon in the Communist struggle for power. In one sense the resumption of business at the old stand was inevitable, given the current tensions between Russia and America. The cold war between the two powers has become an all-out cold war, in which every weapon short of a shooting war is called into use.

Let us assume—what no one in his senses has really doubted for several years—that something like a Comintern has in effect been operating from Moscow. The new manifesto says that a need has been felt for "an exchange of experience between the parties." One asks why such an exchange could not have been carried on, as so much else has been carried on, behind the scenes. The answer is that the effect the Communists want can be achieved only by a public announcement of the unity of the nine Communist parties in their common cause.

One of the key sentences of the manifesto (the whole document is worth the most careful study, phrase by phrase) is this: "The main danger for the working class at this moment lies in the underestimation of its own strength and overestimation of the force of the imperialist camp." This gives the clue to what it is that the masters of the Comintern are trying most to fight—the widely bruited report throughout Europe of the enormous strength of America, economic, military, atomic. Elsewhere the manifesto speaks of a "further sharpening of the universal crisis of capitalism, a weakening of the forces of capitalism." No doubt the signers believe this, as one of those long-term propositions that Marxians are trained to make. But for the immediate future they have no illusions about American capitalism being weak. The Politburo has undoubtedly come to the conclusion that the thing it has most to fear in Europe is fear itself—the fear of American strength which is leading many workers and intellectuals to throw in their lot on America's side and against Russia. The new Comintern is calculated to fight that fear.

There will be many Americans who will ask why the Russians do it, and whether they do not understand the effect it will have on American opinion. The answer, of course, is that whether the Russians understand or not, their eyes are not on America right now. Their eyes are on Europe.

They have written American opinion off. The members of the Politburo, who make all the basic decisions for world Communism including the decision to reconstitute the Comintern, have evidently decided that they can do little to shape American policy or opinion. The "objective facts"— as Marxians like to put it—will shape that. The struggle now is a struggle for Europe. The newly resumed Comintern is an effort to line up as solid a Communist front in Europe as possible, to bolster Russia's strength whether the outcome of the present struggle prove to be peace or war.

Which means that the Russians recognize that the struggle for Europe has now come to its decisive phase. Why now? Partly because of the pressure of the Marshall Plan on European opinion. Partly because the Russians want to shift some of the onus of the Communist decisions in European countries from Russia itself to the praesidium of the new Comintern. Partly, no doubt, because there are conflicting national interests between such Communist parties as the French, the Italian, and the Yugoslav, and some clearinghouse of decisions will serve to keep discipline in the political armies of Communism.

But the main reason is that the struggle to win over the European working class has now reached its decisive stage. Anyone reading the new manifesto carefully must be impressed by the amount of emphasis it places on the Socialists of Europe. "Treasonable," "faithful toadies of the imperialists," "traitors in this common cause," "servile placidity": these are the phrases applied to the Right-Wing socialism of Blum and Ramadier, Attlee and Bevin, Saragat, Renner, Schumacher. If one studies the structure of the manifesto, it is apparent that even the bitter denunciation of the United States as "imperialist" and "anti-democratic" is the prelude to the even more important and violent attack on the Socialists. The effort is to discredit the Socialists by linking them with "American imperialism." To put it most barely, the effort is to sharpen the existing split of the Socialist movement in Europe, and win over as many as possible of the doubtfuls and the waverers among Europe's Socialist workers into the camp of those co-operating with the Communists.

Note also the weapon on which the new Comintern most relies. It is not, as was true of the old Comintern, the weapon of minority revolution. The manifesto has few of the phrases of world class-struggle. The fact is that the men of the new Comintern are themselves in the seats of power, except in France and Italy—and even in those countries they lead movements with large blocs of power. Some of the men who were at the last World Congress of the Comintern in 1935, and who helped dissolve it in 1943, are now members of the ruling group in eastern Europe. They are very skillful in their use of semantics in the manifesto—with the ex-

tremely dubious result that Russia is depicted as wholly "anti-imperial-
ist" and "democratic" and America as wholly "imperialist" and "anti-
democratic." But most of all they show their skill in their appeal to the
passion of nationalism.

The Communists, says the manifesto, "must grasp in their hands the
banner of national independence and sovereignty in their own countries."
This ties in with the attack on American motives in the Marshall Plan, as
aimed at "the economic and political subjugation of Europe through
American imperialism." In other words, the main propaganda effort of
European Communism will be to identify American pressures as anti-
national, and equate Communism with patriotism. This is a formidable
propaganda line. There is little question that in some countries the Communists will lose strength in immediate terms, because they will so openly
be taking orders from a transnational Comintern. But the Russians are
evidently willing to risk this immediate loss, and hope to make up for it
by exploiting the theme of nationalism and patriotism.

The moral for America is a dual one. If we mean not to lose Europe,
we must make our basic alliances with the Socialists of France and Britain, and not with the steel and cartel barons of Germany. And we must
rely not on handouts which influence Parliamentary votes but on the real
economic reconstruction of Europe from within.

OCT. 7, 1947

The Lessons of the Czechoslovak Coup

1. On the Blowing Up of a Bridge

THE WHOLE EPISODE of the Communist coup in Czechoslovakia is now
sufficiently rounded out so that an estimate of it can be made.

There is no question about what happened. It was a revolutionary coup
engineered by the Communists, carried out skillfully and swiftly according to a well-tested pattern. A police-state is being set up which, while it
still allows for some non-Communists in the Cabinet, is moving toward
the Russian model.

The real questions have to do with the reasons for the coup, and its
timing.

One factor was the cold war between Russia and America. No doubt the Russians figured that in order to be prepared for war if and when it comes, they must have the whole of eastern Europe consolidated as part of the Russian economic empire and political power-bloc. Czechoslovakia is too crucial a part of that area for the Communists to take any chance of losing it.

The Russians were determined to show that the Truman Doctrine is pretty futile, and that they can be as tough in their Czechoslovak policy as the Americans in their Greek policy. They were also determined to make certain that the Czechs would never stray back into the Marshall Plan fold, which would have meant that American money would be a powerful anti-Communist weapon.

The Communists were beginning to lose ground inside Czechoslovakia, and may have been fearful of losing more in the May elections. It is a good revolutionary principle that when parliamentary methods start to slip, you must use direct-action methods. The anti-Communists who resigned from the Cabinet to precipitate an electoral crisis made the mistake of forgetting this, and thus gave the Communists their chance to use direct action. With their well-organized trade-union movement, and their control of police and army, and their local action groups, they had the advantage all the way through.

The business of revolution has become a serious business in the postwar world. The Communists work hard at it, they know the techniques, and they have a lot of pride in keeping score. When they saw their chance, they took it.

If these factors together serve to account for the move and its timing, how about the larger meaning of it for us?

One effect it is bound to have is to weaken the parliamentary position of the Communists throughout western Europe, and especially in France and Italy. For the Czech coup has demonstrated for all except the willfully blind that the Communists use a Popular Front only as long as it is useful to them, and smash it at their first chance to capture power.

This is a heavy price for the world Communist movement to pay—this final proof that when the Communist lion and the Socialist lamb lie down together, the lion has no peaceful intentions. The fact that the Communists were willing to pay it means that their move was partly from weakness rather than strength. It means that they have pretty much written off their parliamentary chances during the next phase—the ERP phase— of the history of western Europe. They are doomed to be in the opposition during this phase, and are willing to sacrifice the position of their western European parties in order to consolidate their strength in eastern Europe.

The lesson for America, however, seems to me a far different one from that which is being quite generally drawn. The Communists have no strength as a major party or group in the United States. They are not part of a coalition government, nor is there any question of one. In a nation where there is no strong party of either Communists or Socialists, it is idle to sound the sort of alarm that is being sounded in France and Italy. If anything the Czech coup has weakened the Communists in a future bid they may make for common action with Socialists and liberals, and has weakened them also in the trade-unions. The present hysteria in America about the "Red wave," the "spy" accusations, the deportations, is pointless as well as dangerous.

The real lessons for American liberals are quite different. Czechoslovakia for a time seemed to be a "bridge" between a collectivist economy and a parliamentary state. The Communists have now blown up that bridge. They claim that it was not they who did it—that it was a "people's revolution," and they were only its instruments. Only the politically naïve and politically illiterate will swallow that. A people's revolution under Communism is possible in a feudal country. It is a cruel play on words in a democratic country, such as Czechoslovakia was.

But it would be foolish to underestimate the role that mass feeling played in the Czechoslovak coup. No matter how good their organization, the Communists would not have been able to carry it through if they had not had a substantial section of the trade-unions, the farmers, and the army behind them. It was not a majority to start with, but they may well make it a majority now. The question is: How did they win them over?

They did it because they offered the only image of resolute action toward breaking up the big farms and collectivizing industry. The Americans as a symbol stand for wealth and economic power. But they do not stand, in the thinking of the people of Europe, as a symbol for economic democracy. In the struggle for Europe, our disastrous mistake is that the one weapon which would be most effective against the Communists— the belief of our people in a genuine economic democracy—is a weapon our ruling groups do not dare use. For it might undermine their own power and privilege.

2. Masaryk and the Iron Men

THE MEMORY of Jan Masaryk will live a long time in Czechoslovakia to plague the new iron men whose ruthlessness formed the setting for his death.

The circumstances of his death, so far as we know them now, seem to point to suicide, and not one of those brutal political killings that are dressed up to look like suicide. Whatever else the Communists might have wanted of Masaryk, they did not want this. Not this silent, desperate act of finality, so eloquent in its muteness.

If he had fled his country at the time of the coup, it would have been a blow to them, but they could have handled it. If he had tried to organize resistance, either at home or abroad, they would have branded him as a wrecker of his country's unity, and a traitor to the "people's revolution." He would have done them immense damage, but he would also have helped plunge his people into civil war. Besides, he had waited too long, and an act of open resistance could no longer be effective. It would have been a gesture with bloodshed. He must have chosen instead a gesture that shed no one's blood except his own.

It will plague the new Czech Communist regime. For if it is suicide, Masaryk is so clearly the symbol of the utter hopelessness he finally came to feel for his people's liberty under the new Communist state.

If ever there was a European non-Communist liberal who tried hard to work with the Communists, it was Masaryk. I remember an evening I spent with him from which I carried away some clear impressions of his thinking. His foreign policy was based squarely on the proposition that the Czechs had been foolish to trust themselves to the West before Munich, and that in a world of power politics they now had no recourse but to line up with Russia. He also knew that part of the price which Russian power exacted was a government which included the Communists. His great hope—and his great gamble—was that the balance of power in the cabinet could be maintained long enough to save Czech freedom. Which is to say, long enough so that the Russians and Americans might reach an agreement not to destroy their common world. His hope and his gamble ended at the window of the Czernin Palace.

Was he naïve in his hope? It is hard to pass judgment, but I think that the historian who writes about the role he played will reconstruct it somewhat as follows:

His country had already in 1938 experienced the bitter taste of being caught in an anti-Comintern pact and betrayed by it. The experience had turned a large number of his countrymen toward Communism. It did not turn him. For his father had been the first President of the Czech Republic, and all the beads of his blood strained toward freedom. But he worked with the Communists, trusting that he and they could find common ground in fighting fascism, averting a war, rebuilding their country. He thought they were anti-fascists and Czechs first, and Communists second. Since the Communist coup proved him wrong, almost no word had come from him. Perhaps he still went along, hoping perhaps that in time the Czech people, so tenacious of their liberties, would manage to regain them. We can only surmise from his death that in the fifteen days since the coup he saw the walls of the police-state closing in implacably on the people he loved. He may have felt that many of them had accepted the fact of the coup because he had. Perhaps as a sensitive man he could not face them or himself.

But Masaryk's death is far more than the tragedy of a man, or even of a people. It is the symbol of the plight of European man today, caught between the Russians who will cynically kill him unless he turns anti-capitalist, and the Americans who just as cynically will let him die unless he turns anti-Communist. Witty, traveled, cosmopolitan, unfanatic, Masaryk was the type of the good European. It seems incredible that a man of such temperament should have come to the end of his rope. Yet whether he killed himself or was killed, his death is in either event a sign that the great humanist tradition of Europe, of which he was a good product, is nearing its end. It is gripped in a deep pessimism which we Americans, who feel we can still make our own history and the world's, cannot grasp. For Europe's pessimism is based on the fact that, caught as it is between the Russian and American power drives, it can no longer make its own history.

I suppose that Communists will dismiss Masaryk as a weakling—a man who tried to stand alone and couldn't take it, a man who disdained to destroy his country in fighting the Communists but who could not stomach becoming their instrument. It is part of their creed the world over to despise and ridicule such men, because they cannot understand them. They cannot understand men who live by principles rather than by orders.

Masaryk was a galling problem for the Communists. He worked with them, but they knew he was independent. At any time they knew he might kick over the traces. They couldn't take a risk. Only a few days ago it was reported that he was under stiff pressure to join the Social-Democrats. I can see why. As long as he was a nonparty man, he had to answer only to his own conscience and sense of patriotism. But as a Social-Democrat in Czechoslovakia today he would be answerable to the conscience of Fierlinger,[1] which is the same as answering to Gottwald's[2]

---

[1] Zdenek Fierlinger, leader of the Social-Democrats in Czechoslokavia. Deposed after an internal struggle in his party, he returned to power after the Communist coup.

[2] Klement Gottwald, leader of the Czechoslovak Communists, Prime Minister, and later President of the Czechoslovak Republic.

conscience. This he would not do, and thus he was a problem to the Communists who are seeking to turn Czechoslovakia into a single-party state.

No doubt the Czech Communists see themselves as the Iron Men of the new order. They see themselves in the image of a Lenin, hammering out history in the interests of the people. This is where they are wrong. For the Russian Revolution had a meaning for the Russian people, grew out of their experience, answered to their needs. Even its unfreedom was part of their traditional unfreedom. This does not apply to Czechoslovakia, whose traditions lie with European humanism, not with Russian autocracy. Lenin created something big and new in the world, even if it has since been corrupted. Gottwald and his Iron Men have created nothing new, and they have killed the promising job which Masaryk was so anxious to complete alongside them—the job of building a real democratic collectivism.

Someone will still carry that job through, somewhere in the world. It will be a long road, and Masaryk—for all his blunders—will be one of the minor martyrs along the way. Perhaps his act was not wholly futile. For it will be a rebuke forever to the little sterile men who fancy themselves Iron Men. And thus, even in dying, he found at his high window the last area of space and light in which he could make history.

MARCH 3, 11, 1948

The Sins of Marshal Tito

THERE WAS JOY in the State Department, we are told, when the striped-pants boys got the news of Marshal Tito's chastisement. I think they missed the point. I doubt that Yugoslavia will now come over to our side in the cold war, although undoubtedly Tito would welcome a good trade agreement.

The importance of the blast against Tito lies less in international power-politics than it does in Communist tactics and discipline. Politically it is an affair inside the family, with the quarrelers getting so intense that they don't care whether their wranglings reach the neighbors.

But going beyond power-politics, the clash has an extraordinary world-wide interest and meaning. For the real drama of the Tito episode is a drama of ideas, and the ideas concern us as much as they do the Communists.

Approach it this way. Marxism, as a theory of history and of action, has always placed the international working-class movement first, and held the spirit of nationalism to be an evil thing. Lenin, to be sure, and Stalin after him, did deal with "the national question"—but what Stalin has meant by it has been the cultural autonomy of the various national groups inside the far-flung area of Soviet Russia.

The nationalism of Marshal Tito and his Yugoslav Communists is a very different thing. It is the nationalism of an independent sovereign state which is willing to be a partner in a world Communist bloc, but insists on being an equal partner, and on deciding its own internal affairs.

To the Russian commissars, Zhdanov and Malenkov, the sins of Marshal Tito are many and blatant, and the Cominform document enumerating them is one of those dismally arid, yet curiously absorbing, theological documents which always make the history of heresy fascinating. Tito is, it seems, a Trotskyist because he goes off on ideological frolics of his own, instead of living up to Cominform discipline. He is also a Bukharinite, because—on issues like the economic plan and small farm-holdings—he is retreating toward capitalism and an alliance with the Popular Front elements, instead of carrying through the land revolution and building it on the Communist elements alone.

This sounds as if business were continuing as usual at the old stand of Communist polemics. Actually, however, something new has been added. Throughout Europe, in the Communist countries, a struggle has been going on between the older leaders and a new group of tough young Communists who have come up through World War II and the resistance movements. They regard the older men as romantic fuddy-duddies. These have ideas of their own as to how to run things in their own countries. They are passionate nationalists, and don't think every word coming from Mother Moscow has the sacred quality of the Koran. It was to keep them in line, under discipline, that the Cominform was rebuilt. It is to keep them in line throughout Europe that the dramatic anti-Tito manifesto has been issued.

Added to this is the special nature of the Yugoslav national character and of Yugoslav history. It has been a turbulent history, crisscrossed with insurgencies, riddled with separatist movements. That history did not end with the Communist triumph. The Russians, who have their own history and their own national character, have an almost mystical sense of unity which the Yugoslavs lack. It is natural for the Russians to demand discipline from the Slav bloc. It is also natural for the Yugoslavs, who have for centuries fought mastery by others, to put up a fight against mastery by their own International. I doubt whether Tito is his own free agent here. He must reckon with his younger lieutenants and with the raw material of his own culture.

There are, of course, other issues. There are genuine differences of opinion as to the tactics to be used in what the Marxians call the "transition period" before full socialism is achieved in any country. The Russians, as veterans of revolutionary movements, feel that they know how to carry through a revolution better than the Yugoslav novices.

There is, finally, the issue of world power-politics. The Russians, while waiting for their peace offer to be taken up, are preparing for war as thoroughly as we. They can't afford to go into a war with weak links in the chain of Communist disciplines. Zhdanov sees Tito as a weak link. Hence he must either be mended, or broken and replaced. Since Moscow is the great world center of Communist power, and Tito has nowhere else to go, Moscow may well win out.

Yet it is a healthy experience for the Kremlin titans—or for the masters of any other empire—to know that there are limits to ideological empire. The monolithic will which the men of power always dream of imposing is always a dream, exactly because it must reckon with the rich and intractable material of human life and national cultures. Mother Moscow must learn this—and Mother Wall Street too had better think about it a bit.

JULY 1, 1948

On Peacetime Military Training

1. *Skills, Not Attitudes*

THE TROUBLE with most of the current talk about peacetime conscription is that each side sets out to prove too much. One side says we must enroll every young man in the Army for a year and give him military training, else the nation will perish. I am skeptical. We never have had peacetime conscription, yet the nation has not perished: once we are in a war we do very well at it. The other side says we must keep our young men away from anything relating to war, else our democracy will perish. Again I am a skeptic. We have been in a series of wars, and our democracy has not perished.

What is it that we seek? We want to be able to protect our national security, if war should come. But to say that we must guard our security does not in itself determine the method. If it did, the simplest answer would be for us to maintain forever a massive standing wartime armed force. No one advocates that, and why not? Partly because it would be economically wasteful, but mainly because everyone recognizes that the absence of a big permanent standing army has been part of the American tradition of a free society.

It is clear then that while we want national security, we want it by a method that will not cost us too much socially. What sort of method would that be?

To get at that, let me ask what is the core of military strength in today's world. War is technology. From this it might be argued, as one of my correspondents argues, that "America's best defense is the development of our national resources and our technical knowledge through a program of full employment, full production, and prosperity." I agree this is our "best defense," but surely not adequate defense. The economic potential is the final war strength we have to draw on, but the question is how will we make that war strength mobilizable?

As concerns the young men who will have to fight a war, the answer lies in skills. War today is not primarily a war of drill and discipline. It is a war of machines. The nation that can defend itself is not only the nation with the economic strength to put war machines into the field and in the air and on the sea, but also the nation whose young men know how to use machines in wartime because they have learned how to use machines in peacetime.

I know this is not the viewpoint of those who want a year of military training under the Army for every boy. They say that war is machines and their use, yes, but it is also drilling and discipline and the ability to take and give orders, and the ability to work together. Granted. But you can get the discipline and attitudes when you find war close and have to put into an army the material you have trained. The crux of the training is the skills, not the attitudes.

This is for me the nub of the whole question. Just as a big standing army is alien to our tradition, so continual training in military attitudes is alien to it. Let us train our young people, but let us not confuse training for war as well as peace skills with training for militarism. Let us train them, but let us restrict the training to the minimum basic skills, and let it be done under civilian auspices and not under the Regular Army.

I have read a very moving article on the other side, called "A Letter to Twelve College Presidents," by Captain McGeorge Bundy, in the May *Atlantic Monthly*. It is a passionate letter, the gist of it being that we live in a world of force, that we had better make sure we have it on our side, that we had better back up our foreign policy with it, that the twelve college presidents who are against peacetime conscription "are talking through twelve learned hats," that most soldiers feel thus, and that if civilians don't they will find they have "cut themselves off from the young men of the country."

I can understand Captain Bundy's feeling. He had, as a Yale undergraduate, been fed such lifeless pap about every war being suicidal for every democracy that he revolted passionately against it. Now he, and many soldiers like him, have become fierce realists. They have earned the right to talk thus. But I doubt that we civilians have. I see no reason why we should glorify war attitudes. I wonder what it is about people that makes them decide, when they have to do something, that it is a glorious thing to do, even when it is in fact dirty and bloody and messy? Why do we have to rationalize the grimmest necessities of life, and give a death's-head the noble visage of a saint? Readiness for war is still a tragic necessity. But instead of embracing the war attitudes, let us hold them at arm's length.

Teach our young men and women the skills that will make them effective parts of an armed force if we ever have to use it again. Teach them about radio and electricity, about chemistry and physics and mathematics. Teach them how to take engines apart and put them together. Teach them how to fly. Teach the girls nursing and cooking and child-care.

Do it in addition to their regular schooling. Let the community take them for a year and teach them these skills and toughen their bodies—not in their regular schools and colleges, but in separate camps for this special purpose. But make sure this is done by a civilian authority, and not by the Army. For the Army would inevitably, by its very nature and training, instill in their minds not only the war skills, but the militarist attitudes.

The best thing about the way we have fought wars thus far has been that our makeshift armies have never ceased being civilians at heart. Let us give them skills earlier, but let us never change that essential fact about them. The great glory of America is that in crises it has proved warlike without being war-liking.

2. *The Compton Commission Report*

THE BIG QUESTION, from the start, about universal military training for American youngsters has been the question of whether it would be a step toward national and world security or a step toward military control of the nation. Despite the careful report of the Compton Commission, I am still unconvinced about the need for sending American youngsters of eighteen into military training camps.

On its military side the report makes several things clear:

The Commission believes that the coming war will involve mobilizing every skill and every manpower resource we have, including spy-systems, scientists, laboratories, workers, an atom-bomb force, regular armed forces under a unified command, and (although the Commission says so only in a mincing way, not a direct one) thought control to get national cohesion. Military training will be only one part of this over-all plan. I agree with this as a factual statement.

The Commission believes that even with atom bombs and bacilli, we shall need a mass military force if we go to war. I agree. The notion of a push-button twenty-four-hour war is part of our hunger for dramatic simplicity in thinking. Even if we destroy the Russian and European cities, we shall have to hold down the vast Eurasian land-mass, and most of the rest of the world, too. We shall have to deal with civil wars, resistance movements, hunger, and disease. That will need many millions of young men.

If I go along with the Commission on these military fundamentals, why then do I end by dissenting sharply from the report as a whole? Obviously these military facts build up to one conclusion in the unanimous mind of the Commission members, and to a different conclusion in my mind. The answer is that we differ on some fundamental nonmilitary notions, some of which the Commission examines in its report, some of which it assumes without examining. Let us look at them.

The Commission believes in the theory that the best way to prevent a war is to prepare for it. I should have thought that history had torn the whiskers off this hoary doctrine generations ago. The Germans—Kaiser and Nazis alike—consistently prepared for war and didn't prevent it. That goes for every military empire of the past, starting with Sparta, which was always prepared to the hilt, which found itself and its youngsters living for war—and which always got war. I offer a counterdoctrine, patterned after Horace Greeley's famous "The way to resume is to resume." I say that the way to prevent war is to bend every energy toward preventing it, not to proceed by the dubious indirection of preparing for it.

The Commission believes—too piously, I suspect—that a military training plan can be kept under civilian control in the kind of atmosphere we have today. I think this is wishful. The Commission proposes a three-man board—two of them civilians, one an Army officer. But the training commission will be doing a military job, in a military atmosphere—which means that in the end it will be done in the military way.

This means that before long the Army will be using military training not only as a way to teach the youngsters armed skills but also as a way to indoctrinate them on other scores as well—to fill their minds with the Army's notions about the identity of the coming enemy, his nature, his political system, his social system, his diplomacy, his world plans, and his supposed friends and allies at home. I don't see how this can help happening, even if you pile civilian advisory commission on civilian advisory commission, and then civilian inspectors on top of both. To ask the Army to train the bodies of youngsters without taking over their minds as well is like asking a general to feed only one-half of a horse while the other half is left to a civilian. By the very nature of war today, it involves preparing the mind as well as the body, and using ideas and emotions as weapons and not only bayonets and bombs.

The pay-off on this is the fact that the six-month service when a boy reaches eighteen will be only a starter. After that he does specialized work of one sort or another, presumably for years, or enrolls in the National Guard. Here is where the Army men will have an undisputed domain.

If my reasoning is right, military training must mean military indoctrination and military domination no matter how hard you fight against them. If my reasoning is right, the Compton Commission report is the military camel's nose under the national civilian tent. It won't be long before the whole camel is under.

What the champions of universal training are after is a reservoir of partially trained young men—a reservoir as large as the whole young manhood of the nation. What they are after is to be able to mobilize our full military strength and save perhaps a year—perhaps more—in doing it. They can save this time because of the fact that all the youngsters will already have had six months of camp plus their later training, because of the fact that they will already have had their individuality broken and will be ready to become part of a vast machine, and finally because of the fact that the conscription machinery will have been kept in running order and well-greased. Doing this always involves a heavy price, even in wartime. It involves a particularly heavy price in peacetime. We had better be terribly sure it is necessary before we pay that price.

A people can turn its main energies only in one direction. If we turn them into the war direction, we might as well give up hope of channeling them some day toward peace. In the end a nation becomes what it prepares for.

JUNE 12, 1945; JUNE 12, 1947

The Sixty-five-Day War

HERE, IT IS, Ladies and Gentlemen: The latest model, newest, most up-to-date, short and easy, painless war, with victory guaranteed in sixty-five days or your money back. Step right up, get into the draft line, get on the war band wagon, strike up the hysteria, get your hates ready, put murder in your heart—let's go.

Where do I get this? Well, there's a new look in the statements coming from Army sources. The military leaders have had quite a propaganda problem. Let's put it this way: If they talk about the latest methods of mass massacre, it scares people; if they don't talk about them, then people might get the idea that the Russians will be hard to lick. Either way, it might hurt the brand-new shiny draft and the somewhat bedraggled universal military training.

The Army leaders have come up with the solution. They will let the people in on the newest war gadgets, but in such a way as not to scare them. They will tell the people about the latest death-dealing instruments, but underscore the fact that America has a monopoly on them, so we needn't be afraid of war casualties. It is the Russians who have to be afraid. You can see how brilliant this is by its double-service feature: It reassures the Americans and it scares the dialectics out of the Russians.

Once you grasp that principle firmly, you will understand about the statements that Forrestal and his fellow guardians of American military fortunes have been making. Forrestal himself told Congress flatly that Russia has as yet neither the knowledge nor the capacity to make the atom bomb, and America has both. Of course, this isn't much good in scaring the Russians, because they must already know it. But it serves the other purpose of reassuring Americans who might otherwise get the idea that there might be some bad risks in our current militarism. Air Secretary Symington added his own contribution by stating that we have Alaskan and other bases from which big bombers can take off (guess in what direction), and we have the bombers. That, too, can't be much news to the Russians, but it's meant as good medicine for whatever might be preventing Americans from embracing the big war policies.

But the real pay-off came from an indirect source, not from the service chiefs. Glenn Martin, who makes planes and other things and is close to the generals, has given us a semiofficial preview of what we have in store for whatever nation (guess which) is unlucky enough to be on the firing line when we get started.

Martin says we have amazing guided missiles that can seek out enemy ships or enemy steel plants across thousands of miles and destroy them. He says we have new atom bombs that make the Hiroshima model obsolete. He says we have radioactive atomic clouds that can move with a favoring breeze and destroy the country they pass over. He says we have new bacteria weapons which get into your body, and lie dormant for a while, and then "make the victim ill with an illness from which he does not recover." But the biggest thing he says is that these weapons and others like them will be able to decide the ultimate outcome of the war after sixty-five days.

The conclusion we are obviously meant to draw is that since America has these weapons and Russia does not, victory will be ours almost in a jiffy. If the war starts the middle of June, let us say, it will be all over except for the cleaning-up by the end of August—which means before people come back from their vacations and before the school and college-terms begin.

This appeals to me—this sixty-five-day war. I like the cleanness of it, the precision of it. It solves everything at once. It wipes out the Russians; it solves the danger of Communist ideas in Europe and elsewhere; it preserves capitalism and the corporations; it makes sure there is no gap even for a moment in their war-contract profits; it keeps our young men all occupied either in factory jobs or elsewhere; it leaves no room for foolish liberal ideas at home; it lays the foundation for American world mastery; and it does all these wonderful things without the anguish and the misery and the sheer dirty messiness of a protracted war.

It appeals to me also because I am at heart a dreamer, and this sixty-five-day war is surely the stuff that dreams are made of, the stuff that rounds out our little life with a sleep.

To be sure, that wasn't the way Churchill talked of World War II. He talked of blood and sweat and tears. Nor was it the way Stalin described to his people the task of killing Germans. He didn't make it so clean. Nor was it the way Roosevelt steeled the American people to their grim task after Pearl Harbor. As a matter of fact, it isn't even the way Einstein, Urey, and the other scientists have described the nature of World War III. They somehow made it seem much messier and more murderous and much more uncertain. But Forrestal and Symington are creative minds who do not have to follow the methods of previous war leaders, and who know about these things far better than the scientists do.

I assume, of course, that Glenn Martin is indirectly a spokesman for our service chiefs when he says what he does. Anyone that high up in the hierarchy of war techniques does not reveal information like that unless he has been told to; and he doesn't pick this particular ticklish time to do it unless the timing has been decided upon by others.

But there are some things about this sixty-five-day war that still trouble me.

Let's assume now that we have more of the new weapons than the Russians. Let's assume that in sixty-five days we can blow their cities to bits with the atom bomb, destroy life on the Russian plains with the radio-active clouds, and infect the Russian population with the mysterious new diseases which look harmless at first but from which "the victim does not recover." What kind of animal does that make us? What kind of conquering miracle-men of science who can blot out the lives of millions of other human beings, on the theory (I suppose) that their politics makes sub-men of them? I go with Chancellor Hutchins of the University of Chicago when he says that if we set about fighting a preventive war against Russia, we should first ask the pardon of the Nazis we hanged at Nuremberg.

Another thing troubles me: not a scruple this time, but a somewhat lowly apprehension. Suppose the Russians have some of the modern weapons too. Can Martin—or Forrestal, or Truman—be terribly certain the odds are overwhelmingly and safely on our side, and that we don't therefore have to examine the grounds of this war too hard? Navy Secretary Sullivan, in giving us the sensational news that enemy submarines (guess whose) have been sighted off our coast, also added that the Russians are using the best German scientists to build them. Could this be true of some other things? Perhaps not atom bombs. But is it so terribly hard for doctors to develop death-dealing bacteria in their laboratories? Once the war started, one could scarcely expect the Russians to fight it in the spirit of good clean fun.

Then there is the question of whether Martin—and Forrestal, and Symington, and Sullivan—have quite grasped the real nature of the coming war. You can destroy cities, but you cannot hold down whole peoples; the Nazis found out that it was pretty hard, and remember that this war will be much less clear in its ideological rights and wrongs to the people of Europe and Asia and Latin America than the last war was. Can you count on there being no resistance movement? The kind of cold war the Russians have been fighting has been almost wholly a propaganda war, and the Russians are pretty good at that kind of war. Will they stop being good at it once the shooting starts? Justice Douglas is right when he says that what we face is an *idea backed by force*. Can we destroy it by the newest gadgets of force without an idea behind it?

Just as the generals and the bigwigs in Washington have muffed the real character of the cold war, and therefore failed miserably in fighting it thus far, so they are muffing the real character of the coming war, and may fail just as miserably at that. For it will be only partly a matter of atomic clouds and germs and atoms. It will be basically a world civil war, in which every nation except for Russia and America will be split down the middle. Which means it will be not a sixty-five-day war at all, but a long-drawn-out relentless war of ideas and hates and passions that will spread over the habitable globe, and about which we can foresee neither the outlines nor the outcome.

MARCH 28, 1948

How to Move Toward War

1. *Brink-of-War Economics*

THERE ARE several ways of interpreting the President's Economic Report. You can view it as a sharp warning about the coming "recession" (for "recession" read "bust") delivered to a Republican Congress and a business group, both of whom are traveling merrily toward chaos. Or you can read it as a thoughtful and able inventory of the nation's economic conditions today, an appraisal of trends and dangers, and a forward glance into the future—in short, as one of the significant beginnings of some sort of economic planning for America.

But there is still another way you can read it, and that way seems to me the most important of all. Take it along with the President's Budget Message, and the report of the President's Air Policy Commission. Put these together and you get something more than a trend. You get the alarming pattern of an economy in which the talk is about social welfare and economic health, but in which most of the national funds being spent are being spent for war; an economy in which the only effective planning that is being done is being done for war; an economy which, as the Finletter Commission expresses it, is to be geared to the expectation of a war involving airborne atom bombs or airborne germs by the end of a five-year period.

There has been a good deal of protest, and rightly, about the increasing role of the generals in President Truman's civilian Administration. This has come not only from liberals, but also from conservatives like Hanson Baldwin of the New York *Times,* who believes in the American tradition of keeping the line clear between the military and civilian spheres. But even more important than the role of the generals in the Administration is the role of military expenditures in the economy.

The recognition of this fact will cut through a lot of confused thinking about present-day economic issues. The Republicans and Democrats are accusing each other of being responsible for inflated prices. In terms of the shattering of price-controls, the blame must lie principally on the Republicans. In terms of the tremendous suction-force on available steel, transport, and basic materials, at least a good part of the blame must rest on a military program which is now spending eleven billion a year in the American markets, and reaching out toward thirteen and even fifteen billion.

Or look at it from another angle. The President has been eloquent in his State of the Nation message about the high corporate profits that have been flowing in our economy, and he comes back to the theme in his Economic Report. Yet what chance is there of stopping these high corporate profits so long as military contracts of one kind or another comprise an expenditure which totals twenty-five per cent of the budget for 1948 and will probably go higher before the year is over? And what chance is there of stopping the high profits so long as the atmosphere in which the contracts are awarded is a war atmosphere, with the pervasive military psychology that you always put first things first—and expense is not a first thing?

This is not meant as an attack only on the Administration. It is equally an attack on the Republicans, including even the so-called isolationist Republicans who are always lamenting the Administration's extravagance on foreign policy. It isn't hard to predict that very few of the cuts the Republicans will put through—despite the talk you may hear—will be military cuts. The hatchet will be used ruthlessly by the Taber-Knutson-Taft tightwad boys on the social-service items. It will be used ruthlessly on Marshall Plan aid. But when it comes to the Air Force, the Navy, the Army, the experiments with atom bombs and germ warfare and supersonic flight and rockets and all the other paraphernalia of death, even a tightwad Republican grows as reverent as a Mohammedan in a sacred mosque. These items are the untouchables.[1] They are all the more untouchable because, like the supernatural elements in religious cults, they are also unknowable. They are surrounded by a vast secrecy, and at the portals of the sacred temple stands the guardian who tells you that if you question this you are giving aid and comfort to the Enemy.

This is the key. We are no longer concerned with an ordinary national defense psychology. We are concerned with a brink-of-war psychology, in which the Enemy has been spotted and identified, and we are told that all must be in readiness for the inevitable clash. In ordinary times the generals stay in their own domain. In a brink-of-war psychology, the civilian functions (like, for example, the Civil Aeronautics Board) move over and are absorbed into the military, so that the generals naturally take over. In ordinary times military expenditures are marginal. In a brink-of-war economy they become central to the whole economic structure, including its artificial "prosperity," its artificial "full employment," its runaway price inflation, its swollen profits, its reckless government spending.

I will be told that this may be true, but given the Russian danger there is no other recourse. I answer that an economy in full swing of becoming a war economy isn't likely to be diverted from the path to war—that one of the obstacles to peace is the very existence of our war economy.

When you get used to easy corporate profits, it's hard to get unused to them. When you find how easy it is to bail out the airplane industry by reports calling for bigger and better airplane contracts, it's hard to envisage the possibility that military planes may become a drug on the market. When you find that a peacetime economy may make heavy inroads into the ranks of sixty million employed, and raise problems of unemployment, you go right on solving the employment problem by the war industries.

Actually American capitalism has not functioned well in our century except under a war economy or a brink-of-war economy. That seems to be the only kind of economic planning we are capable of doing. If we mean all our talk about our great economic exploits, it is time to ask whether we ought not to start thinking about the kind of planning which

---

[1] This proved true as prediction, except that the Marshall Plan cuts were less drastic than I had feared.

will mean a peacetime economy of full employment without runaway prices and obscenely high profits.

2. Brink-of-War Leadership

OUR TOP LEADERS are talking of war and demanding mobilization for it. They point to Russia as the enemy, yet they offer no evidence that Russia —ruthless as it is, wherever Communists get control—is a threat to American security. More important still, they offer no evidence that they have been willing during the past year of crisis to sit down with Russian leaders and discuss a world-wide agreement in which each side makes major concessions in the interests of peace and security for both. Most important of all, they have scrapped the idea of the United Nations as a force for collective peace, and are trusting desperately to the show of American armed force as the way to insure peace.

Who are the men who have shaped this grotesque caricature of a peace policy? And what are the impulsions behind their thinking?

First of all, let us be clear about President Truman's role in all this. He is a bewildered man with a job too big for him. He has an image of himself as a man rising boldly to a great national crisis, but it is an absurd image. He rises only to the roles and the utterances mapped out for him by a small group of men around him. I doubt whether he grasps the full meaning of what is going on, and the import of the decisions he makes. It would be wrong to describe him as a captive, for if he is a prisoner he is a willing one. He is rather an instrument of powerful men and powerful groups, who use him as part of a grand design which is clear in their minds but probably not in his.

Since I have no pipeline to the movers and shakers, I have no inside information on who they are. But one scarcely needs such inside information, at a time when every objective fact spells out who they are and the roles they are playing. Let me take them in the order of their seniority in the councils at Washington:

Admiral William D. Leahy, who fills under Truman as he did under Roosevelt the role of the President's liaison with the military forces, is a great power behind the scenes where decisions of high policy are made. He is the man who, according to the evidence in James F. Byrnes's *Speaking Frankly*, did not find even Byrnes's "tough" policy toward Russia tough enough. His big role in military and political high policy dates back to Roosevelt's regime, when he was American envoy to Pétain's France, and later mixed up in the Darlan phase of our policy. He has been a constant force ever since. Roosevelt was greatly influenced by him but could keep him within limits. Truman can't.

General George C. Marshall served brilliantly under Roosevelt as Chief of Staff, and has served not so brilliantly under Truman as Secretary of State. He is a man of great military and administrative abilities, but his mind cannot break outside those limits. On matters of political policy he is as hopelessly lost as any general. His integrity and patriotism are undoubted. But as a Secretary of State he has been a failure. His role in the grand design is that of the figure with immense prestige, and that is how the other men in power are using him. Because of his military accomplishments his voice carries weight with Congress and the press. The tragedy is that on political matters his voice is that of the military.

The youngest of the triumvirate, and the most recent in point of service, is Defense Secretary James V. Forrestal. He has energy and drive, and he knows what he wants. It is he who is the guiding spirit of the National Security Council, which today shapes not only military policy but *also political policy*, as Blair Bolles recently pointed out. It was he who helped make the decision on scrapping the United Nations on the Palestine partition issue. It is he who more than anyone else shaped the decision on Truman's military-draft speech. His career and conditionings have been those of a powerful financier, and his outlook as the head of our military forces represents the fusion of the corporate and the military viewpoints.

It is, of course, a mistake to fix only on individual men. Each of them expresses the viewpoint of a power-group. Together these power-groups represent the new military caste, the big corporate class, the heavy-industry group, the banking group. They have their satellites in church and state, in the press and other opinion industries.

What are their impulsions? They know that America is today one of the two great power-centers of the world. Their fear of the other power-center, Russia, is doubled and tripled by the fact that Russia's anti-capitalism represents a threat to their power and privilege. They are groups whose whole training has been in the realities and the tactics of power. They despise any method of procedure except the method of power— military and financial. They see themselves undoubtedly as dedicated patriots, yet the fact is that everything in their lives has committed them to a definition of leadership that involves power rather than conciliation, gaining their way by "toughness" rather than finding common ground with their rivals. They regard the internationalists as sentimentalists, they have only contempt for the United Nations as a creative force for peace, they despise the idea of democratic world government.

The tragedy of it is that the harder they pursue their methods the more they are bound to fail, for their methods take no account of what really moves men in Europe and Asia who do not see the world in terms of Wall Street and the Pentagon. The tragedy of it also is that even if these men had doubts about their method, the whole American economy is now so decisively geared to war contracts and war expenditures that they fear what would happen to profits and employment if we let go.

Two things worry them most: the baffling spread of Communist power through methods that these men are not trained to understand or to counter. And, even more, that the youngsters of the world, and the mothers and fathers of the world, are not willing to fight a war.

JAN. 15, MARCH 19, 1948

What Is Appeasement?

THE WORD APPEASEMENT has come to be used in a loose and slippery sense, even by some of the people who are ordinarily careful about how they write and talk. It is one of those loaded words—loaded with emotional dynamite. Whenever anyone suggests that Russia and America can come to an agreement on the major issues that are dividing them now, there is an almost inevitable comeback: "But isn't that appeasement? And haven't we learned from our experience with the Nazis and the Japanese that appeasement never solves anything, but only makes the war worse when it does come?"

How about these questions? And just what is appeasement?

Obviously the sense in which the term appeasement is now being generally used covers any kind of concession or conciliation between the United States and Russia. If we were to offer the Russians some concessions on the German problem, or on Greece, or China, or Korea, or Austria, or on trade, and demand from them major concessions in return, this move would be attacked as "appeasement." But is it, really?

Appeasement has a strict and clear meaning. It does not mean just any form of conciliation or concession. Horse-swapping is not appeasement. When major concessions are made by both sides of a controversy, what you have is a form of conciliation or compromise, and compromise has always been considered a basic element of the democratic process and of international peace.

Appeasement refers to concessions made at the point of a gun. It refers to agreements made between two nations in which one of them has no intention of living up to its side of the bargain. The classic instance, of course, is the effort made at Munich in 1938 to appease the Germans under Hitler. The concessions were extorted at the point of a gun. They were granted by Chamberlain and Daladier in the vain hope that when the Czechs were thrown to the Nazis the appetite of Hitler for conquest would be sated, and that he would live up to his so-far-and-no-farther word. There was never any reason to believe that Hitler would stop, or that he *could* stop even if he wanted to.

Is there a parallel to this in the Russian case today? I doubt it, and I shall continue to doubt it until the evidence shows that the parallel is a true one, and not simply a propaganda instrument of the war group.

It is said that the Russians will accept concessions from us, and make none to us in return. Is this true? The evidence up to the present points to the willingness of the Russians to enter a horse-swapping conference with us. Byrnes writes that Molotov wanted such a conference, and that he (Byrnes) refused as a matter of principle. The recent reports, widely spread and never explicitly denied by American sources, indicate that the Russians sent a feeler to our State Department through Robert Murphy, our representative in Germany, asking for a conference between President Truman and Joseph Stalin. The conference was presumably to have been held on neutral ground in Europe. The answer—so the story goes—was that President Truman would not leave Washington. All of this seems to indicate that the Russians are ready for a give-and-take, with major concessions on both sides.[1]

It is said that the Russians would not live up to their part of the bargain. How do we know that? They will certainly try to interpret any ambiguous clause in their own favor, as they did about Potsdam and Yalta, and hold to that interpretation stubbornly. But skillful negotiation could make the agreement so explicit that there could be no weaseling out. If, after that, the Russians still were bent on scuttling the heart of the agreement, we would know that our only choice was to resist them with arms. But to say that now, as it is being said, is to prejudge an issue on which the life and death of our world depend.

[1] This was never explicitly confirmed by the Administration. President Truman denied that there had ever been any *official* Russian approach to him. For a reply, outlining the detailed history of the *unofficial* Murphy incident, see David Lawrence in the New York Sun, April 23, 1948. Several weeks after President Truman's denial came the Smith-Molotov exchange, discussed in the next article.

It is said that the Russians, like the Nazis, have no intention of stopping their expansionism, that they mean to go on until they have conquered the world for Communism—including America. This may or may not be true. The weight of the evidence is against it. Unlike the Nazis, the Russians do not make a cult of militarism and world rule. Unlike the Nazis, they do not have an image of themselves as a racial ruling elite, with all other peoples as submen. Most important of all, the Nazis had an unstable economy which had to expand or die. The Russian economy is stable enough, and as for the internal position of the Russian ruling group, it would be badly weakened rather than strengthened by the strains of another war. It is not true of the Politburo that, for its survival, the Russians must expand or die.

There still remains the question of the revolutionary doctrine of the Kremlin and the Cominform. For two decades Stalin's basic precept has been that of "socialism in one country" rather than that of world revolution. But in the history of Communism, ideas are weapons and doctrines are flexible. It is possible that the Russians have changed over to the idea of world revolution, and are back in the phase of 1919–25. It is natural for Communism to revert to such a phase after a war, and to reap the biggest possible harvest from postwar disintegration and despair. In one sense that is what Communism is trying to do now, and that is one aspect of Russian policy.

But the Russians are realistic enough to know they cannot go much further than they have gone without being stopped by American power. We have made that clear. What we must make equally clear now is that we are willing to talk peace if the Russians really mean peace. They may want to extend their revolutionary power, but they do not want a war. They do not want another twenty million or more of their people killed, they do not want another postponement of their plans for the rebuilding of peacetime industries within their country. In other words, if they are pursuing a policy of world revolution now, it is probably in a limited sense rather than in an all-out sense. It is a policy they are not likely to pursue to the bitter end if it involves a catastrophic war.

The problem now is to make it clear that peace is possible on both sides, with major concessions on each and major commitments on each. The problem is to reconstruct the United Nations as a framework within which to get an agreement that will hold fast.

That is not appeasement. And for that it is not yet too late.

MARCH 30, 1948

Are We Afraid of Peace?

So IT SEEMS, after all, that Ambassador Bedell Smith's words to Molotov —"the door always remains open for discussion and settlement of our differences"—didn't mean anything really serious. It wasn't an open door he was talking of. It was just one of those polite and meaningless phrases that diplomats use to veil their meaning and obscure their intentions.

The Russians took him at his word. That was unkind and undiplomatic of Molotov, who has done many unkind and undiplomatic things before. The President and the Secretary of State have been thrown into confusion by Russia's surprise move. It is disconcerting in diplomacy to be taken at your word, particularly when the word at which you are taken involves a genuine effort at negotiation, and your political enemies at home are lying in wait to accuse you of "appeasement."

The President now says we never intended an offer of general negotiation. Secretary Marshall says the Russians can act through the United Nations, by withdrawing from specific positions they have taken on concrete issues. But any general negotiations, it seems, would be a betrayal of American policy and principle.

All of which prompts me to ask some simple questions. What is it we are trying to avert—war or peace? Why is it that our officials and spokesmen are so panic-stricken when they are put into a position where they may have to negotiate the crucial differences between us and the Russians?

Are they, perchance, afraid of peace?

Why might they be?

I am not going to speculate about motives. What I set down now are some facts from which motives may be deduced.

It is a fact that the State Department officials and the military people feel that America is winning the cold war with Russia. They feel that they have the Russians diplomatically on the run. In fact, General Marshall made that point pretty clear in his news conference when he interpreted Molotov's statement as a confession of Russian weakness and a sign of a change in Russian policy. It is hard to know how far the State Department hopes to go on this score—whether the intent is to postpone negotiations until the Russians clearly confess their defeat; or whether they will follow the Kennan policy, as expressed in the now famous article by Mr. X., of squeezing Russia from every side until the Russian regime itself is overthrown.

It is a fact that the majority opinion of the State Department is now convinced that, in the cold war with Russia, time is on our side. From their standpoint it might therefore be considered a mistake to shorten the time-span still to be traversed in the cold war—even if it involved the calculated risk of a shooting war.

It is a fact that American policy is now committed to a brisk pace of rearming on a massive scale. The Forrestal-Leahy-Marshall group, who are the real movers and shakers in our policy, are committed to rearming as an instrument for diplomatic war, if it can be kept within those limits, or as a preparation for a shooting war if it comes to that.

This rearming involves not only a current budget of fifteen billion a year, and a vast increase in airplane building. It also involves universal military training in some form, and a peacetime manpower draft. The money is appropriated, and the planes are being built. But the manpower measures are still not wholly secure, the movers and shakers have to maintain the sense of the Russians as the imminent enemy bent on our destruction. A series of peace negotiations with the Russians would, of course, shatter that. They would cut the ground from under the psychology of having to arm to the teeth against a ruthless enemy who will not talk peace. That goes far to explain why the President and the State Department have been thrown into confusion by Molotov's move. The Russians are refusing to go through with the role assigned to them on the stage of history as mapped out on our stage-plan.

It is a fact that our economy is now a brink-of-war economy. It is geared not to a phase of negotiations in internal affairs, but to a stage of protracted rearming, according to a five-year rearmament plan. Our current prosperity and full employment flow from this brink-of-war economy. Once we start cutting back on rearmament we start cutting back on war contracts, and who knows what that can lead to. We should then have to face the difficult problems of making an unplanned free enterprise economy work in peacetime. We have hold of a bear by the tail, and we don't dare let go.

Put these four facts together, that I have given above, and they may shed some light on why our leaders seem so afraid of peace.

But there is no reason for the American people to fear peace. The vast majority of Americans, along with ordinary people all over the world, breathed more freely when they read the headlines about possible negotiations. They were plunged into gloom again by the denials of President

Truman and Secretary Marshall. The stakes of war and peace are theirs. It is they who will in the end have to pay the heavy human cost of adventurism abroad and rearming at home; they who will in the end have to become the targets for atom bombs and germ warfare.

They can still keep the door of the peace talks open. They and they alone. But they can do it only if they decide that just as it has been said that war is too important to be left to the generals, so peace is too important to be left to the diplomats.

MAY 13, 1948

Philadelphia to San Francisco

ON THIS DAY, when so much of the world's turmoil and hope is gathered in San Francisco,[1] my thoughts turn back to another fateful day in another city more than a century and a half ago.

The time was May 25, 1787. The place was Philadelphia, in an upper room in the first meeting of the convention to frame a new constitution for the thirteen confederated states. The actors were the delegates chosen by the states—the best talent and courage and insight that could be found. Washington was chairman, Franklin was the elder statesman, Madison and Hamilton and Randolph and James Wilson and Gouverneur Morris were the big figures. We have planes and radio today, fanfare and klieg lights that the men at Philadelphia did not have. But not even a world conference has bigger men than made up that national conference.

They had a big task. There had been a war which was also a revolution. There was an economic depression. The soldiers who had come back home had debts that they didn't want, and wanted land that they didn't have, and there was some talk of setting up new military governments. The states were quarreling with one another. The loose governmental frame they had was not strong enough to resist potential aggression from the outside. The task of the men at Philadelphia was to make a new frame of government.

They had a double mandate that did not quite make sense. One was

[1] The occasion was the opening of the United Nations constituent conference at San Francisco.

to keep the existing leaky Articles of Confederation, and simply patch them up by amendments. The second was to create something "adequate to the exigencies of government and the preservation of the union." Each canceled the other, so very sensibly they scrapped the first and hugged the second. They violated instructions, but they built a nation. This was their first revolutionary decision.

Their second was to provide for force strong enough to guarantee freedom and dissipate fear. They gave the new Government the power to legislate for all on matters that affected all, and the power to levy armies and use them, and the power to tax and punish. There were cries of pain and lamentation from those who felt that a new tyranny was being set up. Then, as now, the shadow of European despotisms lay over American political development. But the impulse to survival proved stronger than the fear of strength. Once the initial framework of government was there, a very much needed Bill of Rights later was agreed on by Congress. But only a strong frame of government could have given the Bill of Rights any meaning. Without survival there can be no freedom.

The third revolutionary decision was to declare the Constitution in force when nine states had ratified it, instead of waiting for all. The founding fathers knew that the way to begin is to begin, and not to wait for perfection. The aged Franklin, on the last day of the Convention (as reported in Madison's Journal), poked fun at the perfectionists who either would have their own way or not play. He told the story of "a certain French lady" who had a dispute with her sister, and who said, "I don't know how it happens, Sister, but I meet with nobody but myself that's always in the right. *Il n'y a que moi qui a toujours raison.*"

They did pretty well, these men. They were not frightened by words, and they had a sense of history and knew they were making it. They worked hard at their task; Madison steeped himself in books on ancient history and politics for weeks before the Convention opened. But though they built on the past, they had the sense that a new "science of politics," as Hamilton put it, was coming into being. And they were men of action who, having created a document as good as they could make it in an imperfect world, then became its champions in the great debate on whether the states should ratify it, and spent the rest of their lives turning the paper scheme into a living government.

I address these reflections about the men at Philadelphia to the men at San Francisco. I do not mean to say, by any stretch of my words, that the two situations are parallel. There are huge discrepancies between them. The men in the states came from somewhat similar stock, and spoke the same language. They had been through a revolution, and had at least some impulse toward unity. Their social structure was the same, and there were no thrusts toward imperialism that divided them.

The men at San Francisco, moreover, have the further disadvantage that most people who think of them start with skepticism. The wary observer has come to feel that there is an air of unreality about these world conventions, and that the real stuff always goes on behind the scenes. I might add that the world is still at the stage where it dare not hope for a real federal structure that limits sovereignty. We would settle for the Articles of Confederation.

I am thinking rather of the spirit with which the men at Philadelphia worked. They were not cynical, not hopeless. They were confident of themselves, and of the capacity of men, by planning, to make order out of anarchy. They aimed as high as they could see, and settled for as much as they could reach. They made bargains and were practical men, but they never ceased to think of their task as a heroic one.

When the Constitution was signed, Benjamin Franklin looked at Washington's chair, "at the back of which [Madison tells us] a rising sun happened to be painted. . . . 'I have,' said he, 'often and often in the course of the session, and the vicissitudes of my hopes and fears as to its issue, looked at that sun behind the President without being able to tell whether it was rising or setting. But now at length I have the happiness to know that it is a rising and not a setting sun.'"

APRIL 25, 1945

The New Federalist

IN A WORLD almost stifling for lack of bold ideas, I find the idea of a world federal government one of the boldest. It has been jeered and ridiculed, dismissed as visionary, attacked as the road to a world dictatorship—but it refuses to be downed. It has survived even the fanaticism of some of its own more extreme supporters. I have been skeptical of it myself, largely because I have felt that the world government movement diverts energies that might be spent on strengthening the United Nations, and that it is best to move toward a world authority a step at a time. But the clock of history is ticking away, and the world is stuck deep in a cold war which is leaving its glacial deposit on the human spirit. We need something with which to break through the ice. This may be it.

Of all the aspects of world federalism, the one that hits Americans hardest is the parallel with our own government. I have been reading three recent books that bear on this, and having a good time switching from one to another, so that in a sense I have read the three as a unit. One is Carl Van Doren's *The Great Rehearsal* (Viking), a play-by-play account of the Philadelphia Convention that framed the Constitution; the second is *The Enduring Federalist* (Doubleday), which is a reprint of most of the famous Federalist Papers, with a commentary by Charles A. Beard; the third is *Peace or Anarchy*, by Cord Meyer, Jr. (Little, Brown), which is a contemporary "Federalist Paper" for our own time, urging a world monopoly of force at the center, and a world federal government operating directly on individuals, but leaving policies outside of war and peace to the constituent members. Each of these books takes on a dimension of depth and relevance when read with the others which it would not have by itself.

Of the three authors, Van Doren and Meyer are impassioned partisans of world federalism, while Beard seems skeptical of it.

Beard admits that most of the present interest in the American federal principle is due to the fear of an atomic war, but his own interest is still primarily domestic, and I cannot see that he has shifted much from his distrust of visionary internationalism and his established conviction that the best motto for America is "Look homeward, angel." Yet the dynamite of ideas contained in the classic papers by Madison and Hamilton and Jay is still there, and they remain not only "the Bible of the Constitution," but also the Bible of a possible world federation.

The reason why Carl Van Doren's volume is a Book-of-the-Month, and why it has been highly praised by two political hopefuls like Justice Douglas and Harold Stassen, does not lie in anything he may have added to the story of the Convention and the great debate on ratification of the Constitution, which has been told and retold by Farrand, Elliott, Warren, Beard, Hockett. It lies in the quiet skill with which he ties up the debates of 160 years ago with the questions in men's minds today.

For example: then as now, there were jealousies and fears between the units being called on to join together; then as now there was the dread of the small states that they would be swallowed up and of the large ones that they would count for less than their real strength; then as now there were charges and countercharges of perfectionism as contrasted with realism; then as now there were fears of a superstate and its tyranny; then as now there were economic rivalries between the states; then as now there were fierce arguments about liberty and survival; then as now there was the looming shadow of a social issue—at that time the issue of slavery

—to divide the constituent states and muddle up the problem of representation.

Yet even when all these are added together, they still don't make what the world federalists are now calling the "deadly parallel" between 1787 and 1948. There is no sense in distorting history in order to sell an idea which is in itself valid enough, without calling in the support of a parallel that has to be stretched pretty hard to be deadly.

For one thing, no matter how romantic you become about the differences between Georgia and New Hampshire in 1787, they were slight compared to the differences between Russia and the United States today. There was a common language, and most of the people of the states were literate: today, as Justice Douglas has put it, "three-quarters of the people of the world could not read their new charter of government, even if it were printed in their own language."

There was in 1787 a common body of traditions, a common background of political thinking and legal training, a common religious feeling; none of them exists today to anything like the same degree. There were common leaders like Washington and Franklin who had become symbols of unity and evoked something close to reverence from all the citizens of all the states; no such leaders exist today. Most of all, the force of nationalism, with its tremendous suction-power, was at that time the unifying force as against state-feeling; today the force of nationalism, as powerful as ever, is the divisive force. The one-world idea has appeal, but nothing like the appeal that nationalist feeling had in 1787; state-loyalties had a divisive force in 1787, but nothing like the hold on men's minds that nationalism has today, particularly when equated with the holy-war psychology that has afflicted both capitalism and communism.

Does this mean there is no basis for world federalism? Not at all. There is as good a basis as you could wish for: a world government is the only thing that can give us a real chance for world survival; and the federal principle is the best one to provide for the necessary power at the center and the necessary autonomy for each member unit.

On the first of these two propositions, I can't see much room for disagreement. If you doubt it, I suggest you read Cord Meyer's book, especially his discussion of the certainty of a world war so long as each side tries to achieve peace by preparing for war. The only real debate on this point is whether you can have a one-world government for a two-world situation. Meyer belongs to the wing of the world government movement which doesn't indulge in Russia-baiting and which insists that we must do everything possible to get Russia to join a world federalism. I hold with him on that.

But this brings us to the debatable part of the second point. Russia has thus far expressed scorn for world government, and put great emphasis on nationalism. Why? I think the Russians feel that a supergovernment would be another instrument by which Western capitalism hopes to freeze the status quo and prevent the fulfillment of the revolutionary process in the world. The question about the federal principle, with power at the center and freedom at the edges, is: How much power at the center, and what kind of freedom at the edges? Will it be the kind of power that will permit a revolutionary socialism to establish itself where no other answer is adequate for the economic problem? Will it be the kind of freedom that will allow the Politburo and the National Association of Manufacturers to exist in the same world? On both questions the answer must be "Yes."

If it be said this is impossible, I answer that it must be tried. If it be said it is difficult, I agree. But the whole course of history has been a surmounting of difficulties by creative minds and wills. The real lesson of 1787 is that we had as leaders a group of men who imitated no one, but struck out on new paths for themselves. The test of our time is whether we can do something like that, with an even bigger job in a far more dangerous time.

JAN. 20, 1944

The Multiple Revolution

THE AMERICAN CHIEF OF STAFF utters some oracular words, to the effect that a war with Russia seems closer and more likely than it did three months ago, and everyone gapes as if something terribly important and terribly definitive had happened. Has it? Is a military man—even one as competent as General Omar Bradley, and one for whose basic sense I have as much regard—really the man to know when and whether a war will break out?

At bottom, our military men—like our civilian political leaders—blunder about in their guesses because they are blind about the nature of the crisis. At bottom, the crisis of our time is a revolutionary one, although the American leaders seem to have missed the fact of the revolutionary changes going on, and the Russian leaders have largely mistaken their character. The Russians make blunders about it, and bad ones, because their training is a dogmatic Marxian one, and because they think mechanically and miss all the intangibles. But at least they are trained to look beyond the diplomatic maneuvers, and beyond the military posturings, to the deeper social forces that give any period in history its stamp.

There is a revolution going on in the world, and it is a multiple revolution.

In its most obvious phase it is an industrial revolution. In the past decade America has developed precision techniques in production such as the world has never seen before. In the last three years, world science and American engineering have discovered a new form of energy—atomic energy—which, when applied to the industrial processes of peacetime, will transform them as radically as production was transformed in the classical Industrial Revolution of the eighteenth century.

What follows from this is the inescapable fact that the means of livelihood will be within the reach of all. No nation will be the trustee of the world's food or the world's wealth. No class will be the necessary trustee of the economic welfare of a people. If national rivalries could be leveled, and peace could be established, the economic problem as a problem of sheer maintenance of the world's population in comfort will cease to be a problem. This marks something like a turning-point in the world's history, but we are so absorbed with economic rivalries that we do not see what lies beyond them.

The revolution in peacetime industry is, by the same token, also a revolution in wartime skills, in the instruments of death. The scientists know this, and the generals know it. But the same knowledge that gives the generals their sense of confidence fills the scientists with dismay. We have not yet achieved that "absolute weapon" of which we talked when the atom bomb was made: a whole succession of weapons of death, each more terrible than the other, still stretches ahead for us before we achieve that absolute. But what we possess is adequate for world destruction. This sets a framework within which the cavortings of the diplomats, the generals, and the politicians—Russian and American alike—seem like the choreography of an idiot dance of death.

The revolution has also its political phases. One of them we have been strangely blind to: the collapse of the basis of colonialism. The shrinking of the British Empire, the generous—and yet also inevitable—act of giving India its independence, the series of colonial wars in the Far East against the Dutch and the French: all these are signs that colonial empires in the old sense are through. They no longer have a political base, as they used to have, in the claim that the colonial peoples did not have the wisdom to govern themselves. For the mother countries have not shown that wisdom either. They no longer have an economic base, as is shown by the continental economy developing in India. They no longer have a moral base, since the colonial peoples now know that subjection means slavery and overlordship means fascism. The liberation of the East—and some day soon the liberation also of Africa—will mean a shift in the racial balance of world power. The yellow and black peoples are coming into their own. And the examples of Gandhi and Nehru in India show that they have not wholly lost that religion-creating primacy which the East has so long held.

As a corollary, there is the revolutionary fact of the decline of Europe as an economic and technological world force. The new type of map which shows Europe as a hump on the Asiatic continent has a symbolic value today. Add to that the maps which show the air routes between America and Europe. For there are only two big economies in the Western world today, and neither of them is European. One is American, the other Russian. The struggle for Germany is the struggle for the residues of the German economic plant. The partition of Germany is a symbol of a much greater partition which is going on—the partition of Europe. Unless we can get a meeting of minds with the Russians, Europe will be split into a western American half and an eastern Russian half. Europe will, I trust, remain as a cultural force, as Greece remained the great cultural force of the Roman world. But its resemblance to the Greek parallel tells a good deal about its economic and political decline.

All of which leads to another phase of the multiple revolution: the new role of America and Russia. The struggle between them is only partially an ideological one. Most directly, it is a struggle to fill the power vacuum created in Europe by the shattering of German power and the crumbling of British power, and the one created in the Far East by the shattering of Japan and the collapse of colonialism. If there is to be a war it will, of course, proceed in terms of a holy war of supposedly incompatible doctrines. But at the core of it there will be a naked struggle for power between the two great continental economic empires of the world.

Behind each of these empires there is a new and revolutionary sense of world mission. The Russians have had that sense of mission ever since Lenin. It has slumbered, and become "socialism in one country," during the periods when Russia was consolidating its power at home. It has now been reawakened into an arrogant, if not outright aggressive, world revolutionary force—one that is pretty cocky about the long-run future at the same time that the Russian leaders are terrified at the immediate consequences of American military and economic power.

The Americans also are assuming a new role of world power, with a new sense of confidence. Whether we like the designation of "imperial" or not, the fact is that our power in the world today is exactly that. We have developed something the world has never exactly seen before: economic proconsuls, of the type of Paul Hoffman and Averell Harriman and Lewis Douglas. In fact, Hoffman's function is a direct link between American business power and American world power. And Harriman's, as a sort of wandering economic proconsul, is an impressive sign of our vigor as well as our confidence. If the Russians want to write Americans off as decadent and inefficient, as Hitler did, they will be grievously in error. The big question is just how we are going to use our amazing strength and vitality. But about the fact of that strength and vitality, only a willfully blind and willfully stupid person could have any doubts.

The Russians, I think, do not underestimate American strength. If it comes to a war, they count on the discipline and passion of their followers all over the world, and they count on the war turning from an atom-bomb lightning coup into a protracted world civil struggle. They figure that the long-range forces are on their side, and for that reason—as well as because of the war weariness of their people—they strongly prefer peace to war.

But if it is peace they want, they will need to change their attitudes in two basic respects. And that goes for the American leaders as well.

One of these is the moral phase of the multiple revolution of our time. What the Communists did in Czechoslovakia, symbolized so tragically by Masaryk's suicide, outraged all except those who hold that any weapon will do in a struggle for power. I think the Czech episode will prove to have been something of a turning point in the moral consciences of sensitive men. This turning point has not yet reached the ruling cabal in the American Government. For what they have done on the Palestine issue [1] is in its own way almost as outrageous morally as what the Communists did in Czechoslovakia.

At present the moral revulsion against the hypocrisies of Great Power politics is taking the form of a new interest in Gandhi's teachings of passive resistance and a new interest in the inviolate values of freedom. Neither of the ruling groups of the Great Powers will understand these. But ordinary people do. The passion for freedom is not dead in the world, as the Haganah fighters are showing in Palestine. And the revulsion against force and fraud is so widespread among decent people of every political persuasion that we may be certain that the sense of honor

[1] The reference was to the back-tracking of the Truman Administration on the United Nations decision to partition Palestine.

and the respect for human life have not been wholly quenched either.

The other element which the movers and shakers in the world are trying to ignore is the growing conviction that world government alone can
answer the problems of power politics. The youngsters especially are
convinced that the nation state as a form of ultimate power is through,
and that only a new world authority can take its place. Secretary Forrestal has expressed his cynical doubt about this, and the men of the
Kremlin regard the movement as only a new form of American imperialism. Both are wrong. In the end it will prove more powerful than both.

APRIL 27,1948

Epilogue: Toward a Tragic Humanism [1]

"THE TWO most important people in Europe today," someone has written, "are Nikolai Lenin and St. Thomas Aquinas." Which is a way of
saying that among the phoenix-ruins of a continent the battle of Europe
is a battle of *mystiques*. When André Malraux, in an already classic
speech delivered at Paris under United Nations Educational, Scientific,
and Cultural Organization auspices on November 4, 1946, sought to
create an image that would cut across both the Communist and the
Catholic—the image of tragic man conscious of his tragedy but seeking
without illusions to rediscover his essential nature—he became the target of the bitterest attacks. In Europe the vested idea-interests have
staked out their claims as the prescriptive interpreters of man's nature
and destiny. In America we have scarcely shown ourselves aware that the
problem exists.

Largely it is because, as a civilization, America is still on the ascending
arc of success and power. Except when we are actually at war, we have
little sense of the need for any fighting faith. We are today, by all the
exterior standards, a supercolossal power: our impact on the world has
reached Hollywood proportions. However much we may pretend to have
abandoned the idea of inevitable progress, taken from the eighteenth-
and nineteenth-century European thinkers, we act on the assumption
that it is true. We do not feel the need for taking thought, because the

[1] This first appeared as an editorial in the spring, 1947, issue of the *American Scholar*.

successive increments of cubits added to our stature will, we are confident, go on without our taking thought. Our political leaders and spokesmen are two-dimensional figures as incapable of tragic greatness as they are shorn of depth.

There is a good deal of talk, mainly surface talk, of the need for new gods and new religions in this era of the breakdown of man's moral sense. But the fact is that the religion-creating fertility is not one given to the Western or Mediterranean cultures in our time. The last two great efforts were those of Nietzsche and Tolstoy, and each in its diverse way was a failure, although each in the process left an exciting record of the attempt. To talk of fashioning new religions today (something more than a new *mystique* in which man dedicates himself to a political cult) is dangerous because it obscures the real creative need.

That need is for an understanding of man himself, as an individual within his collective civilization. I am speaking of an understanding illusionless enough to measure our limits within a universe greater than ourselves, and also our potentials for carving out a creative life within that frame. I am speaking of an understanding frank enough to recognize that man is part of a naturalistic order, an animal with bestial impulses that can be multiplied by the multiple cunning of his brain; but also courageous enough to assert that man is part of a moral order outside of which he loses his meaning, and that he carries an individual responsibility for translating that moral order into collective action.

I call this a tragic humanism. I call it a humanism because it is centered on the natural and the moral order instead of on the supernatural and the ritualistic. I call it tragic because it must strip itself of the barren belief that men are wholly rational, and of the smug assumption that progress and happiness can come out of systems of power as such, whether capitalism, socialism, or communism.

We must face again in our way the tragic fact that the Greeks faced in theirs. The agonized cry of Oedipus when he discovers in what a web he has been caught is not the end of the human enactment, but the beginning. Ahead of us lie the possibilities of an order in which men have made the honor of the group an enlargement of the integrity of the individual, have wrested from the imperatives of power enough room for freedom of mind and play of personality, and have linked the lonely processes of thought and art with the collective goals of all men who share the human condition.

This is not a religion, or even a *mystique*. It is an idea to which the American creative thinker can dedicate himself with passion and wholeness. An idea with passion and wholeness behind it can move the world.

INDEX

A Note About the Author

MAX LERNER's acute analytical mind and warm liberalism have left their mark in several fields. He is known the country over as radio commentator; he has been editor of The Nation and managing editor of Encyclopedia of Social Sciences and is at present contributing editor to The New Republic and columnist for the New York Star, formerly PM. A graduate of Yale (1923), he earned the Ph.D. degree from the Robert Brookings Graduate School of Economics and Government, and he has been on the faculties of Sarah Lawrence College, Harvard University, and Williams College.

His book It Is Later Than You Think (1938, with a revised edition in 1943) gave currency to that often-repeated phrase. The title of his second book, Ideas Are Weapons, has also become a battle-cry among American writers. This was followed by Ideas for the Ice Age, 1941, The Mind and Faith of Justice Holmes, 1943, and Public Journal, 1945. He is now at work on a long study and commentary on American life, to be called America as a Civilization.